MINE EYES HAVE SEEN:

a **FIRST-PERSON HISTORY** *of the* **EVENTS THAT SHAPED AMERICA**

RICHARD GOLDSTEIN

A Touchstone Book
Published by Simon & Schuster

TOUCHSTONE
Rockefeller Center
1230 Avenue of the Americas
New York, NY 10020

TOUCHSTONE and colophon are registered trademarks
of Simon & Schuster Inc.

Designed by Bonni Leon-Berman

Manufactured in the United States of America

1   3   5   7   9   10   8   6   4   2

Library of Congress Cataloging-in-Publication Data
Mine eyes have seen : a first person history of the events that shaped
America / [edited by] Richard Goldstein.
p.   cm.
"A Touchstone book."
Includes bibliographical references and index.
1. United States—History—Sources.   I. Goldstein, Richard.
E173.M67   1997
973—dc21   97-6445
                                                CIP

ISBN 0-684-81599-0

for **NANCY**

CONTENTS

chapter five

THE ROARING TWENTIES, THE DESPERATE THIRTIES

INTRODUCTION

It's a classic image from World War II—Douglas MacArthur almost walking on water at Leyte Gulf, the Philippines, in October 1944, fulfilling his pledge, "I shall return."

When MacArthur made that promise in March 1942, he had just been flown to Australia on President Roosevelt's orders, leaving American troops besieged in a hopeless holdout on Corregidor.

One of them was Private Irving Strobing, twenty-two years old, of the Army Signal Corps. As Japanese shells rained down, he tapped out a final radio message from the rock in Manila Harbor: "Corregidor used to be a nice place, but it's haunted now. The jig is up. Every one of us is bawling like a baby. They are piling dead and wounded in our tunnel."

MacArthur may be inexorably linked with the fate of the Philippines, but back in that first week of May '42, the suffering was endured by others, the men like Private Strobing, individuals largely forgotten by history.

That soldier's account survives nevertheless, as do the remembrances of so many others whose names are lost to history but who bore witness to great events: an actor named Harry Hawk watching another actor, John Wilkes Booth, dash madly across the stage at Ford's Theater; Kate Bighead, an Indian woman riding among the bodies of the Seventh Cavalry at Little Big Horn and wondering afterward if her pony might have kicked dust upon the remnants of George Armstrong Custer; Leo Rosenberg, a publicity man for Westinghouse who read the Harding-Cox presidential-election returns of 1920 over Pittsburgh's KDKA and thus became the nation's first broadcast newsman; Melba Pattillo, braving a spitting racist mob to integrate Little Rock's Central High School behind the bayonet shield of the 101st Airborne Division.

If history is often made by the unsung, it is obviously written largely by those at the top. So here is George Washington complaining bitterly to the Continental Congress over its failure to feed and equip his Valley Forge soldiers. (He had no cause to proclaim "I shall return" since he never left his men.) And here is Robert F. Kennedy at a climactic moment in the Cuban missile crisis, glancing at his brother the President. "His face seemed drawn, his eyes pained, almost gray. . . . I thought of when he was ill and almost died; when he lost his child; when we learned that our oldest brother had been killed. . . ."

But in looking to these eyewitness accounts from American history, I think most of all of Irving Strobing of 605 Barbey Street, Brooklyn.

The newspaper reports accompanying the text of his message from Corregidor said he was a graduate of Thomas Jefferson High School in the borough's working-class East New York section, a tailor's son who had gone on to Brooklyn College before enlisting in the army.

I, too, went to Thomas Jefferson, and I am a graduate of Brooklyn College. So there's a special feeling of kinship here for me.

School ties or no, all of us can find here a link to yesterday's Americans.

This is an age when a prominent black baseball player named Vince Coleman could say, evidently without embarrassment, "Don't know no Jackie Robinson, man."

But most of us, I hope, will offer kudos to the heroes and scoundrels, to the otherwise anonymous Americans, who became caught up in our history and had the imagination to tell the generations to come: Yes, this is how it was.

Richard Goldstein

Chapter One

the MAKING of a NATION

the NEW WORLD

The early European explorers' discovery of the great North American continent to the west was spawned by a quest for the riches of the East.

The navigators of the sixteenth and seventeenth centuries set out in hopes of finding a direct route to Asia and its spices, gold, and precious gems.

In searching for the sea passage that wasn't there, they ranged along America's East Coast, dipping in and out of the rivers and bays, frustrated always, unaware of the great three-thousand-mile expanse before them.

They would find not riches but the native Americans, their earliest encounters sometimes joyful, sometimes bloody.

On January 7, 1524, the Florentine sailor Giovanni Verrazano went to sea from a point near the island of Madeira aboard the ship *La Dauphine*, commissioned by King Francis I of France to find a passage to the Orient.

In early March, he anchored off Cape Fear, North Carolina, and sent some men ashore in a small boat.

Verrazano would tell of the natives they met.

These people go altogether naked except only that they cover their privy parts with certain skins of beasts . . . which they fasten onto a narrow girdle made of grass, very artificially wrought, hanged about with tails of divers other beasts, which round about their bodies hang dangling down to their knees. Some of them wear garlands of birds' feathers. The people are of color russet, and not much unlike the Saracens; their hair black, thick, and not very long, which they tie together in a knot behind, and wear it like a tail. They are well featured in their limbs, of mean stature, and commonly somewhat bigger than we; broad breasted, strong arms, their legs and other parts of their bodies well fashioned, and they are disfigured in nothing. . . . [W]e saw many of them well favored, having black and great eyes, with a cheerful and steady look, not strong of body, yet sharp-witted, nimble and great runners. . . .

Verrazano set out again and then stopped somewhat north of Cape Fear. When the natives made signs of welcome, he sent a crewman swimming ashore with gifts—evidently sheets of paper, glasses, and bells. The rough waves tossed the man as he swam back, and he was washed ashore, close to death. Now the crew watched as the Indians carried the man. He "cried out piteously" in fear as the Indians stripped off his clothes, laid him down on a sand dune in the sun, and put him beside a great fire. His shipmates expected that the man would be roasted and eaten, but the Indians had only benevolence in their hearts, as Verrazano would note.

The young man having recovered his strength, and having stayed awhile with them, showed them by signs that he was desirous to return to the ship; and they with great love clapping him fast about with many embracings, accompanying him unto the sea; and, to put him in more assurance, leaving him alone they went unto a high ground and stood there, beholding him, until he was entered into the boat.

Verrazano's men had a strange way of reciprocating the Indians' friendship. Stopping later at a place Verrazano called Arcadia (for beautiful Arcady of ancient Greece)—evidently Kitty Hawk, North Carolina, site of the Wright brothers' first flight—the crew kidnapped a child and tried to make off with a young woman as well.

That we might have knowledge thereof, we sent 20 men a-land, which entered into the country about two leagues, and they found that the people were fled to the woods for fear. They saw only one old woman with a young maid of 18 or 20 years old, which, seeing our company, hid themselves in the grass for fear; the old woman carried two infants on her shoulders, and behind her neck a child of 8 years old; the young woman was laden likewise with as many. But when our men came unto them, the women cried out; the old woman made signs that the men were fled unto the woods as soon as they saw us; to quiet them and to win their favor, our men gave them such victuals as they had with them to eat, which the old woman received thankfully; but the young woman disdained them all, and threw them disdainfully on the ground. They took a child from the old woman to bring into France, and, going about to take the young woman (which was very beautiful and of tall stature), they could not possibly, for the great outcries that she made, bring her to the sea, and especially having great woods to pass through, and being far from the ship, we purposed to leave her behind, bearing away the child only.

On April 17, Verrazano sailed into a lovely bay and then anchored in a narrows, the spot where a great bridge bearing his name would arise 440 years later. It was the first glimpse by Europeans of New York Harbor.

Verrazano was impressed by the picturesque hills, the current sites of Staten Island and Brooklyn Heights.

In space of 100 leagues sailing, we found a very pleasant place, situated amongst certain little steep hills; from amidst the which hills there ran down into the sea a great stream of water, which within the mouth was very deep. . . .

Verrazano stayed for only a day before heading toward Rhode Island. But he did get a glimpse of the Indians.

The people . . . are clad with feathers of fowls of divers colors. They came toward us very cheerfully, making great shouts of admiration, showing us where we might come to land most safely with our boat. We entered up the said river into the land about half a league, where it made a most pleasant lake [probably the Upper Bay] about 3 leagues in compass; on the which they rowed from the one side to the other, to the number of 30 of their small boats, wherein were many people, which passed from one shore to the other to come and see us. And behold, upon the sudden (as is wont to fall out in sailing) a contrary flaw of wind coming from the sea, we were enforced to return to our ship, leaving this land, to our great discontentment for the great commodity and pleasantness thereof, which we suppose is not without some riches, all the hills showing mineral matters in them.

POCAHONTAS *to the* RESCUE

Back in 1587, an English expedition directed by Sir Walter Raleigh founded a settlement at Roanoke, the present-day Outer Banks of North Carolina. But resupply ships that arrived three years later found no trace of the colonists. They had evidently succumbed to starvation and Indian raids—the so-called Lost Colony.

The English tried again in May 1607, when a hundred colonists arrived in Chesapeake Bay aboard three ships and founded Jamestown. Their ostensible goal was the spread of Christianity, but they were more interested in metallic riches—gold, silver, and copper.

Jamestown, Virginia, would become the first permanent English settlement in America. Its leader, Captain John Smith, an adventurer and onetime Mediterranean privateer, would keep the colony going despite heavy losses to hunger and conflict with the Indians.

Smith, as every schoolchild knows, almost lost his own head—as he told it. Captured by Indians led by Chief Powhatan, he was about to have his skull bashed open when the chief's young daughter, Pocahontas, saved him.

Whether Smith's story—told in the third person—is true in all its details is a matter for endless debate. But it has proved an enduring tale. And though Smith found no riches, the story of the Indian maiden would eventually bring gold to the coffers of the Disney empire.

At last they brought him [Smith] to Werowocomoco, where was Powhatan, their emperor. Here more than two hundred of those grim courtiers stood wondering at him as [if] he had been a monster, till Powhatan and his train had put themselves in their greatest braveries. Before a fire upon a seat like a bedstead he sat covered with a great robe made of raccoon skins, and all the tails hanging by. On either hand did sit a young wench of sixteen or eighteen years, and along on each side the house two rows of men. And behind them as many women, with all their heads and shoulders painted red, many of their heads bedecked with the white down of birds but everyone with something, and a great chain of white beads about their necks.

At his entrance before the king all the people gave a great shout. The queen of Appomattoc was appointed to bring him water to wash his hands, and another brought him a bunch of feathers instead of a towel to dry them. Having feasted him after their best barbarous manner they could, a long consultation was held. But the conclusion was: two great stones were brought before Powhatan, then as many as could lay hands on him, dragged him to them, and thereon laid his head. And being ready with their clubs to beat out his brains, Pocahontas, the king's dearest daughter, when no entreaty could prevail, got his head in her arms and laid her own upon his to save him from death. Whereat the emperor was contented he should live to make him hatchets and her bells, beads, and copper.

Smith would then tell of an errand his new friend Powhatan sent him on.

Two days after, Powhatan having disguised himself in the most fearful manner he could, caused Captain Smith to be brought forth to a great house in the woods, and there upon a mat by the fire to be left alone. Not long after from behind a mat that divided the house was made the most doleful noise he ever heard. Then Powhatan, more like a devil than a man, with some two hundred more as black as himself, came unto him and told him now they were friends and presently he should go to Jamestown to send him two great guns and a grindstone, for which he would give him the country of Capahowasick, and forever esteem him as his son Nantaquaus.

So to Jamestown with twelve guides Powhatan sent him. That night they quartered in the woods, he still expecting (as he had done all this long time of his imprisonment) every hour to be put to one death or other, for all their feasting. But Almighty God (by His divine providence) had mollified the hearts of those stern barbarians with compassion. The next morning betimes they came to the fort, where Smith, having used the savages with what kindness he could, he showed Rawhunt, Powhatan's trusty servant, two demi-culverins [small cannon] and a millstone to carry Powhatan. They found them somewhat too heavy. But when they did see him discharge them, being loaded with stones, among the boughs of a great tree loaded with icicles, the ice and branches came so tumbling down that the poor savages ran away half dead with fear. But at last we regained some conference with them, and gave them such toys and sent to Powhatan, his women, and children such presents as gave them in general full content.

Jamestown survived despite the troubles with Powhatan. Pocahontas later married John Rolfe, who saved the colony by introducing tobacco, which fetched nice prices in London. And Pocahontas's conversion to Christianity helped reconcile the settlers and the Indians.

the GREAT HARBOR

Verrazano's journey had established the existence of a vast North American continent. But he had seen little when he stopped in New York Harbor, merely glimpsing the entrance to a fine river running out of the bay.

In the late summer of 1609, Henry Hudson, an Englishman sailing for the Dutch, embarked on a thirty-day journey up and down that river—which would bear his name—in another of the futile quests for a sea route to Asia.

But Hudson's meanderings aboard the *Half Moon* would range far beyond the Hudson River, running as far north as the coast of Maine and south to the waters off Virginia. They would lead years later to expeditions through the Appalachians and to the burgeoning of the fur trade.

Hudson's journal provided some of the first detailed descriptions of encounters with Indians. There were many ugly incidents—murders, a kidnapping, and the deliberate use of alcohol to take advantage of the natives—but there were friendly gestures as well, among them a moment of mutual admiration in New York Harbor.

I sailed to the shore in one of their canoes, with an old man, who was the chief of a tribe, consisting of forty men and seventeen women; these I saw there in a house well constructed of oak bark, and circular in shape, so that it had the appearance of being well built, with an arched roof. It contained a great quantity of maize or Indian corn, and beans of last year's growth, and there lay near the house for the purpose of drying, enough to load three ships, besides what was growing in the fields. On our coming into the house, two mats were spread out to sit upon, and immediately some food was spread served in well-made red wooden bowls; two men were also despatched at once with bows and arrows in quest of game, who soon after brought in a pair of pigeons which they had shot. They likewise killed a fat dog, and skinned it in great haste with shells that they had got out of the water.

They supposed that I would remain with them for the night, but I returned after a short time on board the ship. The land is the finest for cultivation that I ever in my life set foot upon, and it also abounds in trees of every description. The natives are a very good people, for when they saw I would not remain, they supposed that I was afraid of their bows, and taking their arrows, they broke them in pieces, and threw them into the fire.

the FIRST THANKSGIVING

In November 1620, a band of 102 settlers arrived aboard the *Mayflower* in Cape Cod Bay, debarking at the site of the present Provincetown, Massachusetts. Half of them were Pilgrims, dissenters from the Church of England who had gone to Holland, then sought to start life anew in America.

By mid-December, the Pilgrims—backed by loans from English merchants—had moved on to Plymouth, where they founded the second permanent English colony in the New World.

After a terrible winter that claimed the lives of half the settlers, the survivors were befriended by Indians who taught them how to fish and grow corn. In October 1621, the Pilgrims celebrated their first harvest by feasting with the braves of the Indian grand chief Massasoit.

The festival was described in a letter sent two months later by Edward Winslow, a future governor of Plymouth, to a "loving and old friend" in England.

You will understand that in this little time that a few of us have been here, we have builte seven dwelling houses, and four for the use of the Plantation, and have made preparation for divers others.

We set last spring some twentie acres of Indian corne and sowed some six acres of barley and peas. And according to ye manner of the Indians, we manured our ground with herrings, or rather shads, which we have in great abundance and take with great ease at our doors.

Our corne did prove well and—God be praised!—we had a good increase of Indian corne, and our barley indifferent good. But our peas not worth the gathering, for we feared they were too late sown. They came up very well and blossomed, but the sun parched them in the blossom. . . .

Our harvest being gotten in, our Governor sente four men out fowling that so we might, after a more special manner, rejoyce together after we had gathered the fruit of our labours. These four, in one day, killed as much fowl as, with a little help besides, served the company almost a week, at which time, amongst other recreations, we exercised our armes, many of the Indians coming amongst us.

And amongst the rest, their greatest King, Massasoit, with some ninety men, whom, for three days, we entertained and feasted.

And they went out and killed five deer, which they brought to the Plantation, and bestowed on our Governor and upon the Captaine and others.

And although it be not always so plentifull as it was at this time with us, yet, by the goodness of God, we are so farr from wante that we often wish you partakers of our plentie.

the MIGHTY MISSISSIPPI

By the second half of the seventeenth century, the French had explored the St. Lawrence Valley. But they were determined to go farther as fur traders looked for better routes and Catholic missionaries sought new converts among the Indians.

A great Southern river was believed to lead to the Pacific. In 1673, the task of finding it was given to Louis Joliet, a fur trader and explorer, and the Jesuit missionary Jacques Marquette.

They left the Jesuit post of St. Ignace, on the Straits of Mackinac, in May. Following the Fox River in two canoes, accompanied by five others, they arrived at Prairie du Chien (Wisconsin) on June 17. And there it was—the Mississippi River.

Joliet and Marquette paddled through placid waters two hundred miles downstream, then encountered a large and raging river coming from the west—the Missouri.

Their voyage, reaching as far as the junction with the Arkansas River, was a prelude to La Salle's navigation of the Mississippi to the Gulf of Mexico in 1682 and his claiming for King Louis XIV of France the vast Western lands watered by the river—the territory La Salle called Louisiana.

Marquette's journal told of discovering the Mississippi and would also provide an early description of the buffalo, which he called the "pisikious."

Here we are, then, on this so renowned River, all of whose peculiar features I have endeavored to note carefully. The Missispi River takes its rise in various lakes in the country of the Northern nations. It is narrow at the place where Miskous [the Wisconsin] empties; its Current, which flows southward, is slow and gentle. To the right is a large chain of very high Mountains, and to the left are beautiful lands; in various Places, the Stream is divided by Islands. . . . Its Width is very unequal; sometimes it is three-quarters of a league, and sometimes it narrows to three arpents [under two hundred yards]. We gently followed its Course, which runs toward the south and southeast, as far as the 42nd degree of Latitude. Here we plainly saw that its aspect was completely changed. There are hardly any woods or mountains; the Islands are more beautiful, and are Covered with finer trees. We saw only deer and cattle, bustards, and Swans without wings, because they drop their plumage in this country. From time to time, we came upon monstrous fish, one of which struck our Canoe with such violence that I Thought that it was a great tree, about to break the Canoe in pieces. . . . When we reached the parallel of 41 degrees 28 minutes, following the same direction, we found that Turkeys had taken the place of game; and the pisikious, or wild cattle, That of the other animals.

We call them "wild cattle" because they are very similar to our domestic cattle. They are not longer, but are nearly as large again, and more Corpulent. When Our people killed one, three persons had much difficulty in moving it. The head is very large; The forehead is flat and a foot and a half Wide between the horns, which are exactly like Those of our oxen, but black and much larger. Under the Neck They have a Sort of large Dewlap, which hangs down; and on The back is a rather high hump. The whole of the head, The Neck, and a portion of the Shoulders are covered with a thick mane Like that of horses; It Forms a crest a foot long, which makes them hideous, and, falling over their eyes, Prevents them from seeing what is before them. The remainder of the Body is covered with a heavy coat of curly hair, almost Like That of our sheep, but much stronger and Thicker. It falls off in Summer, and The skin becomes as soft As Velvet. At that season, the savages Use the hides for making fine Robes, which they paint in various colors.

The flesh and the fat of the pisikious are Excellent, and constitute the best dish at feasts. Moreover they are very fierce; and not a year passes without their killing some savages. When attacked, they catch a man on their Horns, if they can, toss Him in the air, and then throw him on the ground, after which they trample him under foot and kill him. If a person fire at Them from a distance, with either a bow or a gun, he must, immediately after the Shot, throw himself down and hide in the grass; for if they perceive him who has fired, they run at him, and attack him. As their legs are thick and rather Short, they do not run very fast, as a rule, except when angry. They are scattered about the prairie in herds; I have seen one of 400.

Marquette and Joliet became the first Europeans to see the mouth of the Missouri River, which they called the Pekitanoui.

. . . sailing quietly in clear and calm Water, we heard the noise of a rapid, into which we were about to run. I have seen nothing more dreadful. An accumulation of large and entire trees, branches, and float-ing islands, was issuing from the Mouth of The river Pekitanoui, with such impetuosity that we could not without great danger risk passing through it. So great was the agitation that the water was very muddy, and could not become clear.

Pekitanoui is a river of considerable size, coming from the northwest, from a great distance; and it discharges into the Missispi. There are Villages of savages along the river, and I hope by its means to discover the vermillion or California sea.

Judging from The Direction of the course of the Missispi, if it Continue the same way, we think that it discharges into the Mexican Gulf. It would be a great advantage to find the river Leading to the Southern Sea, toward California; and, as I have said, this is what I hope to do by means of the Pekitanoui, according to the reports made to me by the savages. From them I have learned that, by ascending this river for 5 or 6 days, one reaches a fine prairie, 20 or 30 leagues long. This must be crossed in a northwesterly direction, and it terminates at another small river,—on which one may embark, for it is not very difficult to transport Canoes through so fine a country as that prairie. This 2nd River Flows toward The southwest for 10 or 15 leagues, after which it enters a Lake, small and deep, which flows toward the West, where it falls into The sea. I have hardly any doubt that it is The Vermillion Sea, and I do not despair of discovering It some day, if God grant me the grace and the health to do so, in order that I may preach the Gospel to all The peoples of this new world who have so Long Groveled in the darkness of infidelity.

the WITCHES of SALEM

It began with strange behavior on the part of three girls—Betty Parris, age nine, the daughter of Samuel Parris, the minister of Salem Village; the minister's niece, Abigail, eleven, and Ann Putnam, twelve, daughter of an influential townsman. A doctor pronounced them bewitched, and the slave girl belonging to the Parris family was jailed on witchcraft charges.

Soon a wave of hysteria erupted and become enmeshed in village feuds as witchcraft trials spread through the Puritan society of Massachusetts.

More than 150 people were formally charged, nineteen "witches" were hanged in 1692, and the husband of one convicted witch was suffocated by stones for refusing to enter a plea.

One of the vilest witches was Martha Carrier—or so it seemed to the influential clergyman Cotton Mather.

Martha Carrier was indicted for the bewitching of certain persons, according to the form usual in such cases, pleading not guilty to her indictment. There were first brought in a considerable number of the bewitched persons, who not only made the court sensible of an horrid witchcraft committed upon them, but also deposed that it was Martha Carrier or her shape that grievously tormented them by biting, pricking, pinching, and choking of them. It was further deposed that while this Carrier was on her examination before the magistrates, the poor people were so tortured that everyone expected their death upon the very spot, but that upon the binding of Carrier they were eased. . . .

Benjamin Abbot gave in his testimony that last March was a twelve-month this Carrier was very angry with him upon laying out some land near her husband's. . . . Presently after this he was taken with a swelling in his foot, and then with a pain in his side, and exceedingly tormented. It bred unto a sore, which was lanced by Doctor Prescot, and several gallons of corruption ran out of it. For six weeks it continued very bad; and then another sore bred in his groin, which was also lanced by Doctor Prescot. Another sore then bred in his groin, which was likewise cut, and put him to very great misery. He was brought unto death's door and so remained until Carrier was taken and carried away by the constable, from which very day he began to mend and so grew better every day and is well ever since.

Allin Toothaker testified that Richard, the son of Martha Carrier, having some difference with him, pulled him down by the hair of the head. When he rose again, he was going to strike at Richard Carrier, but fell down flat on his back to the ground and had not power to stir hand or foot until he told Carrier he yielded; and then he saw the shape of Martha Carrier go off his breast. . . .

Phebe Chandler testified that about a fortnight before the apprehension of Martha Carrier, on a Lord's day while the psalm was singing in the church, this Carrier then took her by the shoulder and shaking her asked her where she lived. She made no answer, although as Carrier, who lived next door to her father's house, could not in reason but know who she was. Quickly after this, as she was at several times crossing the fields, she heard a voice that she took to be Martha Carrier's; and it seemed as if it was over her head. The voice told her she should within two or three days be poisoned. Accordingly, within such a little time, one half of her right hand became greatly swollen and very painful, as also part of her face—whereof she can give no account how it came. It continued very bad for some days, and several times since she has had a greater pain in her breast and been so seized on her legs that she has hardly been able to go. She added that lately, going well to the house of God, Richard, the son of Martha Carrier, looked very earnestly upon her; and immediately her hand, which had formerly been poisoned, as is said above, began to pain her greatly; and she had a strange burning at her stomach, but was then struck deaf so that she could not hear any of the prayer or singing till the two or three last words of the psalm. . . .

One Lacy, who likewise confessed her share in this witchcraft, now testified that she and the prisoner were once bodily present at a witch meeting in Salem village, and that she knew the prisoner to be a witch and to have been at a diabolical sacrament, and that the prisoner was the undoing of her and her children by enticing them into the snare of the devil. . . .

In the time of this prisoner's trial, one Susanna Sheldon in open court had her hands unaccountable tied together with a wheel band so fast that without cutting it could not be loosened. It was done by a specter, and the sufferer affirmed that it was the prisoner's.

Memorandum: This rampant hag, Martha Carrier, was the person of whom the confession of the witches and of her own children among them are agreed that the devil had promised she should be queen of hell.

Life in Salem would ultimately be brought back to the American consciousness as art. In his 1953 play *The Crucible*, Arthur Miller looked at the witchcraft trials as a precursor to the intolerance in American life that spawned McCarthyism.

the BOSTON MASSACRE

With their victory over France in the French and Indian War of 1754–63—the New World version of the Seven Years' War in Europe—the British gained control of the American continent east of the Mississippi Valley.

To pay for its war burdens, Britain imposed a series of taxes upon the colonists under the Sugar Act, the Stamp Act, and then the Townshend Acts.

In response, the Americans boycotted British goods, and the Massachusetts House of Representatives advocated united colonial resistance. The British showed their resolve by sending five regiments to Boston. When a group of locals attacked sentries on March 5, 1770, pelting them with snowballs, soldiers fired into the crowd. Three people died instantly, and two later succumbed to wounds.

A townsman named Richard Palmes witnessed the Boston Massacre.

Between the hours of nine and ten o'clock of the fifth instant, I heard one of the bells ring, which I supposed was occasioned by fire, and enquiring where the fire was, was answered that the soldiers were abusing the inhabitants; I asked where, was first answered at Murray's barracks. I went there and spoke to some officers that were standing at the door. I told them I was surprised they suffered the soldiers to go out of the barracks after eight o'clock; I was answered by one of the officers, pray do you mean to teach us our duty; I answered I did not, only to remind them of it. One of them then said, you see that the soldiers are all in their barracks, and why do you not go to your homes. Mr. James Lamb and I said, Gentlemen, let us go home, and were answered by home, home, home. . . .

But when I got to the town-pump, we were told there was a rumpus at the Custom-house door; Mr. Spear said to me you had better not go, I told him I would go and try to make peace. I immediately went there and saw Capt. Preston at the head of six or eight soldiers in a circular form, with guns breast high and bayonets fixed; the said Captain stood almost to the end of their guns.

I went immediately to Capt. Preston (as soon as Mr. Bliss had left him), and asked him if their guns were loaded, his answer was they are loaded with powder and ball. I then said to him, I hope you do not intend they shall fire upon the inhabitants, his reply was, by no means. When I was asking him these questions, my left hand was on his right shoulder; Mr. John Hickling had that instant taken his hand off my shoulder, and stepped to my left, then instantly I saw a piece of snow or ice fall among the soldiers on which the soldier at the officer's right hand stepped back and discharged his gun. At the space of some seconds the soldier at his left fired next, and the others one after the other. After the first gun was fired, I heard the word "fire," but who said it I know not.

After the first gun was fired, the said officer had full time to forbid the other soldiers not to fire, but I did not hear him speak to them at all; then turning myself to the left I saw one man dead, distant about six feet; I having a stick in my hand made a stroke at the soldier who fired, and struck the gun out of his hand. I then made a stroke at the officer, my right foot slipped, that brought me on my knee, the blow falling short; he says I hit his arm; when I was recovering myself from the fall, I saw the soldier that fired the first gun endeavoring to push me through with his bayonet, on which I threw my stick at his head, the soldier starting back, gave me an opportunity to jump from him into Exchange Lane, or I must have been inevitably run through my body.

I looked back and saw three persons laying on the ground, and perceiving a soldier stepping round the corner as I thought to shoot me, I ran down Exchange lane, and so up the next into King Street, and followed Mr. Gridley with several other persons with the body of Capt. Morton's apprentice, up to the prison house, and saw he had a ball shot through his breast; at my return I found that the officers and soldiers were gone to the main guard. To my best observation there were not seventy people in King Street at the time of their firing, and then very scattering; but in a few minutes after the firing there were upwards of a thousand.

A Boston merchant named John Tudor described the aftermath.

Tuesday A.M. the inhabitants mett at Faneuil Hall & after som pertinant speeches, chose a Committee of 15 Gentlemn to waite on the Levt.

Governor in Council to request the immediate removal of the Troops. The message was in these Words. That it is the unanimous opinion of this Meeting, that the inhabitants & soldiery can no longer live together in safety; that nothing can Ratonaly be expected to restore the pece of the Town & prevent Blood & Carnage, but the removal of the Troops. . . .

[Thursday] Agreeable to a general request of the Inhabitants, were follow'd to the Grave (for they were all Buried in one) in succession the 4 Bodies of Messs Saml Gray, Saml Maverick, James Caldwell & Crispus Attucks, the unhappy Victims who fell in the Bloody Massacre. On this sorrowfull Occasion most of the shops & stores in Town were shut, all the Bells were order'd to toll a solom peal in Boston, Charleston, Cambridge & Roxbery. The several Hearses forming a junction in King Street, the Theatre of that inhuman Tradgedy, proceeded from thence thro' the main street, lengthened by an immence Concourse of people, So numerous as to be obliged to follow in Ranks of 4 & 6 abreast and brought up by a long Train of Carriages. The sorrow Visible in the Countenances, together with the peculiar solemnity, Surpass description, it was suppos'd that the Spectators & those that follow'd the corps amount to 15,000, some supposed 20,000.

The British troops' commander, Captain Robert Preston, and six of his men were tried for murder. John Adams and Josiah Quincy, though spokesmen for the patriots' cause, defended Preston and four of his soldiers, in order to ensure a fair trial, and these were acquitted. The other two were convicted of manslaughter.

the BOSTON TEA PARTY

A monopoly in the distribution of tea in the colonies granted to the East India Company by the British Parliament in May 1773 aroused further anger. Ships taking tea to Philadelphia and New York were forced to turn back. Tea imported to Charleston, South Carolina, was placed in warehouses but spoiled in the face of a boycott.

Mass meetings by colonists in Boston demanded the removal of three tea-laden ships that had arrived off Griffin's wharf. When the colonists sought a response from the royal governor of Massachusetts, Thomas Hutchinson, they were told he had left for his country home in Milton.

On December 16, 1773, two hundred men disguised as Indians boarded the ships and dumped 342 chests of tea into the harbor.

The identities of the Boston Tea Party agitators were kept secret at the time. In 1834, George Hewes, claiming to have been one of the tea-dumpers, recalled the uprising.

When the committee returned and informed the meeting of the absence of the Governor, there was a confused murmur among the members, and the meeting was immediately dissolved, many of them crying out, "Let every man do his duty, and be true to his country"; and there was a general huzza for Griffin's wharf.

It was now evening, and I immediately dressed myself in the costume of an Indian, equipped with a small hatchet, which I and my associates denominated the tomahawk, with which, and a club, after having painted my face and hands with coal dust in the shop of a blacksmith, I repaired to Griffin's wharf. . . . I fell in with many who were dressed, equipped and painted as I was, and who fell in with me and marched in order to the place of our destination.

When we arrived at the wharf, there were three of our number who assumed an authority to direct our operations, to which we readily submitted. . . . The commander of the division to which I belonged, as soon as we were on board the ship, appointed me boatswain, and ordered me to go to the captain and demand of him the keys to the hatches and a dozen candles. I made the demand accordingly, and the captain promptly replied, and delivered the articles; but requested me at the same time to do no damage to the ship or rigging. We then were ordered by our commanders to open the hatches and take out all the chests of tea and throw them overboard, and we immediately proceeded to execute his orders, first cutting and splitting the chests with our tomahawks, so as thoroughly to expose them to the effects of the water.

In about three hours from the time we went on board, we had thus broken and thrown overboard every tea chest to be found in the ship, while those in the other ships were disposing of the tea in the same way, at the same time. We were surrounded by British armed ships, but no attempt was made to resist us.

We then quietly returned to our several places of residence, without having any conversation with each other, or taking any measures to discover who were our associates. . . . There appeared to be an understanding that each individual should volunteer his services, keep his own secret, and risk the consequence for himself.

During the time we were throwing the tea overboard, there were several attempts made by some of the citizens of Boston and its vicinity to carry off small quantities of it for their family use. To effect that object, they would watch their opportunity to snatch up a handful from the deck, where it became plentifully scattered, and put it in their pockets. One Captain O'Connor, whom I well knew, came on board for that purpose, and when he supposed he was not noticed, filled his pockets, and also the lining of his coat. But I had detected him and gave information to the captain of what he was doing. We were ordered to take him into custody, and just as he was stepping from the vessel, I seized him by the skirt of his coat, and in attempting to pull him back, I tore it off; but, springing forward, by a rapid effort he made his escape. He had, however, to run a gauntlet through the crowd upon the wharf, each one, as he passed, giving him a kick or a stroke. . . .

The next morning, after we had cleared the ships of the tea, it was discovered that very considerable portions of it were floating upon the surface of the water; and to prevent the possibility of any of its being saved for use, a number of small boats were manned by sailors and citizens, who rowed them into those parts of the harbor wherever the tea was visible, and by beating it with oars and paddles so thoroughly drenched it as to render its entire destruction inevitable.

The protest merely hardened British policy. Parliament closed the port of Boston and passed the "Intolerable Acts," providing for the quartering of soldiers in colonists' homes and the transfer of politically tinged trials to English courts.

LEXINGTON GREEN

Responding to England's tough line, colonial assemblies sent delegates to Philadelphia to draw up a coordinated response. The First Continental Congress, meeting in the autumn of 1774, called for a new boycott of British goods and passed resolutions voicing the rights of the colonists.

An open break with England was coming closer.

Moving to head off rebellion, English soldiers set out on the night of April 18, 1775, from Boston to arrest the patriot leaders John Hancock and Samuel Adams and seize guns and powder at Concord.

The tolling of bells, the beating of drums, and the "midnight ride" of Paul Revere warned the colonial militia—the Minutemen—assembled on Lexington Green the following morning. When the British arrived, a skirmish ensued—the opening shots of the American Revolution.

Sylvanus Wood, a twenty-three-year-old Minuteman from nearby Woburn, who stood only five feet tall, was on the scene.

I heard the Lexington bell ring, and fearing there was some difficulty there, I immediately arose, took my gun, and with Robert Douglass went in haste to Lexington, which was about three miles distant. When I arrived there, I inquired of Captain [John] Parker, the commander of the Lexington company, what was the news. Parker told me he did not know what to believe, for a man had come up about half an hour before and informed him that the British troops were not on the road. But while we were talking, a messenger came up and told the captain that the British troops were within half a mile. Parker immediately turned to his drummer, William Diman, and ordered him to beat to arms, which was done.

Wood, joining the militiamen, heard an order from Parker.

Every man of you who is equipped, follow me. And those of you who are not equipped, go into the meeting-house and furnish yourselves from the magazine and immediately join our company.

Wood and the others sprang into action.

Parker led those of us who were equipped to the north end of Lexington Common, near the Bedford road, and formed us in single file. I was stationed about in the centre of the company.

While we were standing, I left my place and went from one end of the company to the other and counted every man who was paraded, and the whole number was thirty-eight and no more. Just as I had finished and got back to my place, I perceived the British troops had arrived on the spot between the meeting-house and Buckman's [tavern], near where Captain Parker stood when he first led off his men.

The British troops immediately wheeled so as to cut off those who had gone into the meeting-house. The British troops approached us rapidly in platoons, with a general officer on horseback at their head. The officer came up within about two rods of the centre of the company, where I stood, the first platoon being about three rods distant. They there halted. The officer then swung his sword and said, "Lay down your arms, you damned rebels, or you are all dead men—Fire!"

Some guns were fired by the British at us from the first platoon, but no person was killed or hurt, [the guns] being charged only with powder. Just at this time Captain Parker ordered every man to take care of himself. The company immediately dispersed; and while the company was dispersing and leaping over the wall, the second platoon of the British fired and killed some of our men. There was not a gun fired by any of Captain Parker's, within my knowledge. I was so situated that I must have known it, had any thing of the kind taken place before a total dispersion of our company. . . . One member of the company told me, many years since, that, after Parker's company had dispersed, and he was at some distance, he gave them the "guts of his gun."

Eight Massachusetts men were killed and ten wounded. The British, who claimed afterward that the Americans actually fired first, suffered only one minor casualty. They then headed for Concord.

Wood concluded:

After the British had begun their march to Concord, I returned to the Common and found Robert Roe and Jonas Parker [an older cousin of Captain Parker] lying dead at the north corner of the Common, near the

Bedford road, and others dead and wounded. I assisted in carrying the dead into the meeting-house. I then proceeded toward Concord with my gun.

At the Concord bridge, militiamen ambushed the British troops, killing dozens. In May, colonists under Ethan Allen and Benedict Arnold seized a British arsenal at Fort Ticonderoga, New York. And in June, the Second Continental Congress moved to create an army with George Washington of Virginia as its commander.

the DECLARATION *of* INDEPENDENCE

The gravestone at Monticello reads:

> *Here Was Buried Thomas Jefferson*
> *Author of the Declaration of Independence*
> *Of the Statute of Virginia for Religious Freedom*
> *And Father of the University of Virginia*

At Jefferson's direction, there is no mention of his having been the third president of the United States, the nation's first secretary of state, or the governor of Virginia.

For it was not as a holder of high office but as a political thinker, as an expounder of the democratic philosophy endowing man with the "inalienable rights" of "life, liberty, and the pursuit of happiness," that Jefferson wished to be remembered.

More than a year had passed since the Battle of Lexington. Now delegates from the thirteen colonies who had assembled in Philadelphia at the Second Continental Congress were drawing up the document providing the justification for their unalterable separation from Britain, for the right of men to throw off bonds of oppression.

The committee appointed to draft the Declaration of Independence consisted of Jefferson, John Adams, Benjamin Franklin, Roger Sherman, and Robert R. Livingston. Jefferson had made his mark as an important and facile writer with his "Summary View of the Rights of British America," but Adams would remember how, when he asked Jefferson to draft the declaration, he was mightily reluctant.

Mr. Jefferson came into Congress in June, 1775, and brought with him a reputation for literature, science, and a happy talent of composition. Writings of his were handed about, remarkable for the peculiar felicity of expression. Though a silent member in Congress, he was so prompt, frank, explicit and decisive upon committees and in conversation —not even Samuel Adams was more so—that he soon seized upon my heart; and upon this occasion I gave him my vote, and did all in my power to procure the votes of others. I think he had one more vote than any other, and that placed him at the head of the committee. I had the next highest number, and that placed me second. The committee met, discussed the subject, and then appointed Mr. Jefferson and me to make the draft, I suppose because we were the two first on the list.

The subcommittee met. Jefferson proposed to me to make the draft. I said, "I will not. You should do it." "Oh! no." "Why will you not? You ought to do it." "I will not." "Reasons enough." "What can be your reasons?" "Reason first, you are a Virginian, and a Virginian ought to appear at the head of this business. Reason second, I am obnoxious, suspected, and unpopular. You are very much otherwise. Reason third, you can write ten times better than I can." "Well," said Jefferson, "if you are decided, I will do it as well as I can." "Very well. When you have drawn it up, we will have a meeting."

A meeting we accordingly had, and conned the paper over. I was delighted with its high tone and the flights of oratory with which it abounded. . . . I consented to report it, and do not now remember that I made or suggested a single alteration.

We reported it to the committee of five. It was read, and I do not remember that Franklin or Sherman criticized anything. We were all in haste. Congress was impatient, and the instrument was reported, as I believe, in Jefferson's handwriting, as he first drew it. Congress cut off about a quarter of it, as I expected they would. . . .

Jefferson would recall that Adams did suggest a few changes.

. . . before I reported it to the committee, I communicated it separately to Dr. Franklin and Mr. Adams, requesting their corrections, because they were the two members of whose judgments and amendments I wished most to have the benefit before presenting it to the committee. . . . Their alterations were two or three only, and merely verbal. I then wrote a fair copy, reported it to the committee, and from them, unaltered, to Congress.

Jefferson would be embittered over changes made by the Continental Congress, which eliminated his castigation of King George III for allowing the slave trade to continue.

The pusillanimous idea that we had friends in England worth keeping terms with still haunted the minds of many. For this reason those passages which conveyed censures on the people of England were struck out, lest they should give them offence. The clause, too, reprobating the enslaving [of] the inhabitants of Africa was struck out in complaisance to South Carolina and Georgia, who had never attempted to restrain the importation of slaves, and who, on the contrary, still wished to continue it. Our Northern brethren also, I believe, felt a little tender under those censures; for though their people had very few slaves themselves, yet they had been pretty considerable carriers of them to others.

Jefferson had written the declaration in modest surroundings.

At the time of writing that instrument, I lodged in the house of a Mr. Graaf, a new brick house, three stories high, of which I rented the second floor, consisting of a parlor and bedroom, ready furnished. In that parlor I wrote habitually and in it wrote this paper particularly. . . .
The proprietor, Graaf, was a young man, son of a German, and then newly married. I think he was a bricklayer, and that his house was on the south side of Market Street, probably between Seventh and Eighth Streets, and if not the only house on that part of the street, I am sure there were few others near it.

Years later, with an eye to commemoration of Independence Day by generations to come, Jefferson told of the desk on which he wrote the declaration.

I received a letter from a friend in Philadelphia lately asking information of the house, and room of the house there, in which the Declaration of Independence was written, with a view to future celebrations of the Fourth of July in it. . . . If then things acquire a superstitious value because of their connection with particular persons, surely a connection with the great Charter of our Independence may give a value to what has been associated with that; and such was the idea of the enquirers after the room in which it was written.

Now I happen still to possess the writing-box on which it was written. It was made from a drawing of my own by Ben. Randall, a cabinetmaker in whose house I took my first lodgings on my arrival in Philadelphia in May, 1776, and I have used it ever since. It claims no merit of particular beauty. It is plain, neat, convenient, and, taking no more room on the writing table than a moderate quarto volume, it yet displays itself sufficiently for any writing. . . . Its imaginary value will increase with years, and another half-century . . . may see it carried in the procession of our nation's birthday as the relics of the saints are in those of the Church.

NATHAN HALE DEFIANT

Declaring independence was one thing. Winning it on the battlefield was another.

Much tribulation lay ahead for the Continental Army.

Following the Battle of Harlem Heights, an American officer named Nathan Hale volunteered to seek intelligence on British troop movements around New York City. Caught on Long Island and identified as a soldier—supposedly betrayed by his cousin, Samuel—Hale was taken to New York, questioned by General William Howe, and hanged without trial on September 22, 1776, in the vicinity of the current site of Grand Central Terminal.

Hale would become a legendary figure thanks to his last words, as recorded in the memoirs of William Hull, an American officer who was given an account of the execution by a British soldier.

. . . an officer came to our camp, under a flag of truce, and informed Hamilton, then a captain of artillery, but afterwards the aid[e] of General Washington, that Captain Hale had been arrested within the British lines, condemned as a spy, and executed that morning.

I learned the melancholy particulars from this officer, who was present at his execution and seemed touched by the circumstances attending it.

He said that Captain Hale had passed through their army, both of Long Island and York Island. That he had procured sketches of the fortifications, and made memoranda of their number and different positions. When apprehended, he was taken before Sir William Howe, and these papers, found concealed about his person, betrayed his intentions. He at once declared his name, his rank in the American army, and his object in coming within the British lines.

Sir William Howe, without the form of a trial, gave orders for his execution the following morning. He was placed in the custody of the Provost Marshal, who was a refugee and hardened to human suffering and every softening sentiment of the heart. Captain Hale, alone, without sympathy or support, save that from above, on the near approach of death asked for a clergyman to attend him. It was refused. He then requested a Bible; that too was refused by his inhuman jailer.

"On the morning of his execution," continued the officer, "my station was near the fatal spot, and I requested the Provost Marshal to permit the prisoner to sit in my marquee, while he was making the necessary preparations. Captain Hale entered: he was calm, and bore himself with gentle dignity, in the consciousness of rectitude and high intentions. He asked for writing materials, which I furnished him: he wrote two letters, one to his mother and one to a brother officer." He was shortly after summoned to the gallows. But a few persons were around him, yet his characteristic dying words were remembered. He said, "I only regret that I have but one life to lose for my country."

JOHN PAUL JONES TRIUMPHANT

During the summer of 1777, Scottish-born John Paul Jones began raiding British shipping in behalf of American interests. In January 1779, the French gave Jones a worn-out ship that he refurbished and called *Bonhomme Richard*, in honor of Benjamin Franklin—who had given him some funds—and his *Poor Richard's Almanack*.

Jones commanded the *Bonhomme Richard* as it captured the frigate *Serapis* on September 23, 1779, off the coast of England. Jones's own ship would go down, but it would be a famous victory, prefaced by his retort for the ages: "I have not yet begun to fight."

The encounter—enshrining Jones as the father of the United States Navy—would be described by Midshipman Nathaniel Fanning, captain of the maintop.

It had now got to be about forty-eight minutes since the action began. The enemy's tops being entirely silenced, the men in ours had nothing to do but direct their whole fire down upon the enemy's decks and forecastle; this we did, and with so much success that in about twenty-five minutes we had cleared her decks so that not a man on board the Serapis was to be seen. However, they still kept up a constant fire, with two eighteen pounders upon the lower gun-deck, and two nine pounders upon her upper gun-deck. Her four guns annoyed us very much and did our ship considerable damage. About this time the enemy's light sails, which were filled onto the Serapis's cranes over her quarterdeck sails caught fire; this communicated itself to her rigging and thence to ours; thus were both ships on fire. The firing on both sides ceased till it was extinguished by the contending parties, after which the action was renewed again. . . . By this time, the topmen in our tops had taken possession of the enemy's tops. . . . We transported from our own into the enemy's tops, stink pots, flasks, hand grenadoes, &c., which we threw in among the enemy whenever they made their appearance. The battle had now continued about three hours, and as we had possession of the Serapis's top, which commanded her quarterdeck, we were well assured that the enemy could not hold out much longer, and were momently expecting that they would strike to us, when the following farcical piece was acted on board our ship:

A report was at this time, circulated among our crew between decks, that Captain Jones and all his officers were slain; the gunners were now the commanders of our ship; that the ship had four or five feet of water in her hold; that she was sinking: they advised the gunner to go upon deck, together with the carpenter, and master at arms, and beg of the enemy quarters. These men mounted the quarterdeck, and bawled out as loud as they could, "Quarters, quarters, for God's sake, quarters! our ship is a-sink-in!" and immediately got upon the ship's poop with a view of hauling down our colours. Hearing this in the top, I told my men that the enemy had struck and was crying out for quarters, for I actually thought that the voices of these men sounded as if on board of the enemy; but in this I was soon undeceived. The three poltroons, finding the ensign and ensign-staff gone, they proceeded upon the quarterdeck, and were in the act of hauling down our pendant, still bawling for "quarters!" when I heard our commodore say, in a loud voice, "what d———d rascals are them—shoot them—kill them!" . . . He had just discharged his pistols at the enemy. The carpenter, and the master-at-arms, hearing Jones's voice, skulked below, and the gunner was attempting to do the same, when Jones threw both of his pistols at his head, one of which struck him in the head, fractured his skull, and knocked him down, at the foot of the gangway ladder, where he lay till the battle was over.

Both ships now took fire again; and on board of our ship it set our main top on fire. The water which we had in a tub, in the tops, was expended without extinguishing the fire. We next had recourse to our clothes, by pulling off our coats and jackets, and throwing them upon the fire, and stamping upon them, which smothered it. Both crews were busily employed in stopping the flames, and the firing on both sides ceased. The enemy now demanded if we had struck, as they had heard the three poltroons halloo for quarters. "If you have," said they, "why don't you haul down your pendant"; as they saw our ensign was gone. "Ay, ay," said Jones, "we'll do that when we can fight no longer, but we shall see yours come down first; for you must know, that Yankees do not haul down their colours till they are fairly beaten." The combat now recommenced again with fury; and continued for a few minutes, then the cry of fire was again heard. The firing ceased, and both crews were once more employed in extinguishing it, which was soon affected, when the battle was renewed with what cannon we could manage: hand grenadoes, stink pots, &c., but principally with lances and boarding pikes. With these the combatants killed each other through the ship's port holes, which were pretty large. . . .

And at thirty-five minutes past 12 at night, a single hand grenado having been thrown by one of our men out of the main top of the enemy, struck on one side of the combings of her upper hatchway, and rebounding from that, fell between decks, where it communicated to a quantity of loose powder scattered about the enemy's cannon; and made a dreadful explosion, and blew up about twenty of the enemy. This closed the scene, and the enemy now bawled out "Quarters, quarters, quarters, for God's sake!" It was, however, some time before the enemy's colours were struck. The captain of the Serapis gave repeated orders for his crew to ascend the quarterdeck and haul down the English flag, but no one would stir. . . . The captain of the Serapis therefore ascended the quarterdeck, and hauled down the very flag which he had nailed to the flagstaff. . . . Captain Jones ordered Richard Dale, his first lieutenant, to select out of our crew a number of men, and take possession of the prize. . . .

This ended this ever memorable battle. The officers, headed by the captain of the Serapis, now came on board our ship; the latter [Captain Parsons] enquired for Captain Jones, to whom he was introduced by our purser. . . . Jones, after receiving his sword, made this reply: "Sir, you have fought like a hero, and I make no doubt but your sovereign will reward you in a most ample manner for it" . . . The two captains now withdrew into the cabin, and there drank a glass or two of wine together. Both ships were now separated from each other, and were mere wrecks; the Serapis's three masts having nothing to support them, fell overboard with all the sails, tops, yards, rigging, &c., making a hideous noise in the water. . . .

To see the dead lying in heaps—to hear the groans of the wounded and dying—the entrails of the dead scattered promiscuously around, the blood (American too) over one's shoes, was enough to move pity from the most hardened and callous breast. And although my spirit was somewhat dampened at this shocking sight, yet when I came to reflect *that we were conquerors, and over those who wished to bind America in everlasting chains of slavery; my spirits revived, and I thought perhaps that some faithful historian would at some future period enroll me among the heroes and deliverers of my country. . . .*

the BATTLE *of* SARATOGA

The victory by General Horatio Gates's Continental troops at Saratoga in October 1777 over a force led by General John Burgoyne marked a turning point in the Revolutionary War. It crushed Britain's effort to cut off New England from the Middle Atlantic and Southern states. And the Continentals' triumph led to France's entry on the American side, allowing George Washington to move south en route to his epic victory at Yorktown, Virginia.

A British lieutenant named Thomas Anburey told how Burgoyne's British professionals were let down at Saratoga by the Indian, Canadian, and Tory troops accompanying them.

The Indians were running from wood to wood, and just as soon as our regiment had formed in the skirts of one, several of them came up, and by their signs were conversing about the savage fire on our right. Soon after the enemy attacked us, and at the very first fire the Indians run off through the woods.

As to the Canadians, little was to be depended upon their adherence, being easily dispirited, with an inclination to quit as soon as there was an appearance of danger; nor was the fidelity of the Provincials to be relied on who had joined our army, as they withdrew on perceiving the resistance of the Americans would be more formidable than expected. The desertion of the Indians, Canadians, and Provincials, at a time when their services were most required, was exceedingly mortifying.

At battle's end, Lieutenant Anburey commanded a burial detail.

. . . fifteen, sixteen and twenty buried in one hole. I however observed a little more decency than some parties had done, who left heads, legs

and arms above ground. No other distinction is paid to officer or private, than the officers are put in a hole by themselves. Our army abounded with young officers, in the subaltern line, and in the course of this unpleasant duty, three of the 20th regiment were interred together, the age of the eldest not exceeding seventeen. This friendly office to the dead . . . was nothing to the scene in bringing in the wounded; the one were past all pain, the other in the most excruciating torments, sending forth dreadful groans. They had remained out all night, and from the loss of blood and want of nourishment, were upon the point of expiring with faintness; some of them begged they might lay and die, others again were insensible, some upon the least movements were put in the most horrid tortures, and all had near a mile to be conveyed to the hospitals; others at their last gasp, who for want of our timely assistance must have inevitably expired. These poor creatures, perishing with cold and weltering in their blood, displayed such a scene, it must be a heart of adamant that could not be effected by it, even to a degree of weakness.

In the course of the late action, Lieutenant Harvey, of the 62d, a youth of sixteen, and a nephew to the Adjutant-General of the same name, received several wounds, and was repeatedly ordered off the field by Colonel Anstruther, but his heroic ardor would not allow him to quit the battle, while he could stand and see his brave lads fighting beside him. A ball striking one of his legs, his removal became absolutely necessary, and while they were conveying him away, another wounded him mortally. In this situation the Surgeon recommended him to take a powerful dose of opium, to avoid a seven or eight hours of the most exquisite torture; this he immediately consented to, and when the Colonel entered the tent with Major Harnage, who were both wounded, they asked whether he had any affairs they could settle for him? his reply was "that being a minor, every thing was already adjusted:" but he had one request, which he had just life enough to utter, "Tell my uncle I die like a soldier!"

Family bonds were unraveled by irreconcilable loyalties, just as uniforms of blue and gray would rip families apart during the next century.

But at Saratoga, there would be a reunion. A British sergeant named Roger Lamb saw it happen.

During the time of the cessation of arms, while the articles of capitulation were preparing, the soldiers of the two armies often saluted, and discoursed with each other from the opposite banks of the river (which at Saratoga was about thirty yards wide, and not very deep), a soldier of the 9th regiment, named Maguire, came down to the bank of the river, with a number of his companions, who engaged in conversation with a party of Americans on the opposite shore.

In a short time something was observed very forcibly to strike the mind of Maguire. He suddenly darted like lightning from his companions, and resolutely plunged into the stream. At the very same moment, one of the American soldiers, seized with a similar impulse, resolutely dashed into the water, from the opposite shore. The wondering soldiers on both sides beheld them eagerly swim towards the middle of the river, where they met; they hung on each other's necks and wept; and the loud cries of "My brother! my dear brother!!!" which accompanied the transaction, soon cleared up the mystery, to the astonished spectators. They were both brothers, the first had migrated from this country [England], and the other had entered the army; one was in the British and the other in the American service, totally ignorant until that hour that they were engaged in hostile combat against each other's life.

WINTER *at* VALLEY FORGE

In mid-December 1777, Washington's army moved to winter quarters on the west side of the Schuylkill, near Philadelphia. For the next three months, his men would suffer greatly, perhaps twenty-five hundred perishing from malnutrition, frostbite, and illness. But the army would emerge as a formidable force, and the encampment at Valley Forge would become a national symbol of patriotic sacrifice.

Joseph Plumb Martin, a Continental Army private from Connecticut, wrote ruefully in his diary of the "thanksgiving" the men were ordered to observe, and then of the first night at Valley Forge.

While we lay here there was a Continental Thanksgiving ordered by Congress; and as the army had all the cause in the world to be particularly thankful, if not for being well off, at least that it was no worse, we were ordered to participate in it. We had nothing to eat for two or three days previous, except what the trees of the fields and forests afforded us. But we must now have what Congress said—a sumptuous Thanksgiving to close the year of high living we had now nearly seen brought to a close. Well, to add something extraordinary to our present stock of provisions, our country, ever mindful of its suffering army, opened her sympathizing heart so wide, upon this occasion, as to give us something to make the world stare—it gave each and every man half a gill of rice and a tablespoon full of vinegar!

After we had made sure of this extraordinary superabundant donation, we were ordered out to attend a meeting and hear a sermon delivered upon the occasion. We accordingly went, for we could not help it. I heard a sermon, a "thanksgiving sermon," what sort of one I do not know now, nor did I at the time I heard it. I had something else to think upon. My belly put me in remembrance of the fine Thanksgiving dinner I was to partake of when I could get it. I remember the text, like an attentive lad at church. "And the soldiers said unto him, And what shall we do? And he said unto them, Do violence to no man, nor accuse anyone falsely." The preacher ought to have added the remainder of the sentence to have made it complete, "And be content with your wages." But that would not do, it would be too apropos; however, he heard it as soon as the service was over, it was shouted from a hundred tongues.

The army was now not only starved but naked. The greatest part were not only shirtless and barefoot, but destitute of all other clothing, especially blankets. I procured a small piece of raw cowhide and made myself a pair of moccasins, which kept my feet (while they lasted) from the frozen ground, although, as I well remember, the hard edges so galled my ankles, while on a march, that it was with much difficulty and pain that I could wear them afterwards; but the only alternative I had was to endure this inconvenience or to go barefoot, as hundreds of my companions had to, till they might be tracked by their blood upon the rough frozen ground. We had hard duty to perform and little or no strength to perform it with.

We marched for the Valley Forge in order to take up our winter quarters. We were now in a truly forlorn condition, no clothing, no provisions and as disheartened as need be. We arrived, however, at our destination a few days before Christmas.

It was dark; there was no water to be found and I was perishing with thirst. I searched for water till I was weary, and came to my tent without finding any. Fatigue and thirst, joined with hunger, almost made me desperate. Just after I arrived at my tent, two soldiers, whom I did not know, passed by. They had some water in their canteens which they told me they had found a good distance off, but could not direct me to the place as it was very dark. I tried to beg a draught of water from them but they were as rigid as Arabs. At length I persuaded them to sell me a drink for three pence, Pennsylvania currency, which was every cent of property I could then call my own, so great was the necessity I was then reduced to.

The view from the top was equally bitter. Two days before Christmas, George Washington wrote from Valley Forge to the president of the Continental Congress.

Since the month of July we have had no assistance from the quartermaster-general, and to want of assistance from this department the commissary-general charges great part of his deficiency. To this I am to add, that, notwithstanding it is a standing order, and often repeated, that the troops shall always have two days' provisions from them, that they might be ready at any sudden call; yet an opportunity has scarcely ever offered, of taking an advantage of the enemy, that has not been either totally obstructed, or greatly impeded, on this account. And this, the great and crying evil, is not all. The soap, vinegar, and other articles allowed by Congress, we see none of, nor have we seen them, I believe, since the battle of Brandywine. The first, indeed, we have now little occasion for; few men having more than one shirt, many only the moiety of one, and some none at all. In addition to which, as a proof of the little benefit received from a clothier-general, and as a further proof of the inability of an army, under the circumstances of this, to perform the common duties of soldiers (besides a number of men confined to hospitals for want of shoes, and others in farmers' houses on the same account), we have, but a field-return this day made, no less than two thousand eight hundred and ninety-eight men now in camp unfit for duty, because they are barefoot and otherwise naked. . . .

Washington poured out his anger at the members of Congress warmed by their fires while his soldiers, and evidently his own reputation, suffered.

. . . what makes this matter still more extraordinary in my eye is, that these very gentlemen,—who were well apprized of the nakedness of the troops from ocular demonstration, who thought their own soldiers worse clad than others, and who advised me near a month ago to postpone the execution of a plan I was about to adopt, in consequence of a resolve of Congress for seizing clothes, under strong assurances that an ample supply would be collected in ten days agreeably to a decree of the State (not one article of which, by the by, is yet come to hand),—should think a winter's campaign, and the covering of these States from the invasion of an enemy, so easy and practicable a business. I can assure those gentlemen, that it is a much easier and less distressing thing to draw remonstrances in a comfortable room by a good fireside, than to occupy a cold, bleak hill, and sleep under frost and snow, without clothes or blankets. However, although they seem to have little feeling for the naked and distressed soldiers, I feel superabundantly for them, and, from my soul, I pity those miseries, which it is neither in my power to relieve or prevent.

It is for these reasons, therefore, that I have dwelt upon the subject; and it adds not a little to my other difficulties and distress to find, that much more is expected of me than is possible to be performed, and that upon the group of safety and policy I am obliged to conceal the true state of the army from public view, and thereby expose myself to detraction and calumny.

SURRENDER *at* YORKTOWN

But with help from France, Washington's army would ultimately prevail in the South.

English troops under General Charles Cornwallis scored a major victory at Guilford Courthouse in North Carolina in March 1781, but the British suffered heavy casualties and lost hope of controlling the Carolinas. The troops retreated northward, and in late September, after a French fleet off the Virginia coast knocked out British ships, they were besieged at Yorktown, on the lower Chesapeake Bay.

A blocking force of French vessels under Admiral de Grasse prevented English troops under Sir Henry Clinton from sailing down from New York to rescue Cornwallis, and American and French troops blocked a land escape via the York Peninsula.

Cornwallis (though refusing to appear in person) surrendered his forces on October 19, capitulating to George Washington and the French commander, Comte de Rochambeau. England's bid to crush the Continental Army was dead.

James Thacher, a surgeon's mate from Barnstable, Massachusetts, who joined the Continental Medical Corps at Cambridge in 1775, witnessed the surrender.

At about twelve o'clock, the combined army was arranged and drawn up in two lines extending more than a mile in length. The Americans were drawn up in a line on the right side of the road, and the French occupied the left. At the head of the former, the great American commander, mounted on his noble courser, took his station, attended by his aides. At the head of the latter was posted the excellent Count Rochambeau and his suite. The French troops, in complete uniform, displayed a martial and noble appearance. Their band of music, of which the timbrel formed a part, is a delightful novelty, and produced, while marching to the ground, a most enchanting effect. The Americans, though not all in uniform, nor their dress so neat, yet exhibited an erect, soldierly air, and every countenance beamed with satisfaction and joy. The concourse of spectators from the country was immense, in point of numbers probably equal to the military, but universal silence and order prevailed.

It was about two o'clock when the captive army advanced through the line formed for their reception. Every eye was prepared to gaze on Lord Cornwallis, the object of particular interest and solicitude, but he disappointed our anxious expectations. Pretending indisposition, he made General O'Hara his substitute as the leader of the army. The officer was followed by the conquered troops in a slow and solemn step, with shouldered arms, colors cased, and drums beating a British march. . . .

The royal troops, while marching through the line formed by the allied army, exhibited a decent and neat appearance, as respected arms and clothing. For their commander opened his store, and directed every soldier to be furnished with a new suit complete, prior to the capitulation. But in their line of march, we remarked a disorderly, and unsoldierly conduct, their step was irregular, and their ranks frequently broken.

But it was in the field, when they came to the last act of the drama, that the spirit and pride of the British soldier was put to the severest test; here their mortification could not be concealed. Some of the platoon officers appeared to be exceedingly chagrined when giving the word, "Ground arms," and I am a witness that they performed this duty in a very unofficerlike manner, and that many of the soldiers manifested a sullen temper, throwing their arms on the pile with violence, as if determined to render them useless. This irregularity, however, was checked by the authority of General Lincoln. After having grounded their arms, and divested themselves of their accoutrements, the captive troops were conducted back to Yorktown and guarded by our troops till they be removed to the place of their destination.

WASHINGTON'S FAREWELL

The Treaty of Paris was signed on September 3, 1783, and British troops evacuated New York in late November.

George Washington was to set out for his home at Mount Vernon, Virginia—and presumed retirement from public life—on December 4. But first he stopped at Fraunces Tavern in New York to bid farewell to his officers.

Colonel Benjamin Tallmadge saw the final scene of the Revolutionary War played out.

At 12 o'clock the officers repaired to Francis' Tavern, in Pearl Street, where Genl. Washington had appointed to meet them and take his final leave of them. We had been assembled but a few moments when His Excellency entered the room. His emotion, too strong to be concealed, seemed to be reciprocated by every officer present.

After partaking of a slight refreshment, in almost breathless silence, the General filled his glass with wine, and turning to his officers, he said: "With a heart full of love and gratitude, I now take leave of you. I most devoutly wish that your latter days may be as prosperous and happy as your former ones have been glorious and honorable."

After the officers had taken a glass of wine, Genl. Washington said, "I cannot come to each of you, but shall feel obliged if each of you will come and take me by the hand."

Gen. Knox, being nearest to him, turned to the Commander-in-Chief, who, suffused in tears, was incapable of utterance, but grasped his hand; when they embraced each other in silence. In the same affectionate manner, every officer in the room marched up to, kissed, and parted with his General-in-Chief.

Such a scene of sorrow and weeping I had never before witnessed, and hope I may never be called upon to witness again. . . . Not a word was uttered to break the solemn silence that prevailed or to interrupt the tenderness. . . . The simple thought that we were then about to part from the man who had conducted us through a long and bloody war, and under whose conduct the glory and independence of our country had been achieved, and that we should see his face no more in this world, seemed to me utterly insupportable.

But the time of separation had come, and waving his hand to his grieving children around him, he left the room, and passing through a corps of light infantry who were paraded to receive him, he walked silently on to Whitehall, where a barge was in waiting. We all followed in mournful silence to the wharf, where a prodigious crowd had assembled to witness the departure of the man who, under God, had been the great agent in establishing the glory and independence of these United

States. As soon as he was seated, the barge put off into the river, and when out in the stream, our great and beloved General waved his hat, and bid us a silent adieu.

SHAYS'S REBELLION

America had won the war, but it had hardly created a national government.

The Articles of Confederation, adopted in 1781, provided for a weak central authority that did not even have the power to tax. So, when a depression struck in the mid-1780s with the dissolution of old trading patterns with England and the cooling down of a wartime economy, debt-ridden farmers could look only to their state legislatures for help.

Farmers in western Massachusetts asked the legislature to shut down courts that were allowing foreclosures, and to issue additional paper money. When they were rebuffed, they staged a revolt led by Daniel Shays, a former Continental Army officer, and in January 1787 marched on an arsenal at Springfield.

In a letter to Governor James Bowdoin, General William Shepard told how his unit defended the guns.

The unhappy time is come to which we have been obliged to shed blood. Shays, who was at the head of about twelve hundred men, marched yesterday afternoon about four o'clock, towards the public buildings in battle array. He marched his men in an open column by platoons. I sent several times by one of my aides, and two other gentlemen, Captains Buffington and Woodbridge, to him to know what he was after, or what he wanted. His reply was, he wanted barracks, and barracks he would have and stores. The answer returned was he must purchase them dear, if he had them.

He still proceeded on his march until he approached within two hundred and fifty yards of the arsenal. He then made a halt. I immediately sent Major Lyman, one of my aides, and Capt. Buffington to inform him not to march his troops any nearer the arsenal on his peril, as I was stationed here by order of your Excellency and the Secretary of War, for the defence of the public property; in case he did I should surely fire on him and his men. A Mr. Wheeler, who appeared to be one of Shays' aides, met Mr. Lyman, after he had delivered my orders in the most peremptory manner, and made answer, that that was all he wanted. Mr. Lyman returned with his answer.

Shays immediately put his troops in motion, and marched on rapidly near one hundred yards. I then ordered Major Stephens, who commanded the artillery, to fire upon them. He accordingly did. The first two shots he endeavored to overshoot them, in hopes they would have taken warning without firing among them, but it had no effect on them. Major Stephens then directed his shot through the center of his column. The fourth or fifth shot put their whole column into the utmost confusion. Shays made an attempt to display the column, but in vain. We had one howitzer which was loaded with grapeshot, which when fired, gave them great uneasiness.

Had I been disposed to destroy them, I might have charged upon their rear and flanks with my infantry and the two field pieces, and could have killed the greater part of his whole army within twenty-five minutes. There was not a single musket fired on either side. I found three men dead on the spot, and one wounded, who is since dead. One of our artillery men by inattention was badly wounded. Three muskets were taken up with the dead, which were all deeply loaded.

I have received no reinforcement yet, and expect to be attacked this day by their whole force combined.

the FOUNDING FATHERS

Shays's men were turned back, and he fled to Vermont. But his revolt fueled the movement for a stronger central government to deal with economic crises.

On May 25, 1787, delegates from all the states except Rhode Island gathered in Philadelphia to remedy the defects in the Articles of Confederation.

With George Washington presiding, the delegates—numbering as many as fifty-five at times—would argue through the summer. They were all men of means—merchants and landowners—but in crucial respects their interests diverged. The small states were pitted against the large ones, and the slaveholding South raged against the abolitionists of the North.

But compromises were nailed down, and by the time the delegates finished their work on September 17, the Articles of Confederation were dead. A new Constitution was adopted, a remarkable document that would endure through the numerous storms of history.

James Madison of Virginia—note-taker extraordinaire—kept a record detailing how the Founding Fathers did it.

I chose a seat in front of the presiding member, with the other members on my right and left hand. In this favorable position for hearing all that passed, I noted in terms legible and in abbreviations and marks intelligible to myself what was read from the Chair or spoken by the members; and losing not a moment unnecessarily between the adjournment and reassembling of the Convention I was enabled to write out my daily notes during the session or within a few finishing days after its close in the extent and form preserved in my own hand on my files. . . . I was not absent a single day, nor more than a casual fraction of an hour in any day, so that I could not have lost a single speech, unless a very short one.

But while the delegates were sitting, there was little Madison could say to the outside world, even in his correspondence with Jefferson, then serving as the American envoy to France. He told Jefferson who the delegates were but could convey nothing beyond that.

In furnishing you with this list of names, I have exhausted all the means which I can make use of for gratifying your curiosity. It was thought expedient in order to secure unbiased discussion within doors, and to prevent misconceptions & misconstructions without, to establish some rules of caution which will for no short time restrain even a confidential communication of our proceedings. The names of the members will satisfy you that the States have been serious in this business.

The attendance of Genl. Washington is a proof of the light in which he regards it. The whole community is big with expectation. And there can be no doubt that the result will in some way or other have a powerful effect on our destiny.

Washington was indeed held in awe by the delegates, as an incident early on would illustrate. One day, a delegate dropped a piece of paper containing information on the intensely secret proceedings. Someone picked it up and handed it to Washington. William Pierce, a delegate from Georgia, would later tell how the following day, after debate concluded, Washington arose and laid down a challenge in the face of this breach of security.

"Gentlemen!" he said. "I am sorry to find that some one member of this body has been so neglectful of the secrets of the Convention as to drop in the State House a copy of the proceedings, which by accident was picked up and delivered to me this morning. I must entreat gentlemen to be more careful, lest our transactions get into the newspapers and disturb the public repose by premature speculations. I know not whose paper it is, but there it is, let him who owns it take it."

At the same time he bowed, picked up his hat and quitted the room with a dignity so severe that every person seemed alarmed, for my part I was extremely so, for putting my hand in my pocket I missed my copy of the same paper, but advancing up to the table my fears soon dissipated; I found it to be in the handwriting of another person. When I went to my lodgings at the Indian Queen, I found my copy in a coat pocket which I had pulled off that morning. It is something remarkable that no person ever owned the paper.

When it came time for the delegates to endorse the Constitution, Benjamin Franklin, aged eighty-one, was helped forward, and he was reported to have wept upon signing. After Pennsylvania's Franklin, delegates from six other states slowly moved to the table.

Madison watched the climactic moments unfold.

Whilst the last members were signing it, Doctr. Franklin looking towards the Presidents chair, at the back of which a rising sun happened to be painted, observed to a few members near him that painters had found it difficult to distinguish in their art a rising from a setting sun. I have, said he, often and often in the course of the session, and the vicissitudes of my hopes and fears as to its issue, looked at that behind the President without being able to tell whether it was rising or setting: But now at length I have the happiness to know that it is a rising and not a setting sun.

DINNER *with* GEORGE *and* MARTHA

Following an eight-day journey from Mount Vernon, George Washington took the oath as the first president at New York's Federal Hall on April 30, 1789.

Monarchy was anathema to the new Republic, but Washington's executive mansion could be quite formal when he fêted the cream of American government and society at dinners held each Thursday at 4 P.M.

One of those gatherings, on the afternoon of August 27, 1789, was wryly described by Senator William Maclay of Pennsylvania.

It was the most solemn dinner I ever sat at. Not a health drank; scarce a word said until the cloth was taken away. Then the President, filling a glass of wine, with great formality drank to the health of every individual name by name around the table. Everybody imitated him, charged glasses, and such a buzz of "health, sir" and "health, madam" and "thank you, sir" and "thank you, madam," never had I heard before. Indeed, I had like to have been thrown out in a hurry; but I got a little wine in my glass and passed the ceremony. The ladies sat a good while, and the bottles passed about; but there was a dead silence about. Mrs. Washington at last withdrew with the ladies.

I expected the men would now begin, but the same stillness remained. The President told of a New England clergyman who had lost a hat and wig in passing over a river called the Brunks [Bronx]. He smiled and everybody else laughed. He now and then said a sentence or two on some common subject, and what he said was not amiss. Mr. Jay [John Jay, the chief justice] tried to make a laugh by mentioning the circumstance of the Duchess of Devonshire leaving no stone unturned to carry Fox's election. There was a Mr. Smith, who mentioned how Homer described Aeneas leaving his wife and carrying his father out of flaming Troy. He had heard somebody (I suppose) witty on the occasion; but if he had ever read it, he would have said Virgil. The President kept a fork in his hand, when the cloth was taken away, I thought for the purpose of picking nuts. He ate no nuts, but played with the fork, striking the edge of the table with it. We did not sit long after the ladies retired. The President rose, went up stairs to drink coffee; the company followed. I took my hat and came home.

the BATTLE of LAKE ERIE

The young nation would double its size in 1803 with the annexation of vast lands in the West—the Louisiana Purchase, a $15-million bargain acquisition from France—but the United States had little international stature.

During Jefferson's presidency, America stayed neutral in the wars between Napoleon and the English, but that didn't stop British vessels from accosting United States merchant ships and "impressing" British subjects, or even naturalized Americans, for Royal Navy service.

Jefferson's successor, James Madison, was beset by the continuing issue of impressment, and by pressure from congressional "war hawks" who claimed that the English were scheming with the Indians of the Ohio Valley, led by Tecumseh, to block westward expansion.

War with Britain came in June 1812, while Madison was heading toward a second term.

The U.S. Navy was a puny force, seemingly no match for the British in the battles to control the Great Lakes. So, when Commodore Oliver Hazard Perry went up against the enemy on Lake Erie with a force consisting of two new twenty-gun brigs, *Lawrence* and *Niagara*, the brig *Caledonia 3*, and six schooners, the odds were not with him.

But as Seaman David C. Bunnell would observe, the British were in for a surprise.

We returned to Put-in Bay, and the second day, (Friday) was memorable and ever to be remembered tenth of September 1813. The sun rose in all its glory—but before it set, many a brave tar on both sides was doomed to a watery grave, and many a jovial soul who had "led the merry dance on the light fantastic toe," the evening previous, never danced again—unless we have our frolics after death.

The first intelligence we received of the approach of the enemy's squadron was from the man at the mast head—"Sail ho!"—An officer of the deck replied, "Where away?" "Off Rattlesnake Island." Before the officer had time to inquire what she looked like, the man bawled out again—"Sail ho!—sail ho—six sail in sight sir." As if by instinct, every soul at once exclaimed—"The enemy is in sight."—All was bustle and hurry, but no confusion. The signal was made to weigh the anchors, which was done with surprising alacrity. We had sixty fathoms of cable out, and it was not more than fifteen minutes before we had our sails set and anchors up. The wind was ahead, and the enemy to the windward, but in fifteen minutes after we had got fairly under way, the wind shifted to the opposite point of compass, which brought us to the windward.

Commodore Perry ordered his flag to be hoisted. We knew this flag was on board, but none of us knew what the motto was, until it was unfurled to the breeze—when we discovered the dying words of the brave Lawrence—"DON'T GIVE UP THE SHIP!" [The final words of Captain James Lawrence, commander of the frigate Chesapeake, as he fell in battle against the British ship Shannon on June 1, 1813.]

This flag was eighteen feet long and nine broad—painted blue—the letters on it very large and white. When it was unfurled, the whole squadron gave three cheers. . . .

All were busy in getting every thing in order for the battle—the shot were got up from below—the guns well loaded and primed—and all was in complete readiness. The drums beat to quarters, and every man repaired to his station. The words "Silence—stand to your quarters!" were given, and the signal to form a line. The wind was light, and our line was soon formed, when we bore down upon the enemy in perfect order.

There being only a light wind, we neared the enemy very slowly. . . . The word "silence" was again given—we stood in awful impatience—not a word was spoken—not a sound heard, except now and then an order to trim a sail, and the boatswain's shrill whistle. It seemed like the awful silence that precedes an earthquake. . . . My pulse beat quick—all nature seemed wrapped in awful suspense. . . . At length there was a gun fired from the Detroit, and the action commenced. A gentle zephyr had wafted us near the enemy, and then died away. . . . Our all was at stake. America had never before had an opportunity, since she became a nation, of meeting squadron to squadron.

No sooner had the first gun been fired from the Detroit, than they opened a tremendous fire from their whole line, of round, grape and canister shot. The Scorpion, Tigress and Aerial, having long guns, returned their fire with considerable effect. Our vessel (the Lawrence) carried 20 guns—ten on each side. . . . My comrades fell on all sides. One man who stood next to me was most shockingly wounded—having both his legs shot off, and a number of the spikes from the bulwark drove into his body. He was carried below, and survived until he heard victory proclaimed—he then exclaimed, "I die in peace," and immediately expired.

The whole of the enemy's line kept up an incessant fire, and our impatience became almost insupportable, but our ever watchful Commodore knew what was best to be done, and ordered the long gun to be manned, and fired; it was done in an instant, and the shot reached the enemy. We kept up a fire with it for a few minutes, when an order from our commander put every man in motion—"Stand by"—a second intervened—"Fire." . . .

I paid attention to the gun which I had charge of, and loaded and fired as fast as possible, and at one time in a great hurry, shoved in a crowbar, and I found after the action was over that it did its duty on board the Detroit, by cutting away three shrouds of her main rigging.

At last my gun got so warm that it jumped entirely out of its carriage. Five of my men out of eight were either killed or wounded. I went to the next gun and found but one man left, but by the assistance of my three she was made to play again. I could now only hear an occasional gun fired from our vessel. I looked up to see if our flag was still flying, and with pleasure beheld, partly obscured by smoke, the star spangled banner yet waving, and heard Perry exclaim, "Man the boat."

I looked along the deck, and such a sight at any other time would have made me shudder. The deck was in a shocking predicament. Death had been very busy. It was one continued gore of blood and carnage— the dead and dying were strewed in every direction over it—for it was impossible to take the wounded below as fast as they fell. . . .

On board the Niagara, to which vessel Perry went in the height of the battle . . . Perry made the signal to close with the enemy—we made sail and were soon in close contact with the British, and the action was renewed with great vigor. The only words I recollect of hearing Perry say were—"Take good aim my boys, don't waste your shot." The smoke was so dense that it was impossible to see the enemy—but we were so close that by firing on a level we could not miss—their vessel being so much higher out of the water than ours. The Lawrence struck her colors for a little time, and then hoisted them again.

The action raged with fury on both sides for some time, when Perry, finding that our ammunition began to grow short, resolved to make one finishing blow. He ran down with the intention of boarding, but the Queen Charlotte had run afoul of the Detroit, which rendered her useless, as she could not fire at us without killing their own men—while our shot took effect in both of them. Our flag was shot away, which produced three cheers from the enemy—but they were sadly mistaken— it was soon hoisted again. In short, after a bloody and well contested conflict of three hours and forty eight minutes, the undaunted Union of Great Britain came down. . . .

We had peas boiling for dinner—our place for cooking was on deck, and during the action a shot had penetrated the boiler, and the peas were rolling all over the deck—we had several pigs loose on deck, and I actually saw one of them eating peas that had both his hind legs shot off. . . .

The Sloop Little Belt attempted to make sail and steer for Malden— the Scorpion gave her chase, and fired a "long tom" at her: the first shot struck close to her stern—next entered her starboard quarter, and went *out at her larboard bow, and she surrendered. Thus made the victory complete. . . .*

What a glorious day for my country.

At 4 P.M., Perry sent a message to General William Henry Harrison with words that would ring through naval history: "We have met the enemy and they are ours."

the BRITISH are COMING!
the BRITISH are COMING!

In April 1813, American troops captured the British Canadian city of York (the present-day Toronto) and burned government buildings. It took a while, but the British would retaliate in spectacular fashion. After routing American soldiers at Bladensburg, Maryland—an encounter watched by President Madison, who had fled to the countryside—they entered Washington without opposition in August 1814 and, under General Robert Ross, burned the Capitol, the executive mansion (not yet called the White House), and other public buildings.

In a letter to her sister, Dolley Madison—who had decorated the mansion with a $26,000 grant from Congress—told of the events the day before the British arrived, and then the hours just before she herself escaped.

Dear Sister—My husband left me yesterday morning to join General Winder. He inquired anxiously whether I had courage or firmness to remain in the President's house until his return on the morrow, or succeeding day, and on my assurance that I had no fear but for him, and the success of our army, he left, beseeching me to take care of myself, and of the Cabinet papers, public and private. I have since received two dispatches from him, written with a pencil. The last is alarming, because he desires I should be ready at a moment's warning to enter my carriage, and leave the city; that the enemy seemed stronger than had at first been reported, and it might happen that they would reach the city with the intention of destroying it. I am accordingly ready; I have pressed as many Cabinet papers into trunks as to fill one carriage; our private property must be sacrificed, and it is impossible to procure wagons for its transportation. I am determined not to go myself until I see Mr. Madison safe, so that he can accompany me, as I hear of much hostility towards him. Disaffection stalks around us. My friends and acquaintances are all gone, even Colonel C. with his hundred, who were stationed as a guard in this inclosure. French John [a servant], with his usual activity and resolution, offers to spike the cannon at the gate, and lay a train of powder, which would blow up the British, should they enter the house. To the last proposition I positively object, without being able to make him understand why all advantages in war may not be taken.

Wednesday morning, twelve o'clock—Since sunrise I have been turning my spy-glass in every direction, and watching with unwearied anxiety, hoping to discover the approach of my dear husband and his friends; but, alas! I can descry only groups of military, wandering in all directions, as if there was a lack of arms, or of spirit to fight for their own fireside.

Three o'clock. Will you believe it, my sister? we have had a battle, or skirmish, near Bladensburg, and here I am still, within sound of the cannon! Mr. Madison comes not. May God protect us! Two messengers covered with dust come to bid me fly; but here I mean to wait for him. . . . At this late hour a wagon has been procured, and I have had it filled with plate and the most valuable portable articles belonging to the house. Whether it will reach its destination, the Bank of Maryland, or fall into the hands of British soldiery, events must determine. Our kind friend, Mr. Carroll, has come to hasten my departure, and in a very humor with me, because I insist on waiting until the large picture of General Washington is secured, and it requires to be unscrewed from the wall. This process was found too tedious for these perilous moments; I have ordered the frame to be broken, and the canvas taken out. It is done! and the precious portrait placed in the hands of two gentlemen of New York, for safe keeping. And now, dear sister, I must leave this house, or the retreating army will make me a prisoner in it by filling up the road I am directed to take. When I shall again write to you, or where I shall be tomorrow, I cannot tell!

A month later, President Madison and wife, Dolley, took up temporary residence a few blocks west of the burned executive mansion, at an eight-sided brick home to be known as Octagon House. It was there that the Treaty of Ghent, concluding the war, was signed on December 24, 1814. Since the treaty said nothing about the key issues of impressment and the rights of neutrals, the fighting ended inconclusively. But naval victories, along with the post-treaty rout of the British at New Orleans, helped erase any lingering sense of American inferiority. And the War of 1812 did inspire feelings of national unity, while also producing "The Star-Spangled Banner" of Francis Scott Key.

Chapter Two

the UNION'S "FIERY TRIAL"

FRONTIER POLITICKING

With open land and abundant natural wealth, the frontier provided an equality of opportunity and freedom from the class structures of Europe. Rugged frontiersmen like Daniel Boone, Kit Carson, and Davy Crockett—born in a Tennessee log cabin in 1786—would become almost mythical figures.

Crockett fought with Andrew Jackson against the Creek Indians and would die in another military campaign—at the Alamo. When he wasn't shooting bears (he supposedly bagged 105 in one season), Indians (whom he later sympathized with), or Mexicans, Crockett could be a shrewd politician. In 1827, he ran for the House of Representatives from Tennessee on a lark—and won.

The account of that race is autobiographical, but the memoir in which it appears may actually have been written by Richard Penn Smith. At any rate, it conveys the flavor of frontier life, and helped create the Crockett legend.

I started off to the Cross Roads, dressed in my hunting shirt, and my rifle on my shoulder. Many of our constituents had assembled there to get a taste of the quality of the candidates at orating. Job Snelling, a gander-shanked Yankee, who had been caught somewhere about Plymouth Bay, and had been shipped to the west with a cargo of codfish and rum, erected a large shantee, and set up shop for the occasion. A large posse of the voters had assembled before I arrived, and my opponent had already made considerable headway with his speechifyng and his treating, when they spied me about a rifle shot from the camp, sauntering along as if I was not a party in business. "There comes Crockett," cried one. "Let us hear the colonel," cried another, and so I mounted the stump that had been cut down for the occasion, and began to bushwhack in the most approved style.

I had not been up long before there was such an uproar in the crowd that I could not hear my own voice, and some of my constituents let me know, that they could not listen to me on such a dry subject as the welfare of the nation, until they had something to drink, and that I must treat 'em. Accordingly, I jumped down from the rostrum, and led the way to the shantee, followed by my constituents, shouting, "Huzza for Crockett," and "Crockett for ever!"

When we entered the shantee, Job was busy dealing out his rum in a style that showed he was making a good day's work of it, and I called for a quart of the best, but the crooked critur returned no other answer than by pointing at a board over the bar, on which he had chalked in large letters, "Pay to-day and trust to-morrow." Now that idea brought me up all standing; it was a sort of cornering in which there was no back out, for ready money in the west in those times was the shyest thing in all nature, and it was most particularly shy with me on that occasion.

The voters, seeing my predicament, fell off to the other side, and I was left deserted and alone, as the Government will be, when he no longer has any offices to bestow [a crack against Jackson, whom he now opposed]. I saw, as plain as day, that the tide of popular opinion was against me, and that, unless I got some rum speedily, I should lose my election as sure as there are snakes in Virginny. . . .

I struck into the woods with my rifle on my shoulder, my best friend in time of need, and as good fortune would have it, I had not been out more than a quarter of an hour before I treed a fat coon, and in the pulling of a trigger he lay dead at the root of the tree. I soon whipped his hairy jacket off his back, and again bent my way towards the shantee, and walked up to the bar, but not alone, for this time I had half a dozen of my constituents at my heels. I threw down the coon skin upon the counter, and called for a quart, and Job, though busy in dealing out rum, forgot to point at his chalked rules and regulations, for he knew that a coon was as good a legal tender for a quart, in the west, as a New York shilling, any day in the year.

My constituents now flocked about me, and cried "Huzza for Crockett," "Crockett for ever," and finding the tide had taken a turn, I told them several yarns, to get them in a good humour, and having soon despatched the value of the coon, I went out and mounted the stump, without opposition, and a clear majority of the voters followed me to hear what I had to offer for the good of the nation. Before I was half through, one of my constituents moved that they would hear the balance of my speech, after they had washed down the first part with some more of Job Snelling's extract of cornstalk and molasses, and the question being put, *it was carried unanimously. It wasn't considered necessary to call the yeas and nays, so we adjourned to the shantee, and on the way I began to reckon that the fate of the nation pretty much depended upon my shooting another coon.*

While standing at the bar, feeling sort of bashful while Job's rules and regulations stared me in the face, I cast down my eyes, and discovered one end of the coon skin sticking between the logs that supported the bar. Job had slung it there in the hurry of business. I gave it a sort of quick jerk, and it followed my hand as natural as if I had been the rightful owner. I slapped it on the counter, and Job, little dreaming that he was barking up the wrong tree, shoved along another bottle, which my constituents quickly disposed of with great good humour, for some of them saw the trick, and then we withdrew to the rostrum to discuss the affairs of the nation.

I don't know how it was, but the voters soon became dry again, and nothing would do, but we must adjourn to the shantee, and as luck would have it, the coon skin was still sticking between the logs, as if Job had flung it there on purpose to tempt me. I was not slow in raising it to the counter, the rum followed of course, and I wish I may be shot, if I didn't, before the day was over, get ten quarts for the same identical skin, and from a fellow too, who in those parts was considered as sharp as a steel trap, and as bright as a pewter button.

This joke secured me my election, for it soon circulated like smoke among my constituents, and they allowed, with one accord, that the man who could get the whip hand of Job Snelling in fair trade could outwit Old Nick [the Devil] himself and was the real grit for them in Congress.

JACKSONIAN DEMOCRACY

A battle that should never have been fought created an American hero. Unaware that the treaty concluding the War of 1812 had been signed two weeks earlier, British troops attacked the Americans defending New Orleans in January 1815. Though vastly outnumbered, the soldiers under General Andrew Jackson, using artillery and superb marksmanship, mowed down the British, killing more than two thousand while incurring only eight American deaths.

Jackson was transformed into a national figure and ran for president in 1824, losing to John Quincy Adams in a race decided in the House of Representatives. But in 1828, the presidency was his.

For the first time, the President was neither a Virginian nor a member of the Adams family. This one was a Tennessee frontiersman, a ruthless Indian-fighter who had crushed the Creeks and Seminoles, a land speculator, and a war hero.

He would embody "Jacksonian Democracy," an opening of the political process to the common man, particularly in the West, where the old property rules for voters had been abolished.

The British writer Frances Trollope, who spent nearly four years touring America, observed the rough-hewn character of Westerners when President-elect Jackson arrived in Cincinnati via steamboat en route to his Washington inaugural. Mrs. Trollope was with her husband, who would be in the party accompanying Jackson east.

More than one private carriage was stationed at the water's edge to await the general's orders, but they were dismissed with the information that he would walk to the hotel. Upon receiving this intimation the silent crowd divided itself in a very orderly manner, leaving a space for him to walk through them. He did so, uncovered, though the distance was considerable, and the weather very cold; but he alone (with the exception of a few European gentlemen who were present) was without a hat. He wore his grey hair carelessly, but not ungracefully arranged, and, spite of his harsh gaunt features, he looks like a gentleman and a soldier. He was in deep mourning, having very recently lost his wife; they were said to have been happy together, and I was pained by hearing a voice near me exclaim, as he approached the spot where I stood, "There goes Jackson, where is his wife?" Another sharp voice, at a little distance, cried, "Adams for ever!" And these sounds were all I heard to break the silence.

"They manage these matters better" in the East, I have no doubt, and yet I was still in the West, and still inclined to think that, however meritorious the American character may be, it is not amiable.

Mr T. [Frances Trollope's husband] and his sons joined the group of citizens who waited upon him in the hotel, and were presented to the President in form; that is, they shook hands with him. Learning that he intended to remain a few hours there, or more properly, that it would be a few hours before the steam-boat would be ready to proceed, Mr T. secured berths on board, and returned, to take a hasty dinner with us. At the hour appointed by the Captain, Mr T. and his son accompanied the general on board; and by subsequent letters I learnt that they had conversed a good deal with him, and were pleased by his conversation and manners, but deeply disgusted by the brutal familiarity to which they saw him exposed at every place on their progress at which they stopped; I am tempted to quote one passage, as sufficiently descriptive of the manner, which so painfully grated against their European feelings.

"There was not a hulking boy from a keel-boat who was not introduced to the President, unless, indeed, as was the case with some, they introduced themselves: for instance, I was at his elbow when a greasy fellow accosted him thus:

" 'General Jackson, I guess?'

"The General bowed assent.

" 'Why, they told me you was dead.'

" 'No! Providence has hitherto preserved my life.'

" 'And is your wife alive too?'

"The general, apparently much hurt, signified the contrary, upon which the courtier concluded his harangue by saying 'Ay, I thought it was the one or the t'other of ye.' "

Job-seekers flocked to Washington, demanding that the old order be thrown out. Thus was born the "spoils system" of patronage rewards popularly associated with Jackson.

But job turnover in his administration would actually be minimal. Although Jackson vilified the established monetary interests, he was not about to turn over the government to the kind of riffraff that descended on the White House for his inaugural party.

Margaret Bayard Smith, the wife of a Maryland senator, was there on March 4, 1829, when the common man turned out en masse for Jackson's swearing in at the Capitol.

Stationing ourselves on the central gravel walk we stood so as to have a clear, full view of the whole scene. The Capitol in all its grandeur and beauty. The Portico and grand steps leading to it were filled with ladies. Scarlet, purple, blue, yellow, white draperies and waving plumes of every kind and colour, among the white marble pillars, had a fine effect. . . . The sun had been obscured through the morning by a mist, or haziness. But the concussion in the air, produced by the discharge of the cannon, dispersed it and the sun shone forth in all his brightness. At the moment the General entered the Portico and advanced to the table, the shout that rent the air still resounds in my ears. When the speech was over, and the President made his parting bow, the barrier that had separated the people from him was broken down and they rushed up the steps all eager to shake hands with him. It was with difficulty he made his way through the Capitol and down the hill to the gateway that opens on the avenue. Here for a moment he was stopped. The living mass was impenetrable. After a while a passage was opened, and he mounted his horse which had been provided for his return (he had walked to the Capitol) then such a cortege that followed him! Country men, farmers, gentlemen, mounted and dismounted, boys, women and children, black and white. Carriages, wagons and carts all pursuing him to the President's house . . .

In the afternoon, the Smiths and their friends made their way to the White House, the throngs of Jackson backers having preceded them.

What a scene did we witness! The Majesty of the People had disappeared, and a rabble, a mob, of boys, negros, women, children, scrambling, fighting, romping. What a pity what a pity! No arrangements had been made, no police officers placed on duty and the whole house had been inundated by the rabble mob. We came too late. The President, after having been literally nearly pressed to death and almost suffocated and torn to pieces by the people in their eagerness to shake hands with Old Hickory, had retreated through the back way or south front and had escaped to his lodgings at Gadsby's. Cut glass and china to the amount of several thousand dollars had been broken in the struggle to get the refreshments, punch and other articles had been carried out in tubs and buckets, but had it been in hogsheads it would have been insufficient, ice-creams, and cake and lemonade, for 20,000 people, for it is said that number were there, tho' I think the estimate exaggerated. Ladies fainted, men were seen with bloody noses and such a scene of confusion took place as is impossible to describe,—those who got in could not get out by the door again, but had to scramble out of windows.

At one time, the President, who had retreated and retreated until he was pressed against the wall, could only be secured by a number of gentlemen forming round him and making a kind of barrier of their own bodies, and pressure was so great that Col. Bomford was, one said, afraid they should been pushed down, or on the President. It was then the windows were thrown open, and the torrent found an outlet, which otherwise might have proved fatal.

Ladies and gentlemen only had been expected at this Levee not the people en masse. But it was the People's day, and the People's President and the People would rule.

the IRON HORSE

In the first decades of the nineteenth century, great achievements in transportation and technology transformed the nation. Canals, steamships, and railroads broke down isolation, and the reaper and cotton gin revolutionized agriculture.

The Mohawk & Hudson was the third steam railroad in the United States. Running between Albany and Schenectady, New York, it shortened an all-day, forty-mile trip through numerous locks of the Erie Canal to a quick seventeen miles overland.

On August 9, 1831, the railway made its first run as William H. Brown, an artist who was aboard, sketched the scene. Years later, Brown reminisced.

This locomotive, the DeWitt Clinton, stood upon a track already fired up, and with a train of some five or six passenger-coaches attached to it (two only were represented in our sketch, for want of room). . . . On arriving at the top of the plane at Albany on this memorable occasion

. . . the peculiar appearance of the machine and train (the first ever seen by the author) arrested his attention, and he at once resolved to make a sketch. Drawing from his pocket a letter just received . . . and substituting his hat for a desk, he commenced. . . . The author had taken a hasty, rough drawing of the machine, the tender, the individual standing on the platform of the machine as its engineer, and the shape of the first passenger-coach, when a tin horn was sounded and the word was given, "All aboard," by Mr. John T. Clark, the master of transportation, who acted as conductor on that memorable occasion. . . .

As there were no coverings or awnings to protect the deck-passengers upon the tops of the cars from the sun, the smoke, and the sparks, and as it was the hot season of the year, the combustible nature of their garments, summer coats, straw hats, and umbrellas, soon became apparent, and a ludicrous scene was enacted. . . .

How shall we describe that start, my readers? It was not that quiet, imperceptible motion . . . of the present day. Not so. There came a sudden jerk, that bounded the sitters from their places, to the great detriment of their high-top fashionable beavers, from the close proximity to the roofs of the cars. This first jerk being over, the engine proceeded with considerable velocity for those times, when compared with stage coaches, until it arrived at a water-station, when it suddenly brought up with jerk No. 2, to the further amusement of some of the excursionists. . . .

In a short time the engine (after frightening the horses attached to all sorts of vehicles filled with the people from the surrounding country, congregated all along at every available position near the road . . . after causing thus innumerable capsizes and smash-ups of the vehicles and the tumbling of spectators in every direction) arrived at the head of the inclined plane at Schenectady, amid the cheers and welcomes of thousands.

CONGRESSIONAL MANNERS

The coarseness in American life observed by the British writer Frances Trollope was hardly confined to the West. Charles Dickens, who spent four and a half months traveling in the United States during the early part of 1842, took a look at Congress and came away with a bemused view of a rather unsightly habit.

I visited both Houses nearly every day during my stay in Washington. On my initiatory visit to the House of Representatives, they divided against a decision of the chair; but the chair won. The second time I went, the member who was speaking, being interrupted by a laugh, mimicked it, as one child would in quarreling with another, and added "that he would make honourable gentlemen opposite sing out a little on the other side of their mouths presently." But interruptions are rare; the speaker being usually heard in silence. There are more quarrels than with us, and more threatenings than gentlemen are accustomed to exchange in any civilised society of which we have record; but farmyard imitations have not as yet been imported from the Parliament of the United Kingdom. The feature in oratory which appears to be the most practised, and most relished, is the constant repetition of the same idea, or shadow of an idea, in fresh words; and the inquiry out of doors is not, "What did he say?" but, "How long did he speak?" These, however, are but enlargements of a principle which prevails elsewhere.

The Senate is a dignified and decorous body, and its proceedings are conducted with much gravity and order. Both Houses are handsomely carpeted; but the state to which these carpets are reduced by the universal disregard of the spittoon with which every honourable member is accommodated, and the extraordinary improvements on the pattern which are squirted and dabbled upon it in every direction, do not admit of being described. I will merely observe, that I strongly recommend all strangers not to look at the floor; and if they happen to drop anything, though it be their purse, not to pick it up with an ungloved hand on any account.

It is somewhat remarkable too, at first, to say the least, to see so many honourable members with swelled faces; and it is scarcely less remarkable to discover that this appearance is caused by the quantity of tobacco they contrive to stow within the hollow of the cheek. It is strange enough, too, to see an honourable gentleman leaning back in his tilted chair, with his legs on the desk before him, shaping a convenient "plug" with his penknife, and when it is quite ready for use, shooting the old one from his mouth as from a pop-gun, and clapping the new one in its place.

I was surprised to observe that even steady old chewers of great experience are not always good marksmen, which has rather inclined me to doubt that general proficiency with the rifle, of which we have heard so much in England. Several gentlemen called upon me who, in the course of conversation, frequently missed the spittoon at five paces; and one (but he was certainly short-sighted) mistook the closed sash for the open window at three. On another occasion, when I dined out, and was sitting with two ladies and some gentlemen round a fire before dinner, one of the company fell short of the fire-place six distinct times. I am disposed to think, however, that this was occasioned by his not aiming at that object; as there was a white marble hearth before the fender, which was more convenient and may have suited his purpose better.

GIANTS *of the* SENATE

The United States Senate may not have been especially genteel, but commanding figures debated great issues: John C. Calhoun of South Carolina, spokesman for the states'-rights doctrine, which provided a constitutional justification for perpetuating slavery; Daniel Webster of Massachusetts, upholding the national government against states' rights in his reply to Senator Robert Hayne of South Carolina, declaring, "Liberty *and* union, now and forever, one and inseparable"; Henry Clay of Kentucky, a leader of the congressional "war hawks" of 1812 and architect of the Missouri Compromise, a futile effort to keep the nation together albeit half slaveholding and half free.

Harriet Martineau, a British writer with access to high political circles, took the measure of the Senate's three great men during a visit to Washington in the mid-1830s.

Mr. Calhoun, the cast-iron man, who looks as if he had never been born, and never could be extinguished, would come in sometimes to keep our understandings upon a painful stretch for a short while, and leave us to take to pieces his close, rapid, theoretical, illustrated talk, and see what we could make of it. . . . It is at first extremely interesting to hear Mr. Calhoun talk; and there is a never-failing evidence of power in all he says

75

and does, which commands intellectual reverence: but the admiration is too soon turned into regret,—into absolute melancholy. It is impossible to resist the conviction that all this force can be at best but useless, and is but too likely to be mischievous. His mind has long lost all power of communicating with any other. I know no man who lives in such utter intellectual solitude. He meets men and harangues them, by the fire-side, as in the Senate: he is wrought, like a piece of machinery, set a-going vehemently by a weight, and stops while you answer: he either passes by what you say, or twists it into a suitability with what is in his head, and begins to lecture again.

Of course, a mind like this can have little influence in the Senate, except by virtue, perpetually wearing out, of what it did in its less eccentric days: but its influence at home is to be dreaded. There is no hope that an intellect so cast in narrow theories will accommodate itself to varying circumstances: and there is every danger that it will break up all that it can, in order to remould the materials in its own way.

Mr. Calhoun is as full as ever of his Nullification doctrines; and those who know the force that is in him, and his utter incapacity of modification by other minds, (after having gone through as remarkable a revolution of political opinion as perhaps any man ever experienced) will no more expect repose and self-retention from him than from a volcano in full force. Relaxation is no longer in the power of his will. I never saw any one who so completely gave me the idea of possession. . . . His moments of softness, in his family, and when recurring to old college days, are hailed by all as a relief to the vehement working of the intellectual machine; a relief equally to himself and others. Those moments are as touching to the observer as tears on the face of a soldier.

Mr. Webster owes his rise to the institutions under which he lives,—institutions which open the race to the swift, and battle to the strong; but there is little in him that is congenial with them. He is aristocratic in his tastes and habits: and but little republican simplicity is to be recognized in him. . . .

Mr. Webster speaks seldom in the Senate. When he does, it is generally on some constitutional question, where his reasoning powers and knowledge are brought into play, and where his authority is considered so high, that he has the glorious satisfaction of knowing that he is listened to as an oracle by an assemblage of the first men in the country. Previous to such an exercise, he may be seen leaning back in his chair, not, as usual, biting the top of his pen, or twirling his thumbs, or bursting into sudden and transient laughter at Colonel Benton's oratorical absurdities, but absent and thoughtful, making notes, and seeing nothing that is before his eyes.

When he rises, his voice is moderate, and his manner quiet, with the slightest possible mixture of embarrassment; his right hand rests upon his desk, and the left hangs by his side. Before his first head is finished, however, his voice has risen so as to fill the chamber and ring again, and he has fallen into his favourite attitude, with his left hand under his coat-tail, and the right in full action. At this moment, the eye rests upon him as upon one under the true inspiration of seeing the invisible, and grasping the impalpable. When the vision has passed away, the change is astonishing. He sits at his desk, writing letters or dreaming, so that he does not always discover when the Senate is going to a division. Some one of his party has not seldom to jog his elbow, and tell him that his vote is wanted.

There can scarcely be a stronger contrast than between the eloquence of Webster and that of Clay. . . . His appearance is plain in the extreme, being that of a mere west-country farmer. He is tall and thin, with a weather-beaten complexion, small grey eyes, which convey an idea of something more than his well-known sagacity,—even of slyness. It is only after much intercourse that Mr. Clay's personal appearance can be discovered to do him any justice at all. All attempts to take his likeness have been in vain, though upwards of thirty portraits of him, by different artists, were in existence when I was in America. No one has succeeded in catching the subtle expression of placid kindness, mingled with astuteness, which becomes visible to the eyes of those who are in daily intercourse with him.

His mode of talking, deliberate and somewhat formal, including sometimes a grave humour, and sometimes a gentle sentiment, very touching from the lips of a sagacious man of ambition, has but one fault,—its obvious adaption to the supposed state of mind of the person to whom it is addressed. Mr. Clay is a man of an irritable and impetuous nature, over which he has obtained a truly noble mastery. His moderation is *now his most striking characteristic; obtained, no doubt, at the cost of prodigious self-denial, on his own part, and on that of his friends, of some of the ease, naturalness, and self-forgetfulness of his manners and discourse. But his conversation is rich in information, and full charged with the spirit of justice and kindliness, rising, on occasion, to a moving magnanimity.*

the VIRGINIA SLAVE REVOLT

Long before the Civil War, rebellions were mounted to break the chains of slavery.

A revolt in South Carolina in 1739 brought the deaths of some twenty-five whites. A former slave named Denmark Vesey planned a major uprising in Charleston in 1822, but authorities learned of it and hanged Vesey and thirty-five others.

In August 1831, a thirty-one-year-old slave named Nat Turner, convinced he had been chosen by God to rip away the bondage, led seventy slaves on a rampage through the countryside around Southampton, Virginia, that left fifty-five dead. Turner eluded capture for two months, but finally was seized in a massive manhunt and hanged.

The slaughter—which had been described in chilling detail by Turner in a confession to his jailer, Thomas Gray—prompted the terrified South to toughen its slave codes.

Hark got a ladder and set it against the chimney, on which I ascended, and hoisting a window, entered and came down stairs, unbarred the door, and removed the guns from their places. It was then observed that I must spill the first blood. On which, armed with a hatchet, and accompanied by Will, I entered my master's chamber, it being dark, I could not give a death blow, the hatchet glanced from his head, he sprang from the bed and called his wife, it was his last work, Will laid him dead, with a blow of his axe, and Mrs. Travis shared the same fate, as she lay in bed. The murder of this family, five in number, was the work of a moment, not one of them awoke; there was a little infant sleeping in a cradle, that was forgotten, until we had left the house and gone some distance, when Henry and Will returned and killed it; we got here, four guns that would shoot, and several old muskets, with a pound or two of powder. . . .

After killing another white, Salathul Francis, at a nearby home, Turner and his men moved on again.

We started from there for Mrs. Reese's, maintaining the most perfect silence on our march, where finding the door unlocked, we entered, and murdered Mrs. Reese in her bed, while sleeping; her son awoke, but it was only to sleep the sleep of death, he had only time to say who is that, and he was no more. From Mrs. Reese's we went to Mrs. Turner's, a mile distant, which we reached about sunrise, on Monday morning. Henry, Austin, and Sam went to the still, where, finding Mr. Peebles, Austin shot him, and the rest of us went to the house; as we approached, the family discovered us, and shut the door. Vain hope! Will, with one stroke of his axe, opened it, and we entered and found Mrs. Turner and Mrs. Newsome in the middle of a room, almost frightened to death. Will immediately killed Mrs. Turner, with one blow of his axe. I took Mrs. Newsome by the hand, and with the sword I had when I was apprehended, I struck her several blows over the head, but not being able to kill her, as the sword was dull. Will, turning around and discovering it, despatched her also.

Turner and nine others now approached the Whitehead home while six men headed elsewhere.

We discovered Mr. Richard Whitehead standing in the cotton patch, near the lane fence; we called him over into the lane, and Will, the executioner, was near at hand, with his fatal axe, to send him to an untimely grave. As we pushed on to the house, I discovered some one run round the garden, and thinking it was some of the white family, I pursued them, but finding it was a servant girl belonging to the house, I returned to commence the work of death, but they whom I left had not been idle; all the family were already murdered, but Mrs. Whitehead and her daughter Margaret. As I came round to the door I saw Will pulling

Mrs. Whitehead out of the house, and at the step he nearly severed her head from her body, with his broad axe. Miss Margaret, when I discovered her, had concealed herself in the corner, formed by the projection of the cellar cap from the house; on my approach she fled, but was soon overtaken, and after repeated blows with a sword, I killed her by a blow on the head, with a fence rail.

REMEMBERING *the* ALAMO

At the time of the Nat Turner rebellion, twenty thousand Americans were in the Mexican territory of Texas, many growing cotton with slave labor brought from the South.

Since the Mexico City government was hostile to slavery, the Texans sought to secede as a prelude to creating another American slave state. The Mexican president, Santa Anna, moved to crush the revolt, and in the winter of 1836 his troops attacked a band of 187 Americans and their followers, commanded by Colonel William B. Travis, at a San Antonio mission known as the Alamo.

The defenders held out for ten days, but on March 6 they were massacred. Of the Americans, only a woman, her baby, and a slave belonging to Travis survived. The dead included Davy Crockett and Jim Bowie, inventor of the Bowie knife.

Among the survivors of the Alamo was an eight-year-old Mexican boy named Enrique Esparza. Interviewed at age ninety, he would relive the terror.

You ask me do I remember it. I tell you yes. It is burned into my brain and indelibly scarred there. Neither age nor infirmity could make me forget, for the scene was one of such horror that it could never be forgotten by any one who witnessed its incidents. . . .

It was twilight when we got into the Alamo, and it grew pitch-dark soon afterward. All of the doors were closed and barred. The sentinels that had been on duty without were first called inside and then the openings closed. Some sentinels were posted upon the roof, but these were protected by the walls of the Alamo church and the old convent building. We went into the church portion. It was shut up when we arrived. We were admitted through a small window.

I distinctly remember that I climbed through the window and over a cannon that was placed inside the church immediately behind the window. There were several other cannon there. Some were back of the doors. Some had been mounted on the roof and some had been placed in the Convent. The window was opened to permit us to enter and it was closed immediately after we got inside.

Enrique was in the chapel with his mother while his father, Gregorio, manned a cannon. The boy could hear cannonballs hit the chapel wall and Mexican soldiers hollering.

The end came suddenly and almost unexpectedly and with a rush. It came at night and when all was dark save when there was a gleam of light from the flash and flame of a fired gun. Our men fought hard all day long. Their ammunition was very low. That of many was entirely spent.

Enrique's mother, brothers, and sister huddled in the chapel's main room. His father, on the floor above, was shot dead manning one of three cannons. The next morning, the attack resumed.

Suddenly there was a terrible din. Cannon boomed. Their shot crashed through the doors and windows and breaches in the walls. Then men rushed in on us. They swarmed among us and over us. They fired on us in volleys. They struck us down with their escopetas. . . . Our men groped and grasped the throats of our foemen and buried their knives into their hearts.

While Enrique waited in the chapel alongside his father's body, soldiers burst through the entrance.

By my side was an American boy. He was about my age but larger. As they reached us he rose to his feet. He had been sleeping, but like myself, he had been rudely awakened. As they rushed upon him he stood calmly and across his shoulders drew the blanket on which he had slept. He was unarmed. They slew him where he stood and his corpse fell over me.

Enrique stayed near his father's body.

It was pitch dark in the Eastern end of the structure and the soldiers of Santa Anna seemed to fear to go there. . . . Santa Anna's men stood still and fired into the darkness and until some one brought lanterns. The last I saw of my father's corpse was when one of them held his lantern above it and over the dead who lay about the cannon he had tended.

MARCHING *into* MEXICO

A month after the Alamo massacre, Texans under Sam Houston got their revenge, slaughtering hundreds of Mexicans at the Battle of San Jacinto, their cry "Remember the Alamo." The Texans drove the Mexicans back across the Rio Grande and won their independence.

Texas became an American territory, its prospects for statehood enmeshed in the balance between free and slave states. On February 28, 1845, at the behest of President-elect James K. Polk, Congress passed a joint resolution calling for its admission to the Union as a state. Mexico responded by breaking diplomatic ties.

That provided an opportunity for the proponents of "Manifest Destiny"—the doctrine that it was the United States' mission to expand across the continent. Polk sent several thousand troops under General Zachary Taylor to the Rio Grande in May 1845, and in the spring of 1846 a minor incident with Mexican soldiers brought a declaration of war by Congress. (Texas, meanwhile, was admitted to the Union in December 1845.)

The Mexican War would provide battle experience for young officers who two decades later would confront each other as commanders in the Civil War. Among them was a lieutenant named George Meade who would despair over the bloodthirsty volunteers he was placed in charge of.

They have killed five or six innocent people walking in the streets, for no other object than their own amusement; to be sure they are always drunk, and are in a measure irresponsible for their conduct. They rob and steal the cattle and corn of the poor farmers, and in fact act more like a body of hostile Indians than of civilized whites.

In November 1846, troops under Zachary Taylor captured Saltillo, the capital of Mexico's Coahuila Province. But Meade, serving under Taylor, was appalled by the actions of a Kentucky volunteer regiment whose men had engaged in wide-scale rape and murder.

Without a modification of the manner in which they are officered, they are almost useless in an offensive war. They are sufficiently well drilled for practical purposes, and are, I believe, brave and will fight as gallantly as any man, but they are a set of Goths and Vandals, without discipline, laying waste to the country wherever we go, making us a terror to innocent people, and if there is a spirit or energy in the Mexicans, will finally raise the people against us, who now are perfectly neutral. . . . They cannot take care of themselves; the hospitals are crowded with them, they die like sheep; they waste their provisions, requiring twice as much to supply them as regulars do. They plunder the poor inhabitants of everything they can lay their hands on, and shoot them when they remonstrate, and if one of their number happens to get into a drunken brawl and is killed, they run over the country, killing all the poor innocent people they find in their way, to avenge, as they say, the murder of their brother.

In March 1847, forces under General Winfield Scott besieged Vera Cruz, the most heavily fortified city in the Western Hemisphere. They bombarded it into submission and then pushed through the mountains to the west and conquered Mexico City. American losses at Vera Cruz were minimal, but casualties among Mexican civilians were high.

Scott's inspector general, Ethan Allen Hitchcock, was grieved by the loss of innocent lives.

I am in Camp (Washington) some 2½ miles from Vera Cruz, and we momentarily expect the return of our Commissioners, Generals Worth &

Pillow and Col. Totten, with the Articles duly signed by the Mexicans, surrendering both the city of Vera Cruz & the celebrated Castle of St. Juan D'Ulloa. . . . On the 24th, a heavy battery of guns (6) landed from the navy, opened fire and the day following. The 25th—another heavy battery of 24s commenced fire and more mortars being placed in position the firing during the night of the 25th was very destructive— perfectly terrific—nothing can exceed its horrors.

The enemy commenced firing the day after we landed and continued to fire every day, but with very little effect. They ceased firing usually at night and on the night of the 25th they scarcely fired at all. Our mortars on the contrary (13 in number) poured in a perfect stream of shells into all parts of the City, the very thought of which makes me now shudder. The shells were filled with several pounds of pow[d]er & at night might be seen by their burning fuzes making their passage from the mortars— sometimes 3 or 4 at a time—through an immence arc, rising very high and then descending into the denoted City & probably falling, 4 out [of] 5, into some house through the roof would there burst with an awful explosion, destroying whole families of women & children. It is horrible to think of.

The enemy sent a white flag the morning of the 25th at daylight and all day yesterday & today have been concerned in negociating but we understand that the city & castle are both agreed to be surrendered on our own terms. . . .

I must add that we have lost but two army officers (Captains Al- burtis & Jno. R. Vinton) and a midshipman (Shubrick) with 5 or 6 soldiers & as many seamen. Our approach and our active proceedings have been conducted under the direction of scientific Engineers & every- thing has proceeded according to known rules of the Art of War. Hence the loss has been very slight—of course I mean comparatively—no loss in this infamous war is slight. We have not acted neighborly towards our weak brother.

Writing to his sister, Lieutenant Peter V. Hagner described Vera Cruz on the second day of American occupation after a four-day bombardment.

My previous letters will have told you that we are in possession of Vera Cruz City & dependencies. On the 29th the garrisons of the different forts & the Castle marched out to a plain near the city selected by the Genl. and there between two of the Divisions of the Army stacked their arms, gave their parole—not to fight during the War—& then marched off—southwards. Capt. H. and his officers were appointed to receive the arms. We stood at a white flag in the large open space and upon the head of the Mexican column, reaching our position—it was halted & the arms stacked. We then took an Inventory—Compy by Compy—over 4,000 muskets—swords, colors, musical instruments &c. &c. Then we marched into town—took possession of the vacated Forts—fired salutes —marched in review before the Genl. posted on a balcony in the Plaza —and then commenced the business of putting things to rights.

Genl. Worth, as Gov., is bringing everything into order as fast as possible in a dirty Spanish town now nearly one-third destroyed—full of rubbish—streets piled up with barricades or cut up by our shot & shells —houses shattered terribly in every street—few lazy half-clothed, dirty inhabitants, the most having left the city or hid themselves, as soon as our lines were opened to them. There seems to be no bad feeling towards us—among them. As soon as they get over their fright, they cluster around us and look as amiable as is desirable. . . .

. . . except the arms & guns—and ammunition, they have managed to leave but little public property of much use. The city is paved—built of coral stones & cement—might be made clean & healthful, but is now filthy—& will soon be sickly, unless we can prevent it by speedy policing.

The public establishments are large and costly. We take possession of such of these as we need for storehouses. . . . The city has few or no gardens and as our lines were around them for three weeks they had consumed the most of their fresh provisions, they had plenty of rice & mutton apparently. The poor say they are suffering—and the Genl. has ordered provisions to be distributed. We go to their restaurants in the mean time and pay $1—for a poor dinner—or in the markets pay a picayune for an onion. I don't want to go there—sooner than absolutely necessary. . . . We shall soon move towards the interior. I learn

*there we will have a more agreeable country & a more pleasant time,
I hope.*

the BEAR FLAG REVOLT

When the Mexican War began, there were one thousand American
settlers in California, territory claimed by Mexico but only nominally
governed by it. On June 14, 1846, a handful of Americans at Sonoma,
in the Sacramento Valley, hoisted a white flag with a picture of a bear
on it and declared independence from Mexico—the Bear Flag Revolt.
Commodore John Sloat of the United States Pacific Squadron de-
barked at Monterey on July 7 to claim California for the United States.

The arrival at Yerba Buena (the future site of San Francisco) of the
sloop *Portsmouth,* and the raising of the American flag in a farcical
episode, were chronicled in a log kept by one of its crewman, Joseph
T. Downey. (Commander John B. Montgomery and Lieutenant John
S. Missroom are, respectively, the "Old Man" and the "Autocrat.")

*By 7 bells matters were all arranged, and the party of Marines and
Carbineers landed on the Bank, and after being marshalled in due order,
the Band, consisting of one drum and one fife, struck up Yankee Doodle,
and off we marched keeping time as best we might, to conquer the
redoubtable town of Yerba Buena. As we had anticipated, there was no
foe to dispute our right of possession, for, save here and there a stray
female face peeping from an Adobe wall, no living thing did we see. . . .
On we went then in all the pride and pomp of Martial Array, over hill
and dale, through sand and some little mud, until through the skillful
pilotage of our Old Man, we at last found ourselves brought up all
standing in a hollow square, round the Flag Staff.*

*Here, had time allowed, our Old Man would no doubt have inflicted
a speech if not a sermon upon us, but Fate decreed to the contrary,
consequently the Flag was bent on to the Halyards, and by a flourishing
and patronising invitation, the whole of the male population of Yerba
Buena, comprising, dogs and all, some 25 or 30 souls, were called into
the Square. The oration was delivered, the Proclamation read, and then*

the Autocrat with his own hands hoisted the Colors, while three hearty cheers from the bystanders, a prolonged howl from the dogs, and a salvo of 21 Guns from the Ship completed the Affair. . . .

No sooner was the news spread that the U.S. had taken possession, than all hands gave up to an excess of joy. Bells were rung, guns fired, Whiskey Barrel tapped, and hilarity became the order of the day. . . . Free and independent citizens might be seen in all directions, wending their various ways and some of them making awful deviations from a straight course, all in consequence of their great love of liberty having overtaken them. An express was forthwith despatched with the news and a Flag to New Helvetia, and in less than 48 hours from the first hoisting in Yerba Buena, the Yankee Colors were flying at every important post in Upper California and the U. States in bloodless possession of that beautiful Country.

THOREAU BEHIND BARS

The Mexican War brought the United States much or all of Texas, California, Nevada, Utah, New Mexico, and Arizona. But it had been condemned as a war of aggression and a means to further the cause of the slave states.

In December 1847, a little-known congressman from Illinois denounced the war—the first speech in the House of Representatives by Abraham Lincoln.

At Concord, Massachusetts, a disciple of Ralph Waldo Emerson went to jail for refusing to pay state poll taxes as a gesture of opposition to unjust government policies, in particular the war. He spent only one night behind bars—an aunt paid his fine—and then returned to Walden Pond. To justify his action, Henry David Thoreau would write his essay on civil disobedience. In the next century, its rationale would provide inspiration to the oppressed—to Mahatma Gandhi in India's resistance to the British, and to Martin Luther King, Jr.

I have paid no poll-tax for six years. I was put into a jail once on this account, for one night; and, as I stood considering the walls of solid stone, two or three feet thick, the door of wood and iron, a foot thick, and the iron grating which strained the light, I could not help being struck with the foolishness of that institution which treated me as if I were mere flesh and blood and bones, to be locked up. I wondered that it should have concluded at length that this was the best use it could put me to, and had never thought to avail itself of my services in some way. I saw that, if there was a wall of stone between me and my townsmen, there was a still more difficult one to climb or break through before they could get to be as free as I was. I did not for a moment feel confined, and the walls seemed a great waste of stone and mortar. I felt as if I alone of all my townsmen had paid my tax. They plainly did not know how to treat me, but behaved like persons who are underbred.

In every threat and in every compliment there was a blunder; for they thought that my chief desire was to stand the other side of that stone wall. I could not but smile to see how industriously they locked the door on my meditations, which followed them out again without let or hindrance, and they were really all that was dangerous. As they could not reach me, they had resolved to punish my body; just as boys, if they cannot come at some person against whom they have a spite, will abuse his dog. I saw that the State was half-witted, that it was timid as a lone woman with her silver spoons, and that it did not know its friends from its foes, and I lost all my remaining respect for it, and pitied it.

ADVOCATE for the INSANE

A Boston schoolteacher named Dorothea Dix happened one day in 1841 to visit a jail where several persons judged insane were locked up. What she saw turned her into a crusader, an important figure among reformers of the mid-nineteenth century tied to Transcendentalism, a belief that there were intuitive moral truths transcending the need to be justified with concrete proof.

The best-remembered reform movements of the period centered on the abolition of slavery, women's rights, public education, and the eradication of poverty and child labor.

Dorothea Dix would campaign for the dignity of the mentally ill, who had been treated like savages, penned away in horrific conditions and considered incurable. Traveling across the country to investigate conditions, she would persuade eleven states to build asylums to treat mental disease as an illness.

After two years of looking into "treatment" of the mentally ill in Massachusetts, she presented a petition to that state's legislature.

I come to present the strong claims of suffering humanity. I come to place before the Legislature of Massachusetts the condition of the miserable, the desolate, the outcast. I come as the advocate of helpless, forgotten, insane, and idiotic men and women; of beings sunk to a condition from which the most unconcerned would start with real horror; of beings wretched in our prisons, and more wretched in our almshouses. . . .

I proceed, gentlemen, briefly to call your attention to the present state of insane persons confined within the Commonwealth, in cages, closets, cellars, stalls, pens! Chained, naked, beaten with rods, and lashed into obedience . . .

Lincoln. A woman in a cage. Medford. One idiotic subject chained, and one in a close stall for seventeen years. Pepperell. One often doubly chained, hand and foot; another violent; several peaceable now. Brookfield. One man caged, comfortable. Granville. One often closely confined; now losing the use of his limbs from want of exercise. Charlemont. One man caged. Savoy. One man caged. Lenox. Two in the jail, against whose unfit condition there the jailer protests.

Dedham. The insane disadvantageously placed in the jail. In the almshouse, two females in stalls, situated in the main building; lie in wooden bunks filled with straw; always shut up. One of these subjects is supposed curable. The overseers of the poor have declined giving her a trial at the hospital, as I was informed, on account of expense. . . .

Danvers. November. Visited the almshouse. A large building, much out of repair. Understand a new one is in contemplation. Here are from fifty-six to sixty inmates, one idiotic, three insane; one of the latter in close confinement at all times.

Long before reaching the house, wild shouts, snatches of rude songs, imprecations and obscene language, fell upon the ear, proceeding from the occupant of a low building, rather remote from the principal building to which my course was directed. Found the mistress, and was conducted to the place which was called "the home" of the forlorn maniac, a young woman, exhibiting a condition of neglect and misery blotting out the faintest idea of comfort, and outraging every sentiment of decency. She had been, I learnt, "a respectable person, industrious and worthy. Disappointments and trials shook her mind, and, finally, laid prostrate reason and self-control. She became a maniac for life. She had been at Worcester Hospital for a considerable time, and had been returned as incurable." The mistress told me she understood that, "while there, she was comfortable and decent." Alas, what a change was here exhibited! . . . There she stood with naked arms and disheveled hair, the unwashed frame invested with fragments of unclean garments, the air so extremely offensive, though ventilation was afforded on all sides save one, that it was not possible to remain beyond a few moments without retreating for recovery of the outward air. . . .

Gentlemen, I commit to you this sacred cause. Your action upon this subject will affect the present and future condition of hundreds and of thousands.

In this legislation, as in all things, may you exercise that "wisdom which is the breath of the power of God."

the LASH of SLAVERY

He was born on Maryland's Eastern Shore in February 1818, the son of a slave woman and a white father, probably his master. Taught to read by the wife of one of his later masters, he taught himself to write while working in the Baltimore shipyards. At age twenty, he fled to New York City, then to New Bedford, Massachusetts, where he worked in shipbuilding.

After making an impromptu speech to an antislavery convention in Nantucket, Frederick Douglass embarked on his life's work: he became a powerful speaker and writer in behalf of the abolitionist cause.

In 1845, he published his *Narrative*, providing a graphic account of the horrors of slavery.

I have had two masters. My first master's name was Anthony. I do not remember his first name. He was generally called Captain Anthony —a title which, I presume, he acquired by sailing a craft on the Chesapeake Bay. He was not considered a rich slaveholder. He owned two or three farms, and about thirty slaves. His farms and slaves were under the care of an overseer. The overseer's name was Plummer. Mr. Plummer was a miserable drunkard, a profane swearer, and a savage monster. He always went armed with a cowskin and a heavy cudgel. I have known him to cut and slash the women's heads so horribly, that even master would be enraged at his cruelty, and would threaten to whip him if he did not mind himself. Master, however, was not a humane slaveholder. It required extraordinary barbarity on the part of an overseer to affect him. He was a cruel man, hardened by a long life of slaveholding. He would at times seem to take great pleasure in whipping a slave.

I have often been awakened at the dawn of day by the most heartrending shrieks of an own aunt of mine, whom he used to tie up to a joist, and whip upon her naked back till she was literally covered with blood. No words, no tears, no prayers, from his gory victim, seemed to move his iron heart from its bloody purpose. The louder she screamed, the harder he whipped; and where the blood ran fastest, there he whipped longest. He would whip her to make her scream, and whip her to make her hush; and not until overcome by fatigue would he cease to swing the blood-clotted cowskin. I remember the first time I ever witnessed this horrible exhibition. I was quite a child, but I well remember it. I never shall forget it whilst I remember any thing. It was the first of a long series of such outrages, by which I was doomed to be a witness and a participant. It struck me with awful force. It was the blood-stained gate, the entrance to the hell of slavery, through which I was about to pass. It was a most terrible spectacle. I wish I could commit to paper the feelings with which I beheld it.

This occurrence took place very soon after I went to live with my old master, and under the following circumstances. Aunt Hester went out one night,—where or for what I do not know,—and happened to be absent when my master desired her presence. He had ordered her not to go out evenings, and warned her that she must never let him catch her in company with a young man, who was paying attention to her, belonging to Colonel Lloyd. The young man's name was Ned Roberts, generally called Lloyd's Ned. Why master was so careful of her may be safely led to conjecture. She was a woman of noble form, and of graceful proportions, having very few equals, and fewer superiors, in personal appearance, among the colored or white women of our neighborhood.

Aunt Hester had not only disobeyed his orders in going out, but had been found in company with Lloyd's Ned; which circumstance, I found, from what he said while whipping her, was the chief offence. Had he been a man of pure morals himself, he might have been thought interested in protecting the innocence of my aunt; but those who knew him will not suspect him of any such virtue.

Before he commenced whipping Aunt Hester, he took her into the kitchen, and stripped her from neck to waist, leaving her neck, shoulders, and back, entirely naked. He then told her to cross her hands, calling her at the same time a d——d b——h. After crossing her hands, he tied them with a strong rope, and led her to a stool under a large hook on the joist, put in for the purpose. He made her get upon the stool, and tied her hands to the hook. She now stood fair for his infernal purpose. Her arms were stretched up at their full length, so that she stood upon the ends of her toes. He then said to her, "Now, you d——d b——h, I'll learn you how to disobey my orders!" and after rolling up his sleeves, he commenced to lay on the heavy cowskin, and soon the warm, red blood (amid heart-rending shrieks from her, and horrid oaths from him) came dripping to the floor. I was so terrified and horror-stricken at the sight, that I hid myself in a closet, and dared not venture out till long after the bloody transaction was over. I expected it would be my turn next.

The uproar over his memoirs caused Douglass to flee to England, fearful he would be captured as a fugitive slave. But he returned to America two years later, and gained further renown as publisher of the abolitionist newspaper *The North Star* in Rochester, New York. Douglass would help raise black regiments for the Union during the Civil War, and later served as ambassador to Haiti.

SOJOURNER TRUTH SPEAKS

Born in Hurley, New York, in 1797, she spent her younger years as a slave, known as Isabella. She eventually gained her freedom, and by the early 1840s—now calling herself Sojourner Truth—a remarkable woman had gained a mission as well.

She chose her new name convinced she had been divinely selected to travel the land "to declare the truth to the people."

A magnificent orator, Sojourner Truth was a force in the abolitionist struggle and a powerful advocate for women's rights during the two decades preceding the Civil War.

On May 29, 1851, she appeared at a national women's convention in Akron, Ohio, to which many clergymen had also been invited. When none of the women could quiet the heckling they were receiving from the ministers, Sojourner Truth came forward. There was a hush in the church meeting hall as she spoke to the men who had mocked women as too helpless to be entrusted with the vote.

Frances Gage, the president of the convention, would recall the moment.

The leaders of the movement trembled on seeing a tall, gaunt black woman in a gray grass and white turban, surmounted with an uncouth sun-bonnet, march deliberately into the church, walk with the air of a queen up the aisle, and take her seat upon the pulpit steps. A buzz of disapprobation was heard all over the house, and there fell on the listening ear, "An abolition affair!" "Women's rights and niggers!" "Go it, darkey!"

I chanced on that occasion to wear my first laurels in public life as president of the meeting. At my request, order was restored, and the business of the convention went on. Morning, afternoon and evening exercises came and went. Through all these sessions, Old Sojourner, quiet and reticent as the "Lybian Statue," sat crouched against the wall at the corner of the pulpit stairs, her sun-bonnet shading her eyes, her elbows on her knees, her chin resting upon her broad, hard palms. At intermission she was busy selling the "Life of Sojourner Truth," a narrative of her own strange and adventurous life. Again and again, timorous and trembling ones came to me and said with earnestness, "Don't let her speak, Mrs. Gage, it will ruin us. Every newspaper in the land will have our cause mixed up with abolition and niggers, and we shall be utterly denounced." My only answer was, "We shall see when the time comes."

The second day the work waxed warm. Methodist, Baptist, Episcopal, Presbyterian and Universalist ministers came in to hear and discuss the resolutions presented. One claimed superior rights and privileges for man, on the ground of "superior intellect. . . ."

The atmosphere betokened a storm, when, slowly from her seat in the corner rose Sojourner Truth, who, till now, had scarcely lifted her head. "Don't let her speak!" gasped half a dozen in my ear. She moved slowly and solemnly to the front, laid her old bonnet at her feet, and turned her great speaking eyes to me. There was a hissing sound of disapprobation above and below. I rose and announced "Sojourner Truth," and begged the audience to keep silence for a few moments.

The tumult subsided at once, and every eye was fixed on this almost Amazon form, which stood nearly six feet high, head erect, and eyes piercing the upper air like one in a dream. At her first word there was a profound hush. She spoke in deep tones, which, though not loud, reached every ear in the house, and away through the throng at the doors and windows.

"Dat man ober dar say dat womin needs to be helped into carriages, and lifted ober ditches, and to hab de best place everywhar. Nobody eber helps me into carriages, or ober mud-puddles, or gibs me any best place!"

And raising herself to her full height, and her voice to a pitch like rolling thunder, she asked, "And ain't I a woman? Look at me! Look at my arm! (and she bared her right arm to the shoulder, showing her tremendous muscular power). I have ploughed, and planted, and gathered into barns, and no man could head me! And ain't I a woman? I could work as much and eat as much as a man—when I could get it— and bear de lash as well! And ain't I a woman? I have borne thirteen chilern, and seen 'em mos' all sold into slavery, and when I cried out with my mother's grief, none but Jesus heard me! And ain't I a woman?

"Den dey talks 'bout dis ting in de head; what dis dey call it?" ("Intellect," whispered someone near.) "Dat's it, honey. What's dat got *to do wid womin's rights or nigger's rights? If my cup won't hold but a pint, and yourn holds a quart, wouldn't ye be mean not to let me have my little half-measure full?" And she pointed her significant finger, and sent a keen glance at the minister who had made the argument. The cheering was loud and long. . . .*

Amid roars of applause she returned to her corner, leaving more than one of us with streaming eyes, and hearts beating with gratitude. She had taken us up in her arms and carried us over the slough of difficulty, turning the whole tide in our favor. I have never in my life seen anything like the magical influence that subdued the mobbish spirit of the day, and turned the sneers and jeers of an excited crowd into notes of respect and admiration. Hundreds rushed up to shake hands with her, and congratulate the glorious old mother, and bid her God-speed on her mission of "testifyin' agin concerning the wickedness of this 'ere people."

Frances Gage's account—a recollection published twelve years afterward—imprinted the electrifying exclamation "Ain't I a woman?" on the women's-rights cause. Doubts have been raised, however, as to whether Sojourner Truth actually used that phrase. An on-the-spot account of her address in the *Anti-Slavery Bugle* did not mention that rallying cry despite roughly paralleling Gage's recollections on the substance of the remarks. But even if Sojourner Truth didn't actually say "Ain't I a woman?" her life embodied its meaning.

the LINCOLN-DOUGLAS DEBATES

They pressed their points before small-town crowds, but their arguments would reverberate upon the whole nation.

The Democrat, seeking re-election to the United States Senate from Illinois, was well known nationally, having twice tried unsuccessfully for his party's presidential nomination.

His Republican opponent, a former one-term congressman, now a lawyer in Springfield, had yet to emerge in the political spotlight.

And they presented a contrast physically when they confronted each other in a series of four debates in 1858.

Stephen A. Douglas, known as "the Little Giant," was a squat man with a large head. Abraham Lincoln was lanky and awkward.

More important, they were at odds on the slavery question.

Douglas advocated a conciliatory stance toward the South by championing "popular sovereignty," a doctrine holding that the populace of a given territory, and not Congress, should determine whether it should eventually enter the Union as a free or a slave state.

Lincoln voiced the stance of his fledgling "free soil" party—slavery must not spread, it must be confined to the states where it currently existed and would eventually die out.

Lincoln would damage Douglas's standing in the South by maneuvering him, at their Freeport debate, into suggesting that popular sovereignty could supersede the Supreme Court's Dred Scott decision of 1857, finding that Congress could not bar the introduction of slavery in the territories because that would nullify slaveholders' property rights.

Douglas would keep his Senate seat when the Illinois Legislature, which elected the state's senators, remained Democratic. But Lincoln would emerge as a national figure and would win the presidency two years later over Douglas and two other candidates.

Carl Schurz, a German American who would go on to a long career in public life—as a Civil War general, journalist, reformer, and secretary of the interior—attended the debate in Quincy. His comments were colored by his partisanship for the Republicans, but he had a sharp eye for detail.

. . . the country people began to stream into town for the great meeting, some singly, on foot or on horseback, or small parties of men and women, and even children, in buggies or farm wagons; while others were marshaled in solemn procession from outlying towns or districts with banners and drums, many of them headed by maidens in white with tri-colored scarfs, who represented the Goddess of Liberty and the different States of the Union, and whose beauty was duly admired by everyone, including themselves.

On the whole, the Democratic displays were much more elaborate and gorgeous than those of the Republicans, and it was said that Douglas had plenty of money to spend for such things. He himself also traveled in what was called in those days "great style," with a secretary and servants and a numerous escort of somewhat loud companions, moving from place to place by special train with cars specially decorated for the occasion, all of which contrasted strongly with Lincoln's extremely modest simplicity.

There was no end of cheering and shouting and jostling on the streets of Quincy that day. But in spite of the excitement created by the political contest, the crowd remained very good-natured, and the occasional jibes flung from one side to the other were uniformly received with a laugh.

The great debate took place in the afternoon on the open square, where a large, pine-board platform had been built. . . .

The first part of Mr. Lincoln's opening address was devoted to a refutation of some things Douglas had said at previous meetings. This refutation may, indeed, have been required for the settlement of disputed points, but it did not strike me as anything extraordinary, either in substance or in form. Neither had Mr. Lincoln any of those physical advantages which usually are thought to be very desirable, if not necessary, to the orator. His voice was not musical, rather high-keyed, and apt to turn into a shrill treble in moments of excitement; but it was not positively disagreeable. It had an exceedingly penetrating, far-reaching quality. The looks of the audience convinced me that every word he spoke was understood at the remotest edges of the vast assemblage. His gesture was awkward. He swung his long arms sometimes in a very ungraceful manner. Now and then he would, to give particular emphasis to a point, bend his knees and body with a sudden downward jerk, and then shoot up again with a vehemence that raised him to his tip-toes and made him look much taller than he really was. . . .

There was, however, in all he said, a tone of earnest truthfulness, of elevated, noble sentiment, and of kindly sympathy, which added greatly to the strength of his argument, and became, as in the course of his speech he touched upon the moral side of the question in debate, powerfully impressive. Even when attacking his opponent with keen satire or invective, which, coming from any other speaker, would have sounded bitter and cruel, there was still a certain something in his utterance making his hearers feel that those thrusts came from a reluctant heart, and that he would much rather have treated his foe as a friend. . . .

By the side of Lincoln's tall, lank, and ungainly form, Douglas stood almost like a dwarf, very short of stature, but square-shouldered and broad-chested, a massive head upon a strong neck, the very embodiment of force, combativeness, and staying power. . . . On that stage in Quincy he looked rather natty and well groomed in excellently fitting broad cloth and shining linen. But his face seemed a little puffy, and it was said that he had been drinking hard with some boon companions either on his journey or after his arrival. The deep, horizontal wrinkle between his keen eyes was unusually dark and scowling. While he was listening to Lincoln's speech, a contemptuous smile now and then flitted across his lips, and when he rose, the tough parliamentary gladiator, he tossed his mane with an air of overbearing superiority, of threatening defiance, as if to say: "How dare anyone stand up against me?"

As I looked at him, I detested him deeply; but my detestation was not free from an anxious dread as to what was to come. His voice, naturally a strong baritone, gave forth a hoarse and rough, at times even something like a barking, sound. His tone was, from the very start, angry, dictatorial, and insolent in the extreme. In one of his first sentences he charged Lincoln with "base insinuations," and then he went on in that style with a wrathful frown upon his brow, defiantly shaking his head, clenching his fists, and stamping his feet. No language seemed to be too offensive for him, and even inoffensive things he would sometimes bring out in a manner which sounded as if intended to be insulting; and thus he occasionally called forth, instead of applause from his friends, demonstrations of remonstrance from the opposition. But his sentences were well put together, his points strongly accentuated, his argumentation seemingly clear and plausible, his sophisms skillfully woven so as to throw the desired flood of darkness upon the subject and thus beguile an untutored mind, his appeals to prejudice unprincipled and reckless, but shrewdly aimed, and his invective vigorous and exceedingly trying to the temper of the assailed party. On the whole, his friends were well pleased with his performance, and rewarded him with vociferous cheers.

But then came Lincoln's closing speech of half an hour, which seemed completely to change the temper of the atmosphere. He replied to Douglas's arguments and attacks with rapid thrusts so deft and piercing, with humorous retort so quaint and pat, and with witty illustrations so clinch-

ing, and he did it all so good-naturedly, that the meeting, again and again, broke out in bursts of delight by which even many of his opponents were carried away, while the scowl on Douglas's face grew darker and darker.

the FALL of FORT SUMTER

In sending Abraham Lincoln to the presidency in the election of 1860 (Stephen Douglas and John Breckinridge of Kentucky, the South's candidate, split the votes of a divided Democratic Party), the American people voted to restrict slavery and preserve the Union.

But before Lincoln entered the White House, the Union had splintered. Stampeded by extremists who were convinced that he would challenge slavery, the Southern legislatures voted for secession. South Carolina was the first, leaving the Union on December 20. In February 1861, delegates from seven seceding states met at Montgomery, Alabama, formed the Confederate States of America, and elected Jefferson Davis of Mississippi as their president.

On March 4, in his inaugural address, Lincoln told the South, "The Government will not assail you."

Its answer came in the predawn hours of April 12, when a South Carolina militia unit commanded by General Pierre G. T. Beauregard bombarded the Federal garrison of Fort Sumter in Charleston Harbor.

The tension of the preceding days was recorded in a diary kept by Mary Boykin Chesnut, the wife of James Chesnut, Jr., who had resigned his United States Senate seat the previous November and was one of the South Carolinians who had negotiated with the fort's commander, Major Robert Anderson.

APRIL 8

Suddenly loud shouting was heard. We ran out. Cannon after cannon roared. We met Mrs. Allen Green in the passageway with blanched cheeks and streaming eyes. [Former] Governor [John] Means rushed out of his room in his dressing-gown and begged us to be calm. "Governor Pickens," said he, "has ordered in the plenitude of his wisdom, seven cannon to be fired as a signal to the Seventh Regiment. Anderson will hear as well as the Seventh Regiment. Now you can go back and be quiet; fighting in the streets has not begun yet."

So we retired. Dr. Gibbes calls Mrs. Allen Green Dame Placid. There was no placidity to-day, with cannon bursting and Allen on the island. No sleep for anybody last night. The streets were alive with soldiers, men shouting, marching, singing. [Louis T.] Wigfall, the "stormy petrel," is in his glory, the only thoroughly happy person I see. To-day things seem to have settled down a little. One can but hope still. Lincoln, or Seward, has made such silly advances and then far sillier drawings back. There may be a chance for peace after all. Things are happening so fast. My husband has been made an aide-de-camp to General Beauregard. . . .

APRIL 12

I do not pretend to go to sleep. How can I? If Anderson does not accept terms at four, the orders are, he shall be fired upon. I count four, St. Michael's bells chime out and I begin to hope. At half-past four the heavy booming of a cannon. I sprang out of bed, and on my knees prostrate I prayed as I never prayed before.

There was a sound of stir all over the house, pattering of feet in the corridors. All seemed hurrying one way. I put on my double-gown and a shawl and went, too. It was to the housetop. The shells were bursting. In the dark I heard a man say, "Waste of ammunition." I knew my husband was rowing about in a boat somewhere in that dark bay, and that the shells were roofing it over, bursting toward the fort. If Anderson was obstinate, Colonel Chesnut was to order the fort on one side to open fire. Certainly fire had begun. The regular roar of the cannon, there it was. And who could tell what each volley accomplished of death and destruction?

The women were wild there on the housetop. Prayers came from the women and imprecations from the men. And then a shell would light up the scene. To-night they say the forces are to attempt to land. We watched up there, and everybody wondered that Fort Sumter did not fire a shot.

The events were also recorded in a diary kept by Edmund Ruffin, one of the Confederate negotiators.

APRIL 12

Before 4 A.M. the drums beat for parade, & our company was speedily on the march to the batteries which they were to man. At 4:30, a signal shell was thrown from a mortar battery at Fort Johnson, which had been before ordered to be taken as the command for immediate attack—& the firing from all the batteries bearing on Fort Sumter next began in the order arranged—which was that the discharges should be two minutes apart, & the round of all the pieces & batteries to be completed in 32 minutes, & then to begin again. The night before . . . Capt. Cuthbert had notified me that his company requested of me to discharge the first cannon to be fired, which was their 64 lb. Columbiad, loaded with shell. By order of Gen. Beauregard, made known the afternoon of the 11th, the attack was to be commenced by the first shot at the fort being fired by the Palmetto Guard, & from the Iron Battery.

In accepting & acting upon this highly appreciated compliment, that company had made me its instrument. . . . Of course, I was highly gratified by the compliment, & delighted to perform the service—which I did. The shell struck the fort, at the north-east angle of the parapet. The firing then proceeded, as stated, from 14 different batteries, including Fort Moultrie & the floating battery, which had been placed for this purpose in the cove, back of Sullivan's Island. Most of both shot & shells, at first, missed the fort. But many struck, & the proportion of effective balls & shells increased with the practice. To all this firing, not a gun was fired in return, for two hours or more.

Mary Boykin Chesnut described the scene the following morning.

APRIL 13

Nobody has been hurt after all. How gay we were last night. Reaction after the dread of all the slaughter we thought those dreadful cannon were making. Not even a battery the worse for wear. Fort Sumter has been on fire. Anderson has not yet silenced any of our guns. So the aides, still with swords and red sashes by way of uniform, tell us. But the sound of those guns makes regular meals impossible. None of us go to table. Tea-trays pervade the corridors going everywhere. Some of the anxious hearts lie on their beds and moan in solitary misery. Mrs. Wigfall and I

solace ourselves with tea in my room. These women have all a satisfying
faith. "God is on our side," they say. . . .

Not by one word or look can we detect any change in the demeanor
of these negro servants. Lawrence sits at our door, sleepy and respectful,
and profoundly indifferent. So are they all, but they carry it too far. You
could not tell that they had even heard the awful roar going on in the
bay, though it has been dinning in their eyes night and day. People talk
before them as if they were chairs and tables. They make no sign. Are
they stolidly stupid or wiser than we are; silent and strong, biding their
time?

Captain Abner Doubleday, a United States Army officer who would
be remembered mainly for inventing baseball (something he never actually did), weathered the chaos inside Fort Sumter.

It seemed impossible to escape suffocation. Same lay down close to
the ground, with handkerchiefs over their mouths, and others posted
themselves near the embrasures, where the smoke was somewhat lessened
by the draught of air.

The roaring and crackling of the flames, the dense masses of whirling
smoke, the bursting of the enemy's shells, and our own which were
exploding in the burning rooms, the crashing of the shot, and the sound
of masonry falling in every direction, made the fort a pandemonium.
When at last nothing was left of the building but the blackened walls and
smoldering embers, it became painfully evident that an immense amount
of damage had been done. There was a tower at each angle of the
fort. One of these, containing great quantities of shells upon which we
had relied, was almost completely shattered by successive explosions.
The massive wooden gates studded with iron nails were burned, and the
wall built behind them was now a mere heap of debris, so that
the main entrance was wide open for an assaulting party. The sally
ports were in a similar condition, and the numerous windows on the
gorge side which had been planked up had now become all open
entrances.

About 12:48 P.M. the end of the flagstaff was shot down and the flag fell.

Again, Mary Boykin Chesnut.

APRIL 15

I did not know that one could live through such days of excitement. Some one called: "Come out! There is a crowd coming." A mob it was, indeed, but it was headed by Colonels Chesnut and Manning. The crowd was shouting and showing these two as messengers of good news. They were escorted to Beauregard's headquarters. Fort Sumter had surrendered! Those upon the housetops shouted to us "The fort is on fire." That had been the story once or twice before.

When we had calmed down, Colonel Chesnut, who had taken it all quietly enough, if anything more unruffled than usual in his serenity, told us how the surrender came about. Wigfall was with them on Morris Island when they saw the fire in the fort; he jumped in a little boat, and with his handkerchief as a white flag, rowed over. Wigfall went in through a porthole. When Colonel Chesnut arrived shortly after, and was received at the regular entrance, Colonel [Major] Anderson told him he had need to pick his way warily, for the place was all mined. As far as I can make out the fort surrendered to Wigfall. But it is all confusion. Our flag is flying there.

Major Robert Anderson, Fort Sumter's commander, reported his surrender.

Dispatch from the steamer Baltic, off Sandy Hook, to Secretary of War Simeon Cameron, April 18, 1861, dictated to Captain Gustavus Fox.

Having defended Fort Sumter for thirty-four hours, until the quarters were entirely burned, the main gates destroyed by fire, the gorge walls seriously impaired, the magazine surrounded by flames, and its door closed from the effects of the heat, four barrels and three cartridges of powder only being available, and no provisions remaining but pork, I accepted terms of evacuation offered by General Beauregard, being the same offered by him on the 11th instant, prior to the commencement of hostilities, and marched out of the fort on Sunday afternoon, being the 14th instant, with colors flying and drums beating, bringing away company and private property, and saluting my flag with fifty guns.

Robert Anderson, Major, First Artillery

The nation now plunged into what Abraham Lincoln would call "the fiery trial" that "will light us down, in honor or dishonor, to the latest generation."

ROUT *at* BULL RUN

Upon the fall of Fort Sumter, Lincoln declared a "state of insurrection" and called for seventy-five thousand volunteers to serve three months of military duty. But it soon became clear that this would not be a short war.

Virginia seceded on April 20, and Robert E. Lee, refusing to abandon his native state, spurned Lincoln's request that he command the Union troops. Instead, he resigned his commission in the United States Army and took control of the Confederate forces.

On July 21, green Union troops, under inept officers, were routed at Manassas, Virginia—just twenty miles south of Washington—in the first Battle of Bull Run. The Union soldiers moved through the center of the Confederate line, but then were driven back by troops on the right flank commanded by General Thomas J. Jackson. "There is Jackson, standing like a stone wall," said a fellow officer. Thereafter the former professor at the Virginia Military Institute would be known as "Stonewall."

A retreat turned into a stampede as Union troops choked the roads leading back to Washington.

William Howard Russell, a correspondent for the *Times* of London, witnessed the flight.

I had ridden between three and a half and four miles, as well as I could judge, when I was obliged to turn for the third and fourth time into the road by a considerable stream, direction of which was spanned by a bridge, towards which I was threading my way, when my attention was attracted by loud shouts in advance, and I perceived several wagons coming from the battlefield, the drivers of which were endeavoring to force their horses past the ammunition carts going in the contrary direction near the bridge; a thick cloud of dust rose behind them, and running by the side of the wagons were a number of men in uniform, whom I supposed to be the guard. My first impression was that the wagons were returning for fresh supplies of ammunition. But every moment the crowd increased; drivers and men cried out with the most vehement gestures, "Turn back! Turn back! We are whipped." They seized the heads of the horses and swore at the opposing drivers. Emerging from the crowd, a breathless man, in the uniform of an officer, with an empty scabbard dangling by his side, was cut off by getting between my horse and a cart for a moment.

"What is the matter, sir? What is this all about?"

"Why it means we are pretty badly whipped, that's the truth," he gasped, and continued.

. . . I got up out of the road into a cornfield, through which men were hastily walking or running, their faces streaming with perspiration, and generally without arms, and worked my way for about half a mile or so, as well as I could judge, against an increasing stream of fugitives, the ground being strewn with coats, blankets, firelocks, cooking tins, caps, belt, bayonets—asking in vain where General McDowell was. . . .

Russell observed a remarkable scene on the streets of Washington the following day.

I awoke from a deep sleep this morning, about six o'clock. The rain was falling in torrents, and beat with a dull, thudding sound on the leads outside my windows; but, louder than all, came a strange sound, as if the tread of men, a confused tramp and splashing, and a murmuring of voices. I got up and ran to the front room, the windows of which looked on the street, and there, to my intense surprise, I saw a steady stream of men covered with mud, soaked through with rain, who were pouring irregularly, without any semblance of order, up Pennsylvania Avenue towards the Capitol. A dense stream of vapour rose from the multitude; but looking closely at the men, I perceived they belonged to different regiments, New Yorkers, Michiganders, Rhode Islanders, Massachusetters, Minnesotians, mingled pellmell together. Many of them were without knapsacks, crossbelts, and firelocks. Some had neither greatcoats nor shoes, others were covered with blankets. Hastily putting on my clothes, I ran downstairs and asked an "officer," who was passing by, a pale young man, who looked exhausted to death, and who had lost his sword, for the empty sheath dangled at his side, where the men were coming from.

"Where from? Well, sir, I guess we're all coming out of Verginny as far as we can, and pretty well whipped too."

"What! the whole army, sir?"

"That's more than I know. They may stay like that. I know I'm going home. I've had enough of fighting to last my lifetime."

Whilst the rain fell, the tramp of feet went steadily on. As I lifted my eyes now and then from the paper, I saw the beaten, footsore spongy-looking soldiers, officers, and all the debris of the army filing through mud and rain, and forming in crowds in front of the spirit-stores. . . . When the lad came in with my breakfast he seemed a degree or two lighter in colour than usual.

"What's the matter with you?"

"I spects, massa, the Seceshers soon be in here. I'm a free nigger; I must go, sar, afore de come cotch me."

General Scott is quite overwhelmed by the affair, and is unable to stir. General McDowell has not yet arrived. The Secretary of War knows not what to do. Mr. Lincoln is equally helpless, and Mr. Seward, who retains some calmness, is, notwithstanding his military rank and military experience, without resource or expedient. There are a good many troops hanging on about the camps and forts on the other side of the river, it is said; but they are thoroughly disorganised and will run away if the enemy comes in sight without a shot, and then the capital must fall at once.

"MINE EYES HAVE SEEN *the* GLORY"

Julia Ward Howe, an essayist and poet active in the abolitionist and suffragist movements, accompanied her husband, Dr. Samuel Gridley Howe, a physician for a military medical corps, to Munson's Hill, Virginia, on November 18, 1861, to watch a little army ceremony. The Confederates broke things up, but by early the next morning, stirring in her room at Willard's Hotel in Washington, Mrs. Howe had gained inspiration for a powerful emotional weapon that would well serve the Union soldiers.

We were invited one day to attend a review of troops at some distance from the town. While we were engaged in watching the maneuvers, a sudden movement of the enemy necessitated immediate action. The review was discontinued, and we saw a detachment of soldiers gallop to the assistance of a small body of our men who were in imminent danger of being surrounded and cut off from retreat. The regiments remaining on the field were ordered to march to their cantonments. We returned to the city very slowly, of necessity, for the troops nearly filled the road. My dear minister was in the carriage with me, as were several other friends. To beguile the rather tedious drive, we sang from time to time snatches of the army songs so popular at that time, concluding, I think, with:

> *John Brown's body lies a-moldering in the ground;*
> *His soul is marching on.*

The soldiers seemed to like this and answered back, "Good for you!" Mr. Clarke said, "Mrs. Howe, why do you not write some good words for that stirring tune?" I replied that I had often wished to do this but had not as yet found in my mind any leading toward it.

I went to bed that night as usual and slept, according to my wont, quite soundly. I awoke in the gray of the morning twilight, and as I lay waiting for the dawn, the long lines of the desired poem began to twine themselves in my mind. Having thought out all the stanzas, I said to myself, "I must get up and write these verses down, lest I fall asleep and forget them." So with a sudden effort I sprang out of bed and found in the dimness an old stump of a pen which I remembered to have used the day before. I scrawled the verses almost without looking at the paper. I had learned to do this when, on previous occasions, attacks of versification had visited me in the night and I feared to have recourse to a light lest I should wake the baby, who slept near me. I was always obliged to decipher my scrawl before another night should intervene, as it was only legible while the matter was fresh in my mind. At this time, having completed my writing, I returned to bed and fell asleep, saying to myself, "I like this better than most things I have written."

She wrote six stanzas on her husband's stationery, then sent a slightly amended version to *The Atlantic Monthly*, which printed it in February 1862 for the handsome sum of $5. Soon regiments all over the North were singing the words to rhythmic music composed in 1852 by William Steffe, a Methodist preacher.

"The Battle Hymn of the Republic" would be a perfect anthem for the religious and nationalistic fervor of the Union soldiers.

Mine eyes have seen the glory of the coming of the Lord;
He is trampling out the vintage where the grapes of wrath are stored;
He hath loosed the fateful lightning of His terrible swift sword:
His truth is marching on.

GETTYSBURG

Union troops were turned back at Cedar Mountain, Virginia, and at the second Battle of Bull Run, but repulsed Lee's forces at Sharpsburg, Maryland, in the Battle of Antietam, the single bloodiest day of the war. Now, with the Union position strengthened, Lincoln drew up the Emancipation Proclamation on September 22, 1862.

The following June, the Confederates planned another thrust to the North—this time an invasion of Pennsylvania. Success would undermine Union morale, perhaps spur England to recognize the Confederacy, and open a route toward Washington.

Lee's seventy-five thousand troops clashed with a Union force of eighty-eight thousand under General George B. Meade at Gettysburg, a little town astride important roads. The Rebels attacked from Seminary Ridge; the Yanks set up a defense line at Cemetery Ridge. In furious combat during the first three days of July, each side suffered at least twenty thousand casualties.

The climax came when the Confederates were turned back in a frontal assault known as Pickett's Charge. Lee was forced to retreat across the Potomac, and he never again would mount a major challenge. Meade missed a grand opportunity to pursue, but the battle was a turning point in the war.

A Union soldier named Jesse Bowman Young would recall the calm after the storm.

The battle was now over, but nobody knew it! The repulse of Pickett's charge was really the defeat of the Army of Northern Virginia, but . . . the two armies stood at bay, glaring like two wild beasts which had fought one another almost to death, watching for a stroke or a motion, and listening for a growl that might indicate a further continuance of the struggle. General Meade hardly durst venture out against the Confederates after the defeat of Pickett, and General Lee was too weak to undertake any further movement except in retreat, unless he should be attacked. . . .

There have been few such sights and circumstances as those amid which the two armies found themselves at Gettysburg when the fight was over on Friday afternoon, July 3, 1863. . . . Thousands of men were lying unattended, scattered over the field, mingled with broken gun carriages, exploded caissons, hundreds of dead and dying horses, and other ghastly debris of the battlefield. At once the poor victims of shot and shell nearest our lines were brought in; others farther out were in due time reached; and the surgeons and nurses . . . kept up their work of ministering to and caring for the wounded.

It was possible, as night came on, to make a bit of a fire, here and there in the rear, and boil water for a cup of coffee, which was a boon to be grateful for. While the boys sat or lay on the ground, eating a bite of hardtack, and eagerly, in their hunger, devouring the succulent salt pork, which was about the only nourishment to be secured, relays of men with stretchers, and hundreds of others helping the wounded to walk to the rear, passed back and forth with their bloody freight, now and then a groan or a suppressed shriek telling the story of suffering and heroic fortitude.

"Listen, boys!" was the shout of one of the men as they lay on the ground. . . . "The fight must be over—listen! There is a band in the rear beginning to tune up. . . ." It was a sight and a situation long to be remembered. The field was covered with the slain; the full moon looked down with serene, unclouded, and softened luster on the field of Gettysburg, trodden down for miles by the two great armies; surgeons were cutting off limbs, administering whisky, chloroform, and morphine to deaden pain; hundreds of men were going back and forth from the fields where the actual fighting had occurred, to the rear, with the mangled bodies of the wounded; and about 100,000 men—the survivors who were left out of 160,000 in the two armies—were waiting to see what would come on the morrow, when suddenly a band of music began to play in the rear of the Union line of battle, down somewhere on the Taneytown Road.

Down the valley and up the hill and over the field, into the ears of wounded and dying men, and beyond our line into the bivouac of the beaten enemy, the soft, gentle and melting tune . . . "Home, Sweet, Sweet Home" was breathed from the brazen instruments.

On November 19, 1863, Abraham Lincoln dedicated the military cemetery at Gettysburg.

We here highly resolve that these dead shall not have died in vain; that this nation, under God, shall have a new birth of freedom; and that government of the people, by the people, for the people, shall not perish from the earth.

COUNTRYMEN AGAIN

In November 1864, General William T. Sherman began his march from Atlanta to the sea, his troops destroying everything in their path.

Then they turned northward, devastating the Carolinas, burning and occupying Charleston. On April 3, 1865, Union forces entered Petersburg and Richmond, and Jefferson Davis fled the Confederate capital.

His men besieged and starving, Robert E. Lee could fight no more. He arrived at the tiny village of Appomattox Court House, Virginia, on April 9 to meet with Ulysses S. Grant. They were both West Point graduates; they had both served as junior officers in the Mexican War; now they would be fellow Americans once more.

Twenty years after the Civil War, dying of cancer, Grant wrote his memoirs—a jewel of American letters—to save his family from financial ruin. He remembered the moment when Lee laid down his sword.

When I had left camp that morning I had not expected so soon the result that was then taking place, and consequently was in rough garb. I was without a sword, as I usually was when on horseback on the field, and wore a soldier's blouse for a coat, with the shoulder straps of my rank to indicate to the army who I was. When I went into the house I found General Lee. We greeted each other, and after shaking hands took our seats. I had my staff with me, a good portion of whom were in the room during the whole of the interview.

What General Lee's feelings were I do not know. As he was a man of much dignity, with an impassible face, it was impossible to say whether he felt inwardly glad that the end had finally come, or felt sad over the result, and was too manly to show it. Whatever his feelings, they were entirely concealed from my observation; but my own feelings, which had been quite jubilant on the receipt of his letter, were sad and depressed. I felt like anything rather than rejoicing at the downfall of a foe who had fought so long and valiantly, and had suffered so much for a cause, though the cause was, I believe, one of the worst for which a people ever fought, and one for which there was the least excuse. I do not question, however, the sincerity of the great mass of those who were opposed to us.

General Lee was dressed in a full uniform which was entirely new, and was wearing a sword of considerable value, very likely the sword which had been presented by the State of Virginia; at all events, it was an entirely different sword from the one that would ordinarily be worn in the field. In my rough traveling suit, the uniform of a private with the straps of a lieutenant-general, I must have contrasted very strangely with a man so handsomely dressed, six feet high and of faultless form. But this was not a matter that I thought of until afterwards.

We soon fell into a conversation about old army times. He remarked that he remembered me very well in the old army; and I told him that as a matter of course I remembered him perfectly, but from the difference in our rank and years (there being about sixteen years' difference in our ages), I had thought it very likely that I had not attracted his attention sufficiently to be remembered by him after such a long interval. Our conversation grew so pleasant that I almost forgot the object of our meeting. . . .

General Lee, after all was completed and before taking his leave, remarked that his army was in a very bad condition for want of food, and that they were without forage; that his men had been living for some days on parched corn exclusively, and that he would have to ask me for rations and forage. I told him "certainly," and asked for how many men he wanted rations. His answer was "about twenty-five thousand:" and I authorized him to send his own commissary and quartermaster to Appomattox Station, two or three miles away, where he could have, out of the trains we had stopped, all the provisions wanted. . . .

Lee and I then separated as cordially as we had met, he returning to his own lines, and all went into bivouac for the night at Appomattox.

Soon after Lee's departure I telegraphed to Washington as follows:

HEADQUARTERS APPOMATTOX C.H., Va.

April 9th, 1865, 4:30 P.M.

HON. E. M. STANTON, Secretary of War,

Washington,

General Lee surrendered the Army of Northern Virginia this afternoon on terms proposed by myself. The accompanying additional correspondence will show the conditionals fully.

U. S. GRANT,

Lieut.-General.

"YOU'S FREE!"

A white flag was hoisted in the village square at Pamplin, Virginia, a couple of miles from Appomattox Court House. A house servant watched it rise.

"Lee done surrendered!" said the mistress, Sarah Ann.

The servant, Fannie Berry, would long savor the moment.

Never was no time like 'em befo' or since. Niggers shoutin' an' clappin' hands an' singin'! Chillun runnin' all over de place beatin' tins an' yellin'. Ev'ybody happy. Sho' did some celebratin'.

> *Run to de kitchen an' shout in de winder:*
> *Mammy, don't you cook no mo',*
> *You's free! You's free!*
>
> *Run to de henhouse an' shout:*
> *Rooster, don't you crow no mo',*
> *You's free! You's free!*
> *Ol' hen, don't you lay no mo' eggs,*
> *You's free! You's free!*
>
> *Go to de pigpen an' tell de pig:*
> *Ol' pig, don't you grunt no mo',*
> *You's free! You's free!*
>
> *Tell de cows:*
> *Ol' cow, don't you give no mo' milk,*
> *You's free! You's free!*

WARTIME'S TOLL

The casualty lists were appalling: The Union counted 360,000 dead, the Confederacy 260,000. Tens of thousands of young men would be crippled, mounds of amputated limbs stacked at field hospitals.

America's national poet, Walt Whitman, wrote how "the real war will never get into the books." For Whitman, the story lay not in the grand strategy but in the sacrifice and suffering of the soldiers.

For three years, Whitman served as a volunteer visitor to the wounded at Washington hospitals. Devoted to Lincoln and the Union cause, he nonetheless comforted the gray as well as the blue.

I stayed tonight a long time by the bedside of a new patient, a young Baltimorean aged about nineteen years. W.S.P. (2nd Maryland, Southern), very feeble, right leg amputated, can't sleep hardly at all; has taken a great deal of morphine, which, as usual, is costing more than it comes to. Evidently very intelligent and well bred, very affectionate, held on to my hand and put it by his face, not willing to let me leave.

As I was lingering, soothing him in his pain, he says to me suddenly: "I hardly think you know who I am; I don't wish to impose on you—I am a Rebel soldier." I said I did not know that, but it made no difference. Visited him daily for about two weeks after that, while he lived (death had marked him and he was quite alone). I loved him much, always kissed him, and he did me.

In an adjoining ward I found his brother, an officer of rank, a Union soldier, a brave and religious man, Colonel Clifton K. Prentiss, 6th Maryland Infantry, 6th Corps, wounded in one of the engagements at Petersburg, April 2; lingered, suffered much, died in Brooklyn August 20 '65. It was in the same battle both were hit. One was a strong Unionist, the other Secesh; both fought on their respective sides, both badly wounded, and both brought together here after a separation of four years. Each died for his cause.

LINCOLN'S FINAL HOURS

April 14—Good Friday. Abraham Lincoln has supposedly had a recent dream afflicting him with a premonition of death. He meets with his Cabinet during the day, is already looking to a plan for reconciliation with the South. Prevailed upon by his wife, Mary, he goes to Ford's Theater that night to see the play *Our American Cousin.*

Oliver Gatch, an army captain from Ohio, was in the theater audience. He happened to notice a man lingering near the passage to the state box, left unsecured because the lone policeman assigned as the presidential bodyguard had deserted his post.

It was during a lull in the action of a scene that my brother and I, cramped from long sitting in one position, rose from our seats to stretch ourselves. While we were standing in the aisle close to the wall, my brother called my attention to a young man who seemed to be watching the play from a position against the wall near the entrance to the President's box. My brother remarked [about] this young man's striking appearance, and I agreed with him, thinking him the handsomest man I had ever seen. He had a haughty demeanor, but his face was so calm that one would never have thought of suspecting him of any dreadful purpose. I noticed, though, how his eyes flashed and how sharp was their contrast to his pallid countenance. Presently, I saw him edge toward the box without changing his attitude, and then enter the passage-way and close the door behind him.

William Withers, the orchestra leader, was at one of the theater entrances when a shot rang out.

I stood with astonishment, thinking why they should fire off a pistol in Our American Cousin. As I turned around, I saw a man running toward me with his head down. . . . I saw it was John Wilkes Booth. . . .

Should I live a thousand years, I shall never forget the ten seconds of my life that I spent between Booth and his liberty. . . . He looked terrible. His eyes seemed starting from their sockets, and his hair stood on end. In his left hand there was a long dagger. . . .

He glared at me like a wild beast for a few seconds, then lowered his head, and, with arms flying, made a rush. . . . With the dagger, he made a desperate lunge at me. I was so bewildered that I made no move to defend myself and his second stab sent the sharp blade ripping through the collar of my coat, penetrating my vest and under garments and inflicting a flesh wound in my neck.

115

As Booth—a well-known member of a distinguished acting family —had crossed the stage, a cast member, Harry Hawk, was standing onstage opposite the President's box, his soliloquy interrupted.

Booth dragged himself up on one knee and was slashing the long knife around him like one who was crazy. It was then, I am sure, I heard him say, "The South shall be free!" I recognized Booth as he regained his feet and came toward me, waving his knife. I did not know what he had done or what his purpose might be. I did simply what any other man would have done—I ran. My dressing-room was up a short flight of stairs and I retreated to it.

Abraham Lincoln spent his final hours at the Petersen boarding house, across from Ford's Theater, as surgeons, Cabinet members, Mary, and their son Robert waited for the end by bedside candlelight.

The scene would be captured by a twenty-one-year-old army corporal named James Tanner—legless since the second Battle of Bull Run— who had been boarding at a home on Tenth Street next to the Petersen house. Tanner had studied shorthand and was employed at the War Department's Ordnance Bureau. At midnight, hearing a call for someone who could transcribe testimony from witnesses to the assassination, Tanner hobbled over on a pair of peg legs, volunteered his services, and took notes until 4 A.M. Then the corporal set down an account of the President's last moments.

His stertorous breathing subsided a couple of minutes after seven o'clock. From then till the end only the gentle rise and fall of his bosom gave indication that life remained. The Surgeon General was near the head of the bed, sometimes sitting on the edge, his finger on the pulse of the dying man. Occasionally he put his ear down to catch the lessening beats of his heart.

Mr. Lincoln's pastor, the Reverend Dr. Gurley, stood a little to the left of the bed. Mr. Stanton sat in a chair near the foot on the left. . . . I stood quite near the head of the bed and from that position had full view of Mr. Stanton across the President's body.

At my right Robert Lincoln sobbed on the shoulder of Charles Sumner.

Stanton's gaze was fixed intently on the countenance of the dying chief. The first indication that the dreaded end had come was at twenty-two minutes past seven, when the Surgeon General gently crossed the pulseless hands of Lincoln across the motionless breast and rose to his feet.

The Reverend Dr. Gurley stepped forward and lifting his hands began "Our Father and Our God" and I snatched pencil and notebook from my pocket, but my haste defeated my purpose. My pencil point (I had but one) caught in my coat and broke, and the world lost the prayer, a prayer that was only interrupted by the sobs of Stanton as he buried his face in the bedclothes.

As "Thy will be done, Amen" in subdued and tremulous tones floated through the little chamber, Mr. Stanton raised his head, the tears streaming down his face. A more agonized expression I never saw on a human countenance as he sobbed out the words: "He belongs to the angels now."

Edwin Stanton's remark has come down through history as "Now he belongs to the ages." That's how others heard it, but perhaps Tanner recorded what was really said.

Mrs. Lincoln made several visits to the deathbed during the night. Shortly before 7 A.M., she came once more to her husband's side. With her was a close friend, Elizabeth Dixon, the wife of Senator James Dixon of Connecticut.

Just as the day was struggling with the dim candles in the room we went in again. Mrs. Lincoln must have noticed a change for the moment she looked at him she fainted and fell upon the floor. I caught her in my arms & held her to the window which was open. . . . She again seated herself by the President, kissing him and calling him every endearing name—The surgeons counting every pulsation & noting every breath gradually growing less & less—They then asked her to go into the adjoining room, and in twenty minutes came in and said, "It is all over! the President is no more."

Abraham Lincoln's body was taken back to the White House accompanied by an honor guard—General Daniel Rucker of the Quartermaster Department, with a lieutenant and ten privates marching alongside, their firearms reversed.

At eleven o'clock in the morning, an autopsy was performed in a guest room at the northeast corner of the second floor. The top of the President's skull was sawed on a straight line above his ears and then lifted off. Two pathologists from the Army Medical Museum, Assistant Surgeon Edward Curtis and Assistant Surgeon J. Janvier Woodward, did the work.

Curtis would describe the scene.

The room contained but little furniture: a large, heavily curtained bed, a sofa or two, bureau, wardrobe and chairs comprised all there was. Seated around the room were several general officers and some civilians, silent or conversing in whispers, and to one side, stretched upon a rough framework of boards and covered only with sheets and towels, lay—cold and immovable—what but a few hours before was the soul of a great nation. The Surgeon General was walking up and down the room when I arrived and detailed me the history of the case. He said that the President showed most wonderful tenacity of life, and, had not his wound been necessarily mortal, might have survived an injury to which most men would succumb. . . .

Dr. Woodward and I proceeded to open the head and remove the brain down to the track of the ball. The latter had entered a little to the left of the median line at the back of the head, had passed almost directly forwards through the center of the brain, and lodged. Not finding it readily, we proceeded to remove the entire brain, when, as I was lifting the latter from the cavity of the skull, suddenly the bullet dropped out through my fingers and fell, breaking the solemn silence of the room with its clatter, into an empty basin that was standing beneath. There it lay upon the white china, a little black mass no bigger than the end of my finger—dull, motionless and harmless, yet the cause of such mighty changes in the world's history as we may perhaps never realize. . . .

Silently, in one corner of the room, I prepared the brain for weighing. As I looked at the mass of soft gray and white substance that I was carefully washing, it was impossible to realize that it was that mere clay upon whose workings, but the day before, rested the hopes of the nation.

I felt more profoundly impressed than ever with the mystery of that unknown something which may be named "vital spark" as well as anything else, whose absence or presence makes the immeasurable difference between an inert mass of matter owing obedience to no laws but that governing the physical and chemical forces of the universe, and on the other hand, a living brain by whose silent, subtle machinery a world may be ruled.

David R. Locke, an old friend of Lincoln's who had written satirical articles under his pen name, Petroleum V. Nasby, came from Toledo to view the body as it moved through Ohio en route to burial in Springfield, Illinois. There were reports that Lincoln's face had shrunken and decayed. But Locke saw otherwise.

I saw him, or what was mortal of him, on the mournful progress to his last resting-place, in his coffin. The face was the same as in life. Death had not changed the kindly countenance in any line. There was upon it the same sad look that it had worn always, though not so intensely sad as it had been in life. It was as if the spirit had come back to the poor clay, reshaped the wonderfully sweet face, and given it an expression of gladness that he had finally gone "where the wicked cease from troubling, and the weary are at rest." The face had an expression of absolute content, of relief, at throwing off a burden such as few men have been called upon to bear—a burden which few men could have borne. I had seen the same expression upon his living face only a few times, when, after a great calamity, he had come to a great victory. It was the look of a worn man suddenly relieved. Wilkes Booth did Abraham Lincoln the greatest service man could possibly do for him—he gave him peace.

TRACKING DOWN *an* ASSASSIN

John Wilkes Booth and an accomplice, David Herold, fled Ford's Theater on horseback and escaped into Virginia. Federal troops cornered them on April 26 in a tobacco-drying barn at Garrett's farm, near Port Royal. Soldiers commanded by a pair of officers, E. J.

Conger and L. B. Baker, closed in. George Alfred Townsend, a reporter for the *New York World*, was on the scene.

Herold was quite up to the door, within whispering distance of Baker. The latter told him to put out his hands to be handcuffed, at the same time drawing open the door a little distance. Herold thrust forward his hands, when Baker, seizing him, jerked him into the night and straightaway delivered him over to a deputation of cavalrymen. The fellow began to talk of his innocence and plead so noisily that Conger threatened to gag him unless he ceased. Then Booth made his last appeal, in the same clear, unbroken voice:

"Captain, give me a chance. Draw off your men, and I will fight them singly. I could have killed you six times tonight, but I believe you to be a brave man and would not murder you. Give a lame man a show."

Ere he ceased speaking, Colonel Conger, slipping around to the rear, drew some loose straws through a crack, and lit a match upon them. They were dry and blazed up in an instant, carrying a sheet of smoke and flame through the parted planks and heaving in a twinkling a world of light and heat upon the magazine within. The blaze lit up the black recesses of the great barn until every wasp's nest and cobweb in the roof was luminous, flinging streaks of red and violet across the tumbled farm gear in the corner, plows, harrows, hoes, rakes, sugar mills, and making every separate grain in the high bin adjacent gleam like a mote of precious gold. They tinged the beams, the upright columns, the barricades, where clover and timothy, piled high, held toward the hot incendiary their separate straws for the funeral pile. They bathed the murderer's retreat in a beautiful illumination, and while in a bold outline his figure stood revealed, they rose like an impenetrable wall to guard from sight the hated enemy who lit them.

Behind the blaze, with his eye to a crack, Conger saw Wilkes Booth standing upright on a crutch. He likens him in this instant to his brother, Edwin, whom he says he so much resembled that he half believed, for the moment, the whole pursuit to have been a mistake. At the gleam of the fire Wilkes dropped his crutch and his carbine, and on both hands crept up to the spot to espy the incendiary and shoot him dead. His eyes were lustrous like fever, and swelled and rolled in terrible beauty, while his teeth were fixed and he peered with vengeance in his look.

The fire that made him visible concealed his enemy. A second he turned glaring at the fire, as if to leap upon it and extinguish it, but it had made such headway that this was a futile impulse and he dismissed it. As calmly as upon a battlefield a veteran stands amidst a hail of ball and shell and plunging iron, Booth turned at a man's stride and pushed for the door, carbine in poise, and the last resolve of death, which we name despair, set on his high bloodless forehead.

As so he dashed, intent to expire not unaccompanied, a disobedient sergeant, at an eyehole, drew upon him the fatal bead. The barn was all glorious with conflagration, and in the beautiful ruin this outlawed man strode like all we know of wicked valor, stern in the face of death. A shock, a shout, a gathering up of his splendid figure as if to overtip the stature God gave him, and John Wilkes Booth fell headlong to the floor, lying there in a heap, a little life remaining.

"He has shot himself," cried Baker, unaware of the source of the report, and rushing in, he grasped his arms to guard against any feint or strategy. A moment convinced him that further struggle against prone flesh was useless. Booth did not move, nor breathe nor gasp. Conger and two sergeants now entered and, taking up the body, they bore it in haste from the advancing flames and laid it without upon the grass, all fresh with heavenly dew.

"Water," cried Conger, "bring water."

When this was dashed into his face, he revived a little and stirred his lips. Baker put his ear close down and heard him say:

"Tell Mother—I die—for my country."

the SOUTH in RUINS

The Civil War left the Southern states devastated. Atlanta, Richmond, and Charleston had been gutted by fire or bombarded into rubble. The cotton, rice, and sugar crops had been destroyed, the roads and railroads wrecked. The schools were closed, the Confederate currency was worthless.

The slaves were free, but to do what? Before beginning his uncertain new path, a former slave named William Colbert took a last look at the Alabama plantation where he had been in bondage for the past twenty years. It had been looted by Union troops. His old master, Jim Hodison, a cruel man, was now suffering.

Interviewed when he was in his nineties, Colbert reflected on the last time he saw "massa."

All de niggers 'roun' hated to be bought by him kaze he wuz so mean. When he wuz too tired to whup us he had de overseer do it; and de overseer wuz meaner dan de massa.

De massa had three boys to go to war, but dere wuzn't one to come home. All the chillun he had wuz killed. Massa, he los' all his money and de house soon begin droppin' away to nothin'. Us niggers one by one lef' de ole place and de las' time I seed de home plantation I wuz a-standin' on a hill. I looked back on it for de las' time through a patch of scrub pines and it look' so lonely. Dere warn't but one person in sight, de massa. He was a-settin' in a wicker chair in de yard lookin' out ober a small field of cotton and cawn. Dere wuz fo' crosses in de graveyard in de side lawn where he wuz a-settin'. De fo'th one wuz his wife. I lost my ole woman too 37 years ago, and all dis time, I's been a-carrin' on like de massa—all alone.

the PRESIDENCY on TRIAL

In his second inaugural address, Abraham Lincoln had declared: "With malice toward none, with charity for all, with firmness in the right, as God gives us to see the right, let us strive on to finish the work we are in, to bind up the nation's wounds. . . ."

Lincoln's vision of reconciliation would be thwarted by the Radical Republicans of Congress, who divided the South into military regions under Reconstruction laws that imposed retribution upon the South while pursuing full citizenship for blacks.

Lincoln's successor, Andrew Johnson, a former senator from Tennessee, had been the only Southern member of the old Senate to uphold the Union, but had also defended slavery and the Fugitive Slave Law. Now, seeking to protect Southern whites from the racial equality he opposed and resistant to congressional efforts to dominate the executive, he became locked in a struggle with the Senate over policy toward the South.

A dispute with Congress over Johnson's firing of Secretary of War Edwin M. Stanton brought his impeachment (in effect, an indictment) by the House of Representatives. At Johnson's trial before the Senate, the vote of a senator from Kansas—the last undecided man—would be decisive.

Senator Edmund G. Ross had long opposed slavery, and sentiment in Kansas was heavily against Johnson. A vote to oust him would seemingly confirm Ross's moral principles and save his career.

He later told of the hour when he had had to decide.

That day, May 15, 1868, was fateful. There had been none such in nearly a hundred years of the history of the Government. It was to determine judicially a question of varying phases which had never before been brought for solution in the courts—what should constitute "high crimes and misdemeanors in office" on the part of the National Executive; what latitude should be allowed him in the expression of personal opinion in his differences with coordinate branches of the Government; how far he might lawfully go in the exercise of his personal judgment in the administration of the powers and duties of his great office; whether his oath of office permitted him to interpret the Constitution for himself in the absence and anticipation of judicial determination, or whether he should be governed by Congressional interpretation of that instrument. In a large sense, the independence of the executive office as a coordinate branch of the Government was on trial. . . .

The hours seemed to pass with oppressive tedium awaiting the time for the assembling of the Senate and the beginning of the vote. It came at last, and found the galleries thronged to their utmost with a brilliant and eager auditory. Tickets of admission were at an enormous premium. Every chair on the floor was filled with a Senator, a Cabinet officer, a member of the President's counsel, or a representative, for the House had adjourned and its anxious members had at once thronged to the Senate chamber. Every foot of available standing room in the area and about the senatorial seats was occupied. . . .

Pages were flitting from place to place with messages. . . . Little groups were gathered here and there in subdued conversation, discussing the situation and the probable result and its attendant consequences. The intensity of public interest was increased by the general impression that the entire official incumbency and patronage of the Government in all its departments, financial and political, had been pledged in advance and on condition of the removal of the President. . . .

The Chief Justice, with apparent emotion, propounded the query, "How say you, Senator Ross, is the respondent, Andrew Johnson, guilty or not guilty under this article?"

At this point the intensity with which the gaze of the audience was centered upon the figure then on the floor was beyond description or comparison. Hope and fear seem blended in every face, instantaneously alternating, some with revengeful hate predominating as in the mind's eye they saw their dreams of success, of place, and triumph dashed to earth; others lighted with hope that the President would be relieved of the charges against him, and things remain as they were. Not only were the occupants of the galleries bending forward in intense and breathless silence and anxiety to catch the verdict, but the Senators in their seats leaned over their desks, many with hand to ear, that not a syllable or intonation in the utterance of the verdict should be lost.

Conscious that I was at that moment the focus of all eyes, and conscious also of the far-reaching effect, especially upon myself, of the vote I was about to give, it is something more than a simile to say that I almost literally looked down into my open grave. Friends, position, fortune, everything that makes life desirable to an ambitious man, were about to be swept away by the breath of my mouth, perhaps forever. Realizing the tremendous responsibility which an untoward combination of conditions seemed to have put upon me, it is not strange that my answer was carried waveringly over the air and failed to reach the limits of the audience, or that a repetition was called for by distant Senators on the opposite side of the chamber. Then the verdict came—"Not guilty" —in a voice that could not be misunderstood.

Ross had not been convinced that Johnson was guilty of "high crimes and misdemeanors," and he feared that the constitutional separation of powers in the national government would forever be destroyed by a Senate conviction.

After the vote, he wrote to his wife.

Millions of men cursing me today will bless me tomorrow for having saved the country from the greatest peril through which it has ever passed, though none but God can ever know the struggle it has cost me.

Ross did not seek another Senate term, turning instead to journalism and becoming publisher of a weekly newspaper in Coffeyville, Kansas. He had saved the presidency of Andrew Johnson at the cost of his own political life.

SOUTH CAROLINA'S "BLACK PARLIAMENT"

Now full-fledged citizens with the vote, Southern blacks elected fellow former slaves to their state legislatures, and even to Congress, where sixteen black men sat during Reconstruction.

The currents of political change were especially dramatic in South Carolina, where in 1870 blacks obtained half the state's eight executive offices and three congressional seats. Jonathan J. Wright, elected to South Carolina's Supreme Court that year, became the only black man to hold such a position in any state in the Reconstruction era. And blacks constituted a majority of South Carolina's House of Representatives and controlled its key committees.

But by the mid-1870s, sentiment among the Northern Republicans who had imposed Reconstruction began to change, as racism eroded support for black enfranchisement.

James Shepherd Pike, a veteran antislavery journalist and Lincoln's ambassador to the Netherlands during the Civil War, was dispatched by the *New York Tribune* to South Carolina in 1873 to report on Reconstruction. He wrote with feeling of its black legislators facing a radically new world. But his racist-tinged reports depicting widespread corruption—later incorporated in a book called *The Prostrate State*—would be an influential force in the reversal of black progress.

We will enter the House of Representatives. Here sit one hundred and twenty-four members. Of these, twenty-three are white men, representing the remains of the old civilization. These are good-looking, substantial citizens. They are men of weight and standing in the communities they represent. They are all from the hill country. The frosts of sixty and seventy winters whiten the heads of some among them. There they sit, grim and silent. They feel themselves to be but loose stones, thrown in to partially obstruct a current they are powerless to resist. They say little and do little as the days go by. . . .

The dense negro crowd they confront do the debating, the squabbling, the law-making, and create all the clamor and disorder of the body. . . .

Deducting the twenty-three members referred to, who comprise the entire strength of the opposition, we find one hundred and one remaining. Ninety-four are colored, and seven are their white allies. Thus the blacks outnumber the whole body of whites in the House more than three to one. . . . As things stand, the body is almost literally a Black Parliament, and it is the only one on the face of the earth which is the representative of a white constituency and the professed exponent of an advanced type of modern civilization. . . .

The Speaker is black, the Clerk is black, the door-keepers are black, the little pages are black, the chairman of the Ways and Means is black, and the chaplain is coal-black. At some of the desks sit colored men whose types it would be hard to find outside of Congo; whose costume, visages, attitudes, and expression only befit the forecastle of a buccaneer. It must be remembered, also, that these men, with not more than half a dozen exceptions, have been themselves slaves, and that their ancestors were slaves for generations. . . .

They are "quick as lightning" at detecting points of order, and they certainly make incessant and extraordinary use of their knowledge. No one is allowed to talk five minutes without interruption, and one interruption is the signal for another and another, until the original speaker is smothered under an avalanche of them. Forty questions of privilege will be raised in a day. At times, nothing goes on but alternating questions of order and of privilege. The inefficient colored friend who sits in the Speaker's chair cannot suppress this extraordinary element of the debate. Some of the blackest members exhibit a pertinacity of intrusion in raising these points of order and questions of privilege that few white men can equal. Their struggles to get the floor, their bellowings and physical contortions, baffle description. The Speaker's hammer plays a perpetual tattoo all to no purpose. The talking and the interruptions from all quarters go on with the utmost license. Every one esteems himself as good as his neighbor, and puts in his oar, apparently as often for love of riot and confusion as for any thing else. . . .

The Speaker orders a member whom he has discovered to be particularly unruly to take his seat. The member obeys, and with the same motion that he sits down, throws his feet on to his desk hiding himself from the Speaker by the soles of his boots. In an instant he appears again on the floor. After a few experiences of this sort, the Speaker threatens, in a laugh, to call "the gemman" to order. This is considered to be a capital joke, and a guffaw follows. The laugh goes round, and then the peanuts are cracked and munched faster than ever; one hand being employed in fortifying the inner man with this nutriment of universal use, while the other enforces the views of the orator. This laughing propensity of the sable crowd is a great cause of disorder. They laugh as hens cackle—one begins and all follow.

But underneath all this shocking burlesque upon legislative proceedings, we must not forget that there is something very real to this uncouth and untutored multitude. It is not all sham, nor all burlesque. They have a genuine interest and a genuine earnestness in the business of the assembly which we are bound to recognize and respect, unless we would be accounted shallow critics. . . . The whole thing is a wonderful novelty to them as well as to observers. Seven years ago these men were raising corn and cotton under the whip of the overseer. To-day they are raising points of order and questions of privilege. They find they can raise one as well as the other. They prefer the latter. It is easier, and better paid. . . . It means escape and defense from the old oppressors. It means liberty. It means the destruction of prison-walls only too real to them. It is the sunshine of their lives. It is their day of jubilee. It is their long-promised vision of the Lord God Almighty.

Chapter Three

the OLD WEST, *the* NEW AMERICANS

the DONNER PARTY

The 1840s marked the beginning of a historic migration westward as hundreds of thousands of pioneers trekked through prairie trails, deserts, and mountains, lured by the promise of lush new land for farms and instant wealth from vast gold and silver veins.

The perils of terrain and the vagaries of weather, along with the threat of Indian attack, made the journeys arduous at best. For one group of settlers, a fate beyond anything in their darkest imaginings loomed in the snows of the California Sierras. These were the men, women, and children of the Donner Party.

One month after the Anglos in the Sacramento Valley proclaimed the Bear Flag Republic, a group of eighty-nine people—most from the Midwest—began the final leg of a voyage to Sutter's Fort, California.

Led by a man named George Donner, they linked up at Little Sandy Creek in what is now Wyoming for the push through the Sierra Nevadas. Seeking to speed their journey across the mountains, they took an untested shortcut. But it would only delay them—a catastrophic blunder. As the families reached the eastern slopes of the mountains, the first heavy snowfall of the season descended. They were trapped.

For five months, they huddled in a makeshift camp of log cabins as the worst winter on record besieged them with blizzard after blizzard. Now the most harrowing episode of America's push west would unfold. Around Christmastime 1846, barely surviving on twigs, leaves, boiled hides, and charred bones, and watching their fellow settlers slowly die, the survivors resorted to cannibalism.

Patrick Breen, his wife, and their seven children had joined the group after setting out from Iowa, hoping for a land grant near San Francisco Bay. Forty-two of the eighty-nine settlers had died by the time rescue parties arrived from California. But the Breen family made it, and the diary kept by the father became a testament to the suffering of these pioneers.

Friday Nov. 20th 1846. Came to this place on the 31st of last month that it snowed. We went on to the pass. The snow so deep we were

129

unable to find the road, when within 3 miles of the summit. Then turned back to this shanty on the Lake. Stanton came one day after we arrived here. We again took our teams & wagons & made another unsuccessful attempt to cross in company with Stanton. We returned to the shanty it continuing to snow all the time we were here. We now have killed most part of our cattle having to stay here until next spring & live on poor beef without bread or salt. . . .

Wedsd. [December] 30th. Fine clear morning. Froze hard last night. Charley died last night about 10 Oclock. Had with him in money $1.50 two good looking silver watches one razor 3 boxes caps. Keysburg took them into his possession. Spitzer took his coat & waistcoat, Keysburg all his other little effects gold pin one shirt and tools for shaveing.

Thursday 31st. Last of the year, may we with Gods help spend the coming year better than the past which we purpose to do if Almighty God will deliver us from our present dreadful situation which is our prayer if the will of God sees it fitting for us Amen—morning fair now Cloudy wind E by S for three days past. Freezing hard every night. Looks like another snow storm. Snow Storms are dredful to us. Snow very deep. Crust on the snow.

Satd [February] 6th. It snowed faster last night & today than it has done this winter & still Continues without an intermission. Wind SW. Murphys folks or Keysburgs say they cant eat hides. I wish we had enough of them. Mrs. Eddy very weak.

Sund. 7th. Ceased to snow last [night] after one of the most Severe Storms we experienced this winter. The snow fell about 4 feet deep. I had to shovel the snow off our shanty this morning. It thawed so fast & thawed during the whole storm. To day it is quite pleasant. Wind S.W. Milt here to day says Mrs. Reid has to get a hide from Mrs. Murphy & McCutchins child died 2nd of this month.

Mond 8th. Fine clear morning. Wind S.W. Froze hard last [night]. Spitzer died last night about 3 o'clock. We will bury him in the snow. Mrs. Eddy died on the night of the 7th.

Tuesd. 9th. Mrs. Murphy here this morning. Pikes child all but dead. Milt at Murphys not able to get out of bed. Keysburg never gets up says he is not able. John went down to-day to bury Mrs. Eddy & child. Heard nothing from Graves for 2 or 3 days. Mrs. Murphy just now going to Graves. Fine morning. Wind S.E. Froze hard last night. Begins to thaw in the Sun.

Wedndd. 10th. Beautiful morning. Wind W: froze hard last night. To day thawing in the Sun. Milt Elliot died last night at Murphys Shanty about 9 Oclock P:M: Mrs. Reid went there this morning to see after his effects. J Denton trying to borrow meat for Graves. Had none to give. They have nothing but hides. All are entirely out of meat but a little we have. Our hides are nearly all eat up with Gods help spring will soon smile upon us.

Tuesd. 23. Froze hard last night. To day fine & thawey has the appearance of spring all but the deep snow. Wind S:S.E. Shot Towser [a dog] to day & dressed his flesh. Mrs Graves came here this morning to borrow meat dog or ox. They think I have meat to spare but I know to the Contrary. They have plenty hides. I live principally on the same.

Wend. 24th. Froze hard last night. To day Cloudy looks like a storm. Wind blows hard from the W. Commenced thawing. There has not any more returned from those who started to cross the Mts.

Thursd. 25th. Froze hard last night. Fine & sunshiny to day. Wind W. Mrs. Murphy says the wolves are about to dig up the dead bodies at her shanty, the nights are too cold to watch them, we hear them howl.

Frid 26th. Froze hard last night. Today clear & warm. Wind S:E: blowing briskly. Marthas jaw swelled with the toothache: hungry times in camp, plenty hides but the folks will not eat them. We eat them with a tolerable good appetite. Thanks be to Almighty God. Amen. Mrs. Murphy said here yesterday that thought she would Commence on Milt. & eat him. I dont [think] that she has done so yet, it is distressing. The Donners told the California folks that they [would] commence to eat the dead people 4 days ago, if they did not succeed that day or next in finding their cattle then under ten or twelve feet of snow & did not know the spot or near it, I suppose they have done so ere this time.

Satd 27th. Beautiful morning sun shineing brilliantly, wind about S.W. The snow has fell in debth about 5 feet but no thaw but [in] the sun in day time. It freezeing hard every night. Heard some geese fly over last night. Saw none.

Sund. 28th. Froze hard last night. To day fair & sunshine. Wind S.E. 1 solitary Indian passed by yesterday come from the lake had a heavy *pack on his back. Gave me 5 or 6 roots resembleing Onions in shape. Taste some like a sweet potatoe, all full of little tough fibres.*

Mond. March the 1st to [day] fine & pleasant. Froze hard last night. There has 10 men arrived this morning from bear valley with provisions. We are to start in two or three days & Cash our goods here.

GOLD!

A transplanted carpenter from New Jersey named James Marshall was building a sawmill on the American River, east of Sacramento, in the winter of 1848, partners with a Swiss immigrant named John Sutter. On the morning of January 24, Marshall discovered a small shiny object. It was the harbinger of a ribbon of gold running for four hundred miles through streams and rivers in the Sierra Nevada range. By 1849, ninety thousand prospectors had arrived in California from around the world, and a year after that California was admitted to the Union. By the time the Gold Rush ended a decade later, $500 million in deposits had been extracted.

It all began with Marshall's supposedly lucky day.

One morning in January—it was a clear cold morning; I shall never forget that morning—as I was taking my usual walk along the race, after shutting off the water my eye was caught by a glimpse of something shining in the bottom of the ditch. There was about a foot of water running there. I reached my hand down and picked it up; it made my heart thump, for I felt certain it was gold. The piece was about half the size of the shape of a pea. Then I saw another piece in the water. After taking it out I sat down and began to think right hard. I thought it was gold, and yet it did not seem to be of the right color; all the gold coin I had seen was of a reddish tinge; this looked more like brass. I recalled to mind all the metals I had ever seen or heard of, but I could find none that resembled this. Suddenly the idea flashed across my mind that it might be iron pyrites. I trembled to think of it! This question could soon be determined. Putting one of the pieces on hard river stone, I took another and commenced hammering it. It was soft and didn't break; it therefore must be gold, but largely mixed with some other metal, very likely silver; for pure gold, I thought, would certainly have a brighter color. . . .

When I returned to our cabin for breakfast I showed the two pieces to my men. They were all a good deal excited, and had they not thought that the gold only existed in small quantities they would have abandoned everything and left me to finish the job alone. However, to satisfy them, I told them that as soon as we had the mill finished we would devote a week or two to gold hunting and see what we could make out of it. While we were working in the race after this discovery, we always kept a sharp lookout, and in the course of three or four days we had picked up about three ounces—our work still progressing as lively as ever, for none of us imagined at that time that the whole country was sowed with gold. . . .

We thought it our best policy to keep it as quiet as possible till we should have finished our mill, but there was a great number of disbanded Mormon soldiers in and about the fort [Sutter's Fort], and when they came to hear of it, why, it just spread like wildfire, and soon the whole country was in a bustle. I had scarcely arrived at the mill again till several persons appeared with pans, shovels, and hoes, and those that had not iron picks had wooden ones, all anxious to fall to work and dig up our mill; but this we would not permit. As fast as one party disappeared, another one would arrive, and sometimes I had the greatest kind of trouble to get rid of them. I sent them off in all directions, telling them about such and such places where I was certain there was plenty of gold if they would only take the trouble of looking for it. At that time I never imagined the gold was so abundant. I told them to go to such and such places, because it appeared that they would dig nowhere but in such places as I pointed out; and I believe such was their confidence in me that they would have dug on the very top of the mountain if I had told them to do so.

But Marshall would come to a sorry end. Individual trespassers and then highly mechanized mining companies moved onto Sutter's Fort, staking claim to land he considered his. He turned to drink and died in poverty, buried in 1885 on a hill overlooking the spot where, on a January day in 1848, he had peered into a soggy ditch and made history.

the PONY EXPRESS

They raced across prairies, deserts, and mountain ranges, writing a brief but romantic saga in the story of the Old West.

"Wanted—young, skinny, wiry fellows, not over 18. Must be expert riders, willing to risk life daily. Orphans preferred. Wages $25 a week."

So said the advertisement for the Pony Express, a frenetic endeavor organized by the firm of Russell, Majors & Waddell to carry news and mail the two thousand miles from St. Joseph, Missouri, to Sacramento, California.

The first rider set out from Pattee House in St. Joseph on April 3, 1860. But eighteen months later, it was all over. Telegraph lines were being established between California and the Missouri River and were flashing news and letters faster than the most accomplished horseman could carry his packets.

At the age of fifteen, William F. Cody, the boy who as a man would be known as Buffalo Bill—army scout, buffalo hunter, and Wild West showman—tasted adventure in the Pony Express.

The system was really a relay race against time. Stations were built at intervals averaging fifteen miles apart. A rider's route covered three stations, with an exchange of horses at each, so that he was expected at the beginning to cover close to forty-five miles—a good ride when one must average fifteen miles an hour.

The firm undertaking the enterprise had been busy for some time picking the best ponies to be had for money, and the lightest, most wiry and most experienced riders. This was a life that appealed to me, and I struck for a job. I was pretty young in years, but I had already earned a reputation for coming safe out of perilous adventures, and I was hired.

Naturally our equipment was the very lightest. The messages which we carried were written on the thinnest paper to be found. These we carried in a waterproof pouch, slung under our arms. We wore only such clothing as was absolutely necessary.

The first trip of the Pony Express was made in ten days—an average of two hundred miles a day. But we soon began stretching our riders and making better time. Soon we shortened the time to eight days. President Buchanan's last Presidential message in December, 1860, was carried in eight days. President Lincoln's inaugural, the following March, took only seven days and seventeen hours for the journey between St. Joseph and Sacramento.

We soon got used to the work. When it became apparent to the men in charge that the boys could do better than forty-five miles a day the stretches were lengthened. The pay of the rider was from $100 to $125 a month. It was announced that the further a man rode the better would be his pay. That put speed and endurance into all of us.

Stern necessity often compelled us to lengthen our day's work even beyond our desires. In the hostile Indian country, riders were frequently shot. In such an event the man whose relief had been killed had to ride on to the next station, doing two men's ride. Road-agents were another menace, and often they proved as deadly as the Indians.

In stretching my own route I found myself getting further and further west. Finally I was riding well into the foothills of the Rockies. Still further west my route was pushed. Soon I rode from Red Buttes to Sweetwater, a distance of seventy-six miles. Road-agents and Indians infested this country. I never was quite sure when I started out when I should reach my destination, or whether I should never reach it at all.

One day I galloped into the station at Three Crossings to find that my relief had been killed in a drunken row the night before. There was no one to take his place. His route was eighty-five miles across country to the west. I had no time to think it over. Selecting a good pony out of the stables I was soon on my way.

I arrived at Rocky Ridge, the end of the new route, on schedule time, and turning back came on to Red Buttes, my starting-place. The round trip was 320 miles, and I made it in twenty-one hours and forty minutes.

Excitement was plentiful in my two years' service as a Pony Express rider. One day as I was leaving Horse Creek, a party of fifteen Indians jammed me in a sand ravine eight miles west of the station. They fired *at me repeatedly, but my luck held, and I went unscathed. My mount was a California roan pony, the fastest in the stables. I dug the spurs into his sides, and, lying flat on his back, I kept straight on for Sweetwater Bridge eleven miles distant. A turn back to Horse Creek might have brought me more speedily to shelter, but I did not dare risk it.*

The Indians came on behind, riding with all the speed they could put into their horses, but my pony drew rapidly ahead. I had a lead of two miles when I reached the station. There I found I could get no new pony. The stock-tender had been killed by the Indians during the night. All his ponies had been stolen and driven off. I kept on, therefore, to Plonts Station, twelve miles further along, riding the same pony—a ride of twenty-four hours on one mount. At Plonts I told the people what had happened at Sweetwater Bridge. Then, with a fresh horse, I finished my route without further adventure.

STAGECOACH *to the* WEST

Before the railroads spanned the continent, the great stagecoaches provided an adventurous though rocky ride westward.

In the 1820s, craftsmen in Concord, New Hampshire, began turning out what would be the Cadillacs of the West. These were the Concord stages, weighing up to three thousand pounds, drawn by four-to-six-horse teams, and equipped with the choicest hickory woodwork, seats padded with horsehair and brown calf leather, and a shotgun-toting guard watching out for Indians and holdup men.

Just before the Civil War, Mark Twain set out for Nevada from Missouri along with his brother, the secretary of the Nevada Territory. They traveled by stage.

Each of us put on a rough, heavy suit of clothing, woolen army shirt and "stogy" boots included; and into the valise we crowded a few white shirts, some underclothing and such things. My brother, the Secretary, took along about four pounds of United States statutes and six pounds of unabridged Dictionary; for we did not know—poor innocents—that such things could be bought in San Francisco on one day and received in Carson City the next. I was armed to the teeth with a pitiful little Smith & Wesson's seven-shooter, which carried a ball like a homeopathic pill, and it took the whole seven to make a dose for an adult. But I thought it was grand. It appeared to me to be a dangerous weapon. It only had one fault—you could not hit anything with it. One of our "conductors" practiced awhile on a cow with it, and as long as she stood still and behaved herself she was safe; but as soon as she went to moving about, and he got to shooting at other things, she came to grief.

The Secretary had a small-sized Colt's revolver strapped around him for protection against the Indians, and to guard against accidents he carried it uncapped. Mr. George Bemis was dismally formidable. George Bemis was our fellow-traveler. We had never seen him before. He wore in his belt an old original "Allen" revolver, such as irreverent people called a "pepper-box." Simply drawing the trigger back, cocked and fired the pistol. As the trigger came back, the hammer would begin to rise and the barrel to turn over, and presently down would drop the hammer, and away would speed the ball. To aim along the turning barrel and hit the thing aimed at was a feat which was probably never done with an "Allen" in the world. But George's was a reliable weapon, nevertheless, because, as one of the stage-drivers said afterward, "If she didn't get what she went after, she would fetch something else." And so she did. She went after a deuce of spades nailed against a tree, once, and fetched a mule standing about thirty yards to the left of it. Bemis did not want the mule; but the owner came out with a double-barreled shotgun and persuaded him to buy it, anyhow. It was a cheerful weapon—the "Allen." Sometimes all its six barrels would go off at once, and then there was no safe place in all the region round about, but behind it.

We took two or three blankets for protection against frosty weather in the mountains. In the matter of luxuries we were modest—we took none along but some pipes and five pounds of smoking-tobacco. We had two large canteens to carry water in, between stations on the Plains, and we also took with us a little shot-bag of silver coin for daily expenses in the way of breakfasts and dinners.

By eight o'clock everything was ready, and we were on the other side *of the river. We jumped into the stage, the driver cracked his whip, and we bowled away and left "the States" behind us. It was a superb summer morning, and all the landscape was brilliant with sunshine.*

There was a freshness and breeziness, too, and an exhilarating sense of emancipation from all sorts of cares and responsibilities, that almost made us feel that the years we had spent in the close, hot city, toiling and slaving, had been wasted and thrown away. We were spinning along through Kansas, and in the course of an hour and a half we were fairly abroad on the great Plains. Just here the land was rolling—a grand sweep of regular elevation and depressions as far as the eye could reach —like the stately heave and swell of the ocean's bosom after a storm. And everywhere were corn-fields, accenting with squares of deeper green this limitless expanse of grassy land. But presently this sea upon dry ground was to lose its "rolling" character and stretch away for seven hundred miles as level as a floor!

Our coach was a great swinging and swaying stage, of the most sumptuous description—an imposing cradle on wheels. It was drawn by six handsome horses, and by the side of the driver sat the "conductor," the legitimate captain of the craft; for it was his business to take charge and take care of the mails, baggage, express matter, and passengers. We three were the only passengers, this trip. We sat on the back seat, inside. About all the rest of the coach was full of mail-bags—for we had three days' delayed mails with us. Almost touching our knees, a perpendicular wall of mail matter rose up to the roof. There was a great pile of it strapped on top of the stage, and both the fore and hind boots were full.

We had twenty-seven hundred pounds of it aboard, the driver said— "a little for Brigham, and Carson, and 'Frisco, but the heft of it for the Injuns, which is powerful troublesome 'thout they get plenty of truck to read." But as he just then got up to a fearful convulsion of his counte- nance which was suggestive of a wink being swallowed by an earthquake, we guessed that the remark was intended to be facetious, and to mean that we would unload the most of our mail matter somewhere on the Plains and leave it to the Indians, or whosoever wanted it.

the GOLDEN SPIKE

As early as the 1840s, there had been visions of a railroad linking East and West. When gold was discovered in California, the quest began in earnest, but competing routes envisioned by the North and South kept matters bottled up. When the South seceded, Congress acted, creating the Union Pacific and Central Pacific Railroads in 1862 and granting them huge tracts of land and tens of millions in loans.

The Union Pacific built westward from Council Bluffs, Iowa, and the Central Pacific eastward from California. They laid seventeen hundred miles of track, conquering the deserts and the Sierras.

On May 10, 1869, the continent was spanned with the driving of gold and silver spikes joining the two lines at Promontory Point, Utah. Grenville Dodge, the chief engineer for the Union Pacific, was there.

Between Ogden and Promontory each company graded a line, running side by side, and in some places one line was right above the other. The laborers upon the Central Pacific were Chinamen, while ours were Irishmen, and there was much ill feeling between them. Our Irishmen were in the habit of firing their blasts in the cuts without giving warning to the Chinamen on the Central Pacific working right above them. From this cause several Chinamen were severely hurt. Complaint was made to me from the Central Pacific people, and I endeavored to have the contractors bring all hostilities to a close; but for some reason or other they failed to do so. One day the Chinamen, appreciating the situation, put in what is called a "grave" on their work and, when the Irishmen right under them were all at work, let go their blast and buried several of our men. This brought about a truce at once. From that time the Irish laborers showed due respect for the Chinamen, and there was no further trouble.

When the two roads approached in May, 1869, we agreed to connect at the summit of Promontory Point; and the day was fixed so that trains could reach us from New York and California. We laid the rails to the junction point a day or two before the final closing. . . . The trains pulled up facing each other, each crowded with workmen who sought advantageous positions to witness the ceremonies and literally covered the cars. The officers and invited guests formed on each side of the track,

139

leaving it open to the south. The telegraph lines had been brought to that point, so that in the final spiking as each blow was struck, the telegraph recorded it at each connected office from the Atlantic to the Pacific. Prayer was offered; a number of spikes were driven in the two adjoining rails, each one of the prominent persons present taking a hand, but very few hitting the spikes, to the great amusement of the crowd. When the last spike was placed, light taps were given upon it by several officials, and it was finally driven home by the chief engineer of the Union Pacific Railway.

The engineers ran up their locomotives until they touched, the engineer upon each engine breaking a bottle of champagne upon the other one, and thus the two roads were welded into one great trunk line from the Atlantic to the Pacific. Spikes of silver and gold were brought especially for the occasion and later were manufactured into miniature spikes as mementoes of the occasion. It was a bright but cold day. After a few speeches we all took refuge in the Central Pacific cars, where the wine flowed freely and many speeches were made.

A *New York Times* reporter at the Washington, D.C., telegraphic office told how the nation received news of the climactic moment.

The completion of the Pacific Railroad has monopolized public attention here to-day to the exclusion of everything else. The feeling is one of hearty rejoicing. . . . There were no public observances, but the arrangements at the completion of the great work made by the telegraph company to announce the completion of the road simultaneously with the driving of the last spike were perfect. At 2:20 this afternoon, Washington time, all the telegraph offices in the country were notified by the Omaha telegraph office to be ready to receive the signals corresponding to the blows of the hammer that drove the last spike in the last rail that united New York and San Francisco with a band of iron.

Accordingly, Mr. Tinker, Manager of the Western Union Telegraph Office in this city, placed a magnetic bell sounder in the public office of that Company, corner Fourteenth street and the avenue, connected the same with the main lines, and notified the various offices that he was ready. New Orleans instantly responded, the answer being read from the bell taps. New York did the same. At 2:27 o'clock offices over the country began to make all sorts of inquiries of Omaha, to which that office replied:

"To Everybody: Keep quiet. When the last spike is driven at Promontory Point they will say 'Done.' Don't break the circuit, but watch for the signals of the blows of the hammer."

At 2:27 P.M., Promontory Point, 2,400 miles west of Washington, said to the people congregated in the various telegraph offices:

"Almost ready, Hats off, prayer is being offered."

A silence for the prayer ensued. At 2:40, the bell tapped again, and the office at the Point said:

"We have got done praying. The spike is about to be presented."

Chicago replied:

"We understand: all are ready in the East."

Promontory Point: "All ready now; the spike will be driven. The signal will be three dots for the commencement of the blows."

For a moment the instrument was silent; then the hammer of the magnet tapped the bell, "One, two, three," the signal; another pause of a few seconds, and the lightning came flashing eastward, vibrating over 2,400 miles between the junction of the two roads and Washington, and the blows of the hammer upon the spike were measured instantly in telegraphic accents on the bell here. At 2:47 P.M., Promontory Point gave the signal, "Done," and the Continent was spanned with iron.

the GREAT CHICAGO FIRE

With the opening of its Union Stockyards—a centralized, efficient operation for slaughtering beef—and its access to emerging railroads, Chicago surpassed Cincinnati as the world's greatest meat-packing center in the years following the Civil War.

But the calamity of October 8, 1871, threatened the very existence of the Midwest's urban hub.

A fire commonly attributed to the kicking over of a lantern by Mrs. O'Leary's cow killed more than 250, destroyed 17,000 buildings, and left almost 100,000 homeless.

It was an epic disaster, but Chicagoans would not be defeated. They quickly rebuilt, developed a new form of architecture in the steel frame, and in 1893 served as host for the World's Columbian Exposition, an international fair.

John R. Chapin, an artist for *Harper's Weekly*, was at the Sherman House hotel when he heard a fire alarm about 10 P.M. He ignored it and went to sleep. But sometime after midnight, he was awakened by noise in the hall and "a dull roar."

I rose and went to the window, threw open the blinds, and gazed upon a sheet of flame towering one hundred feet above the top of the hotel and upon a shower of sparks as copious as drops in a thunderstorm.

Hesitating but an instant to gaze into the face of the awful but sublime monster that was pursuing me, I turned and fled through the fiery shower —whither I knew not—but away from the fire. Coming to the river, I recognized to the left of me the entrance to the tunnel on Washington Street, and hastened toward it. It was filled already with a crowd of fugitives, all flying with their backs and arms loaded, seeking a place of safety with what they had gathered in the despair of the moment. . . .

Helping now a poor mother who was struggling along with an infant and half a dozen older children, anon assisting an old woman staggering under her burden of household stuff, we at length reached the other side and emerged into a place of safety. . . .

As far as the eye could see toward the south the flames extended in one unbroken sheet, while they were advancing (a wall of fire from one to two hundred feet in height) with terrible rapidity. One glance was sufficient to convince the most hopeful that the city was doomed. . . .

. . . I soon found myself on the Randolph Street Bridge, the point whence my sketch was taken. . . . For nearly two miles to the right of me the flames and smoke were rising from the ruins and ashes of dwellings, warehouses, lumberyards, the immense gasworks; and the view in that direction was bounded by an elevator towering one hundred and fifty feet in the air, which had withstood the fire of the night before, but which was now a living coal, sending upward a sheet of flame and smoke a thousand feet high.

Following the line of fire northward, the next prominent object was the Nevada House, a large brick hotel of six or seven stories in height by about one hundred feet square. For a long time this stood surrounded by the fire, and it seemed likely to resist the attack of the flames; but soon a slight column of smoke climbed up the farther corner, a light tongue of flame followed, and in three minutes thereafter the whole structure was toppling to the ground. . . . Everyone knows how inadequate is human language to express the grandeur of Niagara—we can only feel it. And yet Niagara sinks into insignificance before that towering wall of whirling, seething, roaring flame which swept on, on—devouring the most stately and massive stone buildings as though they had been the cardboard playthings of a child.

. . . someone says, "The elevator is on fire." "No; that's the reflection of the fire." Every eye is turned that way with the utmost anxiety. The smoke is so dense that we can hardly see. It blows aside, and what was the reflection of the fire is now a lurid glare of flame. It is doomed. Two, three minutes more, and it is a monstrous pyramid of flame and thick, black smoke, solid as stone. "My God! look there! there are men on top." "No!" "Wait a moment until the smoke clears away." "Yes, there are—three, five. They're lost! See! they are suffocating. They have crept to the corner. O God! is there no help for them? What are they doing? They are drawing something up; 'tis a rope." They fasten it; and just as the flames burst out around them the first one slides over the parapet and down, followed by one after another until the whole are saved, thank God! A universal cry of relief goes up from the crowd, and we turn to other points.

Late in the afternoon I was reluctantly compelled, for the sake of my family, who knew that I had been stopping at the Sherman, to leave for someplace where I could telegraph of my safety. Seeking out the Indianapolis Depot, I purchased my ticket and awaited the opportunity to depart. Hour after hour passed in the presence of scenes of misery, the fire all the time spreading northward, until, at 7:25 P.M., we started. . . . As we got away and looked back we could realize the extent of the territory, and I send you a sketch of the scene as it appeared from the windows of the train. Forty miles away we still saw the brilliant flames looming above the doomed city.

CUSTER *at* LITTLE BIG HORN

The year 1876 marked a grand time for America—the nation's centennial.

But in early summer, chilling news overshadowed the celebrations— a cavalry force had been annihilated by Indians.

George Armstrong Custer and his Seventh Cavalry—225 soldiers in five companies—had been wiped out to the very last man at the Battle of Little Big Horn in Montana after a frontal assault on several thousand Sioux and Cheyenne.

The braves of Crazy Horse and Sitting Bull were in their glory that afternoon of Sunday, June 25, 1876. But vengeance would come. An enraged national government, already waging war on Indian culture to serve the interests of the railroads, farmers, cattlemen, and prospectors, would become even more relentless.

Kate Bighead, a Cheyenne woman who observed much of the battle at Little Big Horn, remembered the day in an interview in 1927 conducted by Thomas Marquis, an Indian-reservation doctor who sought out old-timers to learn of the nineteenth-century native American culture.

She began by recalling the first time she saw Custer, when the Cheyenne were embattled in the Southwest.

I was in the camp beside the Washita River, in the country the white people call Oklahoma, when Custer and his soldiers came there and fought the Indians. Our Chief Black Kettle and other Cheyennes, many of them women and children, were killed that day. It was early in the morning when the soldiers began the shooting. There had been a big storm, and there was snow on the ground. All of us jumped from our beds, and all of us started running to get away. I was barefooted, as were almost all of the others. Our tepees and all of our property we had to leave behind were burned by the white men.

The next spring Custer and his soldiers found us again. We then were far westward, on a branch of what the white people call Red River, I think. That time there was no fighting. Custer smoked the peace pipe with our chiefs. He promised never again to fight the Cheyennes, so all of us followed him to a soldier fort [Fort Sill, Oklahoma]. Our people gave him the name Hi-es-tzie, meaning Long Hair.

I saw Long Hair many times during those days. One time I was close to where he was mounting his horse to go somewhere, and I took a good look at him. He had a large nose, deep-set eyes, and light-red hair that was long and wavy. He was wearing a buckskin suit and a big white hat. I was then a young woman, 22 years old, and I admired him. All of the Indian women talked of him as being a fine-looking man.

My cousin, a young woman named Me-o-tzi, went often with him to help in finding the trails of Indians. She said he told her his soldier horses were given plenty of corn and oats to eat, so they could outrun and catch the Indians riding ponies that had only grass to eat. All of the Cheyennes liked her, and all were glad she had so important a place in life. After Long Hair went away, different ones of the Cheyenne young men wanted to marry her. But she would not have any of them. She said that Long Hair was her husband, that he had promised to come back to her, and that she would wait for him. . . .

Now it is 1876 and the scene has shifted to the edge of Montana's Little Big Horn River. "Custer's Last Stand" is in its final throes as Kate Bighead watches.

The shots quit coming from the place where the soldiers were lying behind their dead horses. All of the Indians jumped up and ran toward them, supposing all of them were dead. But there were seven of the white men who sprang to their feet and went running toward the river. All of the hundreds of boys came tearing in on their horses, to strike blows upon the dead white men, as that was considered a brave deed for a boy. There was such a rush and mixup that it seemed the whole world had gone wild. There was such a crowd, and there was so much dust and smoke in the air, that I did not see what happened to the seven men who ran down the hillside. Hundreds of Sioux and Cheyenne warriors were after them. The talk I heard afterward was that all of them, and all of the others who had been hidden behind the horses, killed themselves. The

Indians believe that the Everywhere Spirit made all of them go crazy and do this, in punishment for having attacked a peaceful Indian camp.

When I was looking at the last fighting, I saw back along the ridge a living soldier sitting on the ground, in plain view. He was just sitting there and rubbing his head, as if he did not know where he was nor what was going on in the world. While I was watching him, three Sioux men ran to him and seized him. They stretched him out upon his back. They went at this slowly, and I wondered what they were going to do. Pretty soon I found out. Two of them held his arms while the third man cut off his head with a sheath-knife. . . .

I saw several different ones of the soldiers not yet quite dead. The Indians cut off the arms or legs or feet of these, the same as was done for those entirely dead. . . .

I may have seen Custer at the time of the battle or after he was killed. I do not know, and I did not then know of his being there.

But I learned something more about him from our people in Oklahoma. Two of those Southern Cheyenne women who had been in our camp at Little Big Horn told of having been on the battlefield soon after the fighting ended. They saw Custer lying dead there. They had known him in the South. While they were looking at him some Sioux men came and were about to cut up his body. The Cheyenne women, thinking of Me-o-tzi, made signs, "He is a relative of ours," but telling nothing more about him.

So the Sioux men cut off only one joint of a finger. The women then pushed the point of a sewing awl into each of his ears, into his head. This was done to improve his hearing, as it seemed he had not heard what our chiefs in the South said when he smoked the pipe with them. They told him that if ever afterward he should break that peace promise and should fight the Cheyennes, the Everywhere Spirit would surely cause him to be killed.

Through almost sixty years, many a time I have thought of Hi-es-tzie as the handsome man I saw in the South. And I often have wondered if, when I was riding among the dead where he was lying, my pony may have kicked dirt upon his body.

Custer's wife, Elizabeth Bacon Custer, accompanied him in the field for twelve years. A prolific letter-writer and diarist who published three volumes of reminiscences, Libbie Custer would tell of seeing her husband and his men depart for the Little Big Horn from their fort in the Dakota Territory, and then of the day when word arrived of their fate.

The morning for the start came only too soon. My husband was to take Sister Margaret and me out for the first day's march, so I rode beside him out of camp.

. . . we came near Laundress Row, and there my heart entirely failed me. The wives and children of the soldiers lined the road. Mothers, with streaming eyes, held their little ones out at arm's length for one last look at their departing fathers. The toddlers among the children, unnoticed by their elders, had made a mimic column of their own. With their handkerchiefs tied to sticks in lieu of flags, and beating old tin pans for drums, they strode back and forth in imitation of the advancing soldiers. They were fortunately too young to realize why their mothers wailed out their farewells.

When our band struck up "The Girl I Left Behind Me," the most despairing hour seemed to have come. All the sad-faced wives of the officers who had forced themselves to their doors to try to wave a courageous farewell and smile bravely to keep the ones they loved from knowing the anguish of their breaking hearts gave up the struggle at the sound of the music. . . .

With my husband's departure my last happy days in garrison were ended, as a premonition of disaster that I had never known before weighed me down.

A picture of one day of our life in those disconsolate times is fixed indelibly in my memory.

On Sunday afternoon, June 25, our little group of saddened women, borne down with one common weight of anxiety, sought solace in gathering together in our house. We tried to find some slight surcease from trouble in the old hymns: some of them dated back to our childhood days, when our mothers rocked us to sleep to their soothing strains. I remember the grief with which one fair young wife threw herself on the carpet and pillowed her head in the lap of a tender friend. Another sat dejected at the piano and struck soft chords that melted into the notes of the voices.

All were absorbed in the same thoughts, and their eyes were filled with faraway visions and longings. Indescribable yearning for the absent, and untold terror for their safety, engrossed each heart.

At that very hour the fears that our tortured minds had portrayed in imagination were realities, and souls of those we thought upon were ascending to meet their Maker.

On July 5—it took time for the news to come—the sun rose on a beautiful world, but with its earliest beams came the first knell of disaster. A steamer came down the river bearing the wounded [presumably the bodies] from the battle of the Little Big Horn, on Sunday, June 25. This battle wrecked the lives of twenty-six women at Fort Lincoln, and orphaned children of officers and soldiers joined the cry to that of their bereaved mothers.

From that time the life went out of the hearts of the "women who weep," and God asked them to walk on alone and in the shadow.

BILLY *the* KID

William H. Bonney was born in New York City's Bowery area. But he become one of the legendary figures of the Old West—Billy the Kid.

During the Civil War, the Bonney family moved to Kansas. The father soon died, and the mother remarried. She took her son to Colorado and then to the mining camps of New Mexico. At age twelve, Billy showed he was someone to be reckoned with. Enraged by a slighting remark made to his mother by a Silver City blacksmith, he shot the man dead.

Billy eventually turned to cattle rustling, and by the late 1870s he became entangled in the vicious Lincoln County range wars between rival New Mexico cattlemen.

A settler named Annie Lesnett would remember him, however, as a kindly lad—almost the proverbial boy next door.

The only thing to mar my happiness was that the Indians would go on the warpath, and the Lincoln County war was brewing. When Jennie

Mae, my second child, was about nine months old, "The Kid" came to our house with a boy by the name of Jesse Evans, and was introduced as Billie Bonney. Could this be the notorious Billy the Kid? I thought, surely not. He looked just like any other seventeen-year-old boy, and not in the least like a desperado. He was very fond of children, and liked Irvin and Jennie Mae at once. He called my little boy "Pardie" and always wanted to hold the baby. He would take the two of them for a ride on his gray pony. . . .

The Lincoln County War, which was one of the bloodiest in the history of the West, had two sides, one for the Law and the other for Lawlessness. Almost every cattleman in the county was somehow involved. Strange as it may seem, the Kid, an outlaw, joined the forces for law and order.

The lawless side had driven the Kid and his band into the McSween home in Lincoln. . . . The McSween home was soon surrounded by the Murphy gang, and firing became very heavy. . . . [T]hey soaked a barrel with coal oil and rolled it down the hill to set the house afire. The house began to burn, but the battle did not stop. The Kid kept moving his men from room to room until they reached the last room. . . . The Kid ran through the blazing door with a gun in each hand. He jumped from side to side as he ran and made a very elusive target. Not one bullet touched his body, though his clothes were ripped to shreds. His score was one dead and two marked for life—one shot through the jaw and the other lost the lobe of his left ear.

It is impossible to describe the horror of the deeds that were committed during the Lincoln County War. When one party met the other while riding through the hills they just opened fire, either pushing forward or retreating. If all the men were accounted for, their graves might reach from Roswell to White Oaks.

One evening while it was peaceful and quiet on the ranch, the silence was broken by a series of shots. I snatched Jennie Mae and Irvin from their beds and ran toward the river. As I ran past the great triangle used to call cowboys to meals, I paused to give it several strikes; but this was not necessary, for the men—thinking the Indians had attacked—were already on their stomachs working their way toward the house. When the men got into the house and looked around, they found that a box of cartridges that had been on top of the mantel had been knocked by something into the fire. When I told the Kid about this, he asked me if I had a gun.

"Heavens, no," I replied, "I wouldn't know how to shoot even if I had one."

"Take this one," he said, holding one of his guns out to me, "and I'll teach you to shoot when I come back."

Poor boy never came back to our house. The next time I saw him he was a prisoner, guarded by Bell and Olinger. Olinger, knowing that I liked the Kid, invited me to the hanging. I turned my head and blinked fast to keep back the tears. Suddenly the Kid turned to me and said, "Mrs. Lesnett, they can't hang me if I'm not there, can they?"

It was just a few days after this that the Kid killed his two guards at Lincoln, and made his escape.

Having been captured by Sheriff Pat Garrett, Billy the Kid was sentenced to be hanged at Lincoln, New Mexico—supposedly the killer of nineteen men.

But he escaped from jail, fatally shooting his two guards, Johnny Bell and Bob Olinger. Eight weeks later—on July 14, 1881—the sheriff confronted Billy in the middle of the night at a house near Fort Sumner, where he had gone to see a girlfriend.

Billy was fast on the draw, but Garrett was faster. In Garrett's own words:

He raised his pistol quickly. Retreating rapidly across the room he repeated: "Quién es? Quién es?" ["Who is it?"] All this occurred in a moment. Quickly as possible I drew my revolver and fired, threw my body aside, and fired again. The second shot was useless. The Kid fell dead. He never spoke. A struggle or two, a little strangling sound as he gasped for breath and the Kid was with his many victims.

SHOOTOUT *at the* O.K. CORRAL

A drunken lawyer named Allen English was fined $25 by a judge for contempt of court one day back in the 1880s in the Arizona town of Tombstone. "Your honor," English retorted, "twenty-five dollars wouldn't pay for half the contempt I have for this court."

That was old Tombstone all right, home to silver prospectors, cattle thieves, card cheats, whores, gunslingers, and a cemetery called Boot Hill that underscored the lawlessness of Western boomtowns.

The famous gunfight at Tombstone's O.K. Corral—it actually took place a half-block from the rear entrance—symbolized the Wild West at its wildest and would provide a wonderful spectacle for motion-picture producers to come.

On one side stood Wyatt Earp and his brothers Morgan and Virgil —all lawmen of sorts—and their pal the tubercular Doc Holliday, the meanest dentist on earth till Laurence Olivier drilled Dustin Hoffman in *Marathon Man*. Confronting the Earps and Holliday were the McLaury and Clanton boys and their sidekick, Billy Claiborne.

The lead flew furiously outside the O.K. Corral back on October 26, 1881, the thirty-second gun battle climaxing a tangled set of grievances and feuds.

Who fired first?

A Tombstone man named R. F. Coleman told a story that supported the Earps' version of the gunfight.

I was in the O.K. Corral at 2:30 P.M., when I saw the two Clantons and the two McLaury boys in earnest conversation across the street, in Dunbar's corral. I went up the street and notified Sheriff Behan, and told him it was my opinion they meant trouble, and that it was his duty, as Sheriff, to go and disarm them; I told him they had gone to the West End Corral. I then went and saw Marshal Virgil Earp, and notified him to the same effect. I then met Billy Allen, and we walked through the O.K. Corral, about fifty yards behind the Sheriff.

On reaching Freemont street I saw Virgil Earp, Wyatt Earp, Morgan Earp and Doc Holliday, in the center of the street, all armed. I had reached Bauer's meat market; Johnny Behan had just left the cowboys [a euphemism for gunslingers], after having a conversation with them. I went along to Fly's photograph gallery, when I heard Virg. Earp say, "Give up your arm; or throw up your arms." There was some reply made by Frank McLaury, but at the same moment there were two shots fired simultaneously by Doc Holliday and Frank McLaury, when the firing became general, over thirty shots being fired.

Tom McLaury fell first, but raised and fired again before he died. Bill Clanton fell next, and raised to fire again when Mr. Fly took his revolver from him. Frank McLaury ran a few rods and fell. Morgan Earp was shot through and fell, Doc Holliday was hit in the left hip, but kept on firing. Virgil Earp was hit in the third or fourth fire in the leg, which staggered him, but he kept up his effective work. Wyatt Earp stood up and fired in rapid succession, as cool as a cucumber, and was not hit. Doc Holliday was as calm as if at target practice and fired rapidly. After the firing was over, Sheriff Behan went up to Wyatt Earp and said, "I'll have to arrest you." Wyatt replied, "I won't be arrested today. I am right here and am not going away. You have deceived me; you told me those men were disarmed. I went to disarm them."

In testimony at the trial conducted by Magistrate Wells Spicer, a Tombstone jeweler named Wesley Fuller claimed that Billy Clanton and Frank McLaury were defenseless when shot dead.

I was going down Allen street, and saw the parties standing on Freemont street and went down the alley to see Billy Clanton, and tell him to get out of town. I saw Billy Clanton, Frank McLaury and Johnny Behan on Freemont street. . . . The Earps and Holliday were on the corner of Fourth and Allen streets when I saw them armed. Virg. Earp had a shotgun, double barreled; the others had six-shooters. I did not go close enough to tell Billy Clanton anything before the difficulty. I saw the Earps through the alley, just as they got there. I heard some one say, "Throw up your hands!" Billy Clanton threw up his hands and said, "Don't shoot me; I don't want to fight!" At the same time, the shooting commenced.

I did not see Ike Clanton at that time; I did not see Frank McLaury. The Earp party fired the first shot; two shots were fired right away; they were almost together; I think they were both pistol shots. Both parties then commenced firing rapidly. Billy Clanton staggered and fell at the end of the house. I think five or six shots were fired by the Earp party before Billy Clanton and Frank McLaury commenced shooting. They were the only ones of the Clanton-McLaury party I saw fire. At the time the first shots were fired by the Earp party, Billy Clanton's hands were up level with his head. When firing commenced Frank McLaury was standing by and holding his horse. He was doing nothing. I saw his hands; saw no weapon in them; would have seen it if he had one. The first two shots fired were directed at, and that one shot took effect on, Billy Clanton. I saw he was hit; he put his hand down against his stomach, and wheeled around.

The judge dismissed murder charges against the Earps and Holliday.

The following December, Virgil Earp was shot in the arm from ambush and left a cripple. Almost three months after that, Morgan Earp was murdered in another ambush. Wyatt Earp wisely left Tombstone and eventually settled in California, where he wrote his memoirs, speculated in real estate, and died—with his boots off—two weeks short of his eighty-first birthday.

ALEXANDER GRAHAM BELL CALLING

As Americans moved westward, technological advances broke down the isolation of widely separated settlements in the vast continent. Samuel F. B. Morse perfected the telegraph in 1844. And twenty-one years later, Cyrus Field linked America to Europe with completion of the Atlantic cable.

On the afternoon of June 2, 1875, two young inventors were hard at work in a brick building on Boston's Court Street, hoping to create a device they called a "harmonic telegraph." Alexander Graham Bell and Thomas A. Watson were trying to transmit several messages over a single telegraph wire at the same time without interference, envisioning a vast improvement over the single-message telegraph invented by Morse.

But what happened that day went far beyond an enhancement of telegraphy. Bell and Watson would take a first step toward the transmission of human voice.

Watson later recounted how the idea for the telephone was first broached to him by Bell in the late summer of 1874.

Bell said to me, "Watson, I want to tell you of another idea I have which will surprise you!" I listened, I suspect, somewhat languidly, for I must have been working that day about sixteen hours, with only a short nutritive interval . . . but when he went on to say that he had an idea by which he believed it would be possible to talk by telegraph, my nervous system got such a shock that the tired feeling vanished. I have never forgotten his exact words; they have run in my mind ever since like a mathematical formula. "If," he said, "I could make a current of electricity vary in intensity, precisely as the air varies in density during the production of a sound, I should be able to transmit speech telegraphically. . . . "

Then came the spring day when Bell's vision bolted toward reality, a moment that Watson would remember well.

The date when the conception of the undulatory or speech-transmitting current took its perfect form in Bell's mind [was] the greatest day in the history of the telephone, but certainly June 2, 1875, must always rank next; for on that day the mocking fiend inhabiting that demonic telegraph apparatus . . . opened the curtain that hides from man Nature's secrets and gave us a glimpse into that treasury of things not yet discovered. . . .

On the afternoon of June 2, 1875, we were hard at work on same old job, testing some modification of the instruments. Things were badly out of tune that afternoon in that hot garret, not only the instruments, but I fancy, my enthusiasm and my temper, though Bell was as energetic as ever. I had charge of the transmitters as usual, setting them squealing one after the other, while Bell was turning the receiver springs one by one, pressing them against his ear. . . .

One of the transmitter springs I was attending to stopped vibrating and I plucked it to start again. It didn't start and I kept on plucking it, when suddenly I heard a shout from Bell in the next room, and then he came out with a rush, demanding, "What did you do then? Don't change anything. Let me see!"

That strip of magnetized steel by its vibration over the pole of its magnet was generating that marvelous conception of Bell's—a current of electricity that varied in intensity precisely as the air was varying in density within hearing distance of that spring. That undulatory current had passed through the connecting wire to the distant receiver which, fortunately, was a mechanism that could transform that current back into an extremely faint echo of the sound of the vibrating spring that had generated it.

What was still more fortunate, the right man had that mechanism at his ear during that fleeting moment, and instantly recognized the transcendent importance of that faint sound thus electrically transmitted. The shout I heard and his excited rush into my room were the result of that recognition.

The speaking telephone had been born at that moment. Bell knew perfectly well that the mechanism that could transmit all the complex vibrations of one sound could do the same for any sound, even that of speech.

Bell later shifted his operations to 5 Exeter Place in Boston. It was there, on the night of March 10, 1876, that his telephone transmitted its first complete and intelligible sentence, Bell at the mouthpiece and Watson stationed at the receiver.

It made such an impression on me that I wrote that first sentence in a book I have always preserved. The occasion had not been arranged and rehearsed as I suspect the sending of the first message over the Morse telegraph had been years before, for instead of that noble first telegraphic message—"What hath God wrought?"—the first message of the telephone was: "Mr. Watson, come here, I want you." Perhaps, if Mr. Bell had realized that he was about to make a bit of history, he would have been prepared with a more sounding and interesting sentence.

EDISON'S TALKING MACHINES

Thomas A. Edison's invention of the incandescent light bulb would not come until 1879, so he was hardly considered a wizard quite yet when, in 1877, he told of developing a machine that could reproduce voices.

After demonstrating his phonograph in Paris in 1878, Edison was accused of ventriloquism by a member of the French Academy of Sciences named Jean Bouillaud, who said, "It is quite impossible that the noble organs of human speech could be replaced by ignoble, senseless metal."

In an article written a decade later, Philip G. Hubert, Jr., the music critic of the *New York Evening Post*, explained how Edison did it.

The new phonograph takes up, with its table, about the space occupied by a sewing-machine, and might at first be taken for one. Underneath the table is an electric battery or a treadle, according to the power used in moving the cylinder. The wax cylinders, or phonograms, as they are called, are two inches in diameter, and vary in length from one to ten inches, according to the amount of talking which is to be engraved upon them. The smallest size is about that of a napkin ring, and will be sufficient for the ordinary business letter of two or three hundred words. The wax surface is highly polished; when it has been through the apparatus, the marks or engraving upon it can be seen only with a glass. When a message is to be recorded, one of these phonograms is slipped over the permanent steel cylinder, which is set in motion, and the diaphragm, carrying its stylus on the under side, is lowered toward the wax surface until a slight grating sound announces that it touches. Then the talking may begin. It is not necessary to talk louder than in an ordinary conversation, but distinct articulation is required. For reproduction, the stylus is raised, and the "follower" or sounding-spring is brought into contact with the wax. . . .

When it comes to music, the present achievements are wonderful. The phonograph will reproduce any kind of music—singing, the piano, violin, cornet, oboe, etc.—with a beauty of tone and accuracy which will astonish the musician. . . . The phonograph itself cannot cost more than fifty dollars, and the wax cylinders used upon them scarcely more than writing-paper. Once a cylinder has been "engraved," or has had a message recorded upon it, it can be passed through the phonograph any number of times, apparently without deterioration. Mr. Edison has some phonograms, containing pages of Nicholas Nickleby, *which have been read out thousands of times by the phonograph, and no indications of wear are audible. . . .*

As a saving in the time given up to writing, the phonograph promises to far outstrip the typewriter. The business man can dictate to the phonograph as fast as he can talk, and the wax cylinder, inclosed in a suitable box, can be sent off by mail to read out its message perhaps thousands of miles away. Or else, as is now done in Mr. Edison's laboratory in Orange, N.J., the typewriter girl can print out upon paper what her employer has dictated to the phonograph. For the reporter, the editor, and the author who can dictate, a device has been adapted to the phonograph which causes it to stop its message at every tenth word, and to continue only when a spring is touched. Thus, the editor can dictate his article to the phonograph as he does now to his stenographer, and when the printer at the case gets the resulting phonogram the instrument will dictate to him in short sentences. If he cannot set up the sentence at one hearing, it will repeat its ten words. If he is satisfied, it reads out ten words more.

I really see no reason why the newspaper of the future should not come to the subscriber in the shape of a phonogram. It would have to begin, however, with a table of contents, in order that one might not have to listen to a two hours' speech upon the tariff question in order to get at ten lines of a musical notice. But think what a music critic might be able to do for his public! He might give them whole arias from an opera or movement from a symphony, by way of proof or illustration.

Mr. Edison says that by the beginning of 1890 the phonograph will be far less of a curiosity than the telephone is now. For the last year it has been the same story,—the phonographs would be ready for sale next month. It was so a year ago, and it may be so a year from now. But these many delays, which have made people rather skeptical as to the doings of the phonograph, do not make the wonders already achieved less wonderful, or warrant any doubts as to the vast possibilities which the little device contains.

the BROOKLYN BRIDGE

Its beauty has been celebrated in literature, poetry, paintings, song, and motion pictures.

Measuring more than a mile from end to end, its stone towers rising 276 feet—higher than even the tallest buildings of the nineteenth-century landscape it dwarfed—it was a work of grandeur as well as grace.

And it was much more than a link between the cities of New York and Brooklyn. It symbolized the American ideal of progress.

The Brooklyn Bridge was the inspiration of America's leading civil engineer, the German-born John Roebling. But he would never see it rise. His toes were crushed in a pier-side accident in July 1869—as he oversaw preliminary surveys—and he died of lockjaw. His son, Colonel Washington Roebling, would build the bridge though stricken by the "bends" while helping to fight a fire in one of the compressed-air caissons forming bases for the towers.

The man who envisioned the bridge saw New York City as the commercial center of a great nation. But John Roebling's dream went beyond that. He promised to build a great link for the globe, one whose importance would rival the transcontinental railroad and the Suez Canal.

As the great flow of civilization has ever been from East towards the West, with the same certainty will the greatest commercial emporium be located on this continent, which links East to the West, and whose mission it is in the history of mankind to blend the most ancient civilization with the most modern. . . .

Lines of steamers, such as the world never saw before, are now plowing the Atlantic in regular straight line furrows. The same means of communication will unite the western coast of this continent to the eastern coast of Asia. New York will remain the center where these lines meet. . . .

The completed work, when constructed in accordance with my designs, will not only be the greatest bridge in existence, but it will be the greatest engineering work of the continent, and of the age. Its most conspicuous features, the great towers, will serve as landmarks to the adjoining cities, and they will be entitled to be ranked as national monuments. As a great work of art, and as a successful specimen of advanced bridge engineering, this structure will forever testify to the energy, enterprise and wealth of that community which shall secure its erection.

The bridge opened on May 24, 1883, with President Chester A. Arthur leading a grand parade across it as ships blew their horns and tooted whistles.

As evening arrived, a reporter for the *New York Sun* marveled at the setting.

As the sun went down the scene from the bridge was beautiful. It had been a perfect day. Up and down on either side of New York the bright blue water lay gently rippling, while to the south it merged into the great bay and disappeared toward the sea. The vast cities spread away on both sides. Beyond rolled the hilly country until it was lost in the mists of the sky. All up and down the harbor the shipping, piers and buildings were still gaily decorated. On the housetops of both Brooklyn and New York were multitudes of people. . . .

The great buildings in New York loomed up as black as ink against the brilliant background of the sky. The New York bridge pier looked somber and gloomy as night. But in Brooklyn the blaze of the dying sun bathed everything in gold. The great buildings looked like burnished brass. . . . In the west the sun sent its last tribute to the bridge in a series of great bars of golden light that shot up fanlike into the blue sky. Gradually the gold melted away, leaving the heavens cloudless. The sky was a light blue in the west, but grew darker as it rose, until it sank behind Brooklyn in a deep-sea blue.

Slowly the extremities of the twin cities began to grow indistinct. . . .

The Towers of Brooklyn lost their golden hue. They seemed to sink slowly into the city itself. In New York the outlines of the huge buildings became wavering and indistinct.

Then one by one the series of electric lights on the bridge leaped up until the chain was made from Brooklyn to New York. Dot by dot flashes of electric lights sprang up in the upper part of New York. The two great burners at Madison and Union Squares flared up, and the dome of the Post Office in New York set a circlet of diamonds out against the relief of the sky. The streets of the two cities sparkled into life like the jets on a limitless theatrical chandelier, and the windows of the houses popped into notice hundreds at a time. Long strings of lanterns were run over the rigging of the shipping in the harbor, and red and green port and starboard lights seemed numberless. The steamers sped to and fro on the water, leaving long ripples of white foam, which glistened in the light like silver.

the **LADY** *in the* **HARBOR**

New York Harbor lay enveloped in mist the morning of October 28, 1886, as President Grover Cleveland arrived for ceremonies dedicating the Statue of Liberty, a gift from the French people that would symbolize the promise of America.

The base of the statue became shrouded by steam from stacks on the dozens of boats gathered to salute her and from the smoke of a multigun salute. But for José Martí, a fighter for Cuban independence then in the United States as a correspondent for the Argentine newspaper *La Nación*, the mists could not hide the meaning.

Liberty, it is thine hour of arrival! Flags are reflected on faces, heartstrings are plucked by a sweet love, a superior sense of sovereignty brings to countenances a look of peace, nay of beauty. And all these luckless Irishmen, Poles, Italians, Bohemians, Germans redeemed from oppression or misery, hail the monument to Liberty because they feel that through it they themselves are uplifted and restored. . . . In her presence, eyes once again know what tears are. She seemed alive, wrapped in clouds of smoke, covered by a vague brightness, truly like an altar with steamers kneeling at her feet!

Edward Corsi would one day become commissioner of the Ellis Island immigrant-processing center. But back in 1907, he was a ten-year-old glimpsing the Statue of Liberty for the first time as he arrived in America with his family.

My first impressions of the new world will always remain etched in my memory, particularly that hazy October morning when I first saw Ellis Island. The steamer Florida, fourteen days out of Naples, filled to capacity with sixteen hundred natives of Italy, had weathered one of the worst storms in our captain's memory; and glad we were, both children and grownups, to leave the open sea and come at last through the Narrows into the Bay.

My mother, my stepfather, my brother Giuseppe, and my two sisters, Libertà and Helvetia, all of us together, happy that we had come through the storm safely, clustered on the foredeck for fear of separation and looked with wonder on this miraculous land of our dreams.

Giuseppe and I held tightly to stepfather's hands, while Libertà and Helvetia clung to mother. Passengers all about us were crowding against the rail. Jabbered conversation, sharp cries, laughs and cheers—a steadily rising din filled the air. Mothers and fathers lifted up their babies so that they too could see, off to the left, the Statue of Liberty.

I looked at that statue with a sense of bewilderment, half doubting its reality. Looming shadowy through the mist, it brought silence to the decks of the Florida. This symbol of America—this enormous expression of what we all had been taught was the inner meaning of this new country we were coming to—inspired awe in the hopeful immigrants. Many older persons among us, burdened with a thousand memories of what they were leaving behind, had been openly weeping ever since we entered the narrower waters on our final approach toward the unknown. Now somehow steadied, I suppose, by the concreteness of the symbol of America's freedom, they dried their tears.

The French paid for the statue (the cost about $400,000), but funds for the pedestal were raised in America, much of the $250,000 coming from schoolchildren in a drive led by Joseph Pulitzer's *New York World*.

An 1883 art exhibition created to help fund the pedestal included a poem by a young woman who had little in common with the immigrant masses who would be greeted by the lady in the harbor—she was the daughter of a wealthy Jewish family in New York whose roots went back to colonial times. But she was shocked by the pogroms of czarist Russia and worked to help its victims, now starting life anew in America.

That personal experience produced a poem that drew little notice when it was first written. But "The New Colossus" of Emma Lazarus would be affixed to a bronze plaque placed on the Statue of Liberty in 1903, its message an enduring statement of American ideals.

> *Not like the brazen giant of Greek fame,*
> *With conquering limbs astride from land to land;*
> *Here at our sea-washed, sunset gates shall stand*
> *A mighty woman with a torch, whose flame*
> *Is the imprisoned lightning, and her name*
> *Mother of Exiles. From her beacon-hand*
> *Glows world-wide welcome; her mild eyes command*
> *The air-bridged harbor that twin cities frame.*
> *"Keep, ancient lands, your storied pomp!" cries she*
> *With silent lips. "Give me your tired, your poor,*
> *Your huddled masses yearning to breathe free,*
> *The wretched refuse of your teeming shore.*
> *Send these, the homeless, tempest-tossed to me,*
> *I lift my lamp beside the golden door!"*

ELLIS ISLAND

On January 1, 1892, a new immigrant station opened in New York Harbor.

Ellis Island was a replacement for corruption-ridden Castle Garden.

But it was no place of joy for the bewildered masses who passed through, twenty million new Americans by the time it shut down in 1954.

The first hours in the Great Hall—the main registration-and-examination section—were agonizing. The uniformed immigration officers reminded many a Russian Jew of the soldiers of the czar, whose pogroms had sent them to America. The doctors and the officials stirred fear among all the immigrants. Anyone could be sent back home if found to be carrying disease or deemed to be mentally ill, illiterate in a native language, a potential public burden, perhaps even an anarchist.

Soon after the turn of the century, the British author H. G. Wells visited Ellis Island.

I made my way with my introduction along white passages and through traps and a maze of metal lattices that did for a while succeed in catching and imprisoning me, to Commissioner Wachorn, in his quiet, green-toned office. There, for a time, I sat judicially and heard him deal methodically, swiftly, sympathetically, with case after case, a string of appeals against the sentences of deportation pronounced in the busy little courts below. First would come one dingy and strangely garbed group of wild-eyed aliens, and then another: Rumanian gypsies, South Italians, Ruthenians, Swedes, each under the intelligent guidance of a uniformed interpreter, and a case would be started, a report made to Washington, and they would drop out again, hopeful or sullen or fearful as the evidence might trend. . . .

Down-stairs we find the courts, and these seen, we traverse long refectories, long aisles of tables, and close-packed dormitories with banks of steel mattresses, tier above tier, and galleries and passages innumerable, perplexing intricacy that slowly grows systematic with the Commissioner's explanations.

Here is a huge, gray, untidy waiting-room, like a big railway-depot room, full of a sinister crowd of miserable people, loafing about or sitting dejectedly, whom America refuses, and here a second and a third such chamber each with its tragic and evil-looking crowd that hates us, and that even ventures to groan and hiss at us a little for our glimpse of its large dirty spectacle of hopeless failure, and here, squalid enough indeed, but still to some degree hopeful, are the appeal cases as yet undecided. In one place, at a bank of ranges, works an army of men cooks, in another spins the big machinery of the Ellis Island laundry, washing blankets, drying blankets, day in and day out, a big clean steamy space of hurry and rotation. . . .

The central hall is the key of this impression. All day long, through an intricate series of metal pens, the long procession files, step by step, bearing bundles and trunks and boxes, past this examiner and that, past the quick, alert medical officers, the tallymen and the clerks. At every point immigrants are being picked out and set aside for further medical examination, for further questions, for the busy little courts; but the main procession satisfies conditions, passes on. . . .

On they go, from this pen to that, pen by pen, towards a desk at a little metal wicket—the gate of America. . . . The great majority are young men and young women, between seventeen and thirty, good, youthful, hopeful peasant stock. They stand in a long string, waiting to go through that wicket, with bundles, with little tin boxes, with cheap portmanteaus, with odd packages, in pairs, in families, alone, women with children, men with strings of dependents, young couples. All day that string of human beads waits there, jerks forward, waits again; all day and every day, constantly replenished, constantly dropping the end beads through the wicket, till the units mount to hundreds and the hundreds to thousands. . . .

"Look there!" said the Commissioner, taking me by the arm and pointing, and I saw a monster steamship far away, and already a big bulk looming up in the Narrows. "It's the Kaiser Wilhelm der Grosse. *She's got—I forget the exact figures, but let us say—eight-hundred and fifty-three more for us. She'll have to keep them until Friday at the earliest. And there's more behind her, and more strung out all across the Atlantic."*

In one record day this month 21,000 immigrants came into the port of New York alone; in one week over 50,000. This year the total will be 1,200,000 souls.

A contrast to Wells's patronizing view of the immigrants was voiced by a figure who always identified with the underdog.

Fiorello La Guardia took a job as an interpreter at Ellis Island in 1907 to help pay his way through law school. What the future mayor of New York saw in helping process the streams of would-be Americans troubled him deeply.

The immigration laws were rigidly enforced, and there were many heartbreaking scenes on Ellis Island. I never managed during the three years I worked there to become callous to the mental anguish, the disappointment and the despair I witnessed almost daily. . . .

One case haunted me for years. A young girl in her teens from the mountains of northern Italy turned up at Ellis Island. No one understood her particular dialect very well, and because of her hesitancy in replying to questions she did not understand, she was sent to the hospital for observation. I could imagine the effect on this girl, who had always been carefully sheltered and had never been permitted to be in the company of a man alone, when a doctor suddenly rapped on her knees, looked into her eyes, turned her on her back and tickled her spine to ascertain her reflexes. The child rebelled—and how! It was the cruelest case I ever witnessed on the Island. In two weeks' time that child was a raving maniac, although she had been sound and normal when she arrived at Ellis Island.

Louis Adamic, who would become a prominent journalist and author, arrived at Ellis Island in 1913 from Slovenia.

I had written Stefan ("Steve") Radin, brother of my late friend Yanko, whose address in Brooklyn I happened to have, that I was due in New York on December 30th, and would he meet me on Ellis Island, which Peter Molek had told me was the clearing-house for immigrants? . . .

The day I spent on Ellis Island was an eternity. Rumors were current among immigrants of several nationalities that some of us would be refused admittance into the United States and sent back to Europe. For several hours I was in a cold sweat on this account, although, so far as I knew, all my papers were in order, and sewed away in the lining of my jacket were twenty-five dollars in American currency—the minimum amount required by law to be in the possession of every immigrant before entering the country. Then, having rationalized away some of these fears, I gradually worked up a panicky feeling that I might develop measles or smallpox, or some other such disease. I heard that several hundred sick immigrants were quarantined on the island.

The first night in America I spent, with hundreds of other recently arrived immigrants, in an immense hall with tiers of narrow iron-and-canvas bunks, four deep. I was assigned a top bunk. Unlike most of the steerage immigrants, I had no bedding with me, and the blanket which someone threw at me was too thin to be effective against the blasts of cold air that rushed in through the open windows; so that I shivered, sleepless, all night, listening to snores and dream-monologues in perhaps a dozen different languages.

The bunk immediately beneath mine was occupied by a Turk, who slept with his turban wound around his head. He was tall, thin, dark, bearded, hollow-faced and hook-nosed. At peace with Allah, he snored all night, producing a thin wheezing sound, which occasionally, for a moment or two, took on a deeper note.

I thought how curious it was that I should be spending a night in such proximity to a Turk, for Turks were traditional enemies of Balkan peoples, including my own nation. For centuries Turks had forayed into Slovenian territory. Now here I was, trying to sleep directly above a Turk, with only a sheet of canvas between us. . . .

Late in the afternoon of the last day of 1913 I was examined for entry into the United States, with about a hundred other immigrants who had come on the Niagara.

The examiner sat bureaucratically—very much in the manner of officials of the Old Country—behind a great desk, which stood upon a high platform. On the wall above him was a picture of George Washington. Beneath it was an American flag.

The official spoke a bewildering mixture of many Slavic languages. He had a stern voice and a sour visage. I had difficulty understanding some of his questions.

At a small table, piled with papers, not far from the examiner's desk, was a clerk who called out our names, which, it seemed, were written on the long sheets of paper before him.

When my turn came, toward dusk, I was asked the usual questions. When and where was I born? My nationality? Religion? Was I a legitimate child? What were the names of my parents? Was I an imbecile? Was I a prostitute? (I assume that male and female immigrants were subjected to the same questionnaire.) Was I an ex-convict? A criminal? Why had I come to the United States?

I was questioned as to the state of my finances and I produced the required twenty-five dollars.

What did I expect to do in the United States? I replied that I hoped to get a job. What kind of job? I didn't know; any kind of job.

The inspector grunted vaguely, "And who is this person, Stefan Radin —who is meeting you here?"

I answered that Stefan Radin was the brother of a friend of mine, now dead.

Then the inspector waved me out of his presence and the clerk motioned me to go back and sit on one of the benches near by.

I waited another hour. It got dark and the lights were turned on in the room.

Finally, after dozens of other immigrants had been questioned, Steve Radin was called into the examining-room and asked, in English, to state his relationship to me.

He answered, of course, that he was not related to me at all.

Whereupon the inspector fairly pounced upon me, speaking the dreadful botch of Slavic languages. What did I mean by lying to him? He said a great many other things which I did not understand. I did comprehend, however, his threat to return me to the Old Country. It appeared that America had no room for liars: America was glad to welcome to its shores only decent, honest, truthful people.

My heart pounded.

Finally it occurred simultaneously to me and to Steve Radin that the man must be laboring under some misapprehension. And, truly, before another minute elapsed it turned out that the clerk had made a mistake by entering on my paper that I had declared Stefan Radin was my uncle. How the mistake had occurred I do not know; perhaps the clerk had confused my questionnaire form with someone else's.

Finally, perceiving the error, the examiner's face formed in a grimace and, waving his hand in a casual gesture, he ordered me released.

Steve Radin picked up my bag and, in the confusion, I barely remembered to say good-by to Peter Molek, who was going to Pennsylvania.

I was weak in the knees and just managed to walk out of the room, then downstairs and into the ferryboat. I had been shouted at, denounced as a liar by an official of the United States in my second day in the country, before a roomful of people, including Steve Radin, whom, so far, I had merely glimpsed.

But the weakness in my knees soon passed. I laughed, perhaps a bit hysterically, as the little Ellis Island ferryboat bounded over the rough, white-capped waters of the bay toward the Battery.

Steve Radin gaped at me. Then he smiled.

I was in New York—in America.

the SWEATSHOPS of "JEWTOWN"

The "huddled masses" whose plight had so moved Emma Lazarus escaped the threat of pogroms forever by coming to America. But they hardly found a "golden door."

Jammed into filthy and horribly overcrowded tenements, toiling day and night—often with their children beside them—in the fetid "sweatshops" of Manhattan's Lower East Side, the mass of Jewish immigrants had escaped the bonds of Russian oppression only to be chained to the sewing machine.

Jacob Riis, a reporter for the *New York Sun*, exposed their wretched living and working conditions in a series of newspaper articles that would be incorporated into his book *How the Other Half Lives*, published in 1890. His accounts would spur the reforms of the early twentieth century's Progressive Movement.

Riis told of the "sweater"—an exploiter of sorts who was himself a victim of the sweatshop system.

The sweater is simply the middleman, the sub-contractor, a workman like his fellows, perhaps with the single distinction from the rest that he knows a little English; perhaps not even that, but with the accidental possession of two or three sewing-machines, or of credit enough to hire them, as his capital, who drums up work among the clothing-houses. Of workmen he can always get enough. . . .

And the supply across the seas is apparently inexhaustible. Every fresh persecution of the Russian or Polish Jew on his native soil starts greater hordes hitherward to confound economical problems, and recruit the sweater's phalanx. The curse of bigotry and ignorance reaches half-way across the world, to sow its bitter seed in fertile soil in the East Side tenements. If the Jew himself was to blame for the resentment he aroused over there, he is amply punished. He gathers the first-fruits of the harvest here.

The bulk of the sweater's work is done in the tenements, which the law that regulates factory labor does not reach. . . . The tenement has defeated its benevolent purpose. In it the child works unchallenged from the day he is old enough to pull a thread. There is no such thing as a dinner hour; men and women eat while they work, and the "day" is lengthened at both ends far into the night. . . .

Take the Second Avenue Elevated Railroad at Chatham Square and ride up half a mile through the sweaters' district. Every open window of the big tenements, that stand like a continuous brick wall on both sides of the way, gives you a glimpse of one of these shops as the train speeds by. Men and women bending over their machines, or ironing clothes at the window, half-naked. Proprieties do not count on the East Side; nothing counts that cannot be converted into hard cash. . . . At Rivington Street let us get off and continue our trip on foot. It is Sunday evening west of the Bowery. . . . Men stagger along the sidewalk groaning under heavy burdens of unsewn garments, or enormous black bags stuffed full of finished coats and trousers. Let us follow one to his home and see how Sunday passes in a Ludlow Street tenement.

Up two flights of dark stairs, three, four, with new smells of cabbage, of onions, of frying fish, on every landing, whirring sewing machines behind closed doors betraying what goes on within, to the door that opens to admit the bundle and the man. A sweater, this, in a small way. Five men and a woman, two young girls, not fifteen, and a boy who says unasked that he is fifteen, and lies in saying it, are at the machines sewing knickerbockers, "knee-pants" in the Ludlow Street dialect. The floor is littered ankle-deep with half-sewn garments. In the alcove, on a couch of many dozens of "pants" ready for the finisher, a bare-legged baby with pinched face is asleep. A fence of piled-up clothing keeps him from rolling off on the floor. The faces, hands, and arms to the elbows of everyone in the room are black with the color of the cloth on which they are working. The boy and the woman alone look up at our entrance. The girls shoot sidelong glances, but at a warning look from the man with the bundle they tread their machines more energetically than ever. The men do not appear to be aware even of the presence of a stranger.

They are "learners," all of them, says the woman, who proves to be the wife of the boss, and have "come over" only a few weeks ago. . . . The learners work for week's wages, she says. How much do they earn? She shrugs her shoulders with an expressive gesture. The workers themselves, asked in their own tongue, say indifferently, as though the question were of no interest: from two to five dollars. . . .

We have reached Broome Street. . . . One flight up, we knock at the nearest door. In this room a suspender-maker sleeps and works with his family of wife and four children. . . . Coal at ten cents a small pail, meat at twelve cents a pound, one and a half pounds of butter a week at thirty-six cents, and a quarter of a pound of tea in the same space of time, are items of their house-keeping account as given by the daughter. Milk at four and five cents a quart, "according to quality." The sanitary authorities know what that means, know how miserably inadequate is the fine of fifty or a hundred dollars for the murder done in cold blood by the wretches who poison the babes of these tenements with the stuff that is half water, or swill. Their defence is that the demand is for "cheap milk." . . .

Evening has worn into night as we take up our homeward journey through the streets, now no longer silent. The thousands of lighted windows in the tenements glow like dull red eyes in a huge stone wall. From every door multitudes of tired men and women pour forth for a half-hour's rest in the open air before sleep closes the eyes weary with incessant working. Crowds of half-naked children tumble in the street and on the sidewalk, or doze fretfully on the stone steps. As we stop in front of a tenement to watch one of these groups, a dirty baby in a single brief *garment—yet a sweet, human little baby despite its dirt and tatters— tumbles off the lowest step, rolls over once, clutches my leg with unconscious grip, and goes to sleep on the flagstones, its curly head pillowed on my boot.*

the TRIANGLE FIRE

As the years passed, the immigrants began to shift their labors from small tenement sweatshops to large garment factories, places like the Triangle Shirtwaist Company, off New York City's Washington Square Park.

On the morning of Saturday, March 25, 1911, strollers in the park suddenly spotted a puff of smoke coming from the eighth floor of a building at Greene Street and Washington Place. Five hundred people —most of them Jewish and Italian immigrant girls—were at work inside the building, assembling fashionable women's bodice garments for the Triangle company.

Soon flames erupted and the workers were trapped—the doors had been locked. Within moments, 146 people would be dead, fatally burned or crushed in plunging to the sidewalk.

The blaze would prove a landmark for American industrial relations. Out of the tragedy came factory reform and the flourishing of the International Ladies' Garment Workers Union.

William Shepherd, a reporter for the United Press news agency, was passing by when the fire began. He found a telephone in a store across the street and, watching from a plate-glass window, dictated an account to his editor.

Thud—dead! Thud—dead! Thud—dead!

I call them that because the sound and the thought of death came to me each time at the same instant.

A young man helped a girl to the window sill on the ninth floor. Then he held her out deliberately, away from the building, and let her drop. He held out a second girl the same way and let her drop.

He held out a third girl who did not resist. I noticed that. They were all as unresisting as if he were helping them into a street car instead of eternity. He saw that a terrible death awaited them in the flames, and his was only a terrible chivalry.

He brought another girl to the window. I saw her put her arms around him and kiss him. Then he held her into space—and dropped her. Quick as a flash, he was on the window sill himself. His coat fluttered upwards—the air filled his trouser legs as he came down. I could see he wore tan shoes.

Together they went into eternity. Later I saw his face. You could see he was a real man. He had done his best. We found later that in the room in which he stood, many girls were burning to death. He chose the easiest way and was brave enough to help the girl he loved to an easier death. . . .

They were jammed into the windows. They were burning to death in the windows. One by one the window jambs broke. Down came the bodies in a shower, burning, smoking, flaming bodies, with disheveled hair trailing upward. These torches, suffering ones, fell inertly.

The floods of water from the firemen's hoses that ran into the gutter were actually red with blood. I looked upon the heap of dead bodies and I remembered these girls were the shirtwaist makers. I remembered their great strike of last year in which these same girls had demanded more sanitary conditions and more safety precautions in the shops. These dead bodies were the answer.

For many an immigrant bewildered by the ways of America and overwhelmed by poverty and family crises, *The Jewish Daily Forward* was a friend. Readers of the Yiddish-language newspaper sought advice by writing to "A Bintel Brief"—or letter-to-the-editor—section.

The grief and guilt experienced by the survivors of the Triangle fire were reflected in a letter to the *Forward* from a young woman who had experienced a lifetime of woe.

WORTHY EDITOR:

I am a girl twenty-two years of age, but I've already undergone a great deal in my life. When I was born I already had no father. He died four months before my birth. And when I was three weeks old my mother died too. Grandmother, my mother's mother, took me in and soon gave me away to a poor tailor's wife to suckle me.

I was brought up by the tailor and his wife, and got so used to them that I called them Mother and Father. When I grew up I learned from the tailor how to do hand sewing and machine sewing too.

When I was sixteen my grandmother died and left me her small dilapidated house. The rabbi of the town sold it for me for three hundred rubles and gave me the money.

In time one of the tailor's apprentices fell in love with me, and I didn't reject his love. He was a fine, honest, quiet young man and a good earner. He had a golden character and we became as one body and soul. When I turned seventeen my bridegroom came to me with a plan, that we should go to America, and I agreed.

It was hard for me to take leave of the tailor's good family, who had kept me as their own child, and oceans of tears were shed when we parted.

When we came to America my bridegroom immediately started to work and he supported me. He was faithful and devoted. I'll give you an example of his loyalty: once, during the summer in the terrible heat, I slept on the roof. But it started to rain in the middle of the night and I was soaked through to the bone. I got very sick and had to be taken to the hospital. I was so sick that the doctor said I could be saved only by a blood transfusion. My bridegroom said immediately that he was ready to give me his blood, and so, thanks to him, I recovered.

In time I went to work at the "famous" Triangle shop. Later my bridegroom also got a job there. Even at work he wanted to be with me. My bridegroom told me then, "We will both work hard for a while and then we'll be married. We will save every cent so we'll be able to set up a home and then you'll be a housewife and never go to work in the shop again."

Thus my good bridegroom mused about the golden future. Then there was that terrible fire that took one hundred and forty-seven young blossoming lives. When the fire broke out, the screaming, the yelling, the panic all bewildered me. I saw the angel of death before me and my voice was choked in my throat. Suddenly someone seized me with extraordinary strength and carried me out of the shop.

MINE EYES HAVE SEEN

When I recovered I heard calming voices and saw my bridegroom near me. I was in the street, rescued, and saw my girl friends jumping out of the windows and falling to the ground. I clung to my bridegroom and rescuer, but he soon tore himself away from me. "I must save the girls," he said, and disappeared. I never saw him alive again. The next day I identified him, in the morgue, by his watch, which had my picture pasted under the cover. I fainted and they could hardly bring me to.

After that I lay in the hospital for five weeks, and came home shattered. This is the fourth year that I am alone and I still see before me the horrible scenes of the fire. I still see the good face of my dear bridegroom, also the black burned face in the morgue. I am weak and nervous, yet there is now a young man who wants to marry me. But I made a vow that I would never get married. Besides that, I'm afraid that I will never be able to love another man. But this young man doesn't want to leave me, and my friends try to persuade me to marry him and say everything will be all right. I don't believe it, because I think everything can be all right for me only in the grave.

I decided to write to you. I want to hear your opinion.

Respectfully,
A Faithful Reader

ANSWER: It is senseless for this girl to sacrifice her life in memory of her faithful bridegroom, since this would not bring him back to life. What the earth covers must be forgotten. She has suffered enough in her life already and is advised to take herself in hand and begin her life anew.

"HONEST GRAFT"

The poor, untutored immigrant masses—with a myriad of needs—were seemingly at the mercy of government bureaucrats. But not necessarily. The great urban political machines were happy to provide jobs, buckets of coal, baskets of food. In return, they asked for a vote—if not once on election day, perhaps two or three times.

Tammany Hall, the Manhattan Democratic organization, symbolized the power and corruption of the political bosses. The coarse Boss

Tweed, reputed to have bilked New York City's treasury of millions in the late 1860s and early '70s, would become their archetype.

A quarter-century after Tweed went to jail, another Tammany man —George Washington Plunkitt—explained the ways of politics in interviews he gave to a newspaper reporter.

Everybody is talkin' these days about Tammany men growin' rich on graft, but nobody thinks of drawin' the distinction between honest graft and dishonest graft. There's all the difference in the world between the two. Yes, many of our men have grown rich in politics. I have myself. I've made a big fortune out of the game, and I'm gettin' richer every day, but I've not gone in for dishonest graft—blackmailin' gamblers, saloon-keepers, disorderly people, etc.—and neither has any of the men who have made big fortunes in politics.

There's an honest graft, and I'm an example of how it works. I might sum up the whole thing by sayin': "I seen my opportunities and I took 'em."

Just let me explain by examples. My party's in power in the city, and it's goin' to undertake a lot of public improvements. Well, I'm tipped off, say, that they're going to lay out a new park at a certain place.

I see my opportunity and I take it. I go to that place and I buy up all the land I can in the neighborhood. Then the board of this or that makes its plan public, and there is a rush to get my land, which nobody cared particular for before.

Ain't it perfectly honest to charge a good price and make a profit on my investment and foresight? Of course it is. Well, that's honest graft.

Or, supposin' it's a new bridge they're goin' to build. I get tipped off and I buy as much property as I can that has to be taken for approaches. I sell at my own price later on and drop some more money in the bank.

Wouldn't you? It's just like lookin' ahead in Wall Street or in the coffee or cotton market. It's honest graft, and I'm lookin' for it every day in the year. I will tell you frankly that I've got a good lot of it, too.

I'll tell you of one case. They were goin' to fix up a big park, no matter where. I got on to it, and went lookin' about for land in that neighborhood.

I could get nothin' at a bargain but a big piece of swamp, but I took it fast enough and held on to it. What turned out was just what I counted on. They couldn't make the park complete without Plunkitt's swamp, and they had to pay a good price for it. Anything dishonest in that?

Up in the watershed I made some money, too. I bought up several bits of land there some years ago and made a pretty good guess that they would be bought up for water purposes later by the city.

Somehow, I always guessed about right, and shouldn' I enjoy the profit of my foresight? It was rather amusin' when the condemnation commissioners came along and found piece after piece of the land in the name of George Plunkitt of the Fifteenth Assembly District, New York City. They wondered how I knew just what to buy. The answer is—I seen my opportunity and I took it. . . .

I've told you how I got rich from honest graft. Now, let me tell you that most politicians who are accused of robbin' the city get rich the same way.

They didn't steal a dollar from the city treasury. They just seen their opportunities and took them. That is why, when a reform administration comes in and spends a half million dollars in tryin' to find the public robberies they talked about in the campaign, they don't find them.

The books are always all right. The money in the city treasury is all right. Everything is all right. All they can show is that the Tammany heads of departments looked after their friends, within the law, and gave them what opportunities they could to make honest graft. Now, let me tell you that's never goin' to hurt Tammany with the people. Every good man looks after his friends, and any man who doesn't isn't likely to be popular. . . .

The fact is that a reformer can't last in politics. He can make a show for a while, but he always comes down like a rocket. Politics is as much a business as the grocery or the dry-goods or the drug business. You've got to be trained up to it or you're sure to fail. . . .

I've been studyin' the political game for forty-five years, and I don't know it all yet. I'm learnin' somethin' all the time. How, then, can you expect what they call "business men" to turn to politics all at once and make a success of it? It is just as if I went up to Columbia University and started to teach Greek. They usually last as long in politics as I would last at Columbia.

SHOWDOWN *at* HOMESTEAD

Using the Bessemer process he observed in England, the Scottish-born Andrew Carnegie revolutionized steel production in the United States and became one of the nation's richest men.

Like all the giant figures of industry in the latter half of the nineteenth century, Carnegie was intensely antiunion. When workers struck his Homestead, Pennsylvania, steel plant, his manager, Henry Clay Frick, hired strikebreakers and brought in Pinkerton guards to protect them. In an epic encounter in July 1892, the steelworkers attacked the Pinkertons as they came off barges. The guards were beaten off, seven Pinkertons and two union men dying in the melee.

A reporter for the *Pittsburgh Press* was on the scene.

As the Pinkertons neared the top of the bank, they were helped along with kicks and cuffs. One man received a slap from a woman and attempted to strike back. He was at once hit on the head with a stick and the blood flowed freely. Other women punched the fellows in the ribs with parasols and belabored them with switches. The Pinkertons followed each other closely. Many of them were bald headed, others were well dressed, but most of them were tough-looking. No mercy was shown them. . . . The men were punched by every man that could get a lick at them. The Hungarians were particularly vicious and belted the men right and left. They were knocked on the head and struck in the face. The men plunged wildly onward, begging for the mercy which they received not. No distinction was made. They were hit on the heads with hand-billies and clubs and sticks and stricken to the ground. Onward they plunged, bleeding and dazed.

Upon word of the Pinkerton surrender, a crowd moved to the steel mill's main entrance.

Men, women and children in one confused mass surged rapidly toward the works. Many of the women carried brooms and whips. One old woman who has figured before in many troubles of this kind tottered along carrying a huge black jack in her hands, all the time yelling: "Oh, the dirty black sheep, just let me get my hands on them, the dirty, dirty black sheep." Young women who were mild and gentle-looking stood in their gateways and cried to the men as they rushed by: "Give it to the black sheep, kill them all."

The steelworkers won the battle but lost their war. Aided by the Pennsylvania state militia and strikebreakers brought in later, Carnegie kept his plant open, and it would remain union-free for decades to come.

REVOLT *of the* MINERS

Miners were pioneers in the opening of the West—the California gold country of the Forty-Niners, Colorado's Pike's Peak a decade later, the Black Hills of Dakota in the 1870s, the rowdy Tombstone of 1880s Arizona.

The old mining towns with their saloons and dance halls have an aura of romance for modern America. But as solitary prospectors gave way to vast mining enterprises run by ruthless corporations, there were few rewards for the men with the picks and shovels.

Shoshone County, Idaho, developed into an important mining center in the 1890s. It also became a hotbed of labor unrest as miners, seeing their grievances ignored and the law on the side of management, turned desperate. They set out to destroy their very source of livelihood.

James R. Sovereign, the editor of the *Idaho State Tribune*, published at Wallace, in the Coeur d'Alene area, reported on the events of April 29, 1899.

Saturday last witnessed what might properly be considered the close of a seven years' war. About 10.30 a man on horseback came galloping down Bank street from Canyon Creek, and said, "They are coming." Five minutes later the whistle on the Northern Pacific engine pulling the train from Burke and Gem resounded with its usual regularity. On its 9 freight and ore cars were packed 1,000 men, half of whom were masked and armed with Winchester rifles. . . .

Before the train proceeded to Wardner with its human freight on its mission of destruction, armed men walked the streets in quest of an abundant supply of ammunition. It was evident to all that some of the scenes of 1892 were to be repeated, and this time the Bunker Hill and Sullivan Mining Company at Wardner, 12 miles below Wallace, was to be the victim of a forceful demonstration on the part of the organized miners of the Coeur d'Alenes. . . .

The train reached Wardner at 1 o'clock, and the work of clearing the country of all opposition was begun. A detachment of union miners armed with Winchester rifles was dispatched to the mountain side beyond the mill, and the work of placing under the mill 3,000 pounds of dynamite, taken from the magazine of the Frisco mine at Gem, was commenced. At no time did the demonstration assume the appearance or the attitude of a disorganized mob. All the details were managed with the discipline and precision of a perfectly trained military organization. Each miner participating in the affair either wore a strip of white handkerchief in the buttonhole of his coat or a strip of white cloth tied on his right arm.

Sixty armed scabs in the employ of the Bunker Hill company offered the only resistance, and they only gave expression to the most pitiable and lamentable cowardice. Only a few desultory shots from the miners were necessary to send them fleeing over the mountains. At the same time Mr. Burbidge, manager of the mine, might have been seen running toward Kingston, skulking behind every conceivable object and wringing his hands in the desperation of fear. Probably a more humiliating spectacle has not presented itself to the world since the capture of King Charles, nor a more striking evidence of supreme cowardice than was shown by Mr. Burbidge, who heretofore has displayed the defiant air of a tyrant equaled only by Sir Henry Morgan, the leader of the buccaneers of the Spanish Main.

At 2.30 the arrangements were complete, the dynamite was placed under the mill in three departments, the fuse attached, and all was in readiness for the destruction of one of the largest concentrators in the world, costing the company the enormous sum of $250,000. All miners and friends of the miners were warned to take a safe distance from the work of destruction about to begin. The fuses were lighted, and at 2.36

179

there was an awful crash, and broken machinery and fragments of the building were hurled high into the air. Fifteen seconds later another followed, and in about the same time a third. From the force of the third shot debris was hurled in every direction, and a huge canopy was formed in the heavens. Fragments of machinery and broken timbers rained down upon the ruins for several seconds. The shock of each explosion was terrific and was heard 20 miles away. The work of destruction was complete. The great concentrator was as completely demolished as it could have been if months had been spent in preparing the giant explosives for that purpose. The work was planned and executed by men who have received the training of a lifetime in the handling of dynamite.

The explosion was indeed an awe-inspiring scene, and to the eyewitness, were it not for the horrors of destruction, presented a pyrotechnical display which would satisfy the most expert critic of Fourth of July fireworks.

. . . ominous stillness of a few minutes followed. Winchesters and revolvers were everywhere in evidence. The silence was broken by a single shot from a Winchester from some person on top of one of the cars, followed by a deafening fusillade. For five minutes the rattle of musketry was incessant. It was evident, however, from the beginning of the firing that no harm was intended; that the men were simply celebrating the victory they had secured in the destruction of the Bunker Hill concentrator. In the midst of the firing the enemies gave the starting signal and the train moved slowly toward Wallace. . . .

. . . Ranchers and laboring people living in the valley congregated along the track and cheered the men lustily as they passed along. The train reached Wallace about 4 o'clock, and about a hundred of the people of the city were congregated at the depot to witness its arrival. Mayor Smith had taken the precaution to temporarily close the saloons. . . .

During the desultory firing at Wardner, shortly after the train from Wallace arrived, Jack Smythe, a miner at the Frisco mine, was shot and instantly killed. Some say he was shot by scabs in the employ of the Bunker Hill company, others that he was shot by the striking miners through mistake. James Cheyne, a vanner at the Bunker Hill mill, was shot through the hip and died at the Sacred Heart Hospital in Spokane yesterday morning.

President William McKinley called in federal troops at the request of Governor Frank Steunenberg, who declared martial law and moved to crush the miners' revolt although he had been elected with heavy labor support. Order was restored.

But on December 30, 1905, Steunenberg—by then out of office— was killed by a bomb. The confessed assassin implicated William D. "Big Bill" Haywood, secretary-treasurer of the Western Federation of Miners. Defended by Clarence Darrow, Haywood was found not guilty in a highly publicized trial.

a CROSS of GOLD

Just as the immigrant masses among the steelworkers, miners, and sweatshop laborers were exploited in America's rush to industrial might, so, too, were the small farmers of the South and West buffeted by economic change.

Their grievances gave rise to the Populist Party and its demand for "free silver," a return to a standard using silver in addition to gold coins, in order to expand the money supply, bring the farmers higher prices, and ease their debts.

On the steaming night of June 8, 1896, a congressman from Nebraska named William Jennings Bryan arose at the Democratic National Convention in Chicago to sound the "free-silver" cry.

When the Convention convened, I felt as I always do just before a speech of unusual importance. I usually have a feeling of weakness at the pit of my stomach—a suggestion of faintness. I want to lie down. But this being impossible in the Convention, I got a sandwich and a cup of coffee and devoted myself to these as I waited for the debate to begin. . . .

The excitement of the moment was so intense that I hurried to the platform and began at once. My nervousness left me instantly and I felt as composed as if I had been speaking to a small audience on an unimportant occasion. From the first sentence the audience was with me. My voice reached to the uttermost parts of the hall. . . .

The audience seemed to rise and sit down as one man. At the close of a sentence it would rise and shout, and when I began upon another sentence, the room was as still as a church. There was inspiration in the faces of the delegates. . . .

The audience acted like a trained choir—in fact, I thought of a choir as I noted how instantaneously and in unison they responded to each point made. . . .

Bryan told the Eastern gold-standard interests:

You come to us and tell us that the great cities are in favor of the gold standard; we reply that the great cities rest upon our broad and fertile prairies. Burn down your cities and leave our farms, and your cities will spring up again as if by magic; but destroy our farms and the grass will grow in the streets of every city in the country.

Having behind us the producing masses of this nation and the world, supported by the commercial interests, the laboring interests and the toilers everywhere, we will answer their demand for a gold standard by saying to them: You shall not press down upon the brow of labor this crown of thorns, you shall not crucify mankind upon a cross of gold.

Harry Thurston Peck, a prominent editor and literary critic, watched Bryan throw the delegates into a frenzy.

Until now there had spoken no man to whom that riotous assembly would listen with respect. But at this moment there appeared upon the platform Mr. William Jennings Bryan, of Nebraska. . . . As he confronted the 20,000 yelling, cursing, shouting men before him, they felt at once that indescribable, magnetic thrill which beasts and men alike experience in the presence of a master. Serene and self-possessed, and with a smile upon his lips, he faced the roaring multitude with a splendid consciousness of power. Before a single word had been uttered by him, the pandemonium sank to an inarticulate murmur, and when he began to speak, even this was hushed to the profoundest silence. A mellow, penetrating voice, that reached, apparently without the slightest effort, to the farthermost recesses of that enormous hall, gave utterance to a brief exordium. . . . The repose and graceful dignity of his manner, the courteous reference to his opponents, and the perfect clearness and simplicity of his language, riveted the attention of every man and woman in the convention hall. . . . He spoke with the utmost deliberation, so that every word was driven home to each hearer's consciousness, and yet with an ever-increasing force, which found fit expression in the wonderful harmony and power of his voice. His sentences rang out, now with an accent of superb disdain, and with the stirring challenge of a bugle call. . . . The great hall seemed to rock and sway with the fierce energy of the shout that ascended from twenty thousand throats. . . .

The leaderless Democracy of the West was leaderless no more. Throughout the latter part of his address, a crash of applause had followed every sentence; but now the tumult was like that of a great sea thundering against the dikes. Twenty thousand men and women went mad with an irresistible enthusiasm. This orator had met their mood to the very full. He had found magic words for the feeling which they had been unable to express. And so he had played at will upon their very heart-strings, until the full tide of their emotion was let loose in one tempestuous roar of passion.

The writer Charles Warren would tell of the moments after the speech.

There was a pause. Then occurred a wild and hysterical uprising; waves of deafening cheers and yells swept from end to end of the building and back again, unceasing in their tumult. Delegates stood on chairs, uncontrollable, frenzied. A Georgia delegate suddenly tore away the State's blue-tipped rod, raised it high aloft, and started to rush toward the Nebraska delegation. Indian Territory raced down to follow him with its stick. Illinois, South Dakota, Missouri, Virginia, Alabama, Kentucky, Ohio, Iowa, Tennessee, Mississippi, Michigan, Utah, Nevada, California followed. A grand procession of State rods and delegates started around the delegates' enclosure. Bryan was hoisted upon the shoulders of his followers and carried with it. . . . It was fully thirty-five minutes before quiet was restored.

Bryan's "Cross of Gold" speech, one of the great oratorical flights of American history, brought him the Democratic presidential nomination. But amid the furor, he retained his equanimity, as he would later tell it.

The nomination came on the following day on the fifth ballot. I had been so busy all the forenoon that I had not had time to shave. When the bulletin was brought in announcing my nomination, I knew that the crowd would soon turn from the Convention to my headquarters, and I hurried down to the barber for a shave. I mention this as evidence that I was not excited, but the barber was—so much so that he could hardly handle his razor.

But Bryan was a voice from the old America of farms and small towns. The following November, he would be beaten in the presidential election by William McKinley and his Republican gold-standard forces.

America was now a nation of big cities, of big business. And it was looking not to its heartland but to the world.

Chapter Four

the

INTERNATIONAL STAGE

"*a* SPLENDID LITTLE WAR"

The United States had provoked war with Mexico in the 1840s to fuel "Manifest Destiny," its ambitions for continental expansion. A half-century later, the stakes were international when America went to war with Spain.

The Spanish-American War was ostensibly fought to free Cuba of despotic Spanish rule. But it was certainly a product of the imperialist age—a quest for a global naval presence and for markets in the Pacific, where the Spanish had important interests.

President McKinley was not particularly eager for war. But the "yellow journalism" of William Randolph Hearst and Joseph Pulitzer sensationalizing alleged Spanish atrocities in Cuba, the powerful cries for commercial expansion led by Senator Henry Cabot Lodge and other Republicans, and the muscle-flexing of Assistant Navy Secretary Theodore Roosevelt brought him to the brink.

On January 25, 1898, the battleship *Maine* dropped anchor off Havana, its mission reported to be protection of American citizens in Cuba.

On the evening of February 15, an explosion rocked the *Maine*, killing 260 crewmen. Spain maintained that something inside the ship had blown up, but the United States claimed that it had hit a Spanish mine.

On April 25, what Secretary of State John Hay would call "A Splendid Little War" got under way amid cries of "Remember the *Maine.*"

Charles Sigsbee, the captain of the *Maine*, was writing a note that February night when the harbor shook.

I was in my quarters, sitting on the after-side of the table in the admiral's cabin. . . .

I had completed a report called for by Mr. Theodore Roosevelt, Assistant Secretary of the Navy, on the advisability of continuing to place torpedo-tubes on board cruisers and battle-ships. I then wrote a letter home. . . .

At taps ("turn in and keep quiet"), ten minutes after nine o'clock, I laid down my pen to listen for the notes of the bugle, which were singularly beautiful in the oppressive stillness of the night. The marine bugler, Newton, who was rather given to fanciful effects, was evidently doing his best. During his pauses the echoes floated back to the ship with singular directness, repeating the strains of the bugle fully and exactly. . . .

I was inclosing my letter in its envelope when the explosion came. . . . It was a bursting, rending, and crashing roar of immense volume, largely metallic in character. It was followed by a succession of heavy, ominous, metallic sounds, probably caused by the overturning of the central superstructure and by falling debris. There was a trembling and lurching motion of the vessel, a list to port, and a movement of subsidence. The electric lights went out. Then there was intense blackness and smoke.

The situation could not be mistaken: The Maine was blown up and sinking. For a moment the instinct of self-preservation took charge of me, but this was immediately dominated by the habit of command. I went up the inclined deck into the starboard cabin. . . . My first intention was to escape through an air-port, but this was abandoned in favor of the more dignified way of making an exit through the passageway leading forward through the superstructure. . . .

It was soon necessary to retire from the main-deck, for the afterpart of the ship was sinking rapidly. I then went up on the poop-deck. . . .

The flames increased in the central superstructure, and Lieutenant-Commander Wainwright . . . went forward on the poop-awning, making a gallant inspection in the region of the fire, but was soon obliged to report that nothing could be done. The fire-mains and all other facilities were destroyed, and were not available for the service.

We then began to realize more clearly the full extent of the damage. One of the smoke-stacks was laying in the water on the starboard side. . . . As my eyes became more accustomed to the darkness, I could see, dimly, white forms on the water, and hear faint cries for help. Realizing that the white forms were our own men, boats were lowered at once and sent to the assistance of the injured and drowning men. . . .

Presently Lieutenant-Commander Wainwright came to me and reported that our boats had returned alongside the ship at the stern, and that all the wounded that could be found had been gathered in and sent

*to the Spanish cruiser [Alfonso XII] and the City of Washington [a
steamer] and elsewhere. . . .*

*It was a hard blow to be obliged to leave the Maine; none of us desired
to leave while any part of her poop remained above water. We waited
until satisfied that she was resting on the bottom of the harbor. Lieutenant-Commander Wainwright then whispered to me that he thought the
forward ten-inch magazine had been thrown up into the burning material
amidships and might explode at any time, with further disastrous effects.
He was then directed to get everybody into the boats, which was done.
It was an easy operation, one had only to step directly from the deck into
the boat.*

The next day, Captain Sigsbee went back on board and surveyed
the wreckage.

*The forward part of the central superstructure had been blown upward
and somewhat to starboard, and had folded back on its afterpart, carrying
the bridge, pilothouse, and six-inch gun and conning tower with it, and
completely capsizing them. The broad surface that was uppermost was
the ceiling of the berth deck, where many men had swung from beam to
beam in their hammocks the night before. On the white paint of the
ceiling was the impression of two human bodies—mere dust.*

Clara Barton, the founder and president of the American Red
Cross, was in Havana at the request of President McKinley to oversee
American aid to Cubans whom the Spanish had removed to coastal
concentration camps. She was completing paperwork in an apartment
overlooking the harbor when the explosion occurred.

*The house had grown still; the noises on the street were dying away,
when suddenly the table shook from under our hands, the great glass
door opening on to the veranda, facing the sea, flew open; everything in
the room was in motion or out of place. The deafening roar was such a
burst of thunder as perhaps one never heard before. And off to the right,
out over the bay, the air was filled with a blaze of light, and this in turn
filled with black specks like huge specters flying in all directions. Then it*

faded away, the bells rang, the whistles blew, and voices in the street were heard for a moment; then all was quiet again. I supposed it to be the bursting of some mammoth mortar, or explosion of some magazine. A few hours later came the terrible news of the disaster. . . .

We proceeded to the Spanish hospital, San Ambrosia, to find thirty or forty wounded, bruised, cut, burned; they had been crushed by timbers, cut by iron, scorched by fire, and blown sometimes high in the air, sometimes driven down through the red hot furnace room and out into the water, senseless, to be picked up by some boat and gotten ashore. Their wounds were all over them—heads and faces terribly cut, internal wounds, arms, legs, feet and hands burned to the live flesh.

I thought to take the names as I passed among them, and drawing near to the first in the long line, I asked his name. He gave it with his address; then peering out from among the bandages and cotton about his breast and face, he looked earnestly at me and asked: "Isn't this Miss Barton?" "Yes." "I thought it must be. I knew you were here, and thought you would come to us. I am so thankful for us all."

I passed on from one to another, till twelve had been spoken to and the names taken. There were only two of the number who did not recognize me. Their expressions of grateful thanks, spoken under such conditions, were too much. I passed the pencil to another hand and stepped aside.

the ROUGH RIDERS

Theodore Roosevelt quit his naval post, obtained an army commission as a lieutenant colonel, and organized a cavalry outfit known as the Rough Riders.

On July 1, 1898, Roosevelt and his men charged up Kettle Hill and then fought on San Juan Heights above Santiago.

Roosevelt described the prelude to battle in a letter to Senator Henry Cabot Lodge.

For the first hour of the last battle we had a very uncomfortable time. We were lying in reserve under orders, where the bullets of the enemy reached us, and man after man was killed or wounded. I lay on the bank by Lieut. Haskell, talking with him. Finally he did not answer some question of mine; I turned to find that he had been shot through the stomach. I gave an order to one of my men, who stood up and saluted and then fell over my knees with a bullet through his brain. But then came the order to advance, and with it my "crowded hour"; for there followed the great day of my active life. . . .

In a letter to his commanding officer, General Leonard Wood, Roosevelt told what happened next.

The regiment was deployed on both sides of the road, and moved forward until we came to the rearmost lines of the regulars. We continued to move forward until I ordered a charge, and the men rushed the blockhouse and rifle pits on the hill to the right of our advance. They did the work in fine shape, though suffering severely. . . .

We then opened fire on the intrenchments on a hill to our left which some of the other regiments were assailing and which they carried a few minutes later. Meanwhile we were under a heavy rifle fire from the intrenchments along the hills to our front, from whence they also shelled us with a piece of field artillery until some of our marksmen silenced it. When the men got their wind we charged again and carried the second line of intrenchments with a rush. Swinging to the left, we then drove the Spaniards over the brow of the chain of hills fronting Santiago. . . . The Spaniards made one or two efforts to retake the line, but were promptly driven back.

. . . that night we dug a line of intrenchments across our front, using the captured Spaniards' intrenching tools. We had nothing to eat except what we captured from the Spaniards; but their dinners had fortunately been cooked, and we ate them with relish, having been fighting all day. We had no blankets and coats, and lay by the trenches all night. The Spaniards attacked us once in the night, and at dawn they opposed a heavy artillery and rifle fire. . . . The Spanish Mauser bullets made clean wounds; but they also used a copper-jacketed or brass-jacketed bullet which exploded, making very bad wounds indeed. . . .

We went into the fight about 490 strong, 86 were killed or wounded, *and there were about half a dozen missing. The great heat prostrated nearly 40 men, some of them among the best in the regiment. . . .*

The guerrillas in trees not only fired at our troops, but seemed to devote themselves especially to shooting at the surgeons, the hospital assistants with Red Cross badges on their arms, the wounded who were being carried in litters, and the burying parties. Many of the guerrillas were dressed in green uniforms. We sent out a detail of sharpshooters among those in our rear, along the line where they had been shooting the wounded, and killed thirteen. . . .

To attempt to give a list of the men who showed signal valor would necessitate sending in an almost complete roster of the regiment. . . .

But the most conspicuous gallantry was shown by Trooper Rowland. He was wounded in the side in our first fight, but kept in the firing line. He was sent to the hospital next day, but left it and marched out to us, overtaking us, and fought all through this battle with such indifference to danger that I was forced again and again to rate and threaten him for running needless risk.

Great gallantry was also shown by four troopers whom I cannot identify, and by Trooper Winslow Clark, of G. It was after we had taken the first hill—I had called out to rush the second, and, having by that time lost my horse, climbed a wire fence and started toward it. After going a couple of hundred yards, under heavy fire, I found that no one else had come; as I discovered later, it was simply because in the confusion, with men shooting and being shot, they had not noticed me start. I told the five men to wait a moment, as it might be misunderstood if we all ran back, while I ran back and started the regiment; and as soon as I did so the regiment came with a rush. But meanwhile the five men coolly lay down in the opening, returning the fire from the trenches. It is to be wondered at that only Clark was seriously wounded, and he called out, as we parted again, to lay his canteen where he could reach it, but to continue the charge and leave him where he was. All the wounded had to be left until after the fight, for we could spare no men from the firing line.

Though effusive in praising his men, Roosevelt considered his own conduct to have been rather heroic and pressed for the Medal of Honor.

When he didn't get it, he poured out his bitterness in a letter to Senator Lodge.

> . . . the War Department does not intend that I shall have the Medal of Honor. If I didn't earn it, then no commissioned officer ever can earn it. I was not acting in accordance with orders. I had been told to support the attack of the Regulars with my regiment. I moved through the 9th Regiment, of my own accord, and gave the order to charge, and led in person that portion of the line on horseback, being the first man on the Hill, and killing a Spaniard with my own hand. I led in person the next charge on the second line of block-houses; I led in person the third charge; and then at the extreme front commanded the fragments of the six cavalry regiments and brigade until the next morning. . . . [T]hough I had commanded a brigade, and though I had been singled out in reports for special commendation, I was given no brevert rank. For this I don't care, but I am entitled to the Medal of Honor, and I want it.

The storied affair of the Rough Riders would propel Roosevelt to the New York governor's mansion and ultimately the White House. But he never did receive the Medal of Honor. Almost a half-century later, it would be awarded posthumously to his son General Theodore Roosevelt, Jr., who at age fifty-six rallied troops of the Fourth Division in the confused Utah Beach landing on D-Day, then died a month afterward of a heart attack.

REMEMBERING the MAINE

The Spanish-American War lasted only three months, but it yielded a rich international harvest for the United States—possession of Cuba, Puerto Rico, the Philippines, Guam, and Wake Island, all former outposts of the crumbling Spanish Empire.

A decade later, a poignant finale would be written to the story of the Maine.

In 1911, Congress appropriated funds to move her from the bottom of Havana Harbor and then scuttle her at sea. The job was given to

"Dynamite" Johnny O'Brien, a native New Yorker who had become chief of the Havana Harbor pilots. (He got the nickname by carrying a cargo of explosives to Panamanian revolutionaries in 1888.) On March 16, 1912, officials crowded the navy tug *Osceola* and two smaller tugs steering the *Maine*'s wreckage into the ocean as O'Brien directed the operation from what had once been the battleship's superstructure.

The harbor was smooth and there was not enough wind to bother. From the masthead floated the Stars and Stripes, the biggest and handsomest navy ensign I think I ever saw. . . . As I stood alone under the colors there came to me a sudden realization of the wonder of this ceremony in which I was taking part, the like of which the world had never seen nor was likely to see again. I looked across that desolate deck, and there rose in my mind a picture of it bristling with cannon and crowded with strong sailormen, and I never felt so much like crying in my life.

We passed slowly down the line of warships, rails lined with sailors and marines standing at attention, waiting to fall in behind us. . . . To starboard the gray walls of the great Cabana fortress, its ramparts lined with soldiers and its cannon firing minute-guns. A little farther was the historic Morro swarming with spectators. To port was the city of Havana, whose whole population seemed to be thronging the roofs and sea walls. Astern was the escort fleet falling into line, the warships leading, and everywhere the flags were at half-mast.

Four miles out, the procession halted.

At last came the three whistles from the North Carolina, *signaling that the voyage was over, and only the last sad rites remained to be performed. These were delayed a little while to permit all of the vessels of the escort fleet to arrive and group themselves around the grave of the* Maine.

A tug put the working crew aboard again, and at a signal from the Osceola *they opened the sea-cocks in the ship's bottom and raised the sluiceways in the bulkhead and returned to the boat, leaving me again alone. I took one last look around to see that nothing had been forgotten and then signaled the pilot boat to come alongside, dropped onto her, and stood by to wait for the end.*

In 1976, Rear Admiral Hyman G. Rickover investigated the *Maine* disaster, using modern technology to supplement the evidence at hand back in 1898. He concluded that the Spanish were evidently truthful in denying that a mine had blown up the battleship. The most likely source of the explosion, said Rickover, was internal: heat from a fire in the ship's coal bunker adjacent to stored ammunition.

WINGS OVER KITTY HAWK

The inspiration was spawned at a turn-of-the-century bicycle shop in Dayton, Ohio.

Orville and Wilbur Wright, sons of a Protestant bishop, with little formal education but keen mechanical minds, had been tinkering with wheels and sprockets. Soon they began gliding for sport. In 1901, the brothers built a wind tunnel and began aerodynamic experiments. The next step—designing a motor-driven plane.

After a host of mishaps, they took their biplane to a spot where the hills, winds, and sands seemed just right—the North Carolina Outer Banks at Kitty Hawk.

On the frosty morning of December 17, 1903, as Wilbur ran alongside shouting encouragement, Orville lifted off into a stiff headwind from the northeast.

During the night of December 16, 1903, a strong cold wind blew from the north. When we arose on the morning of the 17th, the puddles of water, which had been standing about camp since the recent rains, were covered with ice. The wind had a velocity of 22 to 27 miles an hour. We thought it would die down before long, but when ten o'clock arrived, and the wind was as brisk as ever, we decided that we had better get the machine out. . . .

Wilbur having used his turn in the unsuccessful attempt on the 14th, the right to the first trial now belonged to me. Wilbur ran at the side, holding the wing to balance it on the track. The machine, facing a 27-mile wind, started very slowly. Wilbur was able to stay with it till it lifted from the track after a forty-foot run.

The course of the flight up and down was exceedingly erratic. The control of the front rudder was difficult. As a result the machine would rise suddenly to about ten feet, and then as suddenly dart for the ground. A sudden dart when a little over 120 feet from the point at which it rose into the air ended the flight. This flight lasted only 12 seconds, but it was nevertheless the first in the history of the world in which a machine carrying a man had raised itself by its own power into the air in full flight, had sailed forward without reduction of speed, and had finally landed at a point as high as that from which it started.

Wilbur started the fourth and last flight at just 12 o'clock. The first few hundred feet were up and down as before, but by the time three hundred feet had been covered, the machine was under much better control. The course for the next four or five hundred feet had but little undulation. However, when out about eight hundred feet the machine began pitching again, and, in one of its darts downward, struck the ground. The distance over the ground was measured and found to be 852 feet; the time of the flight 59 seconds.

A decade later, primitive fighter planes and bombers transformed the flying machine into an instrument of war. But sixty-six years after Kitty Hawk, a swatch of cloth used to cover the Wright brothers' wing—put together on their mother's sewing machine—would be carried on a journey of peace: Neil Armstrong took it to the moon.

the RISE *of* THEODORE ROOSEVELT

On September 6, 1901, six months into his second term, President William McKinley was host for a public reception opening the Pan American Exposition at Buffalo. As McKinley greeted a line of visitors, an anarchist named Leon Czolgosz fired two shots into his stomach. McKinley died eight days later, at the age of fifty-eight.

Samuel Ireland was one of two Secret Service agents guarding the President.

A few moments before Czolgosz, the assassin, approached, a man came along with three fingers of his right hand tied up in a bandage, and he had shaken hands with his left. When Czolgosz came up I noticed he was a boyish-looking fellow, with an innocent face, perfectly calm, and I also noticed that his right hand was wrapped up in what appeared to be a bandage. I watched him closely, but was interrupted by the man in front of him, who held on to the President's hand an unusually long time. This man appeared to be an Italian, and wore a heavy black mustache. He was persistent, and it was necessary for me to push him along so that the others could reach the President.

Just as he released the President's hand, and as the President was reaching for the hand of the assassin, there were two quick shots. Startled for a moment, I looked and saw the President draw his right hand up under his coat, straighten up, and, pressing his lips together, give Czolgosz the most scornful and contemptuous look possible to imagine. At the same time I reached for the young man and caught his left arm. The big negro standing just in back of him, and who would have been next to take the President's hand, struck the young man in the neck with one hand, and with the other reached for the revolver, which had been discharged through the handkerchief, and shots from which had set fire to the linen.

Immediately a dozen men fell on the assassin and bore him to the floor. While on the floor Czolgosz again tried to discharge the revolver, but before he could point it at the President it was knocked from his hand by the negro. . . . On the way down to the station Czolgosz would not say a word, but seemed greatly agitated.

The nation may have been mourning its assassinated president, but his successor shed few tears. Ascending from the vice-presidency at age forty-two, now the youngest president in American history, Theodore Roosevelt was bursting with energy and reveling in what he would call the "bully pulpit."

Roosevelt's mood was captured by one of the leading reform journalists of the era, Lincoln Steffens.

The gift of the gods to Theodore Roosevelt was joy, joy in life. He took joy in everything he did, in hunting, camping, and ranching, in politics, in reforming the police or the civil service, in organizing and commanding the Rough Riders. . . .

But the greatest joy in T.R.'s life was his succession to the presidency. I went to Washington to see him; many reformers went there to see the first reformer president take charge. . . .

And he understood, he shared, our joy. He was not yet living in the White House. He used the offices, which were then in the main building, upstairs on the second floor; he worked there by day, but he had to go home at night to his own residence till the McKinleys were moved out and the White House was made ready for Mrs. Roosevelt. His offices were crowded with people, mostly reformers, all day long, and the president did his work among them with little privacy and much rejoicing.

He strode triumphant around among us, talking and shaking hands, dictating and signing letters, and laughing. Washington, the whole country, was in mourning, and no doubt the president felt that he should hold himself down; he didn't; he tried to, but his joy showed in every word and movement. I think that he thought he was suppressing his feelings and yearned for release, which he seized when he could.

One evening after dusk, when it was time for him to go home, he grabbed William Allen White with one hand, me with the other, and saying, "Let's get out of this," he propelled us out of the White House into the streets, where, for an hour or more, he allowed his gladness to explode. With his feet, his fists, his face and with free words he laughed at his luck. He laughed at the rage of Boss Platt and at the tragic disappointment of Mark Hanna; these two had not only lost their President McKinley but had been given as a substitute the man they had thought to bury in the vice-presidency. T.R. yelped at their downfall. And he laughed with glee at the power and place that had come to him.

The assassination of McKinley had affected him, true, but in a romantic way. He described what he would do if an assassin attacked him. He looked about him in the shadows of the trees we were passing under—

he looked for the dastardly coward that might pounce upon him, and, it seemed to me, he hoped the would-be murderer would appear then and there—say at the next dark corner—as he described, as he enacted, what he, the president, would do to him, with his fists, with his feet, with those big, clean teeth. It would have frightened the assassin to see and hear what it was T.R. would have done to him; it may have filled Bill White with terror; what I sensed was the passionate thrill the president was actually finding in the assassination of his assassin.

Roosevelt was an economic conservative but knew that reforms were needed to save the capitalist system. Drawing upon the Populist and Progressive movements, he employed federal power to curb the huge industrial trusts, strike at adulterated foods, and conserve natural resources.

Thanks to hectoring from Lincoln Steffens, Roosevelt's policies would have a catchword: the Square Deal.

T.R. was a politician much more than he was a reformer; in the phraseology of the radicals, he was a careerist, an opportunist with no deep insight into issues, but he was interesting, picturesque.

I accused him of this superficiality once during his first term, when he was keeping his promise to carry out McKinley's policies. That was his excuse for doing "nothing much." He was "being good" so as to be available for a second term.

"You don't stand for anything fundamental," I said, and he laughed. He was sitting behind his desk; I was standing before it. He loved to quarrel amiably with his friends, and it was hard to hit him. So now, to get in under his guard and land on his equanimity, I said with all the scorn I could put into it, "All you represent is the square deal."

"That's it," he shouted, and rising to his feet, he banged the desk with his hands. "That's my slogan; the square deal. I'll throw that out in my next statement. The square deal." And he did.

What did he care how I meant and used it? He knew how it would be taken; he felt in his political sense how all kinds of people would take it as an ideal, as a sufficient ideal, and out he threw it; and he was right.

"A square deal," a phrase shot at him in reproach and criticism, he seized upon and published as his war cry; and a good one, as it proved.

the SAN FRANCISCO EARTHQUAKE

It was 5:12 A.M., April 16, 1906. Enrico Caruso, having performed in *Carmen* at the Grand Opera House of San Francisco the evening before, was jolted from sleep at the Palace Hotel. "I waked up, feeling my bed rocking as though I am in a ship," he would remember. "From the window I see buildings shaking."

Having emerged as a bustling and bawdy town in the Gold Rush days, San Francisco had become the pre-eminent city of the Far West, even an international city of sorts with its polyglot community. But on this day it was virtually destroyed by an earthquake and fire that killed hundreds and left more than 250,000 people homeless.

James Hopper, a reporter for the *San Francisco Call*, joined in the rescue efforts.

The streets were full of people, half-clad, dishevelled, but silent, absolutely silent, as if suddenly they had become speechless idiots. It went down Post Street towards the center of town, and in the morning's garish light I saw many men and women with gray faces. No one spoke. All of them had a singular hurt expression—not one of physical pain, but rather one of injured sensibilities, as if some trusted friend had suddenly wronged them, or as if someone had been rude to them. . . .

A few days later, when I saw a friend who had met me just at this time, he told me that I had been so excited I couldn't talk, that my arms shook and that my eyes were an inch out of their sockets. As I walked slowly down the street, I was very busy taking notes for my paper. "Such and such number, such and such street, cornice down; this building roof down; that building, crumbled." And then I exclaimed, "Good Lord! I'm not going to take a list of ALL the buildings in the city."

It was rather unimportant detail that struck me. In Union Square I saw a man in pink pajamas and pink bathrobe, carrying a pink comforter under his arms, walking barefooted upon the gravel. In the center of the

Square an old man was, with great deliberation, trying to decipher the inscription of the Dewey monument through spectacles from which his lenses had fallen.

I cut across the Square and for the first time heard someone speak. A man said to me "Look!" I looked the way he was pointing, at a three-story wooden building called the Geary, which stood between an unfinished building at the corner of Stockton and Geary Streets and another tall building. The two skyscrapers had shaken off their side walls onto the wooden one nestling between them, and only the facade of the latter stood, like cardboard scenery.

A man stood at one of the windows, trailing to the ground a long piece of cloth that looked no thicker than a ribbon, with the evident intention of sliding down it. I shouted to him to wait a moment, and ran to the door. I found the stairs still intact, stuck along the front wall as if with mucilage.

I scrambled up to the third floor over piles of plaster and laths, and there forgot about the man. For I came to a piece of room in which I found a bed covered with debris. A slim white hand and wrist reached out of the debris, like an appeal.

I threw off the stuff, and found a woman underneath still alive, a little, slender thing whom I had no trouble carrying down to the sidewalk, where someone put her in an express wagon. I went back with another man and we found a second woman, whom we took down on a door. There was another woman in another corner, covered by a pile of bricks. She was dead.

By this time the ruins were fairly swarming with rescuers, and a policeman had to drive many of them away with his club. All the time, however, I could hear a mysterious wailing somewhere in the back. Finally I located it on the second floor. . . . [O]n a platform amid the ruins, a woman with long dishevelled hair was pacing to and fro, repeating in a long, drawn-out wail, over and over again, "Oh, my husband is dead, and a young man is dead, and a woman is dead. . . ."

"Where is your husband?" we roared in her ear, for she seemed unable to hear us. She pointed toward the back. We went toward the back and came to an abrupt end of the hall.

Above us the walls of the homicidal building towered. After a while a *fireman joined us. He seemed stupefied, and like us began to pick up bricks one by one. Finally another fireman came and called him. "Come on, Bill," he said. "There's fires."*

They went off, and then, after we had worked a time longer, a red-headed youth who was digging with us said, "What's de use of diggin out those that's dead?"

His remark struck us all as being so profoundly true that without another word, we all quit.

"*the* BIRTH *of a* NATION"

The motion picture emerged as a popular art form when D. W. Griffith's *The Birth of a Nation* opened at the Liberty Theater in New York City on March 3, 1915.

The two-hour-forty-minute epic, dramatizing American life from the antebellum period through Reconstruction, has been castigated for bigoted racial imagery. Adapted from *The Clansman*, a novel by Thomas Dixon, the movie is said to have helped revive the Ku Klux Klan's influence. But Griffith's stylistic achievements, packing great emotional impact, represented a milestone for the movie industry. And his influence extended well beyond America. A decade later, the renowned Russian filmmaker Sergei Eisenstein would pay tribute to Griffith for his use of devices such as close-ups, varied screen sizes, and symbolic imagery.

A fledgling actor named Joseph Henabery, who would become a leading director, played Abraham Lincoln in *The Birth of a Nation*. Long afterward, he remembered how he persuaded Griffith to give him the part though he was only in his twenties.

Griffith had seen me at rehearsals, and he knew that I'd had some experience. He looked me over from head to foot. I was taller than average, thinner in those days than I am now, and I had a long face. Everybody seems to think that Lincoln had a very long face—which he hadn't. His cheekbones were very wide.

Griffith looked at me and said: "Have you ever made up for Lincoln?"

I said: "Yes, sir." I didn't tell him I'd only made up in private! He called his assistant over. "Get the Lincoln outfit and let this fellow make up."

I worked most all of the afternoon, putting on the make-up. When I came out, people stared at me in amazement; it was the dead come to life. I went over to the open stage where Griffith was working, and got into a position where he could see me.

In those days, a stage was a large platform open to the sky. Overhead were muslin diffusers, which could be drawn across the set to soften the direct glare of the sun.

I just stood on this stage, waiting. Every so often, as Griffith worked with people, he would turn, study me in great detail, and then go back to his work. He did this four or five times. Meanwhile, I was standing there in the boiling hot sun, with heavy clothes and padding in certain places, with a wig, a false nose, spirit gum, hair—I was just roasting.

But he didn't say anything to me, so I thought he didn't much care about it and I left the stage and took off the make-up. Next day, I was out on the lot again and the assistant came up and said, "Where were you yesterday?"

"I was on the stage there."

"Mr. Griffith wanted to see you!"

"He saw me half a dozen times."

"Well, go and put that make-up on again."

I didn't mind; they were paying me five dollars every time I put it on. . . .

The first scenes were not on the Ford's Theater set but in an office of the White House where I was to do a scene with Ralph Lewis, who played Senator Stoneman.

I had no instructions, no script, no idea what I was supposed to do. By this time I was full of Lincoln's story. I had read many books about him, and I knew his physical characteristics, his habits and everything else. And I sat in the chair on my tailbone, sort of hunchbacked. Griffith looked down at me with a frown.

"Don't sit like that," he said.

Now at this time Griffith was such an outstanding figure in the motion-picture business that he was surrounded by a great many yes men. Everything he did, it was: "Yes Mr. Griffith, yes Mr. Griffith." No one was contradictory. By nature, I'm a little combative. I've a lot of Irish in me, and if I'm right I don't mind speaking my piece.

So I said, "Mr. Griffith, I'm sitting in the most frequently mentioned position that Abraham Lincoln sat in. They say that he sat down on his tailbone, with his knees up, like this."

Now Griffith couldn't soak himself in details about every one of his characters, as I could with Lincoln. And he realized that I knew my facts.

"Get a board," he ordered. "Get a board and put it under his feet. Get two boards—make his knees come up high."

He knew that you have to exaggerate sometimes in order to convey an idea.

His attitude changed. He began to relax. He looked a little happier. I think he felt maybe he hadn't picked as much of a lemon as he'd thought. Now he described a part of the scene in which I was supposed to sign some papers on the desk.

"May I say something, Mr. Griffith?" I said. "The books on Lincoln say that when he wrote, or read, it was customary for him to wear glasses."

"Well, have you got them?"

"Yes, sir." I'd dug up an old-fashioned pair of steel-rimmed specs. I showed them to him.

"Use them," he said.

So when the paper was put down I made it part of my business to fish around for my glasses, to take my time putting them on, and then to sign the paper.

Well, now he's happy. He realizes that I have studied the character, and that I know something about the period. When it came to the Ford's Theater scenes, he'd tell me what he was going to do in the long shots, and I'd tell what I'd read that Lincoln would be doing.

Griffith's attitude was simple: "If somebody has made an effort to study his part, then I'm going to make use of what knowledge he has acquired."

When the Lincoln part was finished, I did thirteen bit parts. In one sequence I played in a group of renegade colored people, being pursued by white people—and I was in both groups, chasing myself through the whole sequence. . . .

I'll never forget that first big showing. It was here in Los Angeles, and the picture was still called The Clansman. *The audience was made up largely of professional people—the whole industry's first big showing.*

I have never heard at any exhibition—play, concert or anything—an audience react at the finish as they did at the end of The Clansman. *They literally tore the place apart. Why were they so wildly enthusiastic? Because they felt in their inner souls that something had really grown and developed—and this was a kind of fulfillment.*

the SUFFRAGISTS

Around the turn of the century, women began winning the vote in a number of states, participating in an activist movement with international impact. Suffragists in America were making gains that paralleled the campaigns of British women. But universal women's suffrage in America would be won only after much struggle.

Some ten thousand women protested at the 1913 presidential inaugural of Woodrow Wilson, who opposed giving women the vote. After Wilson was elected to a second term, demonstrations were staged outside the White House. In June 1917, there were mass arrests on charges of "obstructing traffic." Ninety-seven women were sentenced to up to six months in jail. Sent to a workhouse, they were physically abused, often put into solitary confinement, and subjected to force-feeding when they refused to eat.

Mary I. Nolan was one of them.

It was about half past seven at night when we got to Occoquan workhouse. A woman [Mrs. Herndon] was standing behind a desk when we were brought into this office, and there were five or six men in the room. Mrs. Lewis, who spoke for all of us . . . said she must speak to Whittaker, the superintendent of the place.

"You'll sit here all night then," said Mrs. Herndon.

I saw men begin to come upon the porch, but I didn't think anything about it. Mrs. Herndon called my name, but I did not answer.

Suddenly the door literally burst open and Whittaker burst in like a tornado; some men followed him. We could see a crowd of them on the porch. They were not in uniform. They looked as much like tramps as anything. They seemed to come in—and in—and in. One had a face that made me think of an ourang-outang. Mrs. Lewis stood up. Some of us had been sitting and lying on the floor, we were so tired. She had hardly begun to speak, saying we demanded to be treated as political prisoners, when Whittaker said:

"You shut up. I have men here to handle you." *Then he shouted, "Seize her!" I turned and saw men spring toward her, and then some one screamed, "They have taken Mrs. Lewis."*

A man sprang at me and caught me by the shoulder. I am used to remembering a bad foot, which I have had for years, and I remember saying, "I'll come with you; don't drag me; I have a lame foot." But I was jerked down the steps and away into the dark. I didn't have my feet on the ground. I guess that saved me. I heard Mrs. Cosu, who was being dragged along with me, call, "Be careful of your foot."

Out of doors it was very dark. The building to which they took us was lighted up as we came to it. I only remember the American flag flying above it because it caught the light from a window in the wing. We were rushed into a large room that we found opened on a large hall with stone cells on each side. They were perfectly dark. Punishment cells is what they call them. Mine was filthy. It had no window save a slip at the top and no furniture but an iron bed covered with a thin straw pad, and an open toilet flushed from outside the cell.

In the hall outside was a man called Captain Reems. He had on a uniform and was brandishing a thick stick and shouting as we were shoved into the corridor, "Damn you, get in here."

At the end of the corridor they pushed me through a door. Then I lost my balance and fell against the iron bed. Mrs. Cosu struck the wall. Then they threw in two mats and two dirty blankets. There was no light but from the corridor. The door was barred from top to bottom. The walls and floors were brick or stone cemented over. Mrs. Cosu would not let me lie on the floor. She put me on the couch and stretched out on the floor on one of the two pads they threw in. We had only lain there a few minutes, trying to get our breath, when Mrs. Lewis, doubled over and handled like a sack of something, was literally thrown in. Her head struck the iron bed. We thought she was dead. She didn't move. We were crying over her as we lifted her to the pad on my bed, when we heard Miss Burns call:

"Where is Mrs. Nolan?"

I replied, "I am here."

Mrs. Cosu called out, "They have just thrown Mrs. Lewis in here, too."

At this, Mr. Whittaker came to the door and told us not to dare to speak or he would put the brace and bit in our mouths and the straitjacket on our bodies. We were so terrified we kept very still. Mrs. Lewis was not unconscious; she was only stunned. But Mrs. Cosu was desperately ill as the night wore on. She had a bad heart attack and was then vomiting. We called and called. We asked them to send for our own doctor, because we thought she was dying. They paid no attention. A cold wind blew in on us from the outside, and we three lay there shivering and only half conscious until morning.

"One at a time, come out," we heard someone call at the barred door early in the morning. I went first. I bade them good-by. I didn't know where I was going or whether I would ever see them again. They took me to Mr. Whittaker's office, where he called my name.

"Are you willing to put on prison dress and go to the workroom?" said he.

I said, "No."

"Don't you know that I am Mr. Whittaker, the superintendent?" he asked.

"Is there any age limit to your workhouse?" I said. "Would a woman of seventy-three or a child of two be sent here?"

I think I made him think. He motioned to the guard.

"Get a doctor to examine her," he said.

In the hospital cottage I was met by Mrs. Herndon and taken to a little room with two white beds and a hospital table.

"You can lie down if you want to," she said.

I took off my coat and hat. I just lay down on the bed and fell into a kind of stupor. It was nearly noon and I had had no food offered me since the sandwiches our friends brought us in the courtroom at noon the day before.

The doctor came and examined my heart. Then he examined my lame foot. It had a long blue bruise above the ankle, where they had knocked me as they took me across the night before. He asked me what caused the bruise. I said, "Those fiends when they dragged me to the cell last night." It was paining me. He asked if I wanted liniment and I said only hot water. They brought that, and I noticed they did not lock the door. A negro trusty was there. I fell back again into the same stupor.

The next day they brought me some toast and a plate of food, the first I had been offered in over 36 hours. I just looked at the food and motioned it away. It made me sick.

I was released on the sixth day and passed the dispensary as I came out. There were a group of my friends, Mrs. Brannan and Mrs. Morey among others. They had on coarse striped dresses and big, grotesque, heavy shoes. I burst into tears as they led me away.

Wilson's vice-president, Thomas R. Marshall of Indiana, is best remembered for remarking during a desultory Senate debate, "What this country needs is a good five-cent cigar."

Never one to take himself too seriously, Marshall was amused as well by the demands of the suffragists.

His recollection of an encounter with one of the women pressing for the vote reflected the mind-set these crusaders were facing.

One of the most annoying things was the everlasting clatter of the militant suffragettes. . . . The amendment really was submitted to the people in self-defense, to get rid of these women in order that some business might be transacted. They did not call on me very often, however, because it was quite well understood that while I was not opposed to an intelligent woman voting, I was distinctly opposed to universal woman suffrage, and still more strongly opposed to transferring the question of suffrage to the general government. I had two or three interviews, however, which may throw some light on the methods adopted to procure the bill's passage.

One good lady approached me and asked if I could not be for the Suffrage Amendment. She said that I was greatly embarrassing the Democratic women of Indiana; that the Republican senators were for it, and she had decided to see me and ascertain whether I could not advocate it. I told her I could. She brightened up, and said: "Well, that's fine!" I asked her to pause for a moment and answer me whether, if I came out for woman suffrage, she thought that anybody in Indiana would believe I had honestly changed my mind? I called her attention to the fact that I had announced that women had a right to shave and sing bass if they wanted to, but that I was not going to assist in the process. She frankly said she did not think that anybody would believe me. Then I asked her whether she preferred an honest man or a liar? She was the right kind of a woman, and said, so far as she was concerned, I should not be punished for entertaining honest opinions and expressing them.

One night as I came out of the Senate chamber a well-dressed woman stepped up to me, and said: "Mr. Vice-President, how much time have you?" I told her that providence had kindly concealed from my knowledge all information on that subject. She said: "I mean, how much time can you give me?" I said: "That depends on what you desire." She told me that she wanted me to look at her back. I said, "What!" She said: "Yes! I want to show you how I was treated when I was confined in Occoquan for picketing the president." I said: "Madam, you must excuse me! I have no time whatever to give for that purpose. I have reached that age when I confine my examination of backs exclusively to the dinner table!"

While the picketing of the president was going on these enthusiastic women became desirous of adopting the same tactics toward the Senate of the United States. They had some knowledge, however, of the fact that they might find themselves in capital lock-up if they did so without permission. Two of them called on me, therefore, to obtain permission to picket the Senate. I responded by saying that the Congress of the United States had created a Fine Arts Commission; that this commission had exclusive jurisdiction over the erection of works of art in the city of Washington; that nothing could be erected in the public parks and *grounds of the city until the commission had certified that it would beautify and adorn the landscape. I told them if they would take their proposed picketers to this Fine Arts Commission and the commission would certify that they would beautify and adorn the landscape, I would sign a permission therefor; but I warned them that they would have to be better-looking women than those I saw standing in front of the White House, before they could ever hope to obtain this permission.*

They were good sports; laughed it off; went away, I think, satisfied, and the Senate of the United States was saved from marching through an army terrible with banners, proclaiming that what they desired was justice, not mercy.

Thomas Marshall was fighting a losing cause. The Nineteenth Amendment was adopted on August 26, 1920. It stated that "the right of citizens of the United States to vote shall not be denied by the United States or by any State on account of sex."

BIRTH CONTROL PIONEER

Although the Nineteenth Amendment enabled women to participate in political life, they were far from emancipated. Millions were relegated to lives of unremitting domestic toil—while their husbands struggled in back-breaking jobs—as they tried to care for large impoverished families.

In the eyes of Margaret Sanger—herself a product of a large and poor family—women could achieve true economic and social gains, and realize a new sense of dignity, only if they had control over their own bodies.

Sanger established the nation's first birth-control clinic, choosing Brooklyn's Brownsville section, which was teeming with poverty-stricken Jewish-immigrant families.

Working with women who had participated in the suffragist protests, Sanger would ultimately create a national organization battling for safe and reliable contraception, and she would found the International

Planned Parenthood Federation, which by the mid-1990s would have family-planning programs in more than one hundred countries.

But all that was years away. The political and medical establishments would fight her. Federal agents arrested Sanger, and then, one day in 1917, the New York City police arrived at her clinic.

The arrest and raid on the Brooklyn clinic was spectacular. There was no need of a large force of plain clothes men to drag off a trio of decent, serious women who were testing out a law on a fundamental principle. My federal arrest, on the contrary, had been assigned to intelligent men. One had to respect the dignity of their mission; but the New York City officials seem to use tactics suitable only for crooks, bandits and burglars. We were not surprised at being arrested, but the shock and horror of it was that a woman, with a squad of five plain clothes men, conducted the raid and made the arrest. A woman—the irony of it!

I refused to close down the clinic, hoping that a court decision would allow us to continue such necessary work. I was to be disappointed. Pressure was brought upon the landlord, and we were dispossessed by the law as a "public nuisance." In Holland the clinics were called "public utilities."

When the policewoman entered the clinic with her squad of plain clothes men and announced the arrest of Miss Mindell and myself (Mrs. Byrne was not present at the time and her arrest followed later), the room was crowded to suffocation with women waiting in the outer room. The police began bullying these mothers, asking them questions, writing down their names in order to subpoena them to testify against us at the trial. These women, always afraid of trouble which the very presence of a policeman signifies, screamed and cried aloud. The children on their laps screamed, too. It was like a panic for a few minutes until I walked into the room where they were stampeding and begged them to be quiet and not to get excited. I assured them that nothing could happen to them, that I was under arrest but they would be allowed to return home in a few minutes. That quieted them. The men were blocking the door to prevent anyone from leaving, but I finally persuaded them to allow these women to return to their homes, unmolested though terribly frightened by it all.

Crowds began to gather outside. A long line of women with baby carriages and children had been waiting to get into the clinic. Now the streets were filled, and police had to see that traffic was not blocked. The patrol wagon came rattling through the streets to our door, and at length Miss Mindell and I took our seats within and were taken to the police station.

As I sat in the rear of the car and looked out on that seething mob of humans, I wondered, and asked myself what had gone out of the human race. Something had gone from them which silenced them, made them impotent to defend their rights. I thought of the suffragists in England, and pictured the similar results of an arrest there. But as I sat in this mood, the car started to go. I looked out at the mass and heard a scream. It came from a woman wheeling a baby carriage, who had just come around the corner preparing to visit the clinic. She saw the patrol wagon, realized what had happened, left the baby carriage on the walk, rushed through the crowd to the wagon and cried to me: "Come back! Come back and save me!" The woman looked wild. She ran after the car for a dozen yards or so, when some friends caught her weeping form in their arms and led her back to the sidewalk. That was the last thing I saw as the Black Maria dashed off to the station.

SOLDIER *for the* LORD

"It is a fearful thing to lead this great people into war," President Woodrow Wilson told Congress, "but the right is more precious than peace."

Faced with Germany's unrestricted submarine warfare on American shipping, mindful of the nation's sentimental and economic ties to Britain and France, aroused by a German plot inviting Mexico to recover vast territories lost to America, Wilson ended his long dance with neutrality in the fourth year of Europe's Great War.

On April 2, 1917, he asked Congress for a declaration of war. Now the United States would enter the killing grounds overseas in "the war to end all wars."

The popular belief that America was engaged in a holy crusade gained sustenance from a quiet man who accomplished an extraordinary feat. He was Alvin C. York, a pacifist from the hills of Tennessee, a conscientious objector who ultimately decided he would be doing the Lord's work by fighting in a noble cause.

In the final Allied offensive, at the Argonne Forest, York, armed with a rifle, outshot an entire German machine-gun battalion, killing twenty-five men, and then marched off with 132 prisoners in tow.

This hero of World War I would endure over the next two decades as a symbol of an older America, a pious man who shunned acclaim and returned to his rural roots. During World War II, his exploits would be converted into a Hollywood recruiting poster. Gary Cooper carried out the heroics this time, in the movie *Sergeant York*.

York never wavered in his faith that he would survive combat.

I wasn't excited. . . . My daddy used to tell me that if I ever got into trouble all I had to do was to keep cool and I'd come out. . . .

Somehow I knew I wouldn't be killed. I've never thought I would be —never once from the time we started over here.

After he captured his first batch of prisoners in the encounter that would bring him renown, York, accompanied by his men of Company G, 328th Infantry, faced heavy machine-gun fire.

You never heard such a clatter and racket in all your life. I couldn't see any of our boys. Early and Cutting had run along toward the left in front of me just before the battle started, but I didn't know where they were.

If I'd moved I'd have been killed in a second. The Germans [prisoners] were what saved me. I kept up close to them, and so the fellers on the hill had to fire a little high for fear of hitting their own men. The bullets were cracking just over my head and a lot of twigs fell down.

Well, I fired a couple of clips or so—things were moving pretty lively, so I don't know how many I did shoot—and first thing I knew a boche got up and flung a little bomb at me about the size of a silver dollar. It missed and wounded one of the prisoners on the ground, and I got the boche—got him square.

Next thing that happened, a lieutenant rose up from near one of them machine guns and he had seven men with him. The whole bunch came charging down the hill at me. . . .

I had my automatic out by then and let them have it. Got the lieutenant right through the stomach and he dropped and screamed a lot. All the boches who were hit squealed just like pigs. Then I shot the others. . . .

At that distance, I couldn't miss.

He killed that detachment—eight men—before it could charge twenty yards downhill.

As soon as the Germans saw the lieutenant drop, most of them quit firing their machine guns and the battle quieted down. I kept on shooting, but in a minute here comes the major who had surrendered with the first bunch. I reckon he had done shooting at us himself, because I heard firing from the prisoners and afterward I found out that his pistol was empty.

He put his hand on my shoulder . . . and said to me in English: "Don't shoot any more, and I'll make them surrender." So I said, "All right," and he did so, and they did so.

York then marched back with his growing band of prisoners.

Just as we started I passed the body of Corporal Murray Savage. Him and I were cronies—he was my bunkie—but I had to leave him there. I didn't dare take my eye off the mob of prisoners.

In the next batch of Germans that York encountered, one man resisted. He was gunned down, and then York went on.

I had to shoot a man there. When we hit the next nest and I got ready to settle them if they didn't give up, the major tapped me on the shoulder and said, "Don't kill any more and I'll make them surrender." And he did.

We know there are miracles, don't we? Well, this was one. I was taken care of—it's the only way I can figure it out.

CAPTAIN HARRY GIVES 'EM HELL

The encounter in the Vosges Mountains of eastern France the night of August 29, 1918, was only a skirmish, a forgettable exchange of shells in a relatively quiet sector of the war. But for the men of Battery D, Second Battalion, 129th Field Artillery—an outfit from Kansas City, Missouri—it was the first taste of combat. A sergeant panicked, and the troops began to run away. Only the courage of their commander prevented a rout.

At age thirty-four—with few achievements to look back on and few apparent prospects looming beyond the family farm—Battery D's captain would discover that night that he was a man who could lead other men.

After the war, Captain Harry Truman would return to Missouri, but not to the farm. The prestige he would earn back in Jackson County for bringing its boys home would propel him into politics and a stage far beyond his rural roots.

Paul Shaffer, an Army "runner" who delivered a message to Battery D the evening of its baptism in combat, would remember its commander's derring-do.

I reached the battery in nothing flat, as muddy as an alligator, all the skin off my nose. Captain Harry S. Truman was standing there, his tin hat pushed on the back of his head, directing salvos into some spot toward the northeast. He was a banty officer in spectacles, and when he read my message he started runnin' and cussin' all at the same time, shouting for the guns to turn northwest. He ran about a hundred yards to a little knoll, and what he saw didn't need binoculars. I never heard a man cuss so well or so intelligently, and I'd shoed a million mules. He was shouting back ranges and giving bearings.

The battery didn't say a word. They must have figured the cap'n could do the cussin' for the whole outfit. It was a great sight, like the center ring in Barnum and Bailey at the close of the show, everything clockwork, setting fuses, cutting fuses, slapping shells into breeches and jerking lanyards before the man hardly had time to bolt the door. Shell cases were flipping back like a juggler's act, clanging on tin hats of the ammunition passers, the guns just spitting fire—spit-spit-spit-spit.

Then Captain Truman ran down the knoll and cussed 'em to fire even faster. When he ran back up the hill still cussin', I forgot how I didn't want to get killed and I ran with him, even though my bit tongue was hanging out and a tooth sticking through my lip. I couldn't see our infantry. It must have been driven back to the little knoll, trying to crawl around and change front. Beyond it was some mighty fine grazing land, and at the far end a clump of woods, pretty leaves still on the autumn trees. The leaves were falling fast, shells breaking into them. This time Captain Truman had his binoculars on them. I finally made out what he saw. There were groups of Germans at the edge of the woods, stooping low and coming on slowly with machine guns on their hips, held by shoulder straps. He shouted some cusswords filled with figures down to the battery, and shells started breaking into the enemy clumps. Whole legs were soon flying through the air. He really broke up that counterattack. He was still there being shot at when I came to my senses and got off the knoll.

I went back to the sweating battery, but counterbatteries started ranging. They were looking for me and Captain Truman. I knew he had to move soon and I wished I could stay when he brought up the animals. Being from Topeka, I wanted to hear what a Missouri man had to say to his mules. But it wasn't a safe place for an out-of-work blacksmith. So I went back and told my major how Captain Truman and I had broken up a counterattack, and our infantry was now off the dime. I never saw the cussin' captain again until I voted for him in 1948.

BATTLING *the* RED BARON

The exploits of World War I aviators—their "dog fights" with German fighters, the bombing behind the enemy lines, the shooting down of observation balloons—made for exciting newspaper copy back home.

Although a pilot's life expectancy often proved disastrously short, air combat was indeed thrilling in an era when the target was not pinpointed by a mass of electronic gear but confronted close up.

The American fliers gave an important edge to the Allies. They shot down 927 German airplanes and balloons, losing 316 aircraft themselves.

But at times the aviators found themselves outnumbered, as was Lieutenant Hamilton Coolidge, the pilot of a "pursuit plane" (the forerunner of the fighter) one day in late July 1918. He would write a letter telling what happened.

Nine of us on patrol saw a formation of six Boche planes below and our leader signalled to attack. Just as we started down, however, eighteen more Boches appeared over the edge of the clouds. We saw at once that we were in a bad fix. We swung round as quickly as possible, but they were by this time close "on our tails" and the "tracers" began to fly past us. I don't mind saying I was thoroughly scared—twenty-four against nine is poor odds especially when one is over enemy territory. Looking back I could plainly distinguish every feature of the enemy planes nearest me. They were single seats Fokker biplanes. We became somewhat scattered in our hasty retreat, so I can speak only for myself. I kept my motor wide open and kicked my rudder to and fro which gave my machine a zig-zag motion and made it a difficult target. As luck would have it my plane didn't suffer any bullet holes. Fortunately our Spads are very fast: surely that was all that saved us.

On the first morning of the Meuse-Argonne offensive, which cracked the Hindenburg line in the fall of 1918, Coolidge went up in his pursuit plane.

How my old heart just hammered with excitement as I dove down beside that road, not fifty feet high, and recognized those Boche helmets! In a twinkling I was past them, gained a little height to turn in safety, and came diving down upon them from the rear. I just held both triggers down hard while the fiery bullets flew streaming out of the two guns. Little glimpses was all I could catch before I was by. Another turn and down the line again. I had a vague confused picture of streaming fire, of rearing horses, falling men, running men, general mess. Turn again and back upon them. This time I clearly saw two men heel off the seat of a wagon, then more awful mess. A fourth time I turned and came back. One gun stuck but the incendiaries still blazed on. Horses rearing, on fallen men; wagons crosswise in the road; men again dashing for the gutter. I craned my neck to see more and to be sure not to run into trees or houses beyond. Suddenly a ra-ta-ta-ta and a series of whacks like the crack of a whip broke loose. I knew only too well that the bullets were coming very close to crack that way! I rocked and swung and turned and the rattle died away behind. I found myself trembling with excitement and overawed at being a cold-blooded murderer, but a sense of keen satisfaction came too. It was only the sort of thing our poor doughboys have suffered so often.

On October 27, 1918, by then having been promoted to captain, Coolidge was leading a flight group when he was killed by a German anti-aircraft shell near Grandpré, France. Fifteen days later, World War I was over.

WOODROW WILSON'S FAILED CRUSADE

In January 1918, President Wilson went before Congress to outline his "Fourteen Points"—principles for a peace settlement. Foremost among them was creation of an international body to guarantee political independence and territorial integrity "to great and small states alike"— the League of Nations.

The victorious European Allies grudgingly accepted the league as the price for imposing the harsh Treaty of Versailles upon the Germans. But the Republicans in the Senate, kept out of the treaty negotiations by Wilson, refused to ratify American participation.

Wilson embarked upon a cross-country tour to sell the league to the American people and thereby put pressure on the Senate.

After speaking in Pueblo, Colorado, he suffered a stroke. He would never regain his full health, and the isolationists of the Senate would prevail.

Joseph P. Tumulty, Wilson's secretary, was with him when he was stricken.

About four o'clock in the morning of September 26, 1919, Doctor Grayson knocked at the door of my sleeping compartment and told me to dress quickly, that the President was seriously ill. As we walked toward the President's car, the Doctor told me in a few words of the President's trouble and said that he greatly feared it might end fatally if we should attempt to continue the trip and that it was his duty to inform the President that by all means the trip must be cancelled; but that he did not feel free to suggest it to the President without my cooperation and support.

When we arrived at the President's drawing room I found him fully dressed and seated in his chair. With great difficulty he was able to articulate. His face was pale and wan. One side of it had fallen, and his condition was indeed pitiful to behold. Quickly I reached the same conclusion as that of Doctor Grayson, as to the necessity for the immediate cancellation of the trip, for to continue it, in my opinion, meant death to the President. Looking at me, with great tears running down his face, he said: "My dear boy, this has never happened to me before. I felt it coming on yesterday. I do not know what to do." He then pleaded with us not to cut short the trip. Turning to both of us, he said: "Don't you see that if you cancel this trip, Senator Lodge and his friends will say that I am a quitter and that the Western trip was a failure, and the Treaty will be lost."

Reaching over to him, I took both of his hands and said: "What difference, my dear Governor, does it make what they say? Nobody in the world believes you are a quitter, but it is your life that we must now consider. We must cancel the trip, and I am sure that when the people learn of your condition there will be no misunderstanding." He then tried to move over nearer to me to continue his argument against the cancellation of the trip; but he found he was unable to do so. His left arm and leg refused to function. I then realized that the President's whole left side was paralyzed. Looking at me he said: "I want to show them that I can still fight and that I am not afraid. Just postpone the trip for twenty-four hours and I will be all right."

But Doctor Grayson and I resolved not to take any risk, and an immediate statement was made to the inquiring newspaper men that the Western trip was off.

Never was the President more gentle or tender than on that morning. Suffering the greatest pain, paralyzed on his left side, he was still fighting desperately for the thing that was so close to his heart—a vindication of the things for which he had so gallantly fought on the other side. Grim old warrior that he was, he was ready to fight to the death for the League of Nations.

In the dispatches carried to the country, prepared by the fine newspaper men who accompanied us on the trip, it was stated that evidences of a breakdown on the part of the President were plainly visible in the speech he delivered at Pueblo.

I had talked to him only a few minutes before the delivery of that speech, and the only apparent evidence that he was approaching a breakdown was in his remark to me that he had a splitting headache, and that he would have to cut his speech short. As a matter of fact, this last speech he made, at Pueblo, on September 25, 1919, was one of the longest speeches delivered on the Western trip and, if I may say so, was one of the best and most passionate appeals he made for the League of Nations. . . .

In the peroration of the speech he drew a picture of his visit on Decoration Day, 1919, to what he called a beautiful hillside near Paris, where was located the cemetery of Suresnes, a cemetery given over to the burial of the American dead. As he spoke of the purposes for which those departed American soldiers had given their lives, a great wave of emotion, such as I have never witnessed at a public meeting, swept through the whole amphitheatre. As he continued his speech, I looked at Mrs. Wilson and saw tears in her eyes. I then turned to see the effect upon some of the "hard-boiled" newspaper men, to whom great speeches were ordinary things, and they were alike deeply moved. Down in the amphitheatre I saw men sneak their handkerchiefs out of their pockets and wipe the tears *from their eyes. The President was like a great organist playing upon the heart emotions of the thousands of people who were held spellbound by what he said.*

Wilson's recollection of that cemetery visit:

Behind me on the slopes was rank upon rank of living American soldiers, and lying before me on the levels of the plain was rank upon rank of departed American soldiers. Right by the side of the stand where I spoke there was a little group of French women who had adopted those graves, had made themselves mothers of those dear ghosts by putting flowers every day upon those graves, taking them as their own sons, their own beloved, because they had died in the same cause—France was free and the world was free because America had come!

I wish some men in public life who are now opposing the settlement for which these men died could visit such a spot as that. I wish that the thought that comes out of those graves could penetrate their consciousness. I wish that they could feel the moral obligation that rests upon us not to go back on those boys, but to see the thing through, to see it through to the end and make good their redemption of the world. For nothing less depends upon this decision, nothing less than the liberation and salvation of the world.

Chapter Five

the ROARING TWENTIES, *the* DESPERATE THIRTIES

the BLACK SOX SCANDAL

The decade of the 1920s was a time for publicity stunts, for flappers, for widespread lawbreaking spawned by a ridiculous attempt to make America dry. The questionable sacrifices in World War I, and the rejection of international cooperation with the Senate's spurning of the League of Nations, brought a disillusionment with ideals.

Far afield from power politics, one American institution proved a cynic's delight as the 1920s got under way. It seemed that the "national pastime" had been sullied by gamblers and crooked ballplayers when eight members of the Chicago White Sox were accused of taking bribes to lose the 1919 World Series to the Cincinnati Reds.

"Say it ain't so, Joe"—a young boy's supposed plea to the most talented of the Sox, the illiterate outfielder "Shoeless Joe" Jackson—perfectly reflected the innocence that would soon be lost.

Jackson was called in September 1920 as a witness before a Cook County grand jury. A transcript of his testimony was included in Jackson's signed confession, but that document (along with the confessions of three other players) was stolen from the Illinois state's attorney's office before the trial.

Jackson and his teammates would be found not guilty. Nonetheless, they were barred from baseball for life by Commissioner Kenesaw Mountain Landis, their club labeled the "Black Sox."

The transcript of Jackson's grand-jury appearance eventually resurfaced. It related the player's testimony under questioning from Hartley L. Replogle, the assistant state's attorney.

Q: *Did anybody pay you any money to help throw that Series in favor of Cincinnati?*
A: *They did.*
Q: *How much did they pay you?*
A: *They promised me $20,000 and paid me 5.*
Q: *[Did Mrs. Jackson] know that you got $5,000 for helping throw these games?*
A: *She did . . . yes.*
Q: *What did she say about it?*

A: *She said she thought it was an awful thing to do.*
Q: *That was after the fourth game?*
A: *I believe it was, yes.*
[Jackson said that the White Sox pitcher Lefty Williams was the interme-
diary between him and the gamblers.]
Q: *When did he promise the $20,000?*
A: *It was to be paid after each game.*

Jackson said his $5,000 payoff was thrown onto his hotel bed by Williams after the fourth game. He was asked what he told Williams then.

A: *I asked him what the hell had come off here?*
Q: *What did he say?*
A: *He said [Chick] Gandil [the first baseman and ringleader among the players] said we all got a screw . . . that we got double-crossed. I don't think Gandil was crossed as much as he crossed us.*
Q: *At the end of the first game you didn't get any money, did you?*
A: *No, I did not, no, sir.*
Q: *What did you do then?*
A: *I asked Gandil what is the trouble? He says, "Everything is all right." He had it.*
Q: *Then you went ahead and threw the second game, thinking you would get it then, is that right?*
A: *We went ahead and threw the second game. After the third game I says, "Somebody is getting a nice little jazz, everybody is crossed." He said, well, Abe Attel and Bill Burns [gamblers] had crossed him.*

Jackson was then asked about the fourth game of the Series.

Q: *Did you see any fake plays?*
A: *Only the wildness of Cicotte [pitcher Ed Cicotte, one of the fixers].*
Q: *Did you make any intentional errors yourself that day?*
A: *No, sir, not during the whole Series.*
Q: *Did you bat to win?*
A: *Yes.*

Q: *And run the bases to win?*

A: *Yes, sir.*

Q: *And field the balls at the outfield to win?*

A: *I did. . . . I tried to win all the games.*

Q: *Weren't you very much peeved that you only got $5,000 and you expected to get 20?*

A: *No, I was ashamed of myself.*

Q: *Where did you put the $5,000?*

A: *I put it in my pocket.*

Q: *What did Mrs. Jackson say about it?*

A: *She felt awful bad about it, cried about it a while.*

Q: *Had you ever played crooked baseball before?*

A: *No, sir, I never had.*

Q: *You think now Williams may have crossed you, too?*

A: *Well, dealing with crooks, you know, you get crooked every way. This is my first experience and last.*

the GREAT THIRST

President Herbert Hoover called it "a great social and economic experiment, noble in motive."

But his agents had an impossible task in policing "the noble experiment" of Prohibition.

It was, of course, gigantic folly. The adoption of the Eighteenth Amendment—making liquor, beer, and wine illegal—served only to moisten the appetite for alcohol and enrich organized criminals who supplied the bootlegged spirits and ran the speakeasies.

The Volstead Act, which was to enforce Prohibition, went into effect on January 17, 1920. Stanley Walker, the city editor of the *New York Tribune*, captured the atmosphere in Manhattan as midnight rang in a supposedly dry America.

New York, home of the great barrooms, the gorgeous hotels, the gaudiest cabarets in all history, had seen it coming, but even now it didn't seem quite real. Old-timers were puzzled, incredulous, and they asked each other: "Will they really try to enforce that damn fool law?" An experienced bartender named Bleeck buttonholed Representative Christopher D. Sullivan, of the East Side Sullivans, and asked: "Christy, are they really going to enforce it?" And Christy replied: "Yes, I think so. There won't be any more liquor." In later years they laughed at the memory of this curiously naive conversation. . . .

As midnight approached the weather became terribly cold. A bitterly chill wind swept around the corners. Snowplows crunched through the streets. . . .

On this last night, down on New York's lower East Side, Louis Zeltner, a character known as "Wireless Louie," at one time an Alderman and at other times a tipster on the strange goings-on in New York City, was master of ceremonies at a wine-bibbing party at Max's Little Hungary. . . .

Uptown, at Maxim's, the waiters were dressed as pallbearers. At Reisenweber's there was a funeral ball, and Louis Fischer, boss of the place, was one of the saddest men in town. The Cafe de Paris, formerly Rector's, gave a Cinderella ball. . . .

It was at about 11:30 on the night of the Sixteenth that an elderly man wearing a gray overcoat walked east across City Hall Park. His friends knew him as Filthy Phil, because he had been out of polite society so long that he could not utter a simple sentence that was not reeking with blasphemy or venery. He was cursing quietly but savagely—at the authors of prohibition and at the unfathomable caprices of Jehovah. Near the statue of Nathan Hale he encountered an acquaintance and together they crossed the park, traversed Nassau Street and went up one flight. There was a bar, a bartender, and glasses and red liquor. Outside was the blizzard; inside, Phil was at home. Always, he said, there would be places like this. He became very drunk.

The Prohibition Bureau's enforcement agents were ripe for payoffs. And if they weren't corrupt, they were comical, à la Izzy and Moe.

Izzy Einstein and Moe Smith, from New York's Lower East Side, were wonderful sources of newspaper copy, staging their raids with a myriad of disguises and a ton of ruses to match.

Izzy would remember how he and ten fellow agents dressed up as amateur football players and entered a Bronx speakeasy filled with sports fans.

There was an establishment right near Van Cortlandt Park where anybody could buy soft drinks but only people who were known personally could buy anything stronger. I noticed, however, that the patrons were a sports crowd—amateur athletes and fans. That was enough for me. On a Saturday in November I got together a little group of men good and true, and we rigged ourselves out in football togs, smeared with fresh mud. And faces to match. In this regalia we burst into the place announcing with a whoop that now, with the last game of the season over and won, we could break training. Would any saloon-keeper refuse drinks to a bunch of football players in that state of mind?

This fellow didn't anyhow. And he discovered that his season was ended too. . . .

On one occasion, Izzy turned musical for a moment.

A place that no outsider could get into and where booze flowed freely among friends was a sort of club frequented by members of the Musicians Union. You had to have a Union card. Fortunately I was able to borrow one and I went there as a musician willing to buy a drink for anybody who would put me on the trail of a job. They asked me what instrument I played. I said a trombone.

"Play something," they told me, "and let's hear how good you are." I said I'd left my instrument at home. But they borrowed one for me and there was nothing left for me to do but play it, which luckily I could. I played "How Dry I Am."

It satisfied them and they told me that if I'd come back that evening maybe they'd have a job for me.

Instead, I returned with a warrant. . . .

Another time, Izzy used a "Tin Lizzie" as a prop.

A battered Ford proved useful to a couple of other agents and myself in getting us into places as well as getting us around. We'd drive up to a saloon or speakeasy and rush inside asking for the loan of a fountain pen to write a check with. I'd explain that Lizzie was being sold down the river, and my companion, who was to write the check, would insist that the $65 he was paying was a tough bargain because of the condition of the front tires. And I'd come back at him saying I'd guarantee they were good for another thousand miles at the least.

At any rate the deal would be closed and I'd accept the check; whereupon all differences of opinion as to the car's worth would be forgotten in the desire for a little drink in honor of Lizzie's new owner. And we'd get it. Likewise the fellow who served it to us.

Then there was the time a bartender thought he could outsmart Izzy.

The trickest spot I ever got into was up the Hudson at Kingston. There was a hotel there opposite the railroad station where I figured I might make a purchase, but the proprietor was suspicious.

"You look to me like Izzy Einstein," he said.

"Like who?" I asked, trying to pretend that I'd never heard of myself. But he wasn't to be put off.

"I've seen pictures of you and I'd know you anywhere," he insisted. I offered to bet him I wasn't.

"Bet nothing," he scoffed. "I know of a better way of settling it than that." He went over to the sandwich shelf and came back with a ham sandwich. "Here," he said, "eat this with the compliments of the house."

I thanked him, took the sandwich and ate it. He didn't see me blow the ham out. Convinced, he sold me a drink. Then I arrested him.

RADIO ARRIVES

The principle behind radio transmissions predated the twentieth century—Guglielmo Marconi had invented "wireless telegraphy" back in 1896—but the inspiration for using radio waves to provide a mass medium for news and entertainment was a long time in coming.

The first commercial radio station went on the air on November 2, 1920, when Westinghouse broadcast the results of the Harding-Cox presidential voting from its newly licensed station KDKA in East Pittsburgh, actually a shack on the roof of one of its buildings.

Leo H. Rosenberg, a member of the Westinghouse publicity department, read the returns, receiving them from the *Pittsburgh Post.*

As the returns came in to the Post, *they were telephoned to the station and recorded by R. S. McClelland and handed to me for reading into the microphone. The private telephone line was constantly monitored by John Frazier, manager of the telephone department of Westinghouse. . . . Periodically, I would say, "If you are hearing this radio broadcast, please send a postcard to L. H. Rosenberg, Publicity Department, Westinghouse Electric and Manufacturing Company, East Pittsburgh, Pennsylvania." Hundreds of cards were received from all over the United States and some foreign countries, even New Zealand. This was remarkable for a 100-watt station. It was due, we were told, to the bouncing effect of the atmospheric waves.*

A youngster named Robert Saudek who lived a few blocks from the Westinghouse "studio" would be enmeshed in KDKA's pioneering. Years later, he looked back on the great adventure.

I was in the choir at the time the first church service was "radiocast." The first time I ever saw a microphone I saw a dozen microphones, each suspended like a bird cage from a kind of bridge lamp.

Into these black cylinders we poured our shrill song. Into these the Reverend Dr. E. J. van Etten poured his gospels, epistles, collects and sermon. Nobody much except the station's engineers could have been listening, since almost the only sets were in stores and they were closed on Sundays; nevertheless, that morning the great performance revolution began. . . .

Bearing in mind that I had thus performed on the radio before I had ever heard one—that I had seen a microphone before I had put on earphones—you will recognize my excitement when my father, a theatre musician, came home and announced that he had been hired to direct an orchestra over KDKA. My own thrill came from two facts: first, that now my father would have to get up in the morning like other fathers (he had always played till midnight and slept until noon), and second, that we would have to own a radio set.

But first he and my grandfather as tenants-in-common bought a used Dodge touring car so Pop could drive to East Pittsburgh—five miles out of town and the site of KDKA's first studio. . . .

The radio studio itself was very much like the inside of a burlap-lined casket. Burnt orange, a favorite decorator color in 1922, was chosen for the draped silk meringues that billowed from the ceiling to disguise light bulbs. The door was very heavy. A sign on the wall framed the single word, SILENCE. A tall vase of gladioli stood in the corner. And in the center of this still room stood the working part, a microphone whose unruffled, impersonal, inscrutable self-confidence gave the whole place the feeling of an execution chamber. On one wall a glass window provided a clear view of the proceedings for the engineer who threw the switch and operated the rheostat that could go from "soft" to "loud." . . .

My father, who had been a symphony musician, held his standards high—at least as high as a twelve-piece orchestra composed of Westinghouse shopkeepers allowed. With patience and encouragement he would lift them into the arms of Beethoven, Weber, Liszt and Verdi. Among the appreciative letters a printed card from far away would regularly show up to spoil my father's day. "PROGRAM COMING IN FINE," it would report. "PLEASE PLAY 'JAPANESE SANDMAN.'" . . .

At five minutes to ten every night in the week, KDKA had a five-minute program called "The Arlington Time Signals," a monotonously repetitive tone that burped every second for five minutes until, like a child forced to exhale after holding its breath too long, a single, stretched-out beep proclaimed the hour of ten. This expedition into a now-neglected form of programming was treated with such solemnity in the upper echelons at Westinghouse that my father's concerts had to end before 9:55 or he would be "called on the carpet" the next morning for running into the Arlington Time Signals. What the time signals lacked as an aesthetic experience they made up for in purpose, since it was on the sounding of that first blurb that all Westinghouse employees, wherever they were, would pull out their timepieces, stand as still as Lot's wife, and await that last, long gasp by which they would set their turnips. It was considered a public service to relay those baleful tones to the world each night.

I was in Grade 8-B in June, 1924, an election year, and Miss Arbogast was teaching us what a party convention was like. Since my family now had a superheterodyne set equipped with a cone speaker, my father thought it would be instructive as well as inspiring to have the whole eighth grade over to hear the Republican keynote address. He was also persuaded that my teacher, Old Lady Arbogast, might remember the gesture when report cards came due.

The proposal unsettled my mother, since we had just moved to the house and it was not yet presentable; also it was far enough from school that a transportation problem would certainly present itself. The time of the keynote address—noon—would require preparation of fifty lunches, and eating them might conflict with listening to the keynote address.

Sweeping aside all these objections, my father offered to arrange for Mr. Thompson's grocery to make and deliver fifty box lunches (a privilege it declined, leaving the job to my mother) and gallantly volunteered to drive the children from schoolhouse to radio set in a series of round trips; furthermore, as an encore, he would return them to school in time for the afternoon session.

Tuesday, June 10, the day of the address, broke hot and clear. Mother was up early making sandwiches. At 11:30 A.M. my father was to leave the house to get the first load of children, but he was on one of his interminable phone calls to musicians, which no amount of semaphoring could get him to abbreviate. At 11:55 he raced out to the Dodge and set out grimly on his first round trip. While my father was still ferrying children back and forth like Saint Christopher, the keynote address had begun. The voice of Representative Theodore E. Burton (Republican from Ohio) battled its way through the static, bringing neither information nor inspiration to the hungry pupils. Meanwhile, the food was running low, since the rolls had now been converted to ammunition aimed at the successive platoons of children as they arrived.

By the time Miss Arbogast staggered in with the last perspiring load the keynote address was finished, cold cuts were all over the floor, the starving children were in an uproar, and it was clearly time for my father *to start up the shuttle service back to school, which the last carload reached in time to hear the closing bell.*

The keynote address itself, marred by static almost to the point of unintelligibility, was notable chiefly for its employment of the adjective "glorious," which was applied in turn to flag, party, country, tradition, heritage, past, future, and occasion. Yet it was the first time a national convention was ever broadcast, and it was an undeniably glorious event for the eighth grade—with the exception of Miss Arbogast.

the TUBE

There was no single inventor of television—no Bell, no Edison, no Morse. But two men had a legitimate claim to being, in effect, its "father"—Philo Farnsworth and Vladimir Zworykin, whose separate efforts developed the cathode-ray tube.

Farnsworth got the inspiration for an "image dissector tube"—a device scanning electronic lines to create a TV picture—while a teenager in Rigby, Idaho, toiling amid long horizontal lines of sugar beets on the family farm.

Farnsworth's wife, Elma, would recall the experiments that followed as she embarked with him on married life during the 1920s.

We married quite quickly because Phil had to leave for California. On our wedding night he had to see George Everson [a financial backer]. It turned into hours, and I was getting very upset, and then I began to worry for his safety. When he did come back, he apologized for having been gone so long, and he said, "You know, there is another woman in my life."

I didn't say anything, I was so dumbstruck. Then he said, "Her name is television. And in order to have enough time together, I want you to work with me. We are going to be working right on the edge of discovery. It is going to be very exciting, and I want you to be part of it." That's how we started and we were that way all our married life.

During Prohibition, it was quite frowned upon to make your own liquor. I guess we looked a little suspicious to the neighbors. Because of the things we were doing with light, we had to set the blinds when we were demonstrating.

These policemen came to the door—two of the biggest policemen I ever saw. They said, "We have a report that you are operating a still here."

I said, "Well, come on in." Phil took over, and he said to them, "This is what we're doing," and he showed them all that we were trying to do. It was all set up on the dining room table.

George Everson was caught by two policemen at the back door. The two from the front said, "Joe, it's all right. They're doing some kooky things called visions, but they're not doing any selling." George had come in with his hands full of shellac. He was winding coils in the back yard and he had wanted to ask Phil a question. He had his hands up because he didn't want to get shellac on anything, and it looked very suspicious.

The big day was September 7, 1927.

In the previous year, Phil had gotten more backing, and the agreement was that he promised to get a transmission in a year. He came in two weeks early.

It was a beautiful morning. I went into the office to do some sketches in his notebooks.

He called me in. My brother Cliff, who had made the tubes, was in the transmitting room, which was behind a partition. Phil said, "Put in a slide, Cliff," and we saw a line. It was a curvy, thick line. He adjusted it, and it became sharper. He asked Cliff to turn the slide on its side, and the line turned. Phil looked at us and he said, "Well, there you have television."

I could tell he was very excited. He was beaming all over. I was jumping about in my nineteen-year-old excitement.

One of the first things he said was, "Remember, there is a lot to do yet."

There was one colorful person, he was a sort of product of the Gold Rush days. They called him Daddy Fagan, the executive vice president of the Crocker Bank. All of the backers came to the lab, and we were all sitting around waiting while Phil went in to make sure everything was *all right at the transmitter. Mr Fagan called out, "When are we going to see some dollars in this thing, Farnsworth?" And immediately, a dollar sign appeared on the screen.*

Dr. Zworykin was a very charming person. We entertained him in our home. When he saw the first television picture in Phil's lab—this was in 1930, and we had a good picture, a clear picture—he said, "Beautiful, I wish I had invented it myself."

He [Farnsworth] was disappointed at the programming to begin with, but he realized it was in its infancy and had to go through growing pains. When he saw the first man walk on the moon, he said, "It's been all worthwhile."

the DUMBBELL MURDER

The Roaring Twenties spawned a raucous brand of journalism—the tabloid press.

In June 1919, Joseph Medill Patterson launched the first "tab," the *New York Daily News*. Half the size of standard papers, the *News* was easy to handle on the expanding subway system and provided an appealing and lavishly illustrated blend of crime, sex, celebrity gossip, and weirdness for working-class New Yorkers. Five years later, William Randolph Hearst's *New York Daily Mirror* hit the stands to provide competition. Both were huge successes.

The 1927 Snyder-Gray murder case was a wonderful story for the tabloids. Ruth Snyder, a Queens housewife, persuaded her lover, a corset salesman named Judd Gray, to kill her magazine-editor husband after taking out a double-indemnity insurance policy on him.

It was a messy and hardly perfect crime, as Damon Runyon would observe.

A chilly-looking blonde with frosty eyes and one of those marble, you-bet-you-will chins, and an inert, scare-drunk fellow that you couldn't miss among any hundred men as a dead setup for a blonde, or the shell game, or maybe a gold brick.

Mrs. Ruth Snyder and Henry Judd Gray are on trial in the huge weatherbeaten old courthouse of Queens County in Long Island City, just across the river from the roar of New York, for what might be called, for want of a better name, The Dumbbell Murder. It was so dumb.

They are charged with the slaughter four weeks ago of Albert Snyder, art editor of the magazine, Motor Boating, the blonde's husband and father of her nine-year-old daughter, under circumstances that for sheer stupidity and brutality have seldom been equaled in the history of crime.

It was stupid beyond imagination, and so brutal that the thought of it probably makes many a peaceful, home-loving Long Islander of the Albert Snyder type shiver in his pajamas as he prepares for bed.

They killed Snyder as he slumbered, so they both admitted in confessions—Mrs. Snyder has since repudiated hers—first whacking him on the head with a sash weight, then giving him a few whiffs of chloroform, and finally tightening a strand of picture wire around his throat so he wouldn't revive.

This matter disposed of, they went into an adjoining room and had a few drinks of whisky used by some Long Islanders, which is very bad, and talked things over. They thought they had committed "the perfect crime," whatever that may be. It was probably the most imperfect crime on record. It was cruel, atrocious, and unspeakably dumb.

They were red-hot lovers then, these two, but they are strangers now.

Mrs. Snyder, the woman who has been called a Jezebel, a lineal descendant of the Borgia outfit, and a lot of other names, came in for the morning session of court stepping along briskly in her patent-leather pumps, with little short steps.

She is not bad-looking. I have seen much worse. She is thirty-three and looks just about that, though you cannot tell much about blondes. She has a good figure, slim and trim, with narrow shoulders. She is of medium height, and I thought she carried her clothes off rather smartly. She wore a black dress and a black silk coat with a collar of black fur. Some of the girl reporters said it was dyed ermine; others pronounced it rabbit.

They made derogatory comments about her hat. It was a tight-fitting thing called, I believe, a beret. Wisps of her straw-colored hair straggled out from under it. Mrs. Snyder wears her hair bobbed, the back of the *bobbing rather ragged. She is of the Scandinavian type. Her parents are Norwegian and Swedish.*

Her eyes are blue-green and as chilly-looking as an ice-cream cone. If all that Henry Judd Gray says of her actions the night of the murder is true, her veins carry ice water. Gray says he dropped the sash weight after slugging the sleeping Snyder with it once and that Mrs. Snyder picked it up and finished the job. . . .

Gray was neatly dressed in a dark suit, with a white starched collar and subdued tie. He has always been a bit on the dressy side, it is said. He wears big, horn-rimmed spectacles, and his eyes have a startled expression. You couldn't find a meeker, milder-looking fellow in seven states, this man who is charged with one of the most horrible crimes in history. . . .

Mrs. Snyder and Gray have been "hollering copper" on each other lately, as the boys say. That is, they have been telling. Gray's defense goes back to old Mr. Adam, that the woman beguiled him, while Mrs. Snyder says he is a "jackal," and a lot of other things besides that, and claims that he is hiding behind her skirts. . . .

Let no one infer she is altogether without tenderness of heart, for when they were jotting down the confession that was read in the courtroom in Long Island City, Peter M. Daly, an assistant district attorney, asked her:

"Mrs. Snyder, why did you kill your husband?"

He wanted to know.

"Don't put it that way," she said, according to his testimony yesterday. "It sounds so cruel."

"Well, that is what you did, isn't it?" he asked in some surprise.

"Yes," he claims she answered, "but I don't like that term."

A not astonishing distaste, you must admit.

"Well, why did you kill him?" persisted the curious Daly.

"To get rid of him," she answered simply, according to Daly's testimony; and indeed that seems to have been her main idea throughout, if all the evidence the state has so far developed is true. . . .

Right back to old Father Adam, the original, and perhaps the loudest "squawker" among mankind against women, went Henry Judd Gray in telling how and why he lent his hand to the butchery of Albert Snyder. . . .

"She gave me of the tree, and I did eat."

It has been put in various forms since then, as Henry Judd Gray, for one notable instance close at hand, put it in the form of eleven typewritten pages that were read yesterday, but in any form and in any language it remains a "squawk." . . .

As for Henry Judd, I doubt he will last it out. He reminds me of a slowly collapsing lump of tallow. He sat huddled up in his baggy clothes, his eyes on the floor, his chin in hand, while the confession was being read. . . .

It is all very well for the rest of us to say what ought to be done to the blonde throwback to the jungle cat that they call Mrs. Ruth Brown Snyder, but when you get in the jury room and start thinking about going home to tell the neighbors that you have voted to burn a woman—even a blonde woman—I imagine the situation has a different aspect. . . .

Henry Judd Gray said he expects to go to the chair, and adds that he is not afraid of death, an enviable frame of mind, indeed. He says that since he told his story to the world from the witness stand he has found tranquillity, though his tale may also have condemned his blonde partner in blood. But perhaps that's the very reason Henry Judd finds tranquillity.

He sat in his cell in the county jail over in Long Island yesterday, and read from one of the epistles of John. . . .

In another cell, the blonde woman was very mad at everybody because she couldn't get a marcel for her blonde locks, one hair of which was once stronger with Henry Judd Gray than the Atlantic cable.

When the lovers went to the electric chair in January 1928, the *Daily News* scored a coup. It smuggled a photographer named Thomas Howard into the death chamber, a camera hidden below his pants leg. Just as the switch was thrown electrocuting Ruth Snyder, Howard uncovered the lens and snapped the shutter by squeezing a bulb in his pocket. The blurry image, on the front page of the *News*, was a sensation.

The headline told it all in one word: "DEAD!"

a MICKEY MOUSE PRODUCTION

Back in 1920, a nineteen-year-old commercial artist at the Kansas City Film Ad Company began experimenting with animated shorts. After eight years in the world of silent-film animation, Walt Disney was ready to unveil a cartoon that would be very different from anything that had been tried before. For the first time, synchronized sound effects, voice, and music would be melded to tell a story with animated characters.

Disney's 1928 production of *Steamboat Willie* would popularize sound tracks for cartoons just as Al Jolson's *The Jazz Singer* had introduced sound the year before for live-action movies.

But the creators of *Steamboat Willie* had been uncertain whether the thing would work. So, before showing the musical animation to the public, Disney, his brother Roy, and the illustrators Wilfred Jackson and Ubbe Iwerks presented a preview for their wives.

Walt Disney would recall the day the creature who became Mickey Mouse debuted in sound.

Jackson went out and bought a metronome and we moved to the studio and began to work things out. I had a pad of bar music sheets, and I started the metronome and asked Jackson to play a tune on his harmonica. While it ticktocked away, he would play out our frames so we had exactly the right ratio of frames to each bar of music.

I bought a couple of plumber's friends [rubber plungers making a swishy sound] and some slide whistles and ocarinas. We played around with these for a while to work out the sound effects. When I say we, I mean Ub Iwerks, young Jackson, and myself. A few nights later, we asked our wives to come over and see something new. We had no projection room, and our sheet hung on a garage doorway. It was a warm night, so we put our wives in chairs facing the open garage doorway with the sheet hanging over it. Then Roy turned on the projector and began to run Steamboat Willie. Iwerks, I, and Jackson got into the garage behind the sheet, where we could watch the picture from the rear and make our various noises.

Jackson tootled music on his mouth-organ. The rest of us hit cowbells, ocarinas, and whistles and scrubbed away at the washboard. Iwerks had rigged up a microphone to an old radio speaker, so our wives would be able to hear the sound effects clearly.

We beat our brains out synchronizing that cartoon, and when we were through we ran around the sheet, and Roy came running up from the projector, and we looked at our wives expectantly and said, "How was it?" All they said was "Nice" and went on gossiping, as they had done, Roy said bitterly afterward, all through the screening.

the MONKEY TRIAL

In the summer of 1925, a high school teacher named John T. Scopes agreed to test Tennessee's new law against the teaching of evolution. He was prosecuted in the town of Dayton and found guilty in an eight-day trial pitting William Jennings Bryan for the state against Clarence Darrow for the defense.

The Baltimore columnist H. L. Mencken, who persuaded the renowned Darrow to enter the case, would portray it as a clash between narrow fundamentalism and open-minded liberalism, between ignorance and enlightenment. That tone would also be conveyed in the play *Inherit the Wind.*

The "Monkey Trial" and Mencken's vitriolic reporting exacerbated a cultural gap in America. Almost three-quarters of a century later that chasm remains, the debate over "family values" a pointed reminder.

In a column filed from Dayton for the Baltimore *Evening Sun*— titled "Deep in the Coca-Cola Belt"—Mencken wrote sneeringly of the old America.

There is a Unitarian clergyman here from New York, trying desperately to horn into the trial and execution of the infidel Scopes. He will fail. If Darrow ventured to put him on the stand the whole audience, led by the jury, would leap out of the courthouse windows and take to the hills. Darrow himself, indeed, is as much as they can bear. The whisper that he is an atheist has been stilled by the bucolic make-up and by the public report that he has the gift of prophecy and can reconcile Genesis and evolution. Even so, there is ample space about him when he navigates the streets.

The other day a newspaperwoman was warned by her landlady to keep out of the courtroom when he was on his legs. All the local sorcerers predict that a bolt from heaven will fetch him in the end. The night he arrived there was a violent storm, the town water turned brown, and horned cattle in the lowlands were afloat for hours. A woman back in the mountains gave birth to a child with hair four inches long, curiously bobbed in scallops.

The Book of Revelation has all the authority, in these theological uplands, of military orders in time of war. The people turn to it for light upon all their problems, spiritual and secular. If a text were found in it denouncing the anti-evolution law, then the anti-evolution law would become infamous overnight. But so far the exegetes who roar and snuffle in the town have found no such text. Instead they have found only blazing ratifications and reinforcements of Genesis. Darwin is the devil with seven tails and nine horns. Scopes, though he is disguised by flannel pantaloons and a Beta Theta Pi haircut, is the harlot of Babylon. Darrow is Beelzebub in person. . . .

At the last count of noses there were 20,000 Holy Rollers in these hills. The next census, I have no doubt, will show many more. The cities of the lowlands, of course, still resist, and so do most of the country towns, including even Dayton, but once one steps off the state roads the howl of holiness is heard in the woods, and the yokels carry on an almost continuous orgy. . . .

We left Dayton an hour after nightfall and parked our car in a wood a mile or so beyond the little hill village of Morgantown. Far off in a glade a flickering light was visible and out of the silence came a faint rumble of exhortation. We could scarcely distinguish the figure of the preacher; it was like looking down the tube of a dark field microscope. We got out of the car and sneaked along the edge of a mountain cornfield.

Presently we were near enough to see what was going on. From the great limb of a mighty oak hung a couple of crude torches of the sort that car inspectors thrust under Pullman cars when a train pulls in at night. In their light was a preacher, and for a while we could see no one else.

He was an immensely tall and thin mountaineer in blue jeans, his collarless shirt open at the neck and his hair a tousled mop. As he preached he paced up and down under the smoking flambeaux and at each turn he thrust his arms into the air and yelled, "Glory to God!" ...

A young mother sat suckling her baby, rocking as the preacher paced up and down. Two scared little girls hugged each other, their pigtails down their backs. An immensely huge mountain woman, in a gingham dress cut in one piece, rolled on her heels at every "Glory to God." ...

At a signal all the faithful crowded up to the bench and began to pray —not in unison, but each for himself. At another they all fell on their knees, their arms over the penitent. The leader kneeled, facing us, his head alternately thrown back dramatically or buried in his hands. Words spouted from his lips like bullets from a machine gun—appeals to God to pull the penitent back out of hell, defiances of the powers and principalities of the air, a vast impassioned jargon of apocalyptic texts. Suddenly he rose to his feet, threw back his head, and began to speak in tongues —blub-blub-blub, gurgle-gurgle-gurgle. His voice rose to a higher register. The climax was a shrill, inarticulate squawk, like that of a man throttled. He fell headlong across the pyramid of supplicants. ...

From the squirming and jabbering mass a young woman gradually detached herself—a woman not uncomely, with a pathetic homemade cap on her head. Her head jerked back, the veins of her neck swelled, and her fists went to her throat as if she were fighting for breath. She bent backward until she was like a half of a hoop. Then she suddenly snapped forward. We caught a flash of the whites of her eyes. Presently her whole body began to be convulsed—great convulsions that began at the shoulders and ended at the hips. She would leap to her feet, thrust her arms in air, and then hurl herself upon the heap. Her praying flattened out into a mere delirious caterwauling, like that of a tomcat on a petting party. ...

We got tired of it after a while and groped our way back to our automobile. When we got to Dayton, after eleven o'clock—an immensely late hour for these parts—the whole town was still gathered on the courthouse lawn, hanging upon the disputes of theologians. The Bible champion of the world had a crowd. The Seventh Day Adventists missionary had a crowd. A volunteer from faraway Portland, Oregon, made up exactly like Andy Gump, had another and larger crowd. Dayton was enjoying itself. All the usual rules were suspended and the curfew bell was locked up. The prophet Bryan, exhausted by his day's work for Revelations, was snoring in his bed up the road, but enough volunteers were still on watch to keep the battlements manned.

Such is human existence among the fundamentalists, where children are brought up on Genesis and sin is unknown. If I have made the tale too long, then blame the spirit of garrulity that is in the local air. Even newspaper reporters, down here, get some echo of the call. Divine inspiration is as common as the hookworm. I have done my best to show you what the great heritage of mankind comes to in regions where the Bible is the beginning and end of wisdom, and the mountebank Bryan, parading the streets in his seersucker coat, is pointed out to sucklings as the greatest man since Abraham.

from HORSELESS CARRIAGE
to MODEL T

The boomtime 1920s were fueled by the imagination of Henry Ford, a tyrant over his workers, an anti-Semite, and an isolationist in foreign affairs, but a visionary nonetheless.

Though Ford didn't invent the gasoline-powered motorcar, he transformed American life when he figured out a way to produce automobiles faster and more cheaply than anyone else. His gasoline buggies were merely a curiosity on the streets of Detroit in the mid-1890s, but by the 1920s his Model T's turned out on assembly lines were spurring growth, breaking down vast pockets of isolation in America, and opening the way to new forms of leisure.

In the mid-twenties, Ford looked back on the road to the Model T.

In 1892 I completed my first motor car, but it was not until the spring of the following year that it ran to my satisfaction. . . . The car would hold two people, the seat being suspended on posts and the body on elliptical springs. . . . The wheels were twenty-eight-inch wire bicycle wheels with rubber tires. . . .

My "gasoline buggy" was the first and for a long time the only automobile in Detroit. It was considered to be something of a nuisance, for it made a racket and scared horses. Also it blocked traffic. For if I stopped my machine anywhere in town a crowd was around before I could start up again. If I left it alone even for a minute some inquisitive person always tried to run it. Finally, I had to carry a chain and chain it to a lamp post whenever I left it anywhere. And then there was trouble with the police. I do not know quite why, for my impression is that there were no speed-limit laws in those days. Anyway, I had to get a special permit from the mayor and thus for a time enjoyed the distinction of being the only licensed chauffeur in America. I ran that machine about one thousand miles through 1895 and 1896 and then sold it to Charles Ainsley of Detroit for two hundred dollars. That was my first sale. . . .

In 1903, with Tom Cooper, I built two cars solely for speed. They were quite alike. One we named the "999" and the other the "Arrow." . . . I put in four great big cylinders giving 80 H.P.—which up to that time had been unheard of. The roar of those cylinders alone was enough to kill a man. There was only one seat. One life to a car was enough. . . . Going over Niagara Falls would have but been a pastime after a ride in one of them. . . . Cooper said he knew a man who lived on speed, that nothing could go too fast for him. He wired to Salt Lake City and on came a professional bicycle rider named Barney Oldfield. He had never driven a motor car, but he liked the idea of trying it. . . .

It took us only a week to teach him how to drive. The man did not know what fear was. All that he had to learn was how to control the monster. Controlling the fastest car of to-day was nothing as compared to controlling that car. The steering wheel had not yet been thought of. All the previous cars that I had built simply had tillers. On this one I put a two-handed tiller, for holding the car in line required all the strength of a strong man. The race for which we were working was at three miles on the Grosse Point track. . . . The tracks then were not scientifically banked. It was not known how much speed a motor car could develop. No one knew better than Oldfield what the turns meant and as he took his seat, while I was cranking the car for the start, he remarked cheerily: "Well, this chariot may kill me, but they will say afterward that I was going like hell when she took me over the bank." . . .

He never dared to look around. He did not shut off on the curves. He simply let that car go—and go it did. He was about half a mile ahead of the next man at the end of the race!

The "999" did what it was intended to do: It advertised the fact that I could build a fast motor car. A week after the race I formed the Ford Motor Company. . . .

In our first year we built "Model A," selling the runabout for eight hundred and fifty dollars and the tonneau for one hundred dollars more. This model had a two-cylinder opposed motor developing eight horsepower. It had a chain drive, a seventy-two inch wheel base—which was supposed to be long—and a fuel capacity of five gallons. We made and sold 1,708 cars in the first year. . . .

Every one of these "Model A's" has a history. Take No. 420. Colonel D. C. Collier of California bought it in 1904. He used it for a couple of years, sold it, and bought a new Ford. No. 420 changed hands frequently until 1907 when it was bought by one Edmund Jacobs living near Ramona in the heart of the mountains. He drove it for several years in the roughest kind of work. . . . By 1915 No. 420 had passed into the hands of a man named Cantello who took out the motor, hitched it to a water pump, rigged up shafts on the chassis, and now, while the motor chugs away at the pumping of water, the chassis drawn by a burro acts as a buggy. The moral, of course, is that you dissect a Ford but you cannot kill it.

From the day the first motor car appeared on the streets it had to me appeared to be a necessity. It was this knowledge and assurance that led me to build to one end—a car that would meet the wants of the multitudes.

. . . in 1909 I announced one morning, without any previous warning, that in the future we were going to build only one model, that the model was going to be "Model T," and that the chassis would be exactly the same for all cars, and I remarked:

"Any customer can have a car painted any colour that he wants so long as it is black."

LINDBERGH ALONE

If America was looking for a heroic figure in a decade seemingly devoid of idealism, it found one the evening of May 21, 1927.

Charles Lindbergh completed the first solo flight across the Atlantic, landing at Le Bourget Air Field in Paris in a plane he had never before flown at night and with only a flashlight to illuminate his instrument panel.

The United States—and the Parisians as well—went wild. "Lucky Lindy" was everyone's idol.

Is that a cloud on the northeastern horizon, or a strip of low fog—or —can it possibly be land? It looks like land, but I don't intend to be tricked by another mirage. . . .

I'm only sixteen hours out from Newfoundland. I allowed eighteen and a half hours to strike the Irish coast. If that's Ireland, I'm two and a half hours ahead of schedule. . . .

I stare at it intently, not daring to believe my eyes, keeping hope in check to avoid another disappointment, watching the shades and contours unfold into a coastline—a coastline coming down from the north—a coastline bending toward the east—a coastline with rugged shores and rolling mountains. . . .

This must *be Ireland. . . .*

Now the *Spirit of St. Louis* approached Paris.

Four fifty-two on the clock. That's 9:52, Paris time. Le Bourget isn't shown on my map. No one I talked to back home had more than a general idea of its location. "It's a big airport," I was told. "You can't miss it. Just fly northeast from the city." So I penciled a circle on my map, about where Le Bourget ought to be; and now the Spirit of St. Louis is over the outskirts of Paris, pointed toward the center of that circle. . . .

Yes, it's definitely an airport. I see part of a concrete apron in front of a large, half open door. But is it Le Bourget? Well, at least it's a Paris airport. That's the important thing. It's Paris I set out for. If I land on the wrong field, it won't be too serious an error—as long as I land safely. . . .

From each changed angle, as I bank, new details emerge from night and shadow. I see the corners of big hangars, now outlined vaguely, near the floodlights—a line of them. And now, from the far side of the field, I see that all those smaller lights are automobiles, not factory windows. They seem to be blocked in traffic, on a road behind the hangars. It's a huge airport. The floodlights show only a small corner. It must be Le Bourget.

I shift fuel valves to the center wing-tank, sweep my flashlight over the instrument board in a final check, fasten my safety belt, and nose the Spirit of St. Louis down into a gradually descending spiral.

I circle several times while I lose altitude, trying to penetrate the shadows from different vantage points, getting the lay of the land as well as I can in darkness. At one thousand feet I discover the wind sock, dimly lighted, on top of some building. It's bulged, but far from stiff. That means a gentle, constant wind, not over ten or fifteen miles an hour. My landing direction will be over the floodlights, angling away from the hangar line. Why circle any longer? That's all the information I need. No matter how hard I try, my eyes can't penetrate the blanket of night over the central portion of the field. . . .

It's only a hundred yards to the hangars now—solid forms emerging from the night. I'm too high—too fast. Drop wing—left rudder—sideslip —Careful—mustn't get anywhere near the stall. I've never landed the Spirit of St. Louis at night before. It would be better to come in straight. But if I don't sideslip, I'll be too high over the boundary to touch my wheels in the area of light. That would mean circling again—Still too high. I push the stick over to a steeper slip, leaving the nose well down —Below the hangar roofs now—straighten out—A short burst of the engine—Over the lighted area—Sod coming up to meet me—Deceptive high lights and shadows—Careful—easy to bounce when you're tired —Still too fast—Tail too high—Hold off—Hold off—But the lights are far behind—The surface dims—Texture of sod is gone—Ahead, there's nothing but night—Give her the gun and climb for another try? —The wheels touch gently—off again—No, I'll keep contact—Ease the stick forward—Back on the ground—Off—Back—the tail skid too

—Not a bad landing, but I'm beyond the light—can't see anything ahead—Like flying in a fog—Ground loop?—No, still rolling too fast —might blow a tire—The field must be clear—Uncomfortable though, jolting into darkness—Wish I had a wing light—but too heavy on the takeoff—Slower, now—slow enough to ground loop safely—left rudder —reverse it—stick over the other way—the Spirit of St. Louis swings around and stops rolling, resting on the solidness of earth, in the center of Le Bourget.

PANIC on WALL STREET

As the 1920s moved along, America seemed in splendid economic shape. Stock prices sizzled, consumer goods flew off assembly lines in ever-increasing numbers, and new homes arose everywhere.

Then a shock. On October 24, 1929, an alarming selloff hit Wall Street—Black Thursday. Five days later, panic reigned as the stock market took another huge tumble—Black Tuesday.

By the end of October, stockholders had suffered a paper loss of more than $15 billion. By year's end, the value of securities had shrunk by $40 billion.

President Herbert Hoover, businessman and engineer, someone who surely knew the ways of commerce and production, had once proclaimed: "We in America are nearer to the final triumph over poverty than ever before."

But now banks collapsed, factories shut down, farmers went bankrupt.

The Great Depression was on.

Hindsight reveals that amid the prosperity of the 1920s the seeds of economic disaster were ripening. Production outstripped demand, since the laboring classes and farmers never quite got their share of the economic pie and so had limited cash to spend on all those wonderful consumer goods. High tariffs stymied international trade, cutting off foreign markets for American goods. Easy credit brought unbridled speculation and tremendous debt.

Wall Street's collapse did not literally cause the Depression—it reflected the ills of the economic system. But the floor of the New York Stock Exchange was where it all began, right before the eyes of Mildred Wohlforth.

In 1929 I was a reporter and feature writer (sob sister) for William Randolph Hearst's New York Evening Journal. . . .

On Black Thursday, October 1929, when the bottom fell out of the market, my city editor, Amster Spiro, said to me: "Something is going on down on Wall Street. Go see what it's all about." I took the five-cent subway to Wall Street, went to the Stock Exchange and was allowed to watch the frantic proceedings from the visitors' balcony, with a security guard carefully explaining everything to me. He pointed out what each frantic group was buying and selling and told me that crazy buying had destroyed the market and several big traders as well. I didn't see any losers jumping out of windows, but several did just that.

The guard told me that impulse buying, mostly on margin and "by women," had definitely ruined the market. "They don't know a thing about stocks, but that doesn't stop them. Who's killing the market now before our eyes? Stenographers, housewives, chorus girls, that's who! They act like they are out of their minds!" So, since I was assigned to the women's angle of every story, this made my job very easy. I reported the mad goings-on and my Evening Journal story was banner-headed "Stenographers, Chorus Girls, Housewives, All Buying Stocks, Are Responsible for the Crash."

Unfortunately, it wasn't that simple. The "little guy" and perhaps the "little woman" were indeed speculating, but the powerful financiers held the truly huge stakes.

At noon on Black Tuesday, they met secretly to decide whether to halt trading on the New York Stock Exchange. Richard Whitney, then vice-president of the exchange and later its president, called the session.

In order not to give occasion for alarming rumors, this meeting was not held in the Governing Committee Room, but in the office of the president of the Stock Clearing Corporation directly beneath the Stock Exchange floor. . . . The forty governors came to the meeting in groups of two and three as unobtrusively as possible. The office they met in was never designed for large meetings of this sort, with the result that most of the governors were compelled to stand, or to sit on tables. As the meeting progressed, panic was raging overhead on the floor. Every few minutes the latest prices were announced, with quotations moving swiftly and irresistibly downward. The feeling of those present was revealed by their habit of continually lighting cigarettes, taking a puff or two, putting them out and lighting new ones—a practice which soon made the narrow room blue with smoke and extremely stuffy.

A decision was made to have two J. P. Morgan partners—evidently Thomas Lamont and Whitney's brother George—join the session. But Richard Whitney would note how tight security got in the way.

The gentlemen naturally wished to arrive at the meeting as unobtrusively as possible, lest a new crop of rumors be started. But as they attempted to slip quietly in, they were detected by one of the stalwart guards and sternly refused admittance.

One of the governors got the Morgan men through the door. Soon the leaders of the exchange decided to keep it open and hope for the best.

Nine years later, Richard Whitney—a Harvard graduate, a pillar of the American financial community—went to Sing Sing wearing a three-piece suit, a convicted embezzler.

the BONUS ARMY

By the third summer of the Depression, Washington bordered on a state of siege. Some twenty-five thousand jobless and hungry World War I veterans calling themselves the Bonus Expeditionary Force came to the capital in June 1932 with their wives and children to demand that a soldiers' bonus due them in 1945 be paid immediately. (It amounted to about $500 a man.) President Hoover refused to meet with the men and chained the gates outside the White House.

Their leader, Walter W. Waters of Portland, Oregon, once a medic in the 146th Field Artillery, now a laid-off cannery worker, would note on June 7 how his vets had accomplished something even if their demands would not be met.

Eight thousand men and more had already reached the capital. Their ranks on this warm night showed many things—what ten years of life in prosperous America had done. . . .

So they made for America a picture of honest men in poverty. If the B.E.F. had been evicted on the morrow, one of its chief functions would have been accomplished. For Mr. Hoover had said there were no hungry men in America. Either he was wrong or these men imagined their hunger. . . .

Most of the ragtag vets and their families were encamped in Southeast Washington, across the Anacostia River. But several hundred men occupied a couple of dilapidated red-brick buildings on Pennsylvania Avenue at Third Street that were due to be leveled.

On the morning of July 28, police under the command of Pelham D. Glassford, a retired brigadier general who was in fact sympathetic to the veterans, removed them with the help of federal agents.

There was some fighting at that time, but it was merely an omen. In the afternoon, matters got wildly out of hand.

The *Washington Evening Star* had this version:

Two veterans engaged in an altercation in front of the camp supply building, and were immediately surrounded by a howling mob of about 100. Police rushed to the scene and sought to stop the argument. Gen. Glassford, with two policemen at his heels, ran up the stairway along the side of the building to the second floor to get a better view of the trouble. They were immediately followed by about 30 veterans who rushed the stairs and treated Glassford's two aides roughly when they sought to stop the rush.

About this time bricks started flying between groups down on the ground.

Officer George W. Shinault, on the outskirts of the milling mob, near the foot of the stairway, was getting a beating from the veterans. Bricks were flying about him. He drew his pistol and fired. . . . Officer Miles Zamenaciack, who was on the second floor with Glassford, rushed halfway down the stairs and joined in the shooting. A third policeman, J. O. Fife, who was in the midst of the brick fighting on the ground, drew his pistol and started running toward the rear of the building, whence most of the people were coming. About 25 feet from Fife a bonus marcher drew back to hurl a brickbat at him, and, holding his pistol in both hands, Fife fired several times.

Waters would give his own account of the events.

At two o'clock General Glassford and a small group of police returned. They went to a large vacant building next to the one where the eviction had occurred in the morning. They started up a flight of stairs from the outside, intending to go to a top floor and get a bird's-eye view of the scene. General Glassford led the way and a few policemen followed. A small group of veterans, curious, pushing and crowding, followed them closely. The crowd pressed behind them.

Suddenly, without warning, frightened perhaps by the pressure of the following veterans, the last man in the police line whirled about. His gun was in his hand. He fired straight at the veterans behind him and hit the first man. Twice more this policeman, Shinault, pulled the trigger. The policeman in front of him drew his gun, too, and fired one shot, and another veteran dropped, clutching his stomach.

A voice from the top of the stairs cried: "Put down that gun!" It was General Glassford. Shinault whirled around at the sound of the voice. He pointed his gun directly at the General for a moment then, sheepishly, as if caught in some harmless boyish prank, put the gun in his holster.

Not a veteran had threatened him. But two of their number lay silent on the ground and their blood toned the red of the pile of brick dust. Over the entire crowd of milling veterans spread silence. . . . There was no rioting, no brick throwing, no protest—just silence in the face of murder. . . .

Five days later we were to bury William Hushka, the first man shot.

He had been recruited for the B.E.F. out of a breadline in Chicago. Seven days later we were to bury Eric Carlson, the second victim.

Hours after the shootings, an army force that included cavalrymen with sabers unsheathed routed the veterans and burned their camp. It was far from the most glorious moment in the careers of the army commanders—General Douglas MacArthur and Majors Dwight D. Eisenhower and George S. Patton, Jr.

the FIRESIDE CHAT

A believer in "rugged individualism," President Hoover had little to offer the hungry by way of help from Washington. Prosperity was "just around the corner."

In fact, men selling apples were on those corners, and so the American people swept Franklin D. Roosevelt into the White House.

In his acceptance speech at the Democratic National Convention in the summer of 1932, Roosevelt had promised a "New Deal." But before launching his programs, he was determined to stem panic. At his inauguration on March 4, 1933, he told desperate Americans, "The only thing we have to fear is fear itself."

Then he embarked on the "One Hundred Days," a flurry of legislation creating an unprecedented role for the federal government.

The day after his inauguration, Roosevelt called for a nationwide bank holiday in the face of bank closings that cost millions of people their life savings. To explain the need for reform of the failed financial system, he reached out to Americans in a radio address on Sunday evening, March 12.

It was the first of the "Fireside Chats."

The CBS White House correspondent Robert Trout was there.

Ted Church and I walked to the White House and went in the big front door. It was, I think, something of a false step. At later broadcasts we always entered through the doorway of the executive offices in the West Wing. But we were made welcome and shown downstairs.

When we told the President that it was time for him to take his seat at the table where the microphones were, for the first time I saw him go through the routine of clicking the braces, his legs held straight out, then maneuvering to his feet and walking stiff-kneed and so slowly. We broadcasters became so accustomed to that slow walk at public affairs that we came to feel that that was the way a President should walk, with measured dignity.

That night, for the first time, our microphone said "CBS." At last, we had abandoned the Columbia signs. They didn't show up well in the pictures. Instantly, on sitting down, President Roosevelt wanted to know what CBS was. He was used to Columbia. I was impressed by this interest in broadcast matters. Then he lit a cigarette and called for his script.

It could not be found. A search began throughout the living quarters as the clock ticked on. Everyone was anxious, agitated, except FDR. If he was, he didn't show it. At the last moment someone produced a mimeographed press copy of the speech. The staples were pulled out, and we went on the air. That is the copy the President used. After we had left, they found the script—in bed, where the President had been reading it.

FDR read the talk while holding a burning cigarette in one hand. No holder. As it burned nearer and nearer to his fingers, we all began to show signs of nervousness. No need. Just before it burned him, Mr. Roosevelt, without pausing, simply stabbed the cigarette out in an ash tray. Simple stuff now, from a simpler time. But we weren't used to performers like that, especially not a performer who also happened to be the President of the United States.

We proposed two introductory scripts. One was formal, stating the facts coldly. The other was more folksy. It said that what President Roosevelt wanted to do was to come into people's houses by radio as if he were really able to visit them in person (these were not the actual words but the spirit of it), sit down with them and have a fireside chat. That two-word phrase, fireside chat, was put into the copy by Harry Butcher, ex–Iowa farm boy [the CBS manager in Washington]. It was absolutely typical of his way of thinking and talking. . . .

Harry Butcher sent both introductions to the White House. As I *recall, it was on the Friday before the broadcast that Marvin McIntyre [an FDR press aide] telephoned WJSV [the CBS station in Washington] to tell Harry (I didn't call him that then!) that the folksy intro was the one the President liked. So, of course, it was the one I used.*

the DUST BOWL

For years, farmers in the "short-grass" country, where rainfall was usually less than twenty inches a year, had overgrazed their stock and overplowed their fields. Now their luck ran out. A drought combined with fierce windstorms destroyed 250 million acres of farmland in nineteen states by the mid-1930s.

Thousands somehow found the energy to depart the lands their fathers had left them. Their travails were portrayed by John Steinbeck —the Okies of *The Grapes of Wrath*, bound for the promise of California in their ramshackle autos.

The suffering of those who stayed behind was described by a journalist named Meridel Le Sueur, who reported extensively on the plight of the poor during the Depression.

On Decoration day the wind started again, blowing hot as a blast from hell and the young corn withered as if under machine gun fire, the trees in two hours looked as if they had been beaten. The day after Decoration day it was so hot you couldn't sit around looking at the panting cattle and counting their ribs and listening to that low cry that is an awful asking. We got in the car and drove slowly through the sleeping countryside.

Not a soul was in sight. It was like a funeral. The houses were closed up tight, the blinds drawn, the windows and doors closed. There seemed to be a menace in the air made visible. It was frightening. You could hear the fields crack and dry, and the only movement in the down-driving heat was the dead withering of the dry blighted leaves on the twigs. The young corn about four spears up was falling down like a fountain being slowly turned off.

There was something terrifying about this visible sign of disaster. It went into your nostrils so you couldn't breathe: the smell of hunger. It made you count your own ribs with terror. You don't starve in America. Everything looks good. There is something around the corner. Everyone has a chance. That's all over now. The whole country cracks and rumbles and cries out in terrible leanness, stripped with exploitation and terror—and as sign and symbol, bones—bones showing naked and spiritless, showing decay and crisis and a terrific warning, bare and lean. . . .

We kept driving very slowly, about as slowly as you go to a funeral, with no one behind us, meeting no one on the road. The corpse was the very earth. We kept looking at the body of the earth, at the bare and mortgaged and unpainted houses like hollow pupas when the life has gone. They looked stripped as if after a raid. As if a terrible army had just gone through. It used to be hard to look at the fat rich-seeming farms and realize that they were mortgaged to the hilt and losing ground every year, but not now. Now it stands like a visible sign. You can see the marks of the ravagers. The mark of that fearful exploitation stands on the landscape, visible, known, to be reckoned with.

The cows were the only thin flesh visible. They stood in the poor shade of the stripped and dying trees, breathing heavily, their great ribs like the ribs of decaying boats beached and deserted. But you knew that from behind all those drawn blinds hundreds of eyes were watching that afternoon, that no man, woman or child could sit down and read a book or lie down to any dreams. Through all these windows eyes were watching—watching the wheat go, the rye go, the corn, peas, potatoes go. Everywhere in those barricaded houses were eyes drawn back to the burning windows looking out at next winter's food slowly burning in the fields. You look out and see the very food of your next winter's sustenance visibly, physically dying beneath your eyes, projecting into you your future hungers.

The whole countryside that afternoon became terrifying, not only with its present famine but with the foreshadowing of its coming hunger. No vegetables now, and worst of all, no milk. The countryside became monstrous with this double doom. Every house is alike in suffering as in a flood, every cow, every field mounting into hundreds, into thousands, from state to state. You try not to look at the ribs, but pretty soon you are looking only at ribs.

Then an awful thing happened. The sun went down behind the ridge, dropped low, and men and women began to pour out of the houses, the children lean and fleet as rats, the tired lean farm women looking to see what had happened. The men ran into their fields, ran back for water and they began to water their lands with buckets and cups, running, pouring the puny drops of water on the baked earth as if every minute might count now. The children ran behind the cows urging them to eat the harsh dry grass. It looked like an evacuated countryside, with the people running out after the enemy had passed. Not a word was spoken. In intense silence they hurried down the rows with buckets and cups, watered the wilted corn plants, a gargantuan and terrible and hopeless labor. Some came out with horses and ploughs and began stirring up the deadly dust. If the field was a slope, barrels were filled, and a primitive irrigation started. Even the children ran with cups of water, all dogged silent, mad, without a word. A certain madness in it all, like things that are done after unimaginable violence.

We stop and talk to a farmer. His eyes are bloodshot. I can hardly see from the heat and the terrible emotion. . . . How do you think my cows look? he asks. I think they are a little fatter today. I try not to look at his cows with him. Pretty thin, though, he says, pretty thin. I can see the fine jersey pelt beginning to sag and the bones rise out like sticks out of the sea at low tide.

We both know that a farmer across the river shot twenty-two of his cattle yesterday and then shot himself. I look at him and I can see his clavicle and I know that his ribs are rising out of his skin, too. It is visible now, starvation and famine. So they are going to buy the starving cattle and shoot them and feed the rest to the bread lines. A man isn't worth anything—but a cow. . . .

PLEADING *for* BABY CLOTHES

Eleanor Roosevelt was her husband's ambassador to the downtrodden, traveling forty thousand miles a year during the Depression to visit sharecroppers, slum dwellers, hungry children. When a desperate homemaker needed help, she would be more likely to write to Mrs. Roosevelt than to approach the President.

> *Troy, N.Y.*
> *January 2, 1935*

Dear Mrs. Roosevelt,

About a month ago I wrote you asking if you would buy some baby clothes for me with the understanding that I was to repay you as soon as my husband got enough work. Several weeks later I received a reply to apply to a Welfare Association so I might receive the aid I needed. Do you remember?

Please Mrs. Roosevelt, I do not want charity, only a chance from someone who will trust me until we can get enough money to repay the amount spent for the things I need. As a proof that I am really sincere, I am sending you two of my dearest possessions to keep as security, a ring my husband gave me before we were married, and a ring my mother used to wear. Perhaps the actual value of them is not high, but they are worth a lot to me. If you will consider buying the baby clothes, please keep them (rings) until I send you the money you spent. It is very hard to face bearing a baby we cannot afford to have, and the fact that it is due to arrive soon, and still there is no money for the hospital or clothing, does not make it any easier. I Have decided to stay home, keeping my 7 year old daughter from school to help with the smaller children when my husband has work. The oldest little girl is sick now, and has never been strong, so I would not depend on her. The 7 year old one is a good willing little worker and somehow we must manage—but without charity.

If you still feel you cannot trust me, it is allright and I can only say I donot blame you, but if you decide my word is worth anything with so small a security, here is a list of what I will need—but I will need it very soon.

2 shirts, silk and wool, size 2
3 pr. stockings, silk and wool, 4½ or 4
3 straight flannel bands
2 slips—outing flannel
2 muslim dresses
1 sweater

1 wool bonnet
2 pr. wool booties
2 doz. diapers 30 x 30—or 27 x 27
1 large blanket (baby) about 45" or 50"
3 outing flannel nightgaowns

If you will get these for me I would rather no one knew about it. I promise to repay the cost of the layette as soon as possible. We will all be very grateful to you, and I will be more than happy.

Sincerely yours,
Mrs. H.E.C.

PUBLIC ENEMY NO. 1

They were the poster boys and poster girls of the 1930s: Baby Face Nelson, Machine Gun Kelly, Ma Barker and her sons, Bonnie and Clyde, and, of course, John Dillinger.

The bank-robbing desperadoes of the Middle West were transformed into publicity agents for J. Edgar Hoover, stars of a "Public Enemies" list creating an unassailable image for his FBI.

While ignoring the leaders of urban organized crime, who were far more sinister, Hoover scored public-relations coup after coup sending his agents after the rogues of Middle America.

On Sunday evening, July 22, 1934, John Dillinger went to see the gangster movie *Manhattan Melodrama*, starring Clark Gable and Myrna Loy, at Chicago's Biograph Theatre. He had two dates, Anna Sage and Polly Hamilton. They were one too many—Anna betrayed him for a $5,000 reward, and a posse of FBI agents and police erased Dillinger as "Public Enemy No. 1."

The way Polly told it, however, her beau had been simply a sweetie —a guy named Jimmy.

John Dillinger, the outlaw? I didn't know him. The man I knew, and loved, was Jimmy Lawrence, a Board of Trade clerk. A smiling Jimmy

Lawrence, whose mouth twitched at the corners when he told a funny story. The Jimmy Lawrence who gave me an amethyst ring . . .

Lots of things happened that should have told me he was John Dillinger. The scars from having his face altered and removing that mole might have warned me. I asked him about them, though, and he said, "Listen, Countess, I was in an auto accident."

He called me Countess at first, and sometimes Cleopatra. Honey was the name I liked best. . . .

We went to Riverside Park often. He couldn't get enough of the rides. . . . Our car on one of the rides stuck away up at the top in one of the amusement parks one day. That didn't bother him; I guess he wasn't afraid of anything. . . .

Now that I know he was John Dillinger, I can understand why he liked the shooting galleries so. Customers would line up to watch him knock over the targets. . . .

On the last Sunday afternoon of his life, "Jimmy" watched Anna Sage's son Steve play sandlot baseball in a park while Anna and Polly went for bike rides.

We got back in time to see Jimmy being introduced to the crowd. It pleased him so much he bought beer for both teams and distributed the bottles in person right there in Jackson Park, while more policemen than there are bullets in a machine gun were looking for him. He had been awfully kind the night after I read that the Dillinger gang had robbed the South Bend bank of $28,000. That night he bought me gardenias.

When he found out I wasn't feeling very well, he hunted up an electric fan for me and an extra pillow. It was about 5:30 in the evening. I remember there was some argument about how to cook the chicken for dinner, but we got it cooked. He must have had a premonition of death that Sunday we stepped out of the Biograph Theatre. He was so much more considerate, sweeter, I mean, than he had ever been to me before. Then, too, he carried a gun that day.

Jimmy insisted on going to the Biograph because he wanted to see Manhattan Melodrama, the story of a New York gangster, that was playing there. We had a couple of games of pinochle and then started.

The theater was crowded. Jimmy and I got seats together in the third row from the front, but Anna had to sit by herself at the back. If he did have a premonition, Jimmy was a pretty good bluffer. He laughed and joked all the way through the show, and asked me for a kiss in a loud whisper, just to embarrass me. When the show was over, Anna joined us and we started away.

Jimmy had been insisting for a week or more that I take his arm when we walked together. Before he could ask this time, I slipped my arm through his.

As we stepped out, Jimmy seemed to step away from me.

Suddenly a gun roared, right beside me.

I jumped in fright, and Jimmy was lying there shot.

GROUCHO *and the* BOYS

The dreariness of the Depression might fade out of sight for a few hours with a trip to the local movie palace to see *Horse Feathers, A Day at the Races,* or *A Night at the Opera.*

For the Marx Brothers, it had all begun in the heyday of vaudeville at the world's greatest amusement complex. Groucho, Harpo, Chico, Zeppo, and Gummo traced their show-business roots to Coney Island.

The greasepaint mustache, the wisecracks accompanied by an upraised eyebrow and jaunty cigar were a ways off on that summer's day when Julius Marx, the boy who would be Groucho, tried his luck on the Brooklyn boardwalk.

The year? Perhaps it was 1907. But nobody's sure of the date, or even if the story, as related by Groucho long afterward, is entirely true.

My mother decided that we should form an act. She figured the more people in the act, the more money we'd get. So an act was formed with me and Gummo. It was a singing act. We also had a girl named Mabel O'Donnell in the act. I think she had a glass eye. She was stuck on me and she was a fucking nuisance. On top of which she was ugly.

Sometime later my mother decided to put Harpo into the act. She booked our act into Henderson's "Coney Island" and that was where

Harpo appeared on stage for the first time. At the opening performance he shit in his pants.

Next to where we were performing there was some guy who would holler "slocum on the hocum." He kept saying this right through our act and this made Harpo nervous. What it was, actually, was a call to attract attention to this gadget where people would hit the bottom with a sledge hammer and try to ring the bell at the top for a prize. So that was Harpo's debut.

We were hopeless amateurs. On the bill with us was one of the greatest acts in show business. A quartet called The Quartet and they could really sing. We went on before them. Harpo couldn't sing at all and Gummo's voice was changing so although he was supposed to be a baritone, part of the time his voice sounded tenor. We didn't last too long with that act. It was called The Four Nightingales. Then we became The Four Mascots and finally my mother and my Aunt Hannah joined the act and we changed the name to The Six Mascots. Now neither my mother nor her sister had ever been on stage before this. But the more people we had in the act, the more we'd be paid.

I'll never forget one town where we played. The property man was supposed to have put out two golden chairs for my mother and my aunt to sit on. They were supposed to come out and sing a couple of songs. But when they got to the stage there was only one chair. They both tried to sit in the one chair and both of them fell to the floor. And that was the finish of my mother and my aunt in the act.

the *HINDENBURG* AFLAME

Shortly after seven o'clock on the stormy evening of May 7, 1936, the German dirigible *Hindenburg* settled into its mooring at the Lakehurst naval air station in New Jersey, concluding a flight from Frankfurt with ninety-seven people aboard. Suddenly it exploded in a fireball.

Herbert Morrison of Chicago station WLS was on the scene with a disk-recorder, for the arrivals of the *Hindenburg* were something of a news event.

Morrison's frantic, tearful account would become a broadcast-journalism classic.

It's practically standing still now. They've dropped ropes out of the nose of the ship, and they've been taken hold of down on the field by a number of men. It's starting to rain again. The rain had slacked up a little bit. The back motors of the ship are just holding it just enough to keep it from—It burst into flame! Get this, Charley! Get this, Charley!

[Now he is crying.] It's fire, and it's crashing. It's crashing terrible. Oh, my! Get out of the way, please! It's burning and bursting into flames, and it's falling on the mooring mast . . . and all the folks . . . This is terrible, this is one of the worst catastrophes in the world! Oh, flames four or five hundred feet in the sky! It's a terrific crash, ladies and gentlemen, the smoke and the flames now . . . crashing to the ground, not quite to the mooring mast. Oh, the humanity and all the passengers . . . I can't talk, ladies and gentlemen. Honest, it's a mass of smoking wreckage. . . . Lady, I am sorry. . . . Honestly, I can hardly breathe. I'm going to step inside where I cannot see it. Charley, that's terrible. Listen, folks, I'm going to have to stop for a minute because I've lost my voice—this is the worst thing I've ever witnessed.

Morrison's report, later transmitted on the NBC network, provided the first major radio coverage of an air disaster. It also marked the first time a network had used a prerecorded description of a news event, radio having previously confined itself to "live" transcriptions.

The explosion, evidently touched off by a spark igniting bags of hydrogen gas, claimed thirty-six lives. But it brought immortality of sorts for Morrison, whose panic-stricken broadcast is preserved at the Smithsonian Institution.

MARTIANS *in* JERSEY

It was Halloween Eve 1938. Seemingly live dance music was being broadcast on CBS when an "announcer" broke in with a terrifying bulletin: Martians had landed in New Jersey.

The "Martians" were, in fact, the centerpiece in Orson Welles's production of H. G. Wells's *The War of the Worlds* for *The Mercury Theatre on the Air*.

But it was all too real for the more gullible. Scores of listeners fled their homes or placed frantic phone calls to the police.

Naïveté among the American public—this was still a relatively unsophisticated time for mass communications—and the underlying nervousness created by an impending war in Europe combined to create hysteria.

The event raised an unsettling question: if radio had such influence, how might it be used in the years to come?

"Carl Phillips" (newsman):
Ladies and gentlemen, this is the most terrifying thing I have ever witnessed. . . . Wait a minute, someone's crawling. Someone or . . . something. I can see peering out of that black hole two luminous disks. . . . Are they eyes? It might be a face. It might be . . . Good heavens, something's wriggling out of the shadow like a gray snake. Now it's another one, and another one. They look like tentacles to me. There, I can see the thing's body. It's large as a bear and it glistens like wet leather. But that face. It . . . it's indescribable. I can hardly force myself to keep looking at it. The eyes are black and gleam like a serpent. The mouth is kind of V-shaped with saliva dripping from its rimless lips that seem to quiver and pulsate.

Soon the creatures had burned to death a number of witnesses, including poor Carl Phillips. How they managed to do this was explained by an eminent astronomer, Professor Pierson (Orson Welles).

Of their destructive instrument, I might venture some conjectural explanation. For want of a better term, I shall refer to the mysterious weapon as a heat-ray. It's all too evident that these creatures have scientific knowledge far in advance of our own.

Then came startling news from the station's "announcer."

Ladies and gentlemen, I have a grave announcement to make. Incredible as it may seem, both the observations of science and the evidence of our eyes lead to the inescapable assumption that those strange beings who landed in the Jersey farmlands tonight are the vanguard of an invading army from the planet Mars . . . At this time martial law prevails throughout New Jersey and eastern Pennsylvania.

A survey called the Princeton Radio Project later interviewed listeners, trying to find out why so many people had panicked. Archie Burbank, a gas-station operator in Newark, New Jersey, told his story:

My girl friend and I stayed in the car for a while, just driving around. Then we followed the lead of a friend. All of us ran into a grocery store and asked the man if we could go into his cellar. He said, "What's the matter? Are you trying to ruin my business?" So he chased us out. A crowd collected. We rushed to an apartment house and asked the man in the apartment to let us in his cellar. He said, "I don't have any cellar. Get away!" Then people started to rush out of the apartment house all undressed. We got into the car and listened some more. Suddenly, the announcer was gassed, the station went dead so we tried another station but nothing would come on. Then we went to a gas station and filled up our tank in preparation for just riding as far as we could. The gas station man didn't know anything about it. Then one friend, male, decided he would call up the Newark Evening News. He found out it was a play. We listened to the rest of the play and then went dancing.

MARIAN ANDERSON *at the* LINCOLN MEMORIAL

Easter Sunday 1939. The Lincoln Memorial was in its fullest glory— its symbolism never so grand.

The great black contralto Marian Anderson had been barred from performing at Washington's Constitution Hall, which was owned by the Daughters of the American Revolution. The hall had a "white-artists-only" restriction, commonplace for the deeply segregated capital.

When news of the rebuff emerged, Eleanor Roosevelt resigned from the DAR and Interior Secretary Harold Ickes arranged for Miss Anderson to sing at the memorial.

Some seventy-five thousand people gathered there—with millions more listening on radio—in a poignant tableau that proved a marker for the civil-rights movement.

Walter White, the general secretary of the NAACP, was in the crowd.

The concert was scheduled to begin at five o'clock. We drove to the Lincoln Memorial, approaching it from the rear. We had to park the car blocks away because every available place near by had already been preempted. What a sight greeted us when we came around to the front of the Memorial! Every one of the several hundred chairs which had been placed on the lower platform was occupied. Seldom in the history even of Washington had a more distinguished group of sponsors been gathered. But much more important to us was the audience itself. Seventy-five thousand white and colored Americans not only from Washington but from cities, towns, and villages within a radius of hundreds of miles had gathered at the Memorial of the Great Emancipator to hear a singer of whom Toscanini had said, "A voice like yours comes but once in a century."

No member of that audience will ever forget the sight of Miss Anderson emerging from a small anteroom beside Gaudens's statue of Lincoln. She was apparently calm, but those of us who knew her were aware of the great perturbation beneath her serene exterior. . . . A tremendous wave of applause rose from the vast throng, which was silenced only when Miss Anderson gently raised her hand to ask that the concert be permitted to begin. Amplifiers poured out the thunderous chords of the opening bars of "America." Clasping her hands before her Miss Anderson poured out in her superb voice "sweet land of liberty" almost as though it was a prayer.

As the last notes of "Nobody Knows the Trouble I've Seen" faded away the spell was broken by the rush of the audience toward Miss Anderson, which almost threatened tragedy. [Assistant Interior Secretary] Oscar Chapman plowed through the crowd and directed me to the microphone to plead with them not to create a panic. As I did so, but with indifferent success, a single figure caught my eye in the mass of people below which seemed one of the most important and touching symbols of the occasion. It was a slender black girl dressed in somewhat too garishly hued Easter finery. Hers was not the face of one who had been the beneficiary of much education or opportunity. Her hands were particularly noticeable as she thrust them forward and upward, trying desperately, although she was some distance away from Miss Anderson, to touch the singer. They were hands which despite their youth had known only the dreary work of manual labor. Tears streamed down the girl's dark face. Her hat was askew, but in her eyes flamed hope bordering on ecstasy. Life which had been none too easy for her now held out greater hope because one who was also colored and who, like herself, had known poverty, privation, and prejudice, had, by her genius, gone a long way toward conquering bigotry. If Marian Anderson could do it, the girl's eyes seemed to say, then I can, too.

"MR. HOOVER, *this is* LEPKE"

He was the creator of the modern gossip column, the chronicler of Broadway, a man whose fame rivaled that of the celebrities and political figures he wrote and talked about in newspaper columns and radio broadcasts followed by millions in the 1930s and '40s. Walter Winchell could make or break a star, holding forth from Table 50 at the Stork Club on Manhattan's East 53rd Street.

And on an August evening in 1939, he corralled one of the underworld's biggest names.

New York's most feared industrial racketeer, Louis Buchalter—better known as "Lepke"—decided to come out of hiding and take his chances with federal authorities. He surrendered to FBI Director J. Edgar Hoover through the man with the trademark fedora, embellishing Winchell's renown as the most influential newspaperman of his day.

In his syndicated column, Winchell told his readers how he delivered Lepke.

The surrender of public enemy "Lepke" Buchalter to the government last night took place while scores of pedestrians ambled by, and two police radio cars waited for the lights to change, near Twenty-eighth Street and Fifth Avenue.

The time was precisely 10:17 P.M., and the search for the most wanted fugitive in the nation was over. The surrender was negotiated by this reporter, whom G-man John Edgar Hoover authorized to guarantee "safe delivery."

After a series of telephone talks with persons unknown, and with the head of the FBI, Lepke appeared to drop out of the sky, without even a parachute. The time was 10:15. The scene was Madison Square between Twenty-third and Twenty-fourth Streets, where we had halted our car as per instructions.

The following two minutes were consumed traveling slowly north on Fourth Avenue and west on Twenty-seventh Street to Fifth Avenue, where the traffic lights were red—and to the next corner at Twenty-eighth Street, where Mr. Hoover waited alone, unarmed and without handcuffs, in a government limousine. Hoover was disguised in dark sunglasses to keep him from being recognized by passers-by.

The presence of two New York police cruisers, attached to the Fourteenth Precinct, so near the surrender scene startled Hoover as well as Lepke. The G-man later admitted he feared "a leak."

Lepke, who was calmer than this chauffeur, was on the verge of rushing out of our machine into Hoover's arms. The police cruisers, ironically, were the first observed by this reporter in two hours of motoring to complete the surrender.

Not until the final seconds was there a sign of uniformed law. But it was too late. The long arm of government had reached out and claimed another enemy. The Federal Bureau of Investigation and the city of New York had saved $50,000—the reward offered.

While pausing alongside one police car at the Twenty-seventh Street intersection for the lights, Lepke, who was wearing spectacles as part of his disguise, threw them to the corner pavement. They crashed noisily. Two passers-by, middle-aged men with graying temples, stopped and looked up at a building.

Apparently they thought a window had broken above. They never *realized that the man for whom every cop in the land was searching was within touching distance.*

After parking our car behind a machine which was parked behind Hoover's, we shut off the ignition and escorted Lepke into Hoover's car.

"Mr. Hoover," we said, "this is Lepke."

"How do you do?" said Mr. Hoover affably.

"Glad to meet you," replied Lepke. "Let's go."

"To the Federal Building at Foley Square," commanded Hoover. His colored pilot turned swiftly south.

Lepke was a little excited. He seemed anxious to talk—to talk to anybody new—after being in the shadows for over two years with so many hunted men.

"You did the smart thing by coming in, Lepke," comforted Hoover.

"I'm beginning to wonder if I did," Lepke answered. "I would like to see my wife and kids, please?"

Mr. Hoover arranged for them to visit him shortly after Lepke was booked, fingerprinted, and Kodaked. He had $1,700 on him. He gave $1,100 to the boy and $600 to the jailer—for "expenses."

When the government car reached Fourteenth Street, we got out and went to the first phone to notify our editor, who groaned:

"A fine thing! With a World War starting!"

Lepke's decision to surrender wasn't the wisest move he ever made. He was later turned over to New York authorities on murder charges and was executed at Sing Sing on March 4, 1944.

ROYALTY *on the* HUDSON

As Hitler's demands brought Europe to the edge of war in the spring of 1939, President Roosevelt decided on a grand gesture to symbolize the alignment of American interests with those of Britain. He invited King George VI and Queen Elizabeth to visit the United States, the first trip to America by British royalty.

The best-remembered moment would be the June outing at the

President's Hyde Park, New York, home, when the sovereigns became commoners—they were introduced to their first hot dogs.

Outside the public eye, Roosevelt told the king of military steps America could take in the event of war without violating its official neutrality—essentially, naval patrols in the Atlantic.

Also beyond the public gaze—as Eleanor Roosevelt would recall—were some perplexing moments vis-à-vis protocol.

One day before the visit, I invited Lady Lindsay, wife of the British ambassador, to tea and asked her if she was being given any instructions which might be helpful to me. Lady Lindsay was an American whom I had known a long while, and we looked at things from more or less the same point of view. Her sense of humor was keen and she looked at me rather wickedly when she said: "Yes, Sir Alan Lascelles has been to stay with us and he has told us that the king must be served at meals thirty seconds ahead of the queen. He added that the king does not like capers or suet pudding. I told him we did not often have suet pudding in the United States and that I really had not expected the king to like capers." . . .

I told Franklin that British protocol required that the head butler, Fields, stand with a stop watch in his hand and, thirty seconds after he and the king had been served, dispatch a butler to serve the queen and myself, and I inquired what was to happen about the White House rule that the president was always served first. He looked at me with firmness: "We will not require Fields to have a stop watch. The king and I will be served simultaneously and you and the queen will be served next." . . .

One of the young men who had been asked to sing some folk songs had been reported to the FBI as a communist or bolshevik and likely to do something dangerous. The charge was completely untrue and made by someone who wanted to be disagreeable, but when the FBI reported it to the secret service men they had to be true to their traditions and follow the tip through. When the young man came in after dinner he was "frisked" by our secret service men and then by the Scotland Yard people, and apparently was so frightened he could hardly sing. I hoped fervently he would not reach for his handkerchief during the performance, because I was sure both the secret service and Scotland Yard would jump on him. . . .

We sat in the library of the Hyde Park house waiting for them. Franklin had a tray of cocktails ready in front of him, and his mother sat on the other side of the fireplace looking disapprovingly at the cocktails and telling her son that the king would prefer tea. My husband, who could be as obstinate as his mother, kept his tray in readiness, however. Finally the king and queen arrived and I met them at the door and took them to their rooms. In a short time they were dressed and down in the library. As the king approached my husband and the cocktail table, my husband looked up at him and said: "My mother does not approve of cocktails and thinks you should have a cup of tea." The king answered, "Neither does my mother," and took a cocktail. . . .

We had brought up the colored butlers from the White House. My mother-in-law had an English butler who, when he heard that the White House butlers were coming up to help him, was so shocked that the king and queen were to be waited on by colored people that he decided to take his holiday before their majesties came, in order not to see them treated in that manner!

Just exactly what happened to our well-trained White House butlers that night, I shall never know. My mother-in-law had had the extra china that was needed put on a serving table that was not ordinarily used, and suddenly in the middle of dinner the serving table collapsed and the dishes clattered to the floor. . . .

One would think that one mishap of this kind would be enough for one evening, but just after we had gone down to the big library after dinner, there was a most terrible crash as the butler, carrying a tray of decanters, glasses, bowls of ice, and so on, fell down the two steps leading from the hall and slid right into the library, scattering the contents of the tray over the floor and leaving a large lake of water and ice cubes at the bottom of the steps. I am sure Mama wished that her English butler had stayed. . . .

When the king and queen departed, a poignant moment was played out.

The royal couple stood on the rear platform of the train as it pulled out, and the people who were gathered everywhere on the banks of the Hudson and up on the rocks suddenly began to sing "Auld Lang Syne." There was something incredibly moving about this scene—the river in the evening light, the voices of many people singing this old song, and the train slowly pulling out with the young couple waving good-bye. One thought of the clouds that hung over them and the worries they were going to face, and turned away and left the scene with a heavy heart.

Chapter Six

WORLD WAR II YEARS

the MAKING *of* GI JOE

When World War II began, with Hitler's invasion of Poland on September 1, 1939, the United States was far from a military power. Roosevelt was still stymied by the isolationist movement.

Congress would finally authorize a military draft in 1940, and soon thousands of men were arriving at train stations in scores of backwater army towns each morning.

An army private named Marion Hargrove—once the feature editor of the *Charlotte News*—sent vignettes of his basic-training travails at Fort Bragg, North Carolina, back to his newspaper. His tales of army life—misadventures perennially bringing him KP punishment duty—would be compiled in a book. *See Here, Private Hargrove* became a best-seller.

It was often a slapstick account. But in his final vignette, the GI turned from the snafus and reflected on what was to come.

He told of the scene at the Fort Bragg Replacement Center—a coming and going played out every day.

There was a group of new men coming in this morning, down at the railroad siding. Their new uniforms hung strangely upon them, conspicuous and uncertain and uncomfortable—new uniforms on new soldiers.

They were frightened and ill at ease, these men. A week ago they had been civilians and the prospect of the Army had probably hung over them like a Damoclean sword. They had been told, by well-meaning friends, that the Army wouldn't be so bad once they got used to it. The Army will make you or break you, they had been told. The Army really isn't as bad as it's painted, they had heard. All of this, in a diabolical suggestive way, had opened up conjectures to terrify the most indomitable.

This morning, they still hadn't time to get over their fears. They still had no idea what Army life was going to be like. Most of all and first of all, they wondered, "What sort of place is this we're coming into?"

Their spirits were still at their lowest point—past, present or future.

The Replacement Center band, led by wizened little Master Sergeant

Knowles, was there to greet them with a welcome that might dispel from them the feeling that they were cattle being shipped into the fort on consignment. First there were the conventional but stirring military marches, the "Caisson Song" and all the rest. And then there was a sly and corny rendition of the "Tiger Rag," a friendly musical wind that said, "Take it easy, brother."

A little reassured but still suspicious, the men went from the train to the theater, where they would see a program of entertainment and possibly hear a short and casual welcoming address by General Parker.

This afternoon the sound of marching feet came up Headquarters Street from the south and a battery of departing soldiers approached. As they neared the headquarters building, there came the order, "Count cadence—command!" and two hundred voices took up a chant. They passed, counting their footsteps in ringing ordered tones.

Laden with haversacks, they passed in perfect order. Their lines were even, their marching co-ordinated and confident. Their uniforms no longer bore the awkward stamp. Their caps were cocky but correct and their neckties were tucked between the right two buttons.

The cadence count is the scheme of the battery commander who feels proud of the men he has trained, who wants to show them off to the higher-ups in Center Headquarters. "The general might be standing by his window now, watching my men pass," they say. "If he isn't, we should attract his attention."

Just as their arrival marks an emotional ebb, their departure is the flood tide. The men who came in a few weeks ago, green and terrified, leave now as soldiers. The corporal whom they dreaded then is now just a jerk bucking for sergeant. Although they are glad they have been trained with other men on the same level here, the training center which was first a vast and awful place is now just a training center, all right in its way —for rookies. They themselves have outgrown their kindergarten.

The band is at the railroad siding to see them off with a flourish. They pay more attention to the band this time. They know the "Caisson Song." . . .

They see the commanding general standing on the side lines with his aide. He is no longer an ogre out of Washington who might, for all they *know, have the power of life and death over them to administer it at a whim. He is the commanding general, a good soldier and a good fellow, and it was damned white of him to come down to see them off.*

They board the train and they sit waiting for it to take them to their permanent Army post and their part in the war.

As a special favor and for old times' sake, the band swings slowly into the song that is the voice of their nostalgia, "The Sidewalks of New York." Yankee or Rebel, Minnesotan or Nevadan, they love that song.

You can see their faces tightening a little, and a gentle melancholy look come into their eyes as the trombone wails beneath the current of the music. Their melancholy is melancholy with a shrug now. Home and whatever else was dearest to them a few months ago are still dear, but a soldier has to push them into the background when there's a war to be fought.

With the music still playing, the train pulls slowly out and Sergeant Knowles waves it good-bye with his baton.

An old sergeant, kept in the Replacement Center to train the men whose fathers fought with him a generation ago, stands on the side and watches them with a firm, proud look.

"Give 'em hell, boys," he shouts behind them. "Give 'em hell!"

PEARL HARBOR SUNDAY

As 1941 drew to a close, the Roosevelt administration tightened economic sanctions against Japan in a bid to frustrate its war lords' "New Order" aimed at supremacy in Asia.

And America seemed to have the military might to back up a challenge in the Pacific. On Saturday, December 6, Navy Secretary Frank Knox declared: "The American people may be fully confident in their Navy. The U.S. Navy is second to none."

But on Sunday, December 7, the United States Pacific Fleet lay in ruins. The Japanese attack at Pearl Harbor left eight battleships damaged or sunk, more than two hundred planes destroyed on the ground, and twenty-four hundred American sailors, soldiers, and civilians dead.

On Monday, Roosevelt went to Congress for a declaration of war, vowing to avenge "a day that will live in infamy."

By the week's end, the isolationist movement was no more. Though reeling in the Pacific and years away from an invasion of Europe, the United States was at war with Japan and Germany.

On Pearl Harbor Sunday, hundreds of sailors died when a bomb went down the smokestack of the battleship *Arizona*, quickly sending it to the bottom. Elsewhere on Battleship Row, shipyard workers and seamen tried frantically to reach the men who might still be alive inside the *Oklahoma*, lying upside down at the harbor bottom. As the rescuers cut through the hull, they listened for faint taps from crewmen pounding against the bulkheads.

One of them was Stephen Bower Young.

The world was my oyster that Sunday morning in December 1941. I was nineteen, breakfast was over, and liberty would be starting in an hour or so. A quick look out a second-deck porthole of our battleship, the U.S.S. Oklahoma, confirmed my feeling that this was going to be a glorious day. There were still some early morning clouds, but the sun was warm, with just a breath of trade wind ruffling the waters of the harbor. . . .

I was anxious to make that first liberty launch ashore. One of my buddies grinned, "Don't hurry, your girl will wait." . . .

My girl and I were going to Nanakuli, where the surf was much better than Waikiki and the beach not nearly so crowded. For once I had plenty of money—a ten and a one-dollar bill.

I looked at my watch. Two minutes to morning colors. I started toward my locker.

Suddenly the bugle blared over the PA system. . . . It was the call for gun crews to man their anti-aircraft stations.

The harsh excited voice on the PA system froze us in our tracks. "All hands, man your battle stations! On the double! This is no drill! Get going—they're real bombs!"

I headed for my turret battle station. Everyone was running and pushing. The ship shuddered as she was hit somewhere forward.

I clutched at the bulkhead, barely able to stay on my feet as the water flooded in. That was when the dreaded phrase was passed from man to man . . . "Abandon ship, abandon ship." . . .

We could not get out. We were being hit again and again, dreadful, tearing hits. We realized all at once that these were not bombs, but torpedoes. . . .

The list rapidly increased until it seemed that the ship was almost lying on her side. With awful certainty we knew that we were sinking. Suddenly the ship lurched! The deck slipped out from under me and my hands snatched at empty air. As she rolled over, I was pitched into a mass of dead and dying and, with them, buffeted and tossed around. Then the dark waters closed over me as the ship came to rest upside down on the bottom of the harbor.

Eventually I surfaced, gulped for air, and swam desperately in the darkness, surprised to find myself alive. Random shouts mingled with cries for help; then quiet fell abruptly. Water gurgled as it made its way into the ship. I thought we were done for. . . .

We were in a pocket of air that had been trapped as the ship went down. Although our space was only partially flooded, we knew it was simply a matter of time until the air gave out and the water took over. It was rising slowly. We settled back to wait. . . . The situation seemed hopeless. . . .

My watch finally stopped. Time did not matter. I dropped it in the water with a splash. Then I took out a pocketful of change and dropped the coins abruptly into the water. There was a place in town where Oklahoma sailors met to drink beer, sing songs of the Navy, tell sea stories, dance with their girls, laugh, and fight with sailors from other ships. Remembering it, I couldn't resist saying aloud, "How about a cold beer? I'm thirsty."

"Set 'em up, all the way around," a sailor replied.

"Join the Navy and see the world—from the bottom of Pearl Harbor." . . .

As the water rose, the air became more and more foul. I felt a longing to break the silence again.

"Willy," I said, "I'll bet you a dollar we'll suffocate before we drown."

"Okay, you're on," agreed Willy. "I say we drown first."

We each produced a soggy dollar bill, after which we lapsed again into silence. . . .

Suddenly, anger rumbled within me. Why couldn't we have died in the sun where we could have met death head on? That was the way to die, on your feet, like a man. But instead, it was to be a slow, useless death, imprisoned in our dark iron cell.

Still, perhaps to die like this required a special kind of courage. Could I meet the test? "Oh, God," I prayed, "relieve us of our torment. If it is Your will that we die here, please watch over our families and comfort them. We are delivered unto You and ask to be forgiven for our sins."

The hours passed.

Unexpectedly, and from a great distance, came the sound of hammering. Metal against metal! Our hearts jumped. The sound stopped, and we held our breaths. It started again, closer, and died away once more. . . .

Then the noise began again, not sporadically, but like the knock of an automatic tool. Did it mean rescuers?

We hammered at the steel bulkhead with a dog wrench. Three dots—three dashes—SOS!! . . .

A yell sounded from the next compartment. Workers had broken through to them! . . .

"Keep calm, fellows," a worker called out. "We'll get you out!"

They began to cut through the metal. . . . The water had risen to our knees.

"Please hurry, for God's sake! We can't stop this flooding." . . .

The water was now waist high. . . .

Gradually the opening widened as the water pushed at us from behind. It would be just wide enough to scrape through.

"Okay! Come on through!" voices called. We entered the opening in a flood of water. Friendly hands reached for our oil-slicked bodies and pulled us into the next compartment. We were free! Gradually I searched the faces of our rescuers—big Hawaiian Navy Yard workers and some sailors. The Navy indeed took care of its own.

Finally I emerged out of the cold darkness into the warm sunshine of a new day. It was 0900, 8 December.

Standing on the upturned hull, I gazed about me. It was the same

world I had left twenty-five hours before, but as I looked at the smoke
and wreckage of battle, the sunken ships Tennessee, West Virginia and
Arizona astern of us, I felt that life would never be the same, not for me
—not for any of us. I took a few drags on a cigarette. Someone said to
put it out because of all the oil around.

A launch came alongside to take us to a hospital ship. As I stepped
into the boat, I looked down at the ship we had lived in, the ship we had
come so close to dying in, the tomb of friends and shipmates who were
gone forever. The mighty Oklahoma was no more. The flag, the colored
signal pennants would never fly again. Her guns were silent, her turrets
full of men and water. How strange that never in all her life had she ever
fired at an enemy.

The launch chugged out into the harbor. Turning to the sailor who had
bet a dollar with me on how we would die, I grinned at him. "Put the
buck away for a souvenir, Willy. We both lost."

LAST WORD from CORREGIDOR

The early months of war in the Pacific brought a string of disasters for
the United States. Japanese forces took the American possession of
Wake Island just before Christmas, seized Manila in January 1942,
and whipped American and British fleets in the Java Sea at the end of
February.

In early May, after overcoming American and Filipino soldiers on
the Bataan Peninsula, the Japanese stormed the remnants of resistance
on the island of Corregidor in Manila Harbor.

Just before the surrender of Corregidor, radio messages were sent
from the caves by a twenty-two-year-old Army Signal Corps private
named Irving Strobing. Recorded as they were received, presumably
in Honolulu, the messages were played on the "Army Hour" radio
program three weeks later and printed in newspapers.

They are not near yet. We are waiting for God only knows what. How
about a chocolate soda?

... Not many. Not near yet. Lots of heavy fighting going on. We've only got about one hour, twenty minutes before.

We may have to give up by noon. We don't know yet. They are throwing men and shells at us and we may not be able to stand it. They have been shelling us faster than you can count.

We've got about fifty-five minutes and I feel sick at my stomach. I am really low down. They are around now smashing rifles. They bring in the wounded every minute. We will be waiting for you guys to help. This is the only thing I guess that can be done.

General Wainwright is a right guy and we are willing to go on for him, but shells were dropping all night, faster than hell. Damage terrific. Too much for guys to take. Enemy heavy cross-shelling and bombing. They have got us all around and from skies.

From here it looks like firing ceased on both sides. Men here all feeling bad because of terrific nervous strain of the siege. Corregidor used to be a nice place, but it's haunted now. Withstood a terrific pounding.

Just made broadcast to Manila to arrange meeting for surrender. Talk made by General Beebe. I can't say much. Can't think at all. I can hardly think. Say, I have 60 pesos you can have for this weekend.

The jig is up. Everyone is bawling like a baby. They are piling dead and wounded in our tunnel. Arm's weak from pounding key, long hours, no rest, short rations, tired.

I know now how a mouse feels. Caught in a trap waiting for guys to come along and finish it up. Got a treat. Can pineapple. Opening it with Signal Corps knife.

My name Irving Strobing. Get this to my mother, Mrs. Minnie Strobing, 605 Barbey Street, Brooklyn, N.Y. They are to get along O.K. Get in touch with them as soon as possible. Message. My love to Pa [his father, Samuel, a tailor], Joe [his brother Joseph was in the Coast Artillery], Sue [his 18-year-old sister, Sylvia], Mac, Garry, Joy and Paul. Also to all family and friends. God bless 'em all. Hope they be there when I come home. Tell Joe, wherever he is, go give 'em hell for us. My love to you all. God bless you and keep you. Love. Sign my name and tell my mother how you heard from me.

On the following day—May 6, 1942—General Jonathan Wainwright surrendered Corregidor and its 11,000 defenders.

TURNABOUT *at* MIDWAY

The notion that battleships were the heart of a modern navy was demolished on Pearl Harbor Sunday. The American battleships and cruisers destroyed by the Japanese had been attacked not by other battleships but by planes launched from aircraft carriers.

The United States carriers had been spared, fortunately out to sea when the attack occurred. By early 1942, aircraft carriers represented America's best hope for striking back against Japan.

The pattern for naval warfare in the Pacific was set in May 1942 in the Battle of the Coral Sea, north of Australia, when American and Japanese planes dueled with not a single shot fired from a ship.

America's fortunes turned in June, when an immense Japanese fleet was spotted moving toward Midway, an atoll fifteen hundred miles west of Hawaii housing American bases. In a battle fought by fighter planes and bombers sent up from carriers two hundred miles apart, the Japanese lost four aircraft carriers, their first major naval defeat. The United States, suffering severe damage only to the carrier *Yorktown*, took a huge step toward gaining the offensive in the Pacific.

One of the fighter-bombers attacking the Japanese carriers was piloted by Lieutenant Clarence Dickinson.

Our squadron flew in six wedge-shaped sections, inverted V's, three planes in a section, two sections in a division. . . .

About a quarter past twelve Lieutenant Commander McCluskey at the front end and top of the formation picked up the enemy some forty or forty-five miles ahead and to the left. We headed for them as fast as we could go. What McCluskey had distinguished first, almost halfway to the far horizon, on that dense ocean blue were thin, white lines; mere threads, chalk-white. He knew those must be the wakes of the Japanese ships. . . . Because I was less high, it was not until about five minutes after McCluskey saw them that I could see them, too. . . .

This was the Japanese striking force. I could see a huge fleet, so many ships that I knew it was their main body. . . .

This was the culmination of our hopes and dreams. Among those ships, I could see two long, narrow, yellow rectangles, the flight decks of carriers. . . . Then farther off I saw a third carrier. I had expected to see only two and when I saw the third my heart went lower. The southwest corner of the fleet's position was obscured by a storm area. Suddenly another long yellow rectangle came sliding out of that obscurity. A fourth carrier!

I could not understand why we had come this far without having fighters swarming over and around us like hornets. But we hadn't seen a single fighter in the air and not a shot had been fired at us. . . .

Every ship in that fleet bore a distinguishing mark. Each battleship, cruiser and destroyer advertised itself as Japanese with this marking painted on the forward turret. The turret top appeared as a square of white with a round, blood-red center. But on the deck of each carrier, bow or stern, the marking was exactly like that which appears on their planes. . . . On the nearest carrier I could see that this symbol probably would measure sixty feet across; a five-foot band of white, enclosing a fifty-foot disk of red. An enticing target!

There were planes massed on the deck of each carrier and I could clearly see that the flight decks were undamaged, in perfect condition to launch. . . .

By the grace of God, as I put my nose down I picked up our carrier below in front of me. I was making the best dive I had ever made. The people who came back said it was the best dive they had ever made. We were coming from all directions on the port side of the carrier, beautifully spaced. Going down I was watching over the nose of my plane to see the first bombs land on that yellow deck. At last her fighters were taking off and that was when I felt sure I recognized her as the Kaga; and she was enormous. The Kaga and the Akagi were the big names in the Japanese fleet. . . .

As I was almost at the dropping point I saw a bomb hit just behind where I was aiming, that white circle with its blood-red center. . . . I saw the deck rippling, and curling back in all directions exposing a great section of the hangar below. That bomb had a fuse set to make it explode about four feet below the deck. I knew the last plane had taken off or landed on that carrier for a long time to come. . . .

I had determined during that dive that since I was dropping on a Japanese carrier I was going to see my bombs hit. After dropping I kicked my rudder to get my tail out of the way and put my plane in a stall. So I was simply standing there to watch it. I saw the 500-pound bomb hit right abreast of the island. The two 100-pound bombs struck in the forward area of the parked planes and that yellow flight deck. Then I began thinking it was time to get myself away from there and try to get back alive. . . .

As we went away from the Kaga I could see five big fires in the middle of the Japanese fleet. One was either a battle ship or a big cruiser. The destroyer that had been shooting at me was lying still and smoking heavily amidships where her boilers are. But the three biggest fires were the carriers. They were burning fiercely and exploding. I looked back when I was a couple of miles away. In spite of the succession of incidents, this was no more than a few minutes after my bombs had landed on the Kaga. She was on fire from end to end and I saw her blow up at the middle. From right abreast the island a solid ball of fire shot straight up. It passed through fleecy lower clouds which we estimated to be 1,200 feet above the water. Some of our flyers who were up higher saw this solid mass of fire as it burst up through the clouds, and they said the fire rose three or four hundred feet still higher. . . .

I could not afford to wait another second. My gasoline gauges had suddenly assumed an importance greater than the blazing, ruined carriers. I was dubious about our chances from here on. . . . When I left the enemy my inboard tanks registered, each one, thirty gallons. If we had to go more than 150 or 175 miles on the return flight sixty gallons ought to be enough, if I was careful. It might not get me aboard but it would get me back.

the JAPANESE AMERICANS

A fear of homefront sabotage bordering on hysteria and fueled by long-standing prejudice brought a great blot on American standards of justice: the removal of Japanese aliens and Japanese Americans from the West Coast to internment camps in harsh and desolate inland regions.

Perhaps a hundred thousand people of Japanese origin lost their homes, their farms, all their possessions during the war years.

A Californian named George Akimoto would remember the day they came for his father.

My dad was head of a couple of organizations which I guess the F.B.I. considered dangerous or subversive. So one morning, about 7 o'clock, they broke through our front door and came in with submachine guns. One of the deputies—I guess the F.B.I. had recently sworn him in—used to be a bill collector in Stockton and used to collect bills for my dad. He came in with them. They saw my sea scout uniform and said, "What's that?"

I said, "Can't you see the boy scout emblem on that?"

They questioned us, and then they said, "We're going to have to take him." They took my mother's knitting book that was written in Japanese —you know, knit one, purl two. They thought it was a code book. That was the only evidence they took when they took my old man. I could see them just running that thing through the army deciphering machine!

So they took him and put him in the local jail. This was in the wintertime. He didn't even take his topcoat because he thought he would be back in a day or two. Next thing we know, we got a letter from Bismarck, North Dakota. He's up there in a camp freezing his butt off in the snow up there without his topcoat! Eventually he wound up in Santa Fe, New Mexico, actually with prisoners of war from the European theater—Germans, Italians. Then all of a sudden, they released him and he came back to Arkansas where we were.

A lot of things are not mentioned in any of the histories of evacuation. One thing that stays in my mind was when we were in the assembly center, we had some real bad people running the camp—not running the camp, but employees within the camp. One night we got wind of— they're shipping big sides of beef into the camp to feed us, yet we were getting nothing but canned stuff, rations. And once we heard rumors they were smuggling the sides of beef out of camp and somebody was selling them black market. So we sneaked over and watched one night, and sure enough they were loading this truck full of sides of beef. And we heard there was an F.B.I. spy in camp, so we made sure he found out about it; yet nothing was done. I suppose we could have printed something in the paper, but, you know, that would have caused a riot in the camp. . . .

Another thing when we were in Arkansas, the M.P.'s who were put in charge were all complete misfits, guys you couldn't use in combat. So there were guys that weighed three hundred pounds and guys that were so skinny they could hardly walk, and cripples—guys like that guarding us in camp. And when we first went in there, they had watch towers up with machine guns. And one night, one of the guards decided—he was drunk I guess—he sprayed the roof tops with this machine gun. And after that, they removed the machine guns. But, you know, you don't read about things like that.

D-DAY *at* OMAHA BEACH

It was the greatest seaborne invasion in history. As dawn broke on June 6, 1944, the first of 156,000 Allied troops to be landed on the shores of Normandy that day began their approach to the beaches of Nazi-occupied France. They were backed by 5,000 ships and 10,000 planes.

This was D-Day, the beginning of the end for Hitler's Germany.

From the perspective of the present, the breakthrough by American, British, and Canadian forces may seem to have been inevitable. But it was a close thing. "Everything that could have gone wrong had gone wrong," Dwight D. Eisenhower, the Supreme Allied Commander, would remark as he walked along Omaha Beach—the bloodiest American landing sector—to commemorate D-Day's twentieth anniversary.

A storm that had forced a twenty-four-hour postponement of the invasion left overcast skies that foiled the bombers' attempts to soften up German positions overlooking Omaha. And the early naval bombardment was ineffective. The infantrymen would have little protection against the intense firepower raining down from the cliffs.

It was a chaotic morning for men like Sergeant John Robert Slaughter of the Twenty-ninth Division, a nineteen-year-old from Roanoke, Virginia, who was among the first soldiers to hit the beach.

We rail-loaded into our assigned stations on the landing craft and were lowered into the sea by davits. My craft began to take water from spray from seven-foot waves coming in over the bow and from the starboard side. All hands had to help the craft's pumps by bailing water with battle helmets. Cold spume blew in and soon we were shivering.

As the sky lightened, the armada became visible. At 0600, the huge guns of the Allied navies opened up with what must have been one of the greatest artillery barrages ever! The mighty battleship Texas on our starboard side fired in deafening salvos its 14-inch guns. In minutes, giant swells caused by the recoil of those guns almost swamped us. Twin-fuselaged P-38 fighter-bombers were also seen overhead protecting us from the Luftwaffe. This should be a piece of cake!

About 200 or 300 yards from shore we encountered the first enemy artillery fire. How did they survive the bombing and shelling? Near-misses sent water skyward, and then it rained back on us. The British coxswain shouted to step back—he was going to lower the ramp, and for us to quickly disembark. I heard Technical Sergeant Willard Norfleet counter, "These men have heavy equipment and you will take them all the way in." The coxswain begged, "But we'll all be killed." Norfleet unholstered his .45 Colt pistol, put it to the sailor's head and ordered: "All the way in!" The craft proceeded, plowing through the choppy water, until the bow scraped the sandy bottom.

My thinking as we approached the beach: If this boat didn't hurry up and get us in, I would die from seasickness. Thinking I was immune, I had given my puke bag to a buddy who already had filled his. Minus the paper bag, I used the first thing at hand—my steel helmet.

As we approached the beach the ramp was lowered. Mortar and artillery shells exploded on land and in the water. Unseen snipers concealed in the cliffs were shooting down, but most havoc was from automatic weapons. The water was turning red from the blood.

There were dead men in the water and live men acting dead, letting the tide take them in. While lying half in and half out of the water, I noticed a G.I. running from right to left, trying to get across the beach. He was weighted with equipment. An enemy gunner shot him as he stumbled for cover. He screamed for a medic. An aid man moved quickly to help him, and he was also shot. I'll never forget seeing that medic lying next to that wounded G.I. and both of them screaming.

I gathered my courage and started to run. I ran as low as I could, and since I am six feet five inches, I still presented a good target. As I ran through a tidal pool with about six to eight inches of water, I began to stumble. I finally caught my balance and accidentally fired my rifle, barely missing my foot.

Upon reaching the slanted sea wall, I looked back for the first time and got a glimpse of the 5,000-ship armada out in the Channel. It was an awesome sight.

I felt like a naked morsel on a giant sandy platter. The first thing I did was take off my assault jacket and spread my raincoat so I could clean my rifle. It was then I saw bullet holes in my jacket and the raincoat. I lit my first cigarette. I became weak in the knees.

At the base of the bluff, men began to congregate. The regimental commander, Colonel Charlie (Old Hatchetface) Canham, appeared, right arm in a sling and clutching a .45 Colt in his bony left hand. He was shot cleanly through the wrist. Canham didn't look like a soldier, but he was one, and a very tough one at that. He was tall and thin, wire-rim glasses and a pencil-thin mustache.

There was a lieutenant colonel taking refuge from an enemy mortar barrage in a nearby sentinel pillbox. The officer yelled to Canham, "Colonel, you'd better take cover or you're going to get killed!"

Colonel Canham screamed his reply: "Get your ass out of there and get these men off this goddamned beach!"

AFTERNOON *at* WARM SPRINGS

By the winter of 1944, the burdens of the wartime presidency had exacted a heavy toll on Franklin D. Roosevelt. His secretary, Grace Tully, noticed how he sometimes nodded off while doing his work, how his hands were shaking, his shoulders slumping.

In March 1944, the President went to Bethesda Naval Hospital for a checkup. The findings were distressing—an enlarged heart and high blood pressure.

The American public knew nothing of this when Roosevelt ran for a fourth term. But by early 1945, his physical deterioration was evident. Reporting on his trip to the Yalta Conference, Roosevelt sat as he spoke in the House of Representatives—the first time he had been unable to stand before Congress with the aid of braces.

As springtime arrived, Roosevelt went to Warm Springs, Georgia, for a rest. On the afternoon of Thursday, April 12, he was signing papers while sitting for a painting by a woman named Elizabeth Shoumatoff. Among those with him were an aide, William Hassett; his cousins Margaret Suckley and Laura Delano (known respectively as Daisy and Polly); his valet, Arthur Prettyman; a Filipino houseboy; Secret Service agent Charlie Fredericks; and FDR's longtime romantic interest Lucy Rutherford—her presence there unknown, of course, to Eleanor Roosevelt.

Daisy Suckley's diary would tell of that day.

F. appeared just about as planned—Mme. S had her easel set up, we put the Pres.' chair at just the right angle, so the light would be good. We were fussing around, getting things fixed. He came in, looking very fine in a double-breasted grey suit & a crimson tie. His colour was good & he looked smiling & happy & ready for anything. He sat down in his chair while I explained why the chair was facing toward the light, instead of in its usual position, toward the room. . . .

Mme. S. exclaimed: "Mr. President, you look so much better than yesterday, I am glad I did not start working before today." He looked so good looking; much as some of his earlier pictures show him—his features, at once strong and refined.

Mr. Hassett brought some papers to be signed. F. had his feet up on the wicker stool and the usual card table in front of him. He signed everything—Mr. Hassett laying them "out to dry." Mr. Hassett left, leaving the folder of signed letters on the Pres.' table. He began to look over some of them; Mme. S. began to work.

At about 20 mins. of one, the little tray with the cup of gruel and a small pitcher of cream was brought in & put on the table at his right hand—I got up from the sofa and went around to pour the cream for him, mix it a little, & get him started on it. He interrupted his reading for a moment & took some gruel, continued his reading, took more gruel. He enjoyed the gruel, always—he said it seemed to increase his appetite if anything—

Once, I remember, he said, "Wouldn't it be strange if this gruel should be the one thing to put weight on me!" Just a passing thought, of course, but he had his weight on his mind, & he realized that you are failing if your weight continues to decrease when you & your Drs. are trying hard to increase it. Arthur Prettyman also brought in his "green cocktail" which was supposed to increase his appetite, & he swallowed that without interrupting his work.

Mme. S. had given her version of what happened after this. He did say as follows: "We have five more minutes to work"—We all heard it.

My version is as follows: I was crocheting on the sofa, constantly looking up—at him—at Mme. S.—anxious to see the progress of the picture. However, Mme. S. didn't want us to look just yet. I got up for a moment or two, & stood in front of the fireplace behind F's chair. I discovered that from there, I could see the portrait in the little oval mirror which hangs nearest to F's bedroom door—I couldn't see very well, however, & went back to my crocheting on the sofa.

Polly (about 1 P.M.) went into her room to put water in a bowl of roses—I glanced up from my work—

F. seemed to be looking for something: his head forward, his hands fumbling—I went forward & looked into his face. "Have you dropped your cigarette?"

He looked at me with his forehead furrowed in pain and tried to smile. He put his left hand up to the back of his head & said: "I have a terrific pain in the back of my head."

He said it distinctly, but so low that I don't think anyone heard it— My head was not a foot from his—I told him to [put] his head back on his chair—Polly came through her door at that moment. We tilted his chair back, as he was slumping forward, & with Polly & Lucy holding the chair, I took up the telephone & said to the operator . . . "Please get *in touch with Dr. Bruenn & ask him to come at once to the President's cottage," and put down the receiver.*

Mme. S. in the meantime had called in Arthur Prettyman & Joe the Filipino. They picked up F. but found him a dead weight—not at all the way he usually put his arms around the men's shoulders & carried his own weight on them—Polly took F.'s feet & somehow, between us all, we carried him in to his bed, and laid him on 3 pillows.

We did not dare give him the internal stimulant or move him. I was cold as ice in my heart, cold & precise in my voice—I opened his collar & tie & held up the left side of his pillow, rather than move him to the middle of it. I held his right hand. Polly was on his left, her hand on his heart, fanning him. Two or three times he rolled his head from side to side, opened his eyes. Polly thinks he looked at us all in turn. He may have, I could see no signs of real recognition in those eyes—twice he drew up the left side of his face, as if in pain—But it was only a question of 3 or 4 minutes, for he became unconscious as far as one could see—His breathing was rather heavy but his heart seemed to be steady & strong, though quick—

Lucy brought some camphor and held it back & forth before his nostrils, Arthur & Joe stood by. I knew that I had little consciousness except for him. One must not do anything wrong. It was better to do nothing—the Dr. must have come in 15 minutes or so. It is hard to know about minutes in times like this, for one doesn't have the chance, or the thought, to look at a watch. When the doctor came, he asked us all to leave the room so they could get F. undressed & into bed. He was without question unconscious at this time & never regained consciousness—

After a while, the Dr. came out, asked us all what had happened, and telephoned Dr. McIntire in Washington.

Polly telephoned E.R. saying simply: "We are worried about Franklin, he has had a fainting spell. Dr. Bruenn will call you back."

She, of course, knew something serious had happened—Two hours went by—Lucy & Mme. S. left in the auto with Mr. Robbins [Nicholas Robbins, the artist's assistant] within an hour.

Polly, Mr. Hassett & Charlie Fredericks & I stood around, tried to be calm. *The Dr. came out & went back in again. Geo. Fox [a navy physiotherapist], the Dr., Arthur and Joe were in the room almost constantly—At first they were putting hot water bottles & blankets to warm F. Then, the blood pressure, which had gone way up, was brought down somewhat by an injection. F. ceased to be cold.*

About 3.15 F's breathing became very heavy & labored—I had a distinct feeling that this was the beginning of the end—

Dr. Paullin was on his way down from Atlanta. He came in the door. Dr. Bruenn was talking on the phone to Dr. McIntire. He was saying: "If anything, he is a little better."

At that moment the breathing suddenly stopped in F.'s room, someone opened the door & called Dr. Bruenn.

Polly took the telephone from him & asked Dr. "Mac" to hold the wire.

Dr. Paullin was hurried into F.'s room. I looked at my watch: 25 minutes of 4. It was the end—

3:35 P.M. Franklin D. Roosevelt, the hope of the world, is dead.

Vice President Harry S. Truman was at the Senate when Roosevelt died of a cerebral hemorrhage. Steve Early, the presidential press secretary, summoned him to the White House. He did not tell Truman why his presence was urgently requested.

I reached the White House about 5:25 P.M. and was immediately taken in the elevator to the second floor and ushered into Mrs. Roosevelt's study. Mrs. Roosevelt herself, together with Colonel John and Mrs. Anna Roosevelt Boettiger and Mr. Early, were in the room as I entered, and I knew at once that something unusual had taken place. Mrs. Roosevelt seemed calm in her characteristic, graceful dignity. She stepped forward and placed her arm gently about my shoulder.

"Harry," she said quietly, "the President is dead."

For a moment I could not bring myself to speak.

The last news we had had from Warm Springs was that Mr. Roosevelt was recuperating nicely. In fact, he was apparently doing so well that no member of his immediate family, and not even his personal physician, was with him. All this flashed through my mind before I found my voice.

"Is there anything I can do for you?" I asked at last.

I shall never forget her deeply understanding reply.

"Is there anything we can do for you?" she asked. "For you are the one in trouble now."

Arthur Godfrey described the funeral procession for CBS radio as it moved along Pennsylvania Avenue.

The drums are wrapped in black crepe and are muffled, as you can hear. The pace of the musicians is so slow. Behind them, these are the navy boys. And just now, coming past the Treasury, I can see the horses drawing the caisson. . . . And behind it is the car bearing the man on whose shoulders now falls the terrific burdens and responsibilities that were handled so well by the man to whose body we are paying our last respects now. God bless him—President Truman.

Godfrey was unable to continue—he had begun to cry.

the AGE of the ATOM

The Atomic Age began at 5:30 A.M., Mountain War Time, July 16, 1945, when an A-bomb was successfully tested at a site called Trinity, a stretch of semidesert fifty miles from Alamagordo, New Mexico.

On August 6, the B-29 *Enola Gay* dropped the atomic bomb on Hiroshima, and three days later, another bomb fell on Nagasaki.

More than a half-century later, questions linger. Was President Truman justified in dropping the bomb? Did the United States really face the prospect of up to a million casualties in an invasion of Japan, or were the Japanese on the verge of surrender? Given the carnage at Hiroshima, was Nagasaki necessary to persuade the Japanese to end the war?

Only one journalist was present at the dawn of the new age. In the interests of a historical record, William L. Laurence of the *New York Times* was permitted by the government to witness the New Mexico test and was then taken aboard an observer plane over Nagasaki.

From New Mexico:

At that great moment in history, ranking with the moment in the long ago when man first put fire to work for him and started on his march to civilization, the vast energy locked within the hearts of the atoms of matter was released for the first time in a burst of flame such as had never before been seen on this planet, illuminating earth and sky for a brief span that seemed eternal with the light of many supersuns. . . .

It was as though the earth had opened and the skies had split. One felt as though he had been privileged to witness the Birth of the World— to be present at the moment of the Creation when the Lord said: Let There be Light.

From the skies over Nagasaki:

I climbed into the nose of the B-29, the instrument plane which was to follow directly behind the strike plane, No. 77. The quarters were cramped and the only place I could find to sit was a hard metal box. The pilot of my ship was Captain Frederick C. Bock, of Greenville, Michigan, who had majored in philosophy at the University of Chicago. The night outside was dark and uncertain. . . .

We were headed northwest on a straight course for Japan. Only a few stars were visible through the overcast, and from time to time a flash of lightning would illuminate the sky. The weather report had predicted storms ahead part of the way, but clear weather for the final stages. The storm broke just about one hour after we had left Tinian.

On we went through the night. We rode out the storm. On and on we went on a straight course to the Empire. The first signs of dawn came shortly after five o'clock. By 5:50 it was light outside.

It was 9:36 when we began heading for the coast line. The weather planes, half an hour ahead of us, had signaled good visibility over Kokura as well as Nagasaki. But our arrival over Kokura had been delayed by more than three quarters of an hour, and when we got there the weather had changed and thick clouds covered the target. We had located the city by radar, but the orders were to make only a visual drop, which has the advantage of greater accuracy. This meant circling until we found an opening through the clouds over the selected target area. But the winds of destiny decreed otherwise. . . .

We flew southward down the channel and at 11:13 crossed the coast line and headed straight for Nagasaki, about 100 miles to the west. And the nearer we came the greater grew our dejection. Nagasaki too was hidden under a curtain of clouds.

Would we drop the bomb by radar if we could not find an opening on the first and only possible run, and thus risk being off the mark, or would we continue looking for an opening until we had only enough gas left to reach our naval rescue craft in Japanese waters? Maybe we would go even farther—keep on looking for an opening until the last drop and then bail out over enemy territory. What were the misfortunes, or lives, of a handful of men in two B-29's against the chance of shortening the war?

It was up to the pilot and the weaponer to make the decision, and they would have to make it fast. In the aircraft ahead of us two men were just then weighing our fate, and their own, in the balance.

We were then approaching the end of the first run. In a few minutes we would know the answer. The clouds below were still as impenetrable as ever.

And then, at the very last minute, there came an opening. For a few brief moments Nagasaki stood out clearly in broad noontime daylight.

Our watches stood at noon. The seconds ticked away. One, two, three. Ten, twenty, thirty, forty. Fifty. Fifty-seven, fifty-eight, fifty-nine. . . .

It was 12:01 over Nagasaki.

We heard the prearranged signal on our radio, put on our arc welder's glasses and watched tensely the maneuverings of the strike ship about half a mile in front of us.

"There she goes!" someone said.

Out of the belly of No. 77 a black object went downward.

Our B-29 swung around to get out of range; but even though we were turning away in the opposite direction, and despite the fact that it was broad daylight in our cabin, all of us had become aware of a giant flash that broke through the dark barrier of our arc welder's lenses and flooded our cabin with intense light.

After the first flash we removed our glasses, but the light lingered on, a bluish-green light that illuminated the sky all around. A tremendous blast wave struck our ship and made it tremble from nose to tail. This was followed by four more blasts in rapid succession, each resounding like the boom of cannon hitting our plane from all directions.

Observers in the tail of our ship saw a giant ball of fire rise as though from the bowels of the earth, belching forth enormous white smoke rings. Next they saw a giant pillar of purple fire, ten thousand feet high, shooting skyward with enormous speed.

By the time our ship had made another turn in the direction of the atomic explosion the pillar of purple fire had reached the level of our altitude. Only about forty-five seconds had passed.

Awestruck, we watched it shoot upward like a meteor coming from the earth instead of from outer space, becoming ever more alive as it climbed skyward through the white clouds. It was no longer smoke, or dust, or even a cloud of fire. It was a living thing, a new species of being, born right before our eyes.

At one stage of its evolution, covering millions of years in terms of seconds, the entity assumed the form of a giant square totem pole, with its base about three miles long, tapering off to about a mile at the top. Its bottom was brown, its center amber, its top white.

Then, just when it appeared as though the thing had settled down into a state of permanence, there came shooting out of the top a giant mushroom that increased the height of the pillar to a total of 45,000 feet.

The mushroom top was even more alive than the pillar, seething and boiling in a white fury of creamy foam, sizzling upward and then descending earthward, a thousand geysers rolled into one.

It kept struggling in an elemental fury, like a creature in the act of breaking the bonds that held it down. In a few seconds it had freed itself from its gigantic stem and floated upward with tremendous speed, its momentum carrying it into the stratosphere to a height of about sixty thousand feet.

But at that instant another mushroom, smaller in size than the first one, began emerging out of the pillar. It was as though the decapitated monster was growing a new head.

As the first mushroom floated off into the blue it changed its shape into *a flowerlike form, its giant petals curving downward, creamy white outside, rose-colored inside. It still retained that shape when we last gazed at it from a distance of about two hundred miles.*

The boiling pillar of many colors could also be seen at that distance, a giant mountain of jumbled rainbows, in travail. Much living substance had gone into those rainbows.

The quivering top of the pillar protruded to a great height through the white clouds, giving the appearance of a monstrous prehistoric creature with a ruff around its neck, a fleecy ruff extending in all directions as far as the eye could see.

SURRENDER *in* TOKYO BAY

The end came on September 2, 1945, amid remembrances of those terrible moments for the Allies when it had all begun.

The American flag fluttering from the mast of the battleship *Missouri* for the Japanese surrender in Tokyo Bay had flown over the Capitol on December 7, 1941. It had been airlifted for these ceremonies. Webley Edwards of CBS, the pool broadcaster at Japan's capitulation, had announced the raid at Pearl Harbor over a Honolulu radio station. And in the United States delegation accompanying General Douglas MacArthur was General Jonathan M. Wainwright, who had surrendered the Philippines and had only recently been released from a Japanese prisoner-of-war camp.

Among the witnesses to the surrender was Sergeant Dale Kramer, a reporter for *Yank* magazine.

For a while it looked as though the proceedings would go off with almost unreasonable smoothness. Cameramen assigned to the formal surrender ceremonies aboard the battleship Missouri in Tokyo Bay arrived on time, and, although every inch of the turrets and housings and life rafts above the veranda deck where the signing was to take place was crowded, no one fell off and broke a collarbone.

The ceremonies themselves even started and were carried on according to schedule. It took a Canadian colonel to bring things back to normal by signing the surrender document on the wrong line.

No one had the heart to blame the colonel, though. A mere colonel was bound to get nervous around so much higher brass.

The signing aboard the Missouri was a show which lacked nothing in its staging. A cluster of microphones and a long table covered with green cloth had been placed in the center of the deck. On the table lay the big, ledger-size white documents of surrender bound in brown folders.

The assembly of brass and braid was a thing to see—a lake of gold and silver sparkling with rainbows of decorations and ribbons. British and Australian Army officers had scarlet stripes on their garrison caps and on their collars. The French were more conservative, except for the acres of vivid decorations on their breasts. The stocky leader of the Russian delegation wore gold shoulder-boards and red-striped trousers. The Dutch had gold-looped shoulder emblems. The British admirals wore snow-white summer uniforms with shorts and knee-length white stockings. The olive-drab of the Chinese was plain except for ribbons. The least decked-out of all were the Americans. Their hats, except for Adm. Halsey's go-to-hell cap, were gold-braided, but their uniforms were plain sun-tan. Navy regulations do not permit wearing ribbons or decorations on a shirt.

. . . a gig flying the American flag and operated by white-clad American sailors putted around the bow of the ship. In the gig, wearing formal diplomatic morning attire consisting of black cutaway coat, striped pants, and stovepipe hat, sat Foreign Minister Namoru Shigemitsu, leader of the Japanese delegation.

Coming up the gangway, Shigemitsu climbed very slowly because of a stiff left leg, and he limped onto the veranda deck with the aid of a heavy light-colored cane. Behind him came 10 other Japs. One wore a white suit; two more wore formal morning attire; the rest were dressed in the pieced-out uniforms of the Jap Army and Navy. They gathered into three rows on the forward side of the green-covered table. The representatives of the Allied powers formed on the other side.

When they were arranged, Gen. MacArthur entered, stepped to the microphone, and began to speak.

His words rolled sonorously: "We are gathered here, representatives of *the major warring powers, to conclude a solemn agreement whereby peace may be restored.". . .*

The Japanese stood at attention during the short address, their faces grave but otherwise showing little emotion. When the representatives of the Emperor were invited to sign, Foreign Minister Shigemitsu hobbled forward, laid aside his silk hat and cane, and lowered himself slowly into a chair. The wind whipped his thin, dark hair as he reached into his pocket for a pen, tested it, then affixed three large Japanese characters to the first of the documents. He had to rise and bend over the table for the others. . . .

Gen. MacArthur had promised to present Gen. Wainwright, who had surrendered the American forces at Corregidor and until a few days before had been a prisoner of war, with the first pen to sign the surrender. Shigemitsu finished and closed his pen and replaced it in his pocket. . . .

When the big surrender folders were turned around on the table, Gen. MacArthur came forward to affix his signature as Supreme Commander. He asked Gen. Wainwright and Gen. Percival, who had surrendered the British forces at Singapore, to accompany him. Gen. MacArthur signed the first document and handed the pen to Gen. Wainwright. He used five pens in all, ending up with the one from his own pocket.

Sailors have been as avid souvenir collectors in this war as anyone else, but when Adm. Nimitz sat down to sign for the U.S. he used only two pens. After that the representatives of China, the United Kingdom, Russia, Australia, Canada, France, the Netherlands, and New Zealand put down their signatures.

As the big leather document folders were gathered, a GI member of a sound unit recorded a few historic remarks of his own:

"Brother," he said, "I hope those are my discharge papers."

Chapter Seven

COLD WAR CONFLICTS, CIVIL RIGHTS STRUGGLES

UNCLE MILTIE

With World War II over, American industry retooled to meet the demands of consumers—and create new demand for goods and services that had only been dimly glimpsed. Detroit, the great productive engine for planes and tanks, turned back to automobiles. New homes arose in a frenzy of building, the community of Levittown, Long Island, becoming the symbol of the suburbs.

And a new age of entertainment was stirring. In May 1948, *Time* magazine began a section focusing on television, predicting it would "change the American way of life more than anything since the Model T."

TV was envisioned as a force for change in education, in politics, in commerce. But television's first superstar was hardly a revolutionary. He was a vaudeville comic, Broadway headliner, and radio personality.

When Milton Berle took over as the host of *Texaco Star Theater* in 1948, there were five hundred thousand TVs in the country. By the time Berle's show reached midseason, its enormous popularity had brought a doubling in the numer of sets. Every Tuesday at 8 P.M., more than 80 percent of TV viewers were tuned to Berle's madcap variety show. He was Mr. Television to the adults—and Uncle Miltie to the kids.

When the show hit and people started stopping me in the streets, very often I'd get a woman saying to me that she had trouble getting her children to go to sleep at the right time on Tuesdays. Couldn't I please say something to them over television about going to bed when they were supposed to? I always explained that I wasn't allowed to. The sponsor wouldn't like it, and there was an F.C.C. ruling against personal messages, that sort of thing.

When we began the 1949 season, and the sponsor was putting more money into the show, we hired a script girl with a stopwatch to time the dress rehearsal and give us an idea of how much time we should allow for the laughs. Assuming nothing went wrong on the show, we still knew that all she could give us, based on our stop-and-start dress rehearsals, was an educated guess.

That night, on the opening show of the season, I came out to sing the sign-off, "Near You," and do the closing spiel. Ralph Nelson, a great director today, but a floor man on our show then, held up seven fingers to me. It caught me by surprise. "We have seven minutes more to go?" I said over the air. "Okay, somebody bring out a chair."

I started ad-libbing, digging out anything I could think of. Then I said to Nelson, "How are we doing?" It felt like I had used up fifteen minutes.

He held up five fingers.

That's when I remembered those requests from mothers. Since I was running out of things to say, I went into a spiel off the top of my head. "Since this is the beginning of a new season, I want to say something to any of you kiddies who should be in bed, getting a good night's rest before school tomorrow. Listen to your Uncle Miltie, and kiss Mommy and Daddy good night and go straight upstairs like good little boys and girls."

Finally I got the sign-off signal, and maybe two minutes after the show was over I forgot that I had used the name "Uncle Miltie." It was just an ad-lib time-filler, a name I had made up on the spur of the moment.

I didn't remember it until the next day in Boston. I had promised to make an appearance there for the Catholic Youth Organization. They brought me into town from the airport in an open car. At one point the motorcade passed a gang with picks and shovels working in the street, and one of the guys yelled out, "Hey, Uncle Miltie!" That's when I first knew that I had found a tag that stuck with people.

I got the idea confirmed when I was back at the airport and a man with a little boy pointed at me and said, "Look, there's Uncle Miltie."

. . . When I got back to New York, I told the writers what had happened, and on next week's show, when it came sign-off time, I said, "Good night to all you boys and girls, my nephews and nieces, this is your Uncle Miltie saying good night."

I started getting letters addressed to Uncle Miltie, USA, and I knew the handle had taken. So I started writing safety songs and all kinds of poetic advice for the sign-off. I even wrote and published a song, "Uncle Miltie," which somehow didn't replace "The Star-Spangled Banner."

. . . Bishop Fulton J. Sheen had his program on the Dumont channel

at the same time as mine on NBC-TV. One night he began his program by saying, "Good evening, this is Uncle Fultie."

the BERLIN AIRLIFT

The great Soviet ally of World War II would quickly become the great adversary. In June 1948, a milestone event of the Cold War unfolded when Russian troops occupying East Germany cut off road and rail links to West Berlin. The United States, Britain, and France responded with an airlift that would provide Berliners with 2.3 million tons of food, fuel, and machinery ferried on some 277,000 flights, prompting the Soviet Union to abandon its blockade in May 1949.

Alfred Wright of *Time* magazine went along when a C-54 transport piloted by Captain Edward Hensch of Houston and Lieutenant William Baker of Los Angeles took off from the Rhein-Main airport in Frankfurt, West Germany, the afternoon of October 1, 1948, for its second flight of the day to West Berlin's Tempelhof field. He met the airmen at their operations room.

Baker was holding, somewhat awkwardly, a bunch of flowers he had received that morning from a grateful family at Tempelhof airdrome. The Germans are always turning up with flowers and the airmen are always embarrassed (but pleased too). More painful than the actual donation is the necessity of carrying the flowers into the operations room. There is always some arch clown to say: "Getting married?"

. . . Hensch's plane flew over one of the Red Army training grounds. There were tank tracks through the fields and vehicles lined up next to the forest. Said Hensch: "I'd like to come over here with 20,000 pounds of rotten tomatoes some day instead of this load."

The big engine growled on, and Baker, with nothing to do, took a box from the ledge above the instrument panel. He unwrapped it—more presents from grateful Germans: a little porcelain snail, some flowers, and a toy walrus made out of rat's fur. There was a note addressed: An unseen Blokade Flieger. *Hensch could not read it, but he said: "Wait till my wife gets ahold of that. She'll start sending them food packages. She's always sending these Germans presents."*

Just before the beginning of the Tempelhof runway there was a grave-yard crowded with several thousand kids, waving at us. These were the expected beneficiaries of operation "Little Vittles," started by Lieut. Gale S. Halverson, who dropped candy and gum in little parachutes made of handkerchiefs. The town of Mobile, Ala., where Halverson used to be stationed, had taken up a collection, including 50 pounds of handker-chiefs, for "Little Vittles."

. . . Like any suburban commuter, Hensch found his wife waiting in a car by the field. He gave her the flowers, the porcelain snail, the rat's fur walrus and the note. She translated it haltingly. It said: "On the 100th day of the blockade God lives with you flyers. Health, happiness and skill for all of you and a quick return to the old days, and the joyous end of the blockade."

the FIFTH MARINES at the CHOSIN RESERVOIR

On June 25, 1950, some ninety thousand North Korean soldiers stormed across the 38th parallel and invaded South Korea. President Truman quickly committed American troops to a United Nations force led by General Douglas MacArthur, and so—less than five years after the end of World War II—Americans were again fighting in Asia. The Cold War against the communist world had become a very hot one.

By October, MacArthur had staged his brilliant amphibious landing at Inchon, and the North Koreans had been pushed back across the border. Now, instead of settling for a situation akin to that before the invasion, U.N. troops followed them, hoping to bring down the communist government.

In November, communist China entered the war, pouring a million men across the Yalu River from Manchuria. Late that month, Chinese forces stormed the frigid mountainous area near North Korea's Chosin Reservoir, surrounding troops from the First Marine Division and the army's Seventh Infantry Division. The Marines suffered some forty-four hundred battle casualties and seven thousand cases of frostbite before survivors fought their way out in blizzards and horrendous cold.

Private First Class Jack Wright of the Fifth Marines was among the men who battled through combat conditions that tested the corps every bit as fiercely as Guadalcanal, Okinawa, and Iwo Jima had just a few years before.

We were ordered to take the top of the hill. We started up. Below the crest were three deep foxholes. A Chinese soldier jumped out of one of them. I tried to bayonet him. With all the clothes I was wearing and his quilted uniform I couldn't make a dent in the guy. Another Marine behind me shot him. Down in these foxholes we found about five Item Company Marines who had been captured the night before. Their hands had been tied behind them with wire and had turned black. None of them were in a very healthy condition. Our corpsmen untied their hands and got them down to the road where they were put on a truck.

We were then ordered to move forward and take the next hill. I noticed something. My feet felt like they'd gone to sleep and I wasn't feeling the cold in them anymore. I stumbled along trying to wake my feet up, to get some circulation going in them. It felt like I was walking on someone else's feet. Inside of stepping over rocks, I tripped over them. I was tired. I was hungry. I was thirsty. We all carried water and C rations; only thing was, you couldn't drink or eat them. They were frozen solid. The last real sleep we'd had was days before in the valley. I continued to stumble along. Every time I fell, the guy next to me would stop. Pretty soon people were hollering at me to keep going. This is when I realized I was the left guide, and when I stopped, the entire skirmish line stopped. I noticed other Marines stumbled like I did.

The line finally reached the top of the hill. We found one Chinese. Couldn't have been more than sixteen years old. His unit had abandoned him. His feet had froze up and burst open. He lay quietly. I couldn't tell whether he was crying or growling. The noise he made was weird. One corpsman looked, then shook his head. I walked away. There was a shot. This was the first time I knew a prisoner had been shot out of mercy and not out of meanness.

The squad leader came over. "Wright, what'n hell is the matter with you? Why couldn't you stand up?" "Well, my feet are asleep." "Stand up here. Stomp 'em." I stood up and stomped. Almost fell on my face. He called the corpsman over. "Keep moving around, Wright, and see what happens." I moved around until I realized I was on the ridgeline. "Oh, hell . . ." I sat down, but moved my legs and feet and all that stuff. Nothing happened. The corpsman walked over with the platoon sergeant. The sergeant said, "Wright, go down to the convoy and turn yourself in." "Aw, hell, Sarge, ain't nothin' wrong. My feet went to sleep, that's all." "Wright, get your ass down to the road. Maybe if enough of you people turn in, they'll get some relief up here for us."

I found our company corpsman at the bottom of the hill. "Yeah, I know," he said. Didn't bother to check me, just wrote out an evac tag and hung it on me. "What the hell's that for?" "Don't you know what's wrong with you?" "My feet went to sleep. Big deal." "You got frozen feet, Wright." I just stared at him. "Frozen feet?" "Yeah. Consider yourself evacuated." "Now, how'n hell am I gonna get evacuated?" He pointed to the long line of trucks strung out along the road. "Take your choice."

Right in front of me was a jeep pulling a trailer that had three Marines riding in it. One of them told me to hop on the trailer. One old guy got out of the jeep. I'll never forget him. He looked like he'd been in the Corps and been a Marine since 1776. He said, "Take your boot off." I took my boot off. Hell, I wasn't going to argue with that guy. When I pulled the socks off, a layer of skin also came off. The old guy unbuttoned his parka and dungaree jacket and took my foot and placed it on his bare belly. That's how one Marine will take care of another, even if he doesn't know him. Told me to wiggle my toes. I wiggled. He stood for a minute. Then he growled, "Wiggle your toes." "I am." "Oh, damn," he said, "that this should have to happen." Out of his pack the guy produced two pair of nice, clean ski socks. The socks I'd been wearing I'd worn since they were issued to me down on the coast, an eternity ago. He had me put on the new socks, then my shoepacs. He said, "Shoepacs are the most useless damn things the government ever dreamed up." It was true. Shoepacs were darn good as long as you didn't move. Once you did, your feet sweated, the sweat couldn't evaporate, and your feet froze.

From that point on, I joined the walking wounded. . . .

Wright later hitched a ride.

We pulled into the outskirts of Hungnam. I asked an MP directing traffic the location of 3d Battalion, 5th Marines. He pointed away from the direction the personnel carrier was headed. I shook hands with the Army corporal, said good-bye to everyone else, and hopped off.

In a little while I picked up a ride going the direction I wanted to go in. Two hours later I found my unit, or what was left of it. I reported in to my company first sergeant. He looked up from the papers on his field desk. "Wright, you're damn lucky." I asked him why, considering the shape I was in. He showed me a long list he'd been working on of men missing in action or killed in action. My name was on it. He asked what had happened to me. I showed him the evac tag I was still wearing. He asked, "Well, what are you gonna do?" I tore the tag off and handed it to him. "To hell with it, S'arnt. Ain't worth it." He told me where I would find my platoon area.

I hobbled down there, but I didn't see anyone I knew. That afternoon they called a muster. Third Platoon fell in, all three of us—Robert Solen, Don Murrell and me. We'd been the three runts of the platoon. Right there and then 3d Platoon went out of existence. We were assigned to 2d Platoon. That was it.

the ROSENBERGS

The height of the Cold War brought one of the most sensational criminal cases in American history—the espionage trial of Julius Rosenberg; his wife, Ethel; and Morton Sobell, accused of conspiring to pass the secrets of the atomic bomb to the Soviet Union in 1945.

The key government witnesses at the 1951 trial in Manhattan Federal Court were David Greenglass, Mrs. Rosenberg's brother, who had been an Army sergeant at Los Alamos, New Mexico, where the bomb was developed; and Harry Gold, a onetime Philadelphia biochemist.

Greenglass and Gold had already pleaded guilty to spying for the Soviets.

Some of the most riveting testimony involved a prosaic object—a Jell-O box—that was to be used as a source of identification when Gold met with Greenglass.

Greenglass's wife, Ruth, testified that she had taken a portion of that box from the Rosenbergs in New York and brought it to her husband in New Mexico.

Gold later told the jury of delivering the other half of the Jell-O box to Greenglass with the words "I came from Julius" and obtaining A-bomb information from Greenglass that he passed on to Anatoli Yakovlev, a Soviet vice-consul in New York who would be indicted in the Rosenberg case though he fled the country in December 1946.

Gold also linked himself and Yakovlev with Klaus Fuchs, a top British scientist at Los Alamos who had pleaded guilty in London to espionage and was serving a fourteen-year sentence in Britain.

In testimony on March 15, 1951, Gold told of meeting with Yakovlev in New York, a session that led to a trip to New Mexico.

Yakovlev then gave me a sheet of paper; it was onionskin paper, and on it was typed the following: First, the name "Greenglass," just "Greenglass." Then a number "High Street"; all that I can recall about the number is—It was a low number and the last figure, the second figure was "0" and the last figure was either 5, 7 or 9, and then underneath that was "Albuquerque, New Mexico." The last thing that was on the paper was "Recognition signal. I come from Julius."

In addition to this, Yakovlev gave me a piece of cardboard, which appeared to have been cut from a packaged food of some sort. It was cut in an odd shape and Yakovlev told me that the man Greenglass, whom I would meet in Albuquerque, would have the matching piece of cardboard. Yakovlev told me that just in case the man Greenglass would not be present when I called in Albuquerque, that his wife would have the information and that she would turn it over to me. Yakovlev gave me an envelope which he said contained $500 and he told me to give it to Greenglass. Yakovlev told me that I should follow a very devious route on my way to Santa Fe and to Albuquerque.

Gold then told of meeting with Fuchs in Santa Fe on June 2, 1945, and receiving "a bunch of papers" from him. Later that day, he went to Albuquerque.

I arrived in Albuquerque early in the evening of the 2nd of June, and about 8:30 that night went to the designated address on High Street. There I was met by a tall elderly whitehaired and somewhat stooped man. I inquired about the Greenglasses, and he told me that they were out for the evening but he thought they would be in early on Sunday morning. On Sunday about 8:30 I went again to the High Street address. I was admitted and I recall going up a very steep flight of steps, and I knocked on a door.

It was opened by a young man of about 23 with dark hair. He was smiling. I said, "Mr. Greenglass?" He answered in the affirmative. I said, "I came from Julius," and I showed him the piece of cardboard in my hand, the piece of cardboard that had been given me by Yakovlev in Volks' Cafe. He asked me to enter. I did. Greenglass went to a woman's handbag and brought out from it a piece of cardboard. We matched the two of them. At this point, after we had matched the two pieces of cardboard, I introduced myself to Greenglass as Dave from Pittsburgh; that was all. Greenglass introduced me to the young woman who was there and said she was his wife Ruth. Then I gave Mr. Greenglass the envelope which Yakovlev had given me in Volks' Cafe. This envelope was the one that contained $500. Greenglass took the envelope from me.

Greenglass told me that there were a number of people at Los Alamos that he thought would make very likely recruits; that is, they were also people who might be willing to furnish information on the atom bomb to the Soviet Union, and he started to give me the names of these people, the names of some of these people. I cut him very short indeed. I told him that such procedure was extremely hazardous, foolhardy, that under no circumstances should he ever try to proposition anyone on his own into trying to get information for the Soviet Union.

I told him to be very circumspect in his conduct and to never even drop the slightest hint to anyone that he himself was furnishing information on the atom bomb to the Soviet Union. The last thing that took place that morning was that just as I was preparing to go, Mrs. Greenglass told me that just before she had left New York City to come to Albuquerque she had spoken with Julius.

Gold was then shown a photograph and asked if he could identify the people in it.

Yes. The man with his arm around the woman is David Greenglass. The woman is Mrs. Ruth Greenglass. Mr. Greenglass gave me an envelope which he said contained the information for which I had come, the information on the atom bomb. I took the envelope. I arrived in New York on the 5th of June, 1945, in the evening. I met Mr. Yakovlev along Metropolitan Avenue in Brooklyn. Yakovlev wanted to know if I had seen the both of them, said, "the doctor and the man." I said that I had. Yakovlev wanted to know had I got information from the both of them, and I said that I had. Then I gave Yakovlev the two manila envelopes, the one labeled "Doctor," which had the information I had received from Fuchs in Santa Fe; the one labeled "Other," which had the information I had received from David Greenglass in Albuquerque, on 3rd of June, 1945. Yakovlev told me that the information which I had given him some two weeks previous had been sent immediately to the Soviet Union. He said that the information which I had received from Greenglass was extremely excellent and very valuable.

The Rosenbergs and Sobell were convicted of conspiracy to commit espionage. Sobell received a prison term, but Julius and Ethel Rosenberg were sentenced to death. Protests were mounted in their behalf amid allegations they were victims of Cold War hysteria and anti-Semitism. But on June 19, 1953, still proclaiming their innocence, they were electrocuted at Sing Sing.

the END *of* JOE McCARTHY

Few people in public life summoned the courage to confront Senator Joseph McCarthy as he sowed a climate of fear with his communist witch-hunting.

One of those who did stand up to him was a Boston lawyer named Joseph N. Welch.

In the spring of 1954, the Wisconsin senator's venom played out before a nationwide audience in the army-McCarthy hearings, one of television's first "spectaculars."

Welch, a partner in the law firm of Hale & Dorr, had been appointed a special counsel to the army, which was defending itself against McCarthy's accusations of lax security practices. McCarthy's key aide, Roy Cohn, had in turn been accused of seeking to obtain preferential treatment from the army for his former assistant G. David Schine after his induction into the service.

During Welch's appearance before the McCarthy committee on June 9, McCarthy pointedly observed that a young associate in Welch's firm, Fred Fisher—briefly a member of the army legal team at the hearing—had belonged to the National Lawyers Guild "long after it had been exposed as the legal arm of the Communist Party." (The guild had not, in fact, been on the attorney general's list of subversive groups.)

Senator Charles E. Potter, a Republican committee member from Michigan, would remember Welch's electrifying retort.

[Welch:] "Little did I dream you could be so reckless and so cruel as to do an injury to that lad. It is true that he is still with Hale and Dorr. It is true that he will continue to be with Hale and Dorr. It is, I regret to say, equally true that I fear he shall always bear a scar needlessly inflicted by you. If it were in my power to forgive you for your reckless cruelty, I would do so. I'd like to think I am a gentleman, but your forgiveness will have to come from someone other than me."

I watched Joe McCarthy while Welch was talking. His head was down and he was glaring up at Welch with pure venom. Roy Cohn was trying to get his attention and he knew it, but the enemy within himself was in complete charge now. It was a moment when he might have won the whole ball game with a quiet, sincere apology to Welch and Fred Fisher, but that would have been completely out of character and beyond his understanding. He had never apologized to anyone in his life and now he did the worst thing possible—he continued the attack.

His voice was climbing to that high-pitched whine that he always used under stress as he said, "May I say that Mr. Welch talks about this being cruel and reckless. He was just baiting; he had been baiting Mr. Cohn here for hours, requesting that Mr. Cohn, before sundown, get out of any department of government anyone who is serving the Communist cause. I just gave this man's record, and I want to say, Mr. Welch, that it has been labeled long before he became a member, as early as 1944—"

Welch interrupted. *"Senator, may we not drop this? We know he belonged to the Lawyers' Guild, and Mr. Cohn nods his head at me. I did you, I think, no personal injury, Mr. Cohn."*

Cohn said that he had not.

"I meant to do you no personal injury," Welch said, *"and if I did, I beg your pardon. Let us not assassinate this lad further, Senator. You have done enough. Have you no sense of decency, sir, at long last? Have you left no sense of decency?"*

McCarthy answered that quickly—he had, indeed, no sense of decency. Although Roy Cohn was shaking his head at McCarthy, his dark eyes imploring Joe to stop, and although Karl Mundt was trying to put an end to it, McCarthy plunged on. The key word was, of course, *"decency."* Welch knew instinctively where decency stopped and indecency began, where prosecution became assassination. Prosecution by due process of law is part of civilized government; assassination belongs in the mud of savagery.

"I would like to finish this," McCarthy said, and I wondered if he realized that what he was finishing was Joseph Raymond McCarthy.

Still Joe blundered on. *"Let me ask Mr. Welch,"* he said. *"You brought him down, did you not, to act as your assistant?"*

But Welch had had enough.

"Mr. McCarthy, I will not discuss this with you further. You have sat within six feet of me and could have asked me about Fred Fisher. You have brought it out. If there is a God in Heaven, it will do neither you nor your cause any good. I will not discuss it further. I will not ask Mr. Cohn any more questions. You, Mr. Chairman, may, if you will, call the next witness."

The audience, as if it were watching a high moment in a theater, broke *into loud applause. Several policemen who had been assigned to the Caucus Room to prevent any demonstrations stood silent and motionless. The bounce was gone out of Roy Cohn as he rose and left the witness chair, moving like a tired old man. McCarthy, his face frozen, sat staring down at the table. He must have known now that he had wounded himself seriously, and I am sure that that was his only regret.*

Mundt called a recess of five minutes and Joe Welch, his head bowed, walked out of the room. Several of the audience blocked him at the door to shake his hand.

McCarthy was completely alone now. He had isolated himself even from those who had blindly supported him. Finally he caught the eye of a newspaper reporter standing nearby and spread his hands, palms upward, asking, "What did I do?"

His tragedy was that he would never know the answer to that question.

Fred Fisher would become a partner with Hale & Dorr and would enjoy a long and prominent career in the law. McCarthy would be censured by his fellow senators in December 1954 for conduct "contrary to senatorial traditions." He died three years later.

the U-2 SINKS *a* SUMMIT

May Day may have been a workers' holiday for the communist world, but on May 1, 1960, a pilot named Francis Gary Powers was hard at work some seventy thousand feet above the Soviet Union.

An American civilian flying for the Central Intelligence Agency, Powers was in the cockpit of the secret U-2 plane, taking photographs of Soviet missile installations.

This time, he would not return to his base in Pakistan. A missile brought the plane down. Powers parachuted safely, then decided not to swallow the poison the CIA had thoughtfully provided for him.

The timing of the mission was a disaster—it came just as President Eisenhower was preparing for a summit meeting with Soviet leader Nikita Khrushchev. With a CIA spy in tow, Khrushchev canceled the summit. Eisenhower's hopes for a nuclear-test-ban treaty and détente with the Russians were crushed.

Powers was sentenced to ten years in prison, but after serving seventeen months he was exchanged for the Soviet master spy Rudolf Abel.

In March 1962, Powers told the Senate Armed Services Committee how the Russians got their man.

I can remember feeling, hearing and just sensing an explosion, but there was no—just a slight acceleration of the aircraft was all that I felt in the aircraft itself. I immediately looked up from the instruments and everywhere I looked was orange.

I don't know whether the whole sky was orange, or just the reflection of an orange light in the canopy, but I had never seen anything like this before, and I was sure there was an explosion. I felt that the explosion was external to the aircraft and behind me, but I really didn't know.

. . . The right wing dropped slightly, not very much. I used the controls.

The wing came back up level and just before or after it got level, the nose started going down, and very slowly. . . . I immediately assumed at the time that the tail section of the aircraft had come off because it—a very violent maneuver happened in here. . . . I feel sure that both wings came off.

I didn't have much time to look, and I was being thrown around the cockpit very much at this time. . . . I had pulled the control column all the way back into my lap, and it did no good. . . . And a very violent maneuver during this time . . . ended up in a spin. . . .

I don't know how much of the aircraft was left at the time. But all I could see by looking out of the cockpit was sky. The G forces were very strong. . . .

My first reaction was to reach for the destruct switches, and I reached up. I don't know whether I touched them or not, but I thought that I had better see if I can get out of here before using this.

I know that there was a seventy-second time delay between the actuation of the switches and the time that the explosion would occur. . . .

I tried to get into position in the ejection seat so that I could use it. In this particular aircraft there isn't much clearance between the pilot's knees and the top of the windshield, and I was being thrown forward, and if I had used the ejection seat at that time, I would have probably lost both legs just above the knees. . . .

I just stopped struggling and tried to think, and this was the first time that I realized that maybe I could just open the canopy, loosen the seat belt and climb out.

And along in here, I saw 34,000 feet on the altimeter, and it was still moving very fast.

I immediately reached up, opened the canopy. One side came loose first—I think it was the right side. The other handle loosened the left side and it floated off—I believe it was to the left. . . .

I opened the seat belt, and I was immediately thrown forward and half way out of the aircraft.

Well, then, I tried to get back into the aircraft so that I could actuate these destruction switches. I couldn't—the G forces were too great and I could not pull myself back over the top of the windshield. . . .

So then I decided just to try to get out. I gave several lunges and something snapped and I was floating free. It was almost immediately that the parachute opened. . . .

I remembered I had a map in my pocket. I took this map out, looked at it, tore it into small pieces and scattered it in the air.

I also thought of the coin with the poison pin in it. This had been given me just prior to the flight, and it had been my option whether to take this or not, and I chose to take it. I got to thinking that when I got on the ground if I were captured they would surely find this coin, but maybe with just the pin flying loose in the pocket it would be overlooked, so I opened up the coin, got the pin out and just dropped it in my pocket.

Powers landed in a field, twenty-five feet from two men working on a tractor. He was turned over to the authorities, then taken for interrogation to a city that he assumed was Sverdlovsk.

There they performed a thorough search and found the needle at this place. I tried to invent a story there that I didn't know where I was, I was off course, but they brought out the packages that I had in my survival pack or on my person, with maps of the Soviet Union, Russian rubles and several other items that indicated the nature of the mission. It was then that I decided to follow the instructions that I had received earlier and tell them that I was a member of the C.I.A. and the nature of the mission.

It was quite obvious that they knew it anyway.

After his release, Powers would fly again, piloting a traffic helicopter for KNBC-TV in Los Angeles. On August 1, 1977, he was killed when his craft ran out of fuel and crashed. He was buried in Arlington National Cemetery.

the GREAT DEBATES

It wasn't exactly Lincoln versus Douglas—image overshadowed the issues, and the panel-discussion format confined matters to quick verbal jousts.

But political history was made the night of September 26, 1960, in the Chicago studio of the CBS affiliate WBBM-TV when Richard M. Nixon and John F. Kennedy confronted each other in the first televised presidential debate.

TV may have decided a presidential election for the first time. Nixon looked uncomfortable, and his failure to use effective makeup left a five o'clock shadow. Kennedy projected vigor and self-assurance. The consensus among viewers was that the relatively inexperienced Massachusetts senator seized the moment from the vice-president.

Douglass Cater of *The Reporter* magazine was among the journalists who covered the four debates, and he was a panelist for one of them.

Covering the televised Great Debates on the spot was an eerie experience. We gathered in dim, cavernous halls, barred by armed guards from access to the scene of activity. We watched the show on monitors, silent for the most part, occasionally giving way to mirth. At the end of each debate, a pool reporter came out and dictated to us a meticulously detailed account of what he had seen and heard. ("Senator Kennedy took two deep breaths just before the program started. Vice President

Nixon———" "Hey, you're going too fast! What was that again?" "I said Nixon appeared to wet his lips and then at twelve minutes after the hour he wiped his face for the first time. He wiped it four times in all.")

When I served on the panel of interrogators in the third debate, I was somewhat baffled by the glimpse of reality I got. It was a strange mixture of planned method and unplanned content. The networks spared no expense or effort to perfect a split-screen arrangement allowing two candidates, who were a whole continent apart on that particular day, to appear to stand side by side. Each of us was given careful explanations of how the production was to be handled. A whole army of technicians worked to remove distortion in presenting the picture to what proved to be an audience of sixty million–odd citizens. Mr. Nixon's studio had been made frigid to eliminate undue perspiration.

Nobody showed much concern with what the program was to be about. The panel consisted of two men from the networks and two journalists chosen by lot. The only qualification was to have accompanied each candidate at some time during the campaign. We prepared ourselves in isolation from one another. Only during the final anxious moments in the make-up room—where we submitted to the same pancake and lip-rouge adornment as Mr. Nixon—did we decide to reveal in confidence to fellow panel members what our opening question was to be. In the words of the announcer, it was unrehearsed.

For me at least, it was a frustrating assignment. Beforehand I had entertained Walter Mitty dreams of posing a question so trenchant and so to the heart of the matter that no candidate could attempt circumlocution. But trenchancy, I found, was not easily come by. The format of the Great Debate was neither fish nor fowl, not permitting the relentless interrogation of the "Meet the Press" type of quiz show or the clash of ideas that can occur in a genuine debate. The candidates had quickly mastered its special form of gamesmanship. No matter how narrow or broad the question, we could watch by the timing device the way each of them extracted his last second of allotted image projection in making his response. The panel's role was hardly more than to designate categories —animal, vegetable or mineral—on which the two might or might not discourse. . . .

The dialogue was largely a paste-up job containing bits and snippets *from campaign rhetoric already used many times. As the series wore on, the protagonists were like two weary wrestlers who keep trying to get the same holds. What became clear was how limited the vocabulary of the debate really was and how vague were the candidates' ideas about what to do. Kennedy, we learned over and over, wants to get America moving again. Nixon argues that it is moving, and, in an unfortunate phrase, "We can't stand pat.". . .*

Who was judged more sincere? What may have been a major test was Nixon's soliloquy on Harry Truman's language and little children. It provoked loud guffaws among the press corps at the studio. But maybe other good Americans were deeply stirred by this pious man who promised, if elected, not to utter strong words in the White House. (He did, however, utter a few in the studio directly after the program, when he accused Kennedy of violating his no-notes proviso; afterward he told reporters that his spontaneous expressions were off the record.)

Last but not least, was the viewer really edified by the frantic clash on foreign policy? Neither of the men showed any regard for the fact that some things are better left unsaid if one of them expects to conduct that foreign policy next January. It was like a bastardized version of Art Linkletter's "People Are Funny" in which the contestant had to tell how he would deal with Castro in 150 seconds flat.

the CUBAN MISSILE CRISIS

It was a moment that seemed the inevitable consequence of that fireball unleashed over Hiroshima seventeen years before. The United States and the Soviet Union had built up enormous stockpiles of atomic weapons, and now, in October 1962, the world was on the brink of nuclear war.

A U-2 plane had detected offensive missiles being installed by the Russians in Cuba, and soon, intelligence officials believed, the missiles would be armed with nuclear warheads.

President Kennedy ordered a "quarantine" (in effect, a blockade) of Cuba and demanded that Nikita Khrushchev dismantle the missiles.

On the morning of Wednesday, October 24, Kennedy met at the

White House with his top advisers as Russian ships neared the five-hundred-mile barrier he had imposed off Cuba. American naval forces would soon have to intercept the ships or withdraw.

The President's brother, Attorney General Robert F. Kennedy, was in the room.

This was the moment we had prepared for, which we hoped would never come. The danger and concern that we all felt hung like a cloud over all of us and particularly over the President. . . .

It was now a few minutes after 10:00 o'clock. Secretary McNamara announced that two Russian ships, the Gagarin and the Komiles, were within a few miles of our quarantine barrier. The interception of both ships would probably be before noon Washington time. Indeed, the expectation was that at least one of the vessels would be stopped and boarded between 10:30 and 11:00 o'clock.

Then came the disturbing Navy report that a Russian submarine had moved into position between the two ships. . . .

The carrier Essex was to signal the submarine by sonar to surface and identify itself. If it refused, said Secretary McNamara, depth charges with a small explosive would be used until the submarine surfaced.

I think these few minutes were the time of gravest concern for the President. Was the world on the brink of a holocaust? Was it our error? A mistake? Was there something further that should have been done? Or not done? His hand went up to his face and covered his mouth. He opened and closed his fist. His face seemed drawn, his eyes pained, almost gray. We stared at each other across the table. For a few fleeting seconds, it was almost as though no one else was there and he was no longer the President.

Inexplicably, I thought of when he was ill and almost died; when he lost his child; when we learned that our oldest brother had been killed; of personal times of strain and hurt. The voices droned on, but I didn't seem to hear anything until I heard the President say: "Isn't there some way we can avoid having our first exchange with a Russian submarine—almost anything but that?"

"No, there's too much danger to our ships. There is no alternative," said McNamara. "Our commanders have been instructed to avoid hostil-

ities if at all possible, but this is what we must be prepared for, and this is what we must expect."

We had come to the time of final decision. "*We must expect that they will close down Berlin—make the final preparations for that,"* the President said. *I felt we were on the edge of a precipice with no way off. This time, the moment was now—not next week—not tomorrow, "so we can have another meeting and decide"; not in eight hours, "so we can send another message to Khrushchev and perhaps he will finally understand."*

No, none of that was possible. One thousand miles away in the vast expanse of the Atlantic Ocean the final decisions were going to be made in the next few minutes. President Kennedy had initiated the course of events, but he no longer had control over them. He would have to wait —we would have to wait. The minutes in the Cabinet Room ticked slowly by. What could we say now—what could we do?

Then it was 10:25—a messenger brought in a note to [Director of Central Intelligence] John McCone. "Mr. President, we have a preliminary report which seems to indicate that some of the Russian ships have stopped dead in the water.". . .

The meeting droned on. But everyone looked like a different person. For a moment the world had stood still, and now it was going around again.

BREAKING BASEBALL'S COLOR BARRIER

Blacks faced a bitter paradox during World War II. They were asked to fight totalitarianism while relegated to second-class status in the segregated armed forces.

For one army lieutenant—a former all-around athlete at the University of California at Los Angeles—the indignity would not be borne without protest. Jack Roosevelt Robinson was court-martialed for refusing to move to the back of an army bus on a Texas base.

When the war ended, Jackie Robinson's prodigious athletic skills and his character would make him a pioneer in the civil-rights struggle.

Branch Rickey, the president of the Brooklyn Dodgers, gave Robinson the chance to be the first black man to play organized baseball since the nineteenth century.

Rickey knew that Robinson would have to struggle with his combative and proud nature and show enormous restraint in the face of racial taunting. "I'm looking for a ballplayer with guts enough not to fight back," said the Dodger executive.

Robinson took up the challenge, and after a year with the Dodgers' Montreal farm club he made his major-league debut on April 15, 1947. A few days after that, he faced his first big test.

Early in the season, the Philadelphia Phillies came to Ebbets Field for a three-game series. I was still in my slump and events of the opening game certainly didn't help. Starting to the plate in the first inning, I could scarcely believe my ears. Almost as if it had been synchronized by some master conductor, hate poured forth from the Phillies dugout.

"Hey, nigger, why don't you go back to the cotton field where you belong?"

"They're waiting for you in the jungles, black boy!"

"Hey, snowflake, which one of those white boys' wives are you dating tonight?"

"We don't want you here, nigger."

"Go back to the bushes!"

Those insults and taunts were only samples of the torrent of abuse which poured out from the Phillies dugout that April day.

I have to admit that this day, of all the unpleasant days in my life, brought me nearer to cracking up than I ever had been. Perhaps I should have become inured to this kind of garbage, but I was in New York City and unprepared to face the kind of barbarism from a northern team that I had come to associate with the Deep South. The abuse coming out of the Phillies dugout was being directed by the team's manager, Ben Chapman, a Southerner. I felt tortured and I tried just to play ball and ignore the insults. But it was really getting to me. What did the Phillies want from me? What, indeed, did Mr. Rickey expect of me? I was, after all, a human being. What was I doing here turning the other cheek as though I weren't a man? In college days I had a reputation as a black man who never tolerated affronts to his dignity. I had defied prejudice in the Army. How could I have thought that barriers would fall, that, indeed, my talent could triumph over bigotry?

For one wild and rage-crazed minute I thought, "To hell with Mr. Rickey's 'noble experiment.' It's clear it won't succeed. I have made every effort to work hard to get myself into shape. My best is not enough for them." I thought what a glorious, cleansing thing it would be to let go. To hell with the image of the patient black freak I was supposed to create. I could throw down my bat, stride over to that Phillies dugout, grab one of those white sons of bitches and smash his teeth in with my despised black fist. Then I could walk away from it all. I'd never become a sports star. But my son could tell his son someday what his daddy could have been if he hadn't been too much of a man.

Then, I thought of Mr. Rickey—how his family and friends had begged him not to fight for me and my people. I thought of all of his predictions, which had come true. Mr. Rickey had come to a crossroads and made a lonely decision. I was at a crossroads. I would make mine. I would stay.

the MONTGOMERY BUS BOYCOTT

She was born into rural poverty in Tuskegee, Alabama, attending an overcrowded one-room schoolhouse where the black children were present only five months of the year. They spent the rest of the time in the cotton fields.

But she had persevered, would become active in the NAACP, and now, on this December day of 1955, she was riding home on a segregated Montgomery, Alabama, bus, returning from her job as a seamstress at a downtown department store.

When the driver asked Rosa Parks to give up her seat to a white person, she refused.

Having to take a certain section because of your race was humiliating, but having to stand up because a particular driver wanted to keep a white person from having to stand was, to my mind, most inhumane.

More than seventy-five, between eighty-five and I think ninety percent of the patronage of the buses were black people, because more white people could own and drive their own cars than blacks.

I happened to be the secretary of the Montgomery branch of the N.A.A.C.P. as well as the N.A.A.C.P. Youth Council adviser. Many cases did come to my attention that nothing came out of 'cause the person that was abused would be too intimidated to sign an affidavit, or to make a statement. Over the years, I had had my own problems with the bus drivers. In fact, some did tell me not to ride their buses if I felt that I was too important to go to the back door to get on. One had me evicted from the bus in 1943, which did not cause anything more than just a passing glance.

On December 1, 1955, I had finished my day's work as a tailor's assistant in the Montgomery Fair department store and I was on my way home. There was one vacant seat on the Cleveland Avenue bus, which I took, alongside a man and two women across the aisle. There were still a few vacant seats in the white section in the front, of course. We went to the next stop without being disturbed. On the third, the front seats were occupied and this one man, a white man, was standing. The driver asked us to stand up and let him have those seats, and when none of us moved at his first words, he said, "You all make it light on yourselves and let me have those seats." And the man who was sitting next to the window stood up, and I made room for him to pass by me. The two women across the aisle stood up and moved out.

When the driver saw me still sitting, he asked if I was going to stand up and I said, "No, I'm not."

And he said, "Well, if you don't stand up, I'm going to call the police and have you arrested."

I said, "You may do that."

He did get off the bus, and I still stayed where I was. Two policemen came on the bus. One of the policemen asked me if the bus driver had asked me to stand and I said yes.

He said, "Why don't you stand up?"

And I asked him, "Why do you push us around?"

He said, "I do not know, but the law is the law and you're under arrest."

Rosa Parks's defiance set in motion a black boycott of Montgomery's bus lines led by a pair of young ministers—Martin Luther King, Jr., and Ralph Abernathy. The boycott would be a landmark protest in the civil-rights movement, and it would continue until its goals had been achieved. On November 14, 1956, the United States Supreme Court declared Montgomery's segregation laws unconstitutional.

CENTRAL HIGH, LITTLE ROCK

In the predawn hours of D-Day, the 101st Airborne Division had jumped into the fields of Normandy, the vanguard of the democracies' great invasion of Hitler's Europe.

Thirteen years later, the "Screaming Eagles"—rifles and bayonets at the ready—were summoned once again for the cause of freedom, but this time at home.

Setting the tone for the South's massive resistance to the 1954 Supreme Court decision outlawing school segregation, Arkansas Governor Orval Faubus—defying a federal-court decree—had ordered his National Guard to block nine black students from entering Little Rock's Central High School for the fall-1957 term.

Faced with a challenge to the authority of the United States government, President Eisenhower federalized the Arkansas Guardsmen and called out the 101st Airborne to put the students into the school.

One of them was a sixteen-year-old named Melba Pattillo.

There were tears in Mother's eyes as she whispered good-bye. "Make this day the best you can," she said.

"Let's bow our heads for a word of prayer." One of our ministers stepped from among the others and began to say comforting words. I noticed tears were streaming down the faces of many of the adults. I wondered why they were crying just at that moment when I had more hope of staying alive and keeping safe than I had since the integration began.

"Protect these youngsters and bring them home. Flood the Holy Spirit into the hearts and minds of those who would attack our children."

"Yes, Lord," several voices echoed.

One of the soldiers stepped forward and beckoned the driver of a station wagon to move it closer to the driveway. Two jeeps moved forward, one in front of the station wagon, one behind. Guns were mounted on the hoods of the jeeps.

We were already a half hour late for school when we heard the order *"Move out,"* and the leader motioned for us to get into the station wagon. As we collected ourselves and walked toward the caravan, many of the adults were crying openly. When I turned to wave to Mother Lois, I saw tears in her eyes. I couldn't go back to comfort her.

Suddenly, all the soldiers went into action, moving about with precise steps. I hoped I would be allowed to ride in the jeep, although it occurred to me that it didn't have a top so it wouldn't be safe. Sure enough, all nine of us were directed to sit in the station wagon.

Sarge, our driver, was friendly and pleasant. He had a Southern accent, different from ours, different even from the one Arkansas whites had. We rolled away from the curb lined with people waving to us. Mama looked even more distraught. I remembered I hadn't kissed her good-bye.

The driver explained that we were not riding in a caravan but a jeep convoy. I could hear helicopters roaring in the distance. Sarge said they were following us to keep watch. We nine said very little to each other, we were too busy asking Sarge about the soldiers. At times the car was so silent I could hear my stomach growl. It was particularly loud because nervousness had caused me to get rid of my breakfast only moments after I'd eaten it.

Our convoy moved through streets lined with people on both sides, who stood as though they were waiting for a parade. A few friendly folks from our community waved as we passed by. Some of the white people looked totally horrified, while others raised their fists to us. Others shouted ugly words.

As we neared the school, I could hear the roar of a helicopter directly overhead. Our convoy was joined by more jeeps. I could see that armed soldiers and jeeps had already blocked off certain intersections approaching the school. Closer to the school, we saw more soldiers and many more hostile white people with scowls on their faces, lining the sidewalk and shaking their fists. But for the first time I wasn't afraid of them.

We pulled up to the front of the school. Groups of soldiers on guard were lined at intervals several feet apart. A group of twenty or more was running at breakneck speed up and down the street in front of Central High School, their rifles with bayonets pointed straight ahead. Sarge said they were doing crowd control—keeping the mob away from us.

Sarge said we should wait in the station wagon because the soldiers would come for us. As I looked around, I saw a group of uniformed men walking toward us, their bayonets pointed straight up. Their leader beckoned to us as one of them held open the car door. As I stepped outside the car, I heard a noise behind me. In the distance, there was that chillingly familiar but now muffled chant, "Two, four, six, eight. We ain't gonna integrate." I turned to see reporters swarming about across the street from the school. I looked up to see the helicopters hovering overhead, hanging in midair with their blades whirring. The military leader motioned to us to stand still.

About twenty soldiers moved toward us, forming an olive-drab square with one end open. I glanced at the faces of my friends. Like me, they appeared to be impressed by the imposing sight of military power. There was so much to see, and everything was happening so quickly. We walked through the open end of the square. Erect, rifles at their sides, their faces stern, the soldiers did not make eye contact as they surrounded us in a protective cocoon. After a long moment, the leader motioned us to move forward.

Hundreds of Central High students milled about. I could see their astonishment. Some were peering out of windows high above us, some were watching from the yard, others were on the landing. Some were tearful, others angry.

I felt proud and sad at the same time. Proud that I lived in a country that would go this far to bring justice to a Little Rock girl like me, but sad that they had to go to such great lengths. Yes, this is the United States, I thought to myself. There is a reason that I salute the flag. If these guys just go with us this first time, everything's going to be okay.

We began moving forward. The eerie silence of that moment would *forever be etched in my memory. All I could hear was my own heartbeat and the sound of boots clicking on the stone.*

Everyone seemed to be moving in slow motion as I peered past the raised bayonets of the 101st soldiers. I walked on the concrete path toward the front door of the school, the same path the Arkansas National Guard had blocked us from days before. We approached the stairs, our feet moving in unison to the rhythm of the marching click-clack sound of the Screaming Eagles. Step by step we climbed upward—where none of my people had ever before walked as students. We stepped up to the front door of Central High School and crossed the threshold into that place where angry segregationist mobs had forbidden us to go.

Chapter Eight

AMERICA *in* TURMOIL

DALLAS, NOVEMBER 22

The images are still clear: President Kennedy waving to the crowds from the open limousine; Jacqueline Kennedy scrambling as her husband slumped over; Lyndon B. Johnson raising his right hand to take the oath of office on Air Force One; Lee Harvey Oswald clutching his stomach after being shot by Jack Ruby; John-John saluting his father's casket.

But not so clear for many—even three decades later—is the trail that led to the Kennedy assassination. Numerous books have suggested all sorts of conspiracies, have tried to debunk the finding of the Warren Commission that Oswald acted alone that Friday afternoon, November 22, 1963. It's a puzzle that will never entirely be solved.

Among the thousands in the streets for the President's visit to Dallas was a forty-five-year-old steamfitter named Howard Brennan. While waiting for the presidential motorcade to turn into Elm Street from Houston Street, Brennan glanced up at an office building and noticed a man whom he would identify at a police lineup that night. Brennan would later tell how Lee Harvey Oswald left a corner window on the sixth floor and returned "a couple of times."

As I looked at the man, it struck me how unsmiling and calm he was. He didn't seem to feel one bit of excitement. His face was almost expressionless. . . . He seemed preoccupied.

Soon after Kennedy's car moved down an incline toward a triple underpass, a shot rang out, but Brennan thought at first that it was a motorcycle backfire.

Well, then, something, just right after this explosion, made me think that it was a firecracker being thrown from the Texas Book Store. . . .

I looked up then at the Texas School Book Depository Building. What I saw made my blood run cold. Poised in the corner window of the sixth floor was the same young man I had noticed several times before the motorcade arrived. There was one difference—this time he held a rifle in his hands, pointing toward the Presidential car. He steadied the rifle against the cornice and while he moved quickly, he didn't seem to be in any kind of panic. All this happened in the matter of a second or two. Then came the sickening sound of a second shot. . . . I wanted to cry, I wanted to scream, but I couldn't utter a sound.

He was aiming again and I wanted to pray, to beg God to somehow make him miss the target. . . . What I was seeing, the sight became so fixed in my mind that I'll never forget it as long as I live. . . . Then another shot rang out.

To my amazement the man still stood there in the window. He didn't appear to be rushed. There was no particular emotion visible on his face except for a slight smirk. It was a look of satisfaction, as if he had accomplished what he set out to do. . . . He simply moved away from the window until he disappeared from my line of vision.

Merriman Smith, the White House correspondent for United Press International, was at Warm Springs when President Roosevelt died. Now he would win a Pulitzer Prize for his coverage of another president's death.

It was a balmy, sunny noon as we motored through downtown Dallas behind President Kennedy. The procession cleared the center of the business district and turned into a handsome highway that wound through what appeared to be a park.

I was riding in the so-called White House press "pool" car, a telephone company vehicle equipped with a mobile radio-telephone. I was in the front seat between a driver from the telephone company and Malcolm Kilduff, acting White House press secretary for the President's Texas tour. The other pool reporters were wedged in the back seat.

Suddenly we heard three loud, almost painfully loud cracks. The first sounded as if it might have been a large firecracker. But the second and third blasts were unmistakable. Gunfire.

The President's car, possibly as much as 150 or 200 yards ahead, seemed to falter briefly. We saw a flurry of activity in the Secret Service follow-up car behind the Chief Executive's bubble-top limousine.

Next in line was the car bearing Vice President Lyndon B. Johnson.

Behind that, another follow-up car bearing agents assigned to the Vice President's protection. We were behind that car.

Our car stood still for probably only a few seconds, but it seemed like a lifetime. One sees history explode before one's eyes and for even the most trained observer, there is a limit to what one can comprehend.

I looked ahead at the President's car but could not see him or his companion, Gov. John B. Connally of Texas. Both men had been riding on the right side of the bubble-top limousine from Washington. I thought I saw a flash of pink which would have been Mrs. Jacqueline Kennedy.

Everybody in our car began shouting at the driver to pull up closer to the President's car. But at this moment, we saw the big bubble-top and a motorcycle escort roar away at high speed.

We screamed at our driver, "Get going, get going." We careened around the Johnson car and its escort and set out down the highway, barely able to keep in sight of the President's car and the accompanying Secret Service follow-up car.

They vanished around a curve. When we cleared the same curve we could see where we were heading—Parkland Hospital, a large brick structure to the left of the arterial highway. We skidded around a sharp left turn and spilled out of the pool car as it entered the hospital driveway.

I ran to the side of the bubble-top.

The President was face down on the back seat. Mrs. Kennedy made a cradle of her arms around the President's head and bent over him as if she were whispering to him.

Gov. Connally was on his back on the floor of the car, his head and shoulders resting in the arms of his wife, Nellie, who kept shaking her head and shaking with dry sobs. Blood oozed from the front of the Governor's suit. I could not see the President's wound. But I could see blood spattered around the interior of the rear seat and a dark stain spreading down the right side of the President's gray suit.

From the telephone car, I had radioed the Dallas bureau of U.P.I. that three shots had been fired at the Kennedy motorcade. Seeing the bloody scene in the rear of the car at the hospital entrance, I knew I had to get to a telephone immediately.

Clint Hill, the Secret Service agent in charge of the detail assigned to Mrs. Kennedy, was leaning over into the rear of the car.

"How badly was he hit, Clint?" I asked.

"He's dead," Hill replied curtly.

I have no further memory of the scene in the driveway. I recall a babble of anxious voices, tense voices—"Where in hell are the stretchers . . . Get a doctor out here . . . He's on the way . . . Come on, easy there." And from somewhere, nervous sobbing.

I raced down a short stretch of sidewalk into a hospital corridor. The first thing I spotted was a small clerical office, more of a booth than an office. Inside, a bespectacled man stood shuffling what appeared to be hospital forms. At a wicket much like a teller's cage, I spotted a telephone on the shelf.

"How do you get outside?" I gasped. "The President has been hurt and this is an emergency call."

"Dial nine," he said, shoving the phone toward me.

It took two tries before I successfully dialed the Dallas U.P.I. number. Quickly I dictated a bulletin saying the President had been seriously, perhaps fatally, injured by an assassin's bullets while driving through the streets of Dallas.

Litters bearing the President and the Governor rolled by me as I dictated, but my back was to the hallway and I didn't see them until they were at the entrance of the emergency room about 75 or 100 feet away.

I knew they had passed, however, from the horrified expression that suddenly spread over the face of the man behind the wicket.

As I stood in the drab buff hallway leading into the emergency ward trying to reconstruct the shooting for the U.P.I. man on the other end of the telephone and still keeping track of what was happening outside the door of the emergency room, I watched a swift and confused panorama sweep before me.

Kilduff of the White House press staff raced up and down the hall. Police captains barked at each other, "Clear this area." Two priests hurried in behind a Secret Service agent, their narrow purple stoles rolled up tightly in their hands. A police lieutenant ran down the hall with a large carton of blood for transfusions. A doctor came in and said he was responding to a call for "all neurosurgeons."

The priests came out and said the President had received the last sacrament of the Roman Catholic Church. They said he was still alive, but not conscious. Members of the Kennedy staff began arriving. They had been behind us in the motorcade, but hopelessly bogged for a time in confused traffic.

Telephones were at a premium in the hospital and I clung to mine for dear life. I was afraid to stray from the wicket lest I lose contact with the outside world.

My decision was made for me, however, when Kilduff and Wayne Hawks of the White House staff ran by me, shouting that Kilduff would make a statement shortly in the so-called nurses room a floor above and at the far end of the hospital.

I threw down the phone and sped after them. We reached the door of the conference room and there were loud cries of "Quiet!" Fighting to keep his emotions under control, Kilduff said, "President John Fitzgerald Kennedy died at approximately one o'clock."

Smith witnessed the swearing in of Lyndon B. Johnson at the Dallas airport.

Aboard Air Force One on which I had made so many trips as a press association reporter covering President Kennedy, all of the shades of the larger main cabin were drawn and the interior was hot and dimly lighted.

Kilduff propelled us to the President's suite two-thirds of the way back in the plane. The room is used normally as a combination conference and sitting room and could accommodate eight to ten people seated.

I wedged inside the door and began counting. There were 27 people in this compartment. Johnson stood in the center with his wife, Lady Bird. U.S. District Judge Sarah T. Hughes, 67, a kindly faced woman with a small black Bible in her hands, waited to give the oath.

The compartment became hotter and hotter. Johnson was worried that some of the Kennedy staff might not be able to get inside. He urged people to press forward, but a Signal Corps photographer, Capt. Cecil Stoughton, standing in the corner on a chair, said if Johnson moved any closer, it would be virtually impossible to make a truly historic photograph.

It developed that Johnson was waiting for Mrs. Kennedy, who was composing herself in a small bedroom in the rear of the plane. She appeared alone, dressed in the same pink wool suit she had worn in the morning when she appeared so happy shaking hands with airport crowds at the side of her husband.

She was white-faced but dry-eyed. Friendly hands stretched toward her as she stumbled slightly. Johnson took both of her hands in his and motioned her to his left side. Lady Bird stood on his right, a fixed half-smile showing the tension.

Johnson nodded to Judge Hughes, an old friend of his family and a Kennedy appointee.

"Hold up your right hand and repeat after me," the woman jurist said to Johnson.

Outside, a jet could be heard droning into a landing.

Judge Hughes held out the Bible and Johnson covered it with his large left hand. His right arm went slowly into the air and the jurist began to intone the Constitutional oath. "I do solemnly swear I will faithfully execute the office of President of the United States. . . ."

"*a* PROBLEM THAT HAD NO NAME"

During World War II, millions of American women entered the workplace for the first time, in many cases performing tough and grimy tasks hardly in line with their supposed fragility. But when the boys came back, Rosie the Riveter returned to the kitchen.

Two decades later, women were still seen essentially as wives and mothers.

Betty Friedan, a *summa cum laude* graduate of Smith College, was seemingly fulfilling every woman's dream. She had a fine family, lived in the suburbs, and wrote magazine articles, albeit primarily on "women's topics." But she was dissatisfied with her life, with what she called "a problem that had no name."

In her introduction to the tenth-anniversary edition of *The Feminine Mystique*, originally published in 1963, she would tell how those feelings brought about the book that inspired the women's-rights movement.

It seems such a precarious accident that I ever wrote the book at all—but in another way, my whole life had prepared me to write that book. All the pieces finally came together. In 1957, getting strangely bored with writing articles about breast feeding and the like for Redbook *and the* Ladies' Home Journal, *I put an unconscionable amount of time into a questionnaire for my fellow Smith graduates of the class of 1942, thinking I was going to disprove the current notion that education had fitted us ill for our role as women. But the questionnaire raised more questions than it answered for me—education had not exactly geared us to the role women were trying to play, it seemed. The suspicion arose as to whether it was the education or the role that was wrong.* McCall's *commissioned an article based on my Smith alumnae questionnaire, but the then male publisher of* McCall's, *during that great era of togetherness, turned the piece down in horror, despite underground efforts of female editors. The male* McCall's *editors said it couldn't be true.*

I was next commissioned to do the article for Ladies' Home Journal. *That time I took it back, because they rewrote it to say just the opposite of what, in fact, I was trying to say. I tried it again for* Redbook. *Each time I was interviewing more women, psychologists, sociologists, marriage counselors, and the like and getting more and more sure I was on the track of something. But what? I needed a name for whatever it was that kept us from using our rights, that made us feel guilty about anything we did not as our husbands' wives, our children's mothers, but as people ourselves. I needed a name to describe that guilt. Unlike the guilt women used to feel about sexual needs, the guilt they felt now was about needs that didn't fit the sexual definition of women, the mystique of feminine fulfillment—the feminine mystique.*

The editor of Redbook *told my agent, "Betty has gone off her rocker. She has always done a good job for us, but this time only the most neurotic housewife could identify." I opened my agent's letter on the subway as I was taking the kids to the pediatrician. I got off the subway to call my agent and told her, "I'll have to write a book to get this into print." What I was writing threatened the very foundations of the women's magazine world—the feminine mystique.*

When Norton contracted for the book, I thought it would take a year to finish it; it took five. I wouldn't have even started it if the New York Public Library had not, at just the right time, opened the Frederick Lewis Allen Room, where writers working on a book could get a desk, six months at a time, rent free. I got a baby-sitter three days a week and took the bus from Rockland County to the city and somehow managed to prolong the six months to two years in the Allen Room, enduring much joking from other writers at lunch when it came out that I was writing a book about women. Then, somehow, the book took me over, obsessed me, wanted to write itself, and I took my papers home and wrote on the dining-room table, the living-room couch, on a neighbor's dock on the river, and kept on writing it in my mind when I stopped to take the kids somewhere or make dinner, and went back to it after they were in bed. . . .

I was surprised myself at what I was writing, where it was leading. After I finished each chapter, a part of me would wonder, am I crazy? But there was also a growing feeling of calm, strong, gut-sureness as the clues fitted together, which must be the same kind of feeling a scientist has when he or she zeroes in on a discovery in one of those true-science detective stories.

Only this was not just abstract and conceptual. It meant that I and every other woman I knew had been living a lie, and all the doctors who treated us and the experts who studied us were perpetuating that lie, and our homes and schools and churches and politics and professions were built around that lie. If women were really people—no more, no less— then all the things that kept them from being full people in our society would have to be changed. And women, once they broke through the feminine mystique and took themselves seriously as people, would see their place on a false pedestal, even their glorification as sex objects, for the putdown it was.

Yet if I had realized how fantastically fast that would really happen— already in less than ten years' time—maybe I would have been so scared that I might have stopped writing. It's frightening when you're starting on a new road that no one has been on before. You don't know how far it's going to take you until you look back and realize how far, how very far you've gone. When the first woman asked me, in 1963, to autograph The Feminine Mystique, saying what by now hundreds—thousands, I *guess—of women have said to me, "It changed my whole life," I wrote, "Courage to us all on the new road." Because there is no turning back on that road. It has to change your whole life; it certainly changed mine.*

ABOVE *the* HO CHI MINH TRAIL

Back in 1954, President Eisenhower rejected a request by the French that he send American troops to Indochina in the final throes of France's lost colonial war. The United States was not willing to get bogged down in another Asian land campaign.

But by the early 1960s, the Cold War view of communism as a monolithic force was outweighing that wariness. Now the United States had sent military advisers to the South Vietnamese, who were under grave pressure from the communist North Vietnamese government and its Viet Cong allies. A major step toward war came in August 1964, when the Johnson administration staged its first bombing raid on North Vietnam, and obtained legislative backing via the Gulf of Tonkin Resolution, approved by Congress in response to a confusing military encounter off the Vietnamese coast.

By the summer of 1965, the American troop buildup in Vietnam was in full swing. But there would always be hopes that bombing could pound the enemy into submission. Over the next decade, more bombs would be dropped on North Vietnam than had fallen on Nazi Germany.

In December 1986, Dick Rutan and his girlfriend, Jeana Yeager, smashed the last great aviation barrier, becoming the first persons to fly around the world in a plane that never refueled.

Before he became a test pilot, Rutan was an air-force hot shot, flying F-100 ground-support fighters in the Vietnam War in 1967 and '68. He completed 325 missions, winning five Distinguished Flying Crosses and a Silver Star.

Rutan belonged to a unit calling itself Commando Saber, its call sign "Misty." The men known as "Misties" would fly over the Ho Chi Minh Trail—the conduit for the movement of men and supplies from North to South Vietnam, mostly through Laos.

Accompanying the bombs—according to Rutan—was a long chain of lies.

My first impression when we crossed the DMZ was that somebody had turned the goddamn place into the moon. I've never seen so many bomb craters in my whole life. I was appalled. And the thing that really got me was the city of Dong Hoi. It was the first major city north of the DMZ. It was a citadel city. You could see the citadel. They had a nice port there. You could see it was a fairly large town. But they had bombed that thing right into the Stone Age. All you could see was foundations. There was not a stick standing. Totally destroyed. Absolutely, completely destroyed. There wasn't a living soul there. And I thought—Why in the world? Why? Why did we do that? . . .

In some of the areas in Laos, along the Ho Chi Minh Trail, they'd pick stranglehold areas like road intersections. When they'd start out, the road wasn't even visible from the air because it was down in deep jungle. They'd find where the road was and bomb an area two miles around there into nothing but dirt. Not a living thing. A wing of F-104s or F-105s would just go and bomb a point on the road. They'd bomb and bomb and bomb. Or on a mountainside, they'd try to make a slide come down to close the road. And I'll tell you—I spent three tours in Misty. I was a Misty FAC longer than anybody. And I never one time saw a road closed or cut. All that was a total waste of effort. Absolute total waste. The North Vietnamese had those roads open within a handful of minutes. I'd go up there and I'd see a major strike going in. Pulverize the road. Wouldn't even be a road left. I'd come back later and all of a sudden, out would come a little bulldozer going right over the bomb craters. Didn't hardly slow it down.

But they were turning jungle into dust. For nothing. It did not work. But you had to be there to see that it didn't work. Until the Misties got up there, the bombers would go in, and their photo recon would say, "Oh, boy, the bombs are on target, a whole squadron of airplanes put all their bombs on this road and they all had good hits." But they'd bomb and leave. The Misties were up there all day, and we saw what happened. I'd come over in the morning, and the road would be just pristine. I'd call the AB Triple-C—that's the airborne command and control center, a C-130 that would orbit overhead. I'd say, "Hey, the road's not cut. There's trucks going by." That'd really upset 'em. Because they just relayed to Westmoreland, and I'm sure Westmoreland told his boss, "We just strangled the whole Ho Chi Minh Trail." It was a joke. It was the most gross waste of bombs I've ever seen in my life.

The other thing that bothered me was the night bombing. There were people who were totally night-dedicated. Those guys would go up fragged for some truck park at night, and if they couldn't find it, they'd invariably drop their ordnance on villages. We'd go in and check with the AB Triple-C at dawn. And the guys would say, "Oh, God, Misty, we had a fantastic truck kill last night." I'd say, "Where is it?" "Two klicks south of the intersection of Brown Route and Green Route." We'd go over there expecting to find truck hulks and stuff. Nothing. The road is clean. But we'd look four or five or eight miles away, and there'd be a village in flames. With all kinds of fresh bomb craters. I'd radio, "They just hit a village last night." They'd argue with me over the air. The night command post was called Moonbeam. He'd say, "No, no, no, you're wrong. They hit trucks." Well, I knew more about that area than they ever thought about. I knew every square inch of it. I'd just tell him, "Look, you son of a bitch, I'm right here looking at it. Don't give me this garbage. There's no trucks at all. There's nothing on Green Route, it's empty and clean. There's a village, and it's in flames."

MASSACRE *at* MY LAI

It was a story that seemed the stuff of Nazi Germany, a story Americans didn't want to believe.

Three platoons of United States soldiers moved into the South Vietnamese village of My Lai on March 16, 1968, looking for Viet Cong troops. All they found were unresisting men, women, and children. These they rounded up and slaughtered—perhaps as many as five hundred, according to army investigations.

Only one soldier was ever convicted at a court-martial: Lieutenant

William Calley, one of the platoon leaders, was sentenced to life in prison. But he would serve only three years—under house arrest at an army post.

The massacre was first revealed by Seymour Hersh, a former *New York Times* reporter then working free-lance. His account appeared in more than thirty newspapers, and he would win a Pulitzer Prize for it. But for most Americans, the shocking details came directly from one of the soldiers. Private Paul Meadlo told of My Lai in an interview with Mike Wallace broadcast over CBS radio on November 24, 1969, and carried on CBS television the following day.

Q *[Mike Wallace]: How many people did you round up?*

A *[Paul Meadlo]: Well, there was about forty, forty-five people that we gathered in the center of the village. And we placed them in there, and it was like a little island, right there in the center of the village, I'd say. And—*

Q: *What kind of people—men, women, children?*

A: *Men, women, children.*

Q: *Babies?*

A: *Babies. And we all huddled them up. We made them squat down, and Lieutenant Calley came over and said, You know what to do with them, don't you? And I said Yes. So I took it for granted that he just wanted us to watch them. And he left, and came back about ten or fifteen minutes later, and said, How come you ain't killed them yet? And I told him that I didn't think you wanted us to kill them, that you just wanted us to guard them. He said, No, I want them dead. So—*

Q: *He told this to all of you, or to you particularly?*

A: *Well, I was facing him. So, but the other three, four guys heard it and so he stepped back about ten, fifteen feet, and he started shooting them. And he told me to start shooting. So I started shooting. I poured about four clips into the group.*

Q: *You fired four clips from your . . .*

A: *M-16.*

Q: *And that's about—how many clips—I mean how many—*

A: *I carried seventeen rounds to each clip.*

Q: *So you fired something like sixty-seven shots.*

A: *Right.*

Q: *And you killed how many? At that time?*

A: *Well, I fired them on automatic, so you can't—you just spray the area on them and so you can't know how many you killed 'cause they were going fast. So I might have killed ten or fifteen of them.*

Q: *Men, women, and children?*

A: *Men, women, and children.*

Q: *And babies?*

A: *And babies . . .*

Q: *Now you're rounding up more?*

A: *We're rounding up more, and we had about seven or eight people. And we was going to throw them in the hootch, and, well, we put them in the hootch and then we dropped a hand grenade down there with them. And somebody holed up in the ravine, and told us to bring them over to the ravine, so we took them back out, and led them over to—and by that time we already had them over there, and they had about seventy, seventy-five people all gathered up. So we threw ours in with them and Lieutenant Calley told me, he said, Meadlo, we got another job to do. And so he walked over to the people, and he started pushing them off and started shooting. . . .*

Q: *Started pushing them off into the ravine?*

A: *Off into the ravine. It was a ditch. And so we started pushing them off and we started shooting them, so, all together, we just pushed them all off, and just started using automatics on them. And then—*

Q: *Again—men, women, children?*

A: *Men, women, and children.*

Q: *And babies?*

A: *And babies. And so we started shooting them, and somebody told us to switch off to single shot so that we could save ammo. So we switched off to single shot, and shot a few more rounds. . . .*

Meadlo then talked about the events of the following day.

A: . . . *the next morning we started leaving, leaving the perimeter, and I stepped on a land mine next day, next morning.*

Q: *And you came back to the United States.*

Q: *I came back to the United States, and lost a foot out of it. . . .*

Q: *Did you feel any sense of retribution to yourself the day after?*

A: *Well, I felt that I was being punished for what I'd done, the next morning. Later on in that day, I felt like I was being punished.*

Q: *Why did you do it?*

A: *Why did I do it? Because I felt like I was ordered to do it, and it seemed like that, at the time I felt like I was doing the right thing, because like I said I lost a lot of buddies. I lost a damn good buddy, Bobby Wilson, and it was on my conscience. So, after I done it, I felt good, but later on that day, it was getting to me. . . .*

Q: *How do you shoot babies?*

A: *I don't know, it's just one of them things. . . .*

Q: *How many people would you imagine were killed that day?*

A: *I'd say about 370.*

Q: *. . . and you yourself were responsible for how many of them?*

A: *I couldn't say.*

Q: *Twenty-five? Fifty?*

A: *I couldn't say. . . . Just too many.*

Q: *They weren't begging or saying, "No, no," or—*

A: *Right, they was begging and saying, "No, no." And the mothers was hugging their children and—but they kept right on firing. Well, we kept right on firing. They was waving their arms and begging. . . .*

Q: *. . . we've raised just a dickens about what the Nazis did, or what the Japanese did, but particularly what the Nazis did in the Second World War, the brutalization and so forth, you know. It's hard for a good many Americans to understand that young, capable American boys could line up old men, women, and children and babies and shoot them down in cold blood. How do you explain that?*

A: *I wouldn't know.*

Q: *Did you ever dream about all of this that went on?*

A: *Yes, I did . . . and I still dream about it.*

Q: *What kind of dreams?*

A: *I see the women and children in my sleep. Some days, some nights, I can't even sleep. I just lay there thinking about it.*

a BALCONY *in* MEMPHIS

A rainy evening—April 3, 1968. The Church of God in Christ—Memphis, Tennessee. The Reverend Dr. Martin Luther King, Jr., has arrived in the city to support a strike by black sanitation workers. King mesmerizes an audience of five hundred people, delivering a ninety-minute address.

"I don't know what will happen now. We've got some difficult days ahead. But it really doesn't matter with me now, because I've been to the mountaintop. Like anybody, I would like to live a long life. But I'm not concerned about that now. I just want to do God's will. . . . I'm happy tonight. I'm not worried about anything, I'm not fearing any man. Mine eyes have seen the glory of the coming of the Lord."

The following afternoon, King was at the Lorraine Motel in Memphis with the Reverend Ralph David Abernathy, with whom he had founded the Southern Christian Leadership Conference. They were discussing plans for a second march in Memphis to support the sanitation workers, the first one having ended in violence. King stepped onto a balcony to chat with the Reverend Jesse Jackson and another associate, the Reverend Ben Branch, who were in the courtyard.

Abernathy remained inside his room.

I had sprinkled Aramis on my hands and was lifting them to my face when I heard a loud crack, and my hands jerked reflexively. It sounded like a backfire from a car, but there was just enough difference to chill my heart. I wheeled, looked out the door, and saw only Martin's feet. He was down on the concrete balcony.

I bolted out the door and found him there, face up, sprawled and unmoving. Stepping over his frame, I knelt down, gathered him in my arms, and began patting him on his left cheek. Even at the first glance I could see that a bullet had entered his right cheek, leaving a small hole.

"Hit the ground!" someone shouted from the parking lot below.

"Oh, God!" someone else yelled, and I heard scuffling feet.

I looked down at Martin's face. His eyes wobbled, then for an instant focused on me.

"Martin. It's all right. Don't worry. This is Ralph. This is Ralph."

His eyes grew calm and he moved his lips. I was certain he understood and was trying to say something. Then, in the next instant, I saw the understanding drain from his eyes and leave them absolutely empty. I looked more carefully at the wound and noticed the glistening blood and a flash of white bone.

Then [the Reverend Billy] Kyle was standing over me, terror in his face.

"Billy, quick! Go call an ambulance!"

He disappeared inside, and I glanced at the courtyard below, consciously aware for the first time that somebody somewhere had fired a gun. It had been only a matter of seconds, but no one was visible in the parking lot. Jesse, Ben Branch, and the others had apparently taken cover—where, I didn't know.

I scanned the street, the rooftop, but I saw no one with a gun. The seconds ticked off. A couple of cars drove leisurely by. I cradled Martin and tried not to think what might happen next.

Then somewhere I heard a loud wail. I peered into the motel room and saw Billy Kyle, face down on the bed, screaming.

"This is no time to lose our heads," I said as calmly as I could. *"Get an ambulance."*

"I can't get a line," he yelled. *"Something's wrong with the phone."*

Later I would learn that the black woman operating the motel switchboard at the time of the shot had suffered a heart attack and died, thereby making outgoing calls impossible. However, somebody somewhere called an ambulance.

I felt as if I were on that balcony cradling Martin for hours, but it was actually less than ten minutes from the time the shot rang out until the time the rescue squad arrived. After a couple of minutes I heard shouts from the courtyard below, then tentative conversation. At some point police arrived from the far end of the parking lot.

Meanwhile, a man from Community Service Relations had come up the stairs, frightened enough to be crawling on his hands and knees, but *brave enough to bring a blanket to be spread over Martin for the treatment of shock. Then Andy Young followed and knelt beside me.*

He looked down at Martin, then cried out, "Oh, God! Ralph. It's over!"

the STONEWALL RAID

New York City's public-morals police figured they were in for a routine bust the evening of June 27, 1969, when they raided the Stonewall Inn, a homosexual hangout on Greenwich Village's Christopher Street owned by organized crime and replete with drag queens.

But when six policemen tried to make arrests for liquor-law violations, two hundred bar patrons pounded them with bottles and bricks. A melee bringing out police reinforcements raged for half the night.

No one would ever be sure why gays battled back that evening— they had always submitted meekly to authority. This was, after all, an era when the American Psychiatric Association was still listing homosexuality as a mental disorder, a time when the *New York Daily News* could get away with a headline on the Stonewall episode reading "Homo Nest Raided, Queen Bees Are Stinging Mad."

Within a few days, however, gays not only had fought back spontaneously, but were organizing openly. Some five hundred people gathered for New York's first gay-rights rally.

The response to the Stonewall raid would become accepted as the start of the gay-liberation movement.

Two decades later, the United States Postal Service announced a special cancellation with the postmark: "Stonewall Sta./20 Years 1969–89/Lesbian and Gay Pride."

A college student named Morty Manford was one of those inside the Stonewall.

The Stonewall was my favorite place. It was a dive. It was shabby, and the glasses they served the watered-down drinks in weren't particularly clean. The place attracted a very eclectic crowd. Patrons included every type of person: some transvestites, a lot of students, young people, older people, businessmen. It was an interesting place. I met friends at the Stonewall regularly. There was a dance floor and a jukebox. There was a back-room area, which in those days meant there was another bar in back. There were tables where people sat.

The night of the raid, some men in suits and ties entered the place and walked around a little bit. Then whispers went around that the place was being raided. Suddenly, the lights were turned up, and the doors were sealed, and all the patrons were held captive until the police decided what they were going to do. I was anxious, but I wasn't afraid. Everybody was anxious, not knowing whether we were going to be arrested or what was going to happen.

It may have been ten or fifteen minutes later that we were all told to leave. We had to line up, and our identification was checked before we were freed. People who did not have identification or were under age and all transvestites were detained. Those who didn't meet whatever standards the police had were incarcerated temporarily in the coatroom. The coat closet. Little did the police know the ironic symbolism of that. But they found out fast.

As people were released, they stayed outside. They didn't run away. They waited for their friends to come out. People who were walking up and down Christopher Street, which was a very busy cruising area at that time, also assembled. The crowd in front of the Stonewall grew and grew.

I stayed to watch. As some of the gays came out of the bar, they would take a bow, and their friends would cheer. It was a colorful scene. Tension started to grow. After everybody who was going to be released was released, the prisoners—transvestites and bar personnel, bartenders, and the bouncers—were herded into a paddy wagon that was parked right on the sidewalk in front of the bar. The prisoners were left unguarded by the local police; they simply walked out of the paddy wagon to the cheer of the throng. There's no doubt in my mind that those people were deliberately left unguarded. I assume there was some sort of a relationship between the bar management and the local police, so they really didn't want to arrest these people. But they had to at least look like they were trying to do their jobs.

Once all of the people were out and the prisoners went on their merry ways, the crowd stayed. I don't know how to characterize the motives of the crowd at that point, except to say there was curiosity and concern about what had just happened. Then some people in the crowd started throwing pennies across the street at the front of the Stonewall. Then someone apparently threw a rock, which broke one of the windows on the second floor. The Stonewall had a couple of great big plate-glass windows in the front. They were painted black on the inside. And there was a doorway in between them, which was the entrance. The building had a second floor, which I think was used for storage space. With the shattering of the glass of the second-floor window, the crowd collectively exclaimed, "Ooh." It was a dramatic gesture of defiance.

For me, there was a slight lancing of the festering wound of anger that had been building for so long over this kind of unfair harassment and prejudice. It wasn't my fault that many of the bars where I could meet other gay people were run by organized crime. Because of the system of official discrimination on the part of state liquor authorities and the corruption of the local police authorities, these were the only kind of bars that were permitted to serve a gay clientele. None of that was my doing.

The tension escalated. A few more rocks went flying, and then somebody from inside the bar opened the door and stuck out a gun. He yelled for people to stay back. Then he withdrew the gun, closed the door, and went back inside. Somebody took an uprooted parking meter and broke the glass in the front window and the plywood board that was behind it. Then somebody else took a garbage can, one of those wire-mesh cans, set it on fire, and threw the burning garbage into the premises. The area that was set afire was where the coatroom was.

They had a fire hose inside, and they used it. It was a small trash fire. Then they opened the front door and turned the hose on the crowd to try to keep people at a distance. That's when the riot erupted.

Apparently, a fire engine had been summoned because of the trash fire. As it came down the block, uniformed police began to arrive. They came down the street in a phalanx of blue with their riot gear on. In those days the New York City police had a guerrilla-prone cadre known as the Tactical Police Force, the TPF.

Who knows whether the violence would have escalated in the way it did if the TPF had not come in? That's what they always looked for; they wanted confrontation. Chasing after people and hitting them with their billy clubs, I think, provoked a greater response than there would have been otherwise. One way or the other, though, gay people had stood up and rebelled.

I watched. I wasn't looking for a fight. I can't claim credit for the small acts of violence that took place. I didn't break any windows. I wasn't the one who had a knife and cut the tires on the paddy wagon. I didn't hit a cop and get hit by a cop. But it was a very emotional turning point for me. It was the first time I had seen anything like that.

Once they started attacking people and forcing people onto the side streets, I tried to get out of the way. I saw people breaking windows, but I didn't stay too much longer. I returned the next night to see what was going on because the riot was continuing. For me, this festering wound, the anger from oppression and discrimination, was coming out very fast at the point of Stonewall.

MAN on the MOON

A series of Soviet "firsts" in space during the late 1950s and early '60s posed a formidable challenge for the United States. The first spacecraft, Sputnik I, sent aloft in October 1957, and the first manned spaceflight, Yuri Gagarin's orbit on April 12, 1961, were stunning technological achievements with military implications.

Six weeks after Gagarin's ride, President Kennedy went before Congress to state his determination that the United States send a man to the moon by the end of the decade.

On July 20, 1969—eight years and $25 billion later—Apollo 11 fulfilled the pledge, a triumph in the Cold War and a stunning, albeit fleeting, boost for American morale at a time when the nation was racked by the Vietnam War and urban rioting.

The world was transfixed as Colonel Edwin (Buzz) Aldrin and Neil Armstrong made their descent to the powdery gray Sea of Tranquillity, Colonel Michael Collins orbiting above them.

ALDRIN: *Lights on. Down 2¹/₂. Forward. Forward. Good. Forty feet, down 2¹/₂. Picking up some dust. 30 feet, 2¹/₂ down. Faint shadow. 4 forward. 4 forward, drifting to the right a little. 6 . . . [static] . . . down a half.*

CAPCOM *(Deke Slayton)*: *Thirty seconds.*

ALDRIN: *[static] . . . forward. Drifting right . . . [static] . . . Contact light. Okay, engine stop, ACA out of detent.*

ARMSTRONG: *Got it.*

ALDRIN: *Mode controls, both auto, descent engine command override, off. Engine arm, off. 413 is in.*

CAPCOM: *We copy you down, Eagle.*

ARMSTRONG: *Houston, Tranquility Base here. The Eagle has landed.*

CAPCOM: *Roger, Tranquility. We copy you on the ground. You've got a bunch of guys about to turn blue. We're breathing again. Thanks a lot.*

ALDRIN: *Thank you. . . .*

ARMSTRONG: *Houston, that may have seemed like a very long final phase. The AUTO targeting was taking us right into a football field–sized crater, with a large number of big boulders and rocks for about one or two crater diameters around us.*

HOUSTON: *Roger, we copy. It was beautiful from here, Tranquility. Over.*

ALDRIN: *We'll get to details of what's around here, but it looks like a collection of just about every variety of shapes, angularities, granularities, every variety of rock you could find. . . .*

HOUSTON: *Roger, copy. Sounds good to us, Tranquility. . . . Be advised there are lots of smiling faces in this room, and all over the world.*

ALDRIN: *There are two of them up here.*

COLUMBIA *(Collins)*: *And don't forget one in the command module.*

ARMSTRONG: *The guys who said we wouldn't to able to tell precisely where we are, are the winners today. We were a little busy, worrying about program alarms and things like that. . . . I haven't been able to pick out the things on the horizon as a reference as yet.*

HOUSTON *(Slayton)*: *Roger, Tranquility. No sweat. We'll figure it out. Over.*

ARMSTRONG: *Out of the window is a relatively level plain created with a fairly large number of craters of the five to fifty–foot variety and some ridges, small, twenty or thirty feet high, I would guess, and literally thousands of little one and two–foot craters around the area. We see some angular blocks out several hundred feet in front of us that are probably two feet in size. . . . There is a hill in view, just about on the ground track ahead of us, difficult to estimate but might be half a mile or a mile. . . .*

HOUSTON *(Bruce McCandless)*: *Okay, Neil, we can see you coming down the ladder now.*
ARMSTRONG: *Okay, I just checked—getting back up to that first step, Buzz, it's not even collapsed too far, but it's adequate to get back up. . . . It takes a pretty good little jump. . . . I'm at the foot of the ladder. The LM footpads are only depressed in the surface about one or two inches. Although the surface appears to be very, very fine-grained, as you get close to it. It's almost like a powder. Now and then, it's very fine. . . . I'm going to step off the LM now. . . .*
That's one small step for man, one giant leap for mankind.

Armstrong intended to say, and evidently did say, "that's one small step for a man . . ." The "a" was apparently lost in static and so did not appear in the official transcript.

the SPIRIT of WOODSTOCK

The Woodstock music festival is remembered as a symbol of the youth revolt of the 1960s, a rain-drenched celebration of peace and love. Some half a million young people flocked to a six-hundred-acre dairy farm in Bethel, New York, in August 1969 to listen to rock and assert their determination to change their world.

Their political philosopher was Abbie Hoffman, cofounder of the counterculture Yippies. Their music was performed by Janis Joplin, the Grateful Dead, Richie Havens.

But it wasn't all idealism. Some performers demanded cash before they would go on stage. And the festival was conceived as a money-making venture. Tickets were to go for $18 apiece. It was only when the throngs wildly exceeded expectations that almost everyone was admitted free.

Max Yasgur, the farmer who provided the land for the festival, was dubious about going ahead, and some of his neighbors were openly hostile at flower power's invasion of the Catskill region. But as Yasgur's wife, Miriam, would recall, the antagonism served only to convince her husband to welcome the party.

My clearest memory is of this young man coming up the lane on a motorcycle wearing very long, curly hair—something I had not seen on a boy up to that date—a pair of jeans, I think, and a black leather vest, highly decorated, over his bare chest and arms, and boots. And he came to the door and I was a little hesitant as to whether to let him into the house or not, and it turned out to be Michael Lang. And our first impression—you know, we felt very negative about the whole thing, having seen Michael; we weren't going to get involved with "those kinds" of kids.

But it takes Michael about fifteen or twenty minutes to charm you, and having spoken with him for a while, he really put us at ease, despite his appearance. After that, it was a matter of discussing whether or not we really wanted to get involved in this thing, whether we wanted our land to be abused by almost ten thousand people a day for three days, which is what we were told it would be. We didn't feel that the compensation would be the issue at the time. We didn't want any damage to be done to the farm. So we hesitated about it, and they kept trying to convince us, and there were discussions in our lawyer's office and subsequently in our home, I believe, and Max and I decided that we would take it under advisement; we were going to sleep on it and decide whether we really wanted to get involved or not. They were putting it on the basis of these young people who had no place to go, and they sort of appealed to Max's sense of fairness because why should young people be denied a place to go where older people would not be? . . .

My concern basically—Max was always the one to wade in with both feet; he was a person who got very involved—but my concern was for his health. It was not good and I didn't want him to have any added strain over and above what he was doing in the business, which was strenuous enough. . . .

So, we were fifty-fifty or sixty-forty or whatever and went to bed and got up in the morning. Apparently, the talk was around town at this point because several days of discussion had been going on. . . . It doesn't take long for things to get around in a small town. And there were a group of people apparently that were very distressed at the idea that this might happen. So we got up in the morning and in our bedroom we had a balcony which faced 17B, the main highway. There was a big field between the house and the highway, and down at the end of the field we saw a sign had been erected. Now, we knew we didn't have any signs down there. Eventually, of course, we checked it. On the sign it said something like, DON'T BUY YASGUR'S MILK, HE LOVES THE HIPPIES. And I thought, "You don't know Max, because we're going to have a festival."

That did it. He said, "Is it all right with you? We're going to have a festival." We always made joint decisions after he decided what he wanted. Most of the time I said yes because I agreed. If I said no, we then didn't or discussed it further. But I knew that he was not going to get past this sign. And he was leaning toward helping the kids anyway, so I said, "I guess we're going to have a festival." And he said, "Yep, we're going to have a festival." And maybe we wouldn't have if not for the sign, I don't know. I won't ever know. . . .

After the first day, we realized that maybe it was going to work and that things were not turning into the riot I anticipated. And then we got a little bit more comfortable with it. I don't think we got any sleep at all. We would just go up and wash and come back to the office because we were manning phones, we were doing everything we could. Max was helicoptered over there to see what was happening. He couldn't get through the crowds. And there was a veterinarian who had his own helicopter that he used to make calls in the western end of the county or in Pennsylvania, and they paid him to leave the helicopter near our office so that in case of emergency they could get people out. And when things were finally going smoothly, Max said to me, "Would you like to see what it looks like?" And I never have trusted little planes—I've logged *thousands of miles in big planes all over the world, but getting into a little plane was always something of a block for me. And I thought, "I'll never see it otherwise." So I said all right and I got into this little two-man helicopter with no doors and he flew over the festival field to show it to me and it was a sight to remember.*

KENT STATE

As tumultuous as the 1960s were, it seemed that America truly became unhinged in the springtime of 1970.

After President Nixon announced the invasion of neutral Cambodia on Thursday, April 30, protests broke out on campuses around the country. Students at Kent State University in Ohio broke windows in the downtown business district and burned the campus Army ROTC building over the weekend. The National Guard was called in.

By time the month of May ended, a hundred thousand people had converged on Washington to protest the widening of the Vietnam War, and hard-hat construction workers had rampaged through the Wall Street financial district, beating antiwar demonstrators.

But what happened on an Ohio campus on May 4 would come to symbolize America's torment. More than two decades later, the words "Kent State" would still mean much more than simply the name of a university.

Tom Grace was among those caught up in the thirteen seconds of rifle fire that left four students dead.

Some students were throwing rocks at the National Guard, and some of the National Guard were picking up the rocks and throwing them back at the students. I didn't see any National Guardsmen hit by rocks. They seemed to be bouncing at their feet.

Then I remember that the National Guard troop seemed to get into a little huddle before leaving the practice football field. They reformed their lines and proceeded back up the hill. It was almost like the parting of the Red Sea. The students just moved to one side or the other to let the

National Guardsmen pass because no one in their right mind would have stood there, as bayonets were coming.

A lot of people were screaming, "Get out of here, get off our campus," and in the midst of all this were some students, oddly enough, who were still wandering through the area with their textbooks, as if they were completely unaware of what was taking place. I felt that I was still keeping a safe distance. I was 150, 165 feet away. I know that because it's since been paced off.

When the National Guardsmen got to the top of the hill, all of a sudden there was just a quick movement, a flurry of activity, and there was a crack, or two cracks of rifle fire, and I thought, Oh, my God! I turned and started running as fast as I could. I don't think I got more than a step or two, and all of a sudden I was on the ground. It was just like someone had come over and given me a body blow and knocked me right down.

The bullet had entered my left heel and had literally knocked me off my feet. I tried to raise myself and I heard someone yelling, "Stay down, stay down! It's buckshot!" I looked up, and about five or ten feet away from me, behind a tree, was my roommate Alan Canfora. That was the first time I had seen him since we were down on the other side of the commons, chanting antiwar slogans.

So I threw myself back to the ground and lay as prone as possible to shield myself as much as I could, although like most people I was caught right in the open. There was no cover. I just hugged the ground so as to expose as little of my body as possible to the gunfire.

It seemed like the bullets were going within inches of my head. I can remember seeing people behind me, farther down the hill in the parking lot, dropping. I don't know if they were being hit by bullets or they were just hugging the ground. We know today that it only lasted thirteen seconds, but it seemed like it kept going and going and going. And I remember thinking, when is this going to stop? . . .

So I was lying there, and all of a sudden this real husky, well-built guy ran to me, picked me up like I was a sack of potatoes, and threw me over his shoulder. He carried me through the parking lot in the direction of a girls' dormitory. We went by one body, a huge puddle of blood. Head wounds always bleed very badly, and his was just awful.

The female students were screaming as I was carried into the dormitory and placed on a couch, bleeding all over the place. A nursing student applied a tourniquet to my leg. I never really felt that my life was in danger, but I could look down at my foot and I knew that I had one hell of a bad wound. The bullet blew the shoe right off my foot, and there was a bone sticking through my green sock. It looked like somebody had put my foot through a meatgrinder.

The ambulances came. Some attendants came in, put me on a stretcher, and carried me outside. The blood loss had lessened because of the tourniquet that was on my leg. I remember having my fist up in the air as a sign of defiance. They put me into the top tier in the ambulance rather than the lower one, which was already occupied. I remember my foot hitting the edge of the ambulance as I went in. From that moment on, until the time that I actually went under from the anesthesia at Robinson Memorial Hospital, I was probably in the most intense pain that I've ever experienced in my life.

They had the doors closed by this time, and the ambulance was speeding away from the campus. I looked down and saw Sandy Scheuer. I had met Sandy about a week or two beforehand for the first and only time. She had been introduced to me by one of the guys who lived downstairs in my apartment complex. They were casual friends, and she struck me as being a very nice person.

She had a gaping bullet wound in the neck, and the ambulance attendants were tearing away the top two buttons of her blouse and then doing a heart massage. I remember their saying that it's no use, she's dead. And then they just pulled up the sheet over her head.

Chapter Nine

to the MILLENNIUM

the WATERGATE COVER-UP

It was merely a "third-rate burglary attempt" in the words of Ron Ziegler, President Nixon's press secretary.

The June 17, 1972, break-in at Democratic National Committee offices in Washington's Watergate complex—so quickly dismissed by the White House as a dot on the police blotter—was certainly a third-rate effort. The scheme to bug phones and steal campaign plans was botched, and seven men were arrested.

But this would also be history's most famous burglary. The White House's attempt to cover up the burglars' ties to Nixon's political camp and the revelations of "dirty tricks," a "slush fund," and rampant lying would destroy Nixon's presidency.

Perhaps the most riveting testimony came in late June 1973, when John Dean, the White House counsel, told Senator Sam Ervin's Watergate commmittee that Nixon was involved in a cover-up that included payoffs to obtain silence from the burglars.

Dean recalled a meeting he had had with Nixon at the White House on March 21, 1973.

I began by telling the President that there was a cancer growing on the Presidency and that if the cancer was not removed that the President himself would be killed by it. I also told him that it was important that this cancer be removed immediately because it was growing more deadly every day. . . .

I then proceeded to tell him some of the highlights that had occurred during the cover-up. I told him that Kalmbach had been used to raise funds to pay these seven individuals for their silence at the instructions of Ehrlichman, Haldeman, and Mitchell and I had been the conveyor of this instruction to Kalmbach. I told him that after the decision had been made that Magruder was to remain at the reelection committee I had assisted Magruder in preparing his false story for presentation to the grand jury. I told him that cash that had been at the White House had been funneled back to the reelection committee for the purpose of paying the seven individuals to remain silent.

I then proceeded to tell him that perjury had been committed, and for this cover-up to continue would require more perjury and more money. I told him that the demands of the convicted individuals were continually increasing and that with sentencing imminent, the demands had become specific.

I told him that on Monday the 19th, I had received a message from one of the reelection committee lawyers who had spoken directly with Hunt and that Hunt had sent a message to me demanding money. . . . The message was that Hunt wanted $72,000 for living expenses and $50,000 for attorney's fees and if he did not get the money and get it quickly that he would have a lot of seamy things to say about what he had done for John Ehrlichman while he was at the White House. . . .

I concluded by saying that it is going to take continued perjury and continued support of these individuals to perpetuate the cover-up and that I did not believe it was possible to continue it; rather I thought it was time for surgery on the cancer itself and that all those involved must stand up and account for themselves and tell the President himself to get out in front of this matter. . . .

After I finished, I realized that I had not really made the President understand because after he asked a few questions, he suggested that it would be an excellent idea if I gave some sort of briefing to the Cabinet and that he was very impressed with my knowledge of the circumstances but he did not seem particularly concerned with their implications. . . .

On March 13 [an error by Dean, who was still relating events of the March 21 meeting] we discussed both clemency and the fact that there was no money. The way the clemency discussion came up as you will recall is that at the end of another conversation I raised with him the fact that there were demands being made for money, for continued money, there was no money around to pay it. He asked me how, you know, how much it was going to cost. I gave him my best estimate, which I said was $1 million or more. He, in turn, said to me, "Well, $1 million is certainly no problem to raise" and turned to Mr. Haldeman and made a similar comment and then he came back after just a brief discussion on that and I remember very clearly the way he pushed his chair away from his desk as he was looking back at Mr. Haldeman to get, you know, the same message through to Mr. Haldeman, you know, that $1 million is no problem.

Three weeks after Dean testified, a White House aide named Alexander Butterfield created a sensation when he told the Ervin committee that Nixon had taped conversations in the White House.

Claiming "executive privilege," Nixon refused to surrender Watergate tapes to the committee, but the Supreme Court ultimately forced him to give them up.

A tape transcript of Dean's March 21 conversation with Nixon would corroborate the account that the White House counsel gave to the committee.

DEAN: *I think that there is no doubt the seriousness of the problem we've got. We have a cancer within, close to the Presidency, that is growing. It is growing daily. It's compounding, growing geometrically now, because it compounds itself. That will be clear if I, you know, explain some of the details of why it is. Basically, it is because (1) we are being blackmailed; (2) people are going to start perjuring themselves very quickly that have not had to perjure themselves to protect other people in the line. And there is no assurance—*

NIXON: *That that won't bust?*

DEAN: *That that won't bust. So let me give you the sort of basic facts. . . . Well, first of all, there is the problem of the continued blackmail which will not only go on now, but it will go on while these people are in prison, and it will compound the obstruction of justice situation. It will cost money. It is dangerous. People around here are not pros at this sort of thing. This is the sort of thing Mafia people can do; washing money, getting clean money, and things like that. We just don't know about those things, because we are not criminals and not used to dealing in that business.*

NIXON: *That's right.*

DEAN: *It is a tough thing to know how to do.*

NIXON: *Maybe it takes a gang to do that.*

DEAN: *That's right. There is a real problem as to whether we could even do it. Plus there is a real problem in raising money. Mitchell has been working on raising money. He is one of the ones with the most to lose. But there is no denying the fact that the White House, in Ehrlichman, Haldeman and Dean, are involved in some of the early money decisions.*

NIXON: *How much money do you need?*

DEAN: *I would say these people are going to cost a million dollars over the next two years.*

NIXON: *We could get that. On the money, if you need the money you could get that. You could get a million dollars. You could get it in cash. I know where it could be gotten. It is not easy, but it could be done. But the question is who the hell would handle it? Any ideas on that?*

On July 27, 1974, the House Judiciary Committee approved two articles of impeachment against the President. On August 8, Nixon announced his resignation, effective the following day.

Exactly one month later, Nixon's successor, Gerald R. Ford, granted him a "full, free and absolute pardon . . . for all offenses against the United States which he . . . has committed or may have committed or taken part in. . . ."

John Dean would spend four months in jail but would go on to write the best-seller *Blind Ambition*, chronicling the "third-rate burglary" that brought down a president.

GARY GILMORE FACES *the* FIRING SQUAD

A ten-year suspension of capital punishment in the United States ended at 8:07 A.M., January 17, 1977, when a firing squad at the Utah State Penitentiary sent a volley of .30-caliber bullets through the heart of Gary Mark Gilmore.

The United States Supreme Court had ruled in a 1972 Georgia case that death sentences were customarily imposed in a largely arbitrary way, violating the Eighth Amendment's prohibition of "cruel and unusual punishment." But the path to a renewal of executions was opened by a 1976 court ruling that permitted capital punishment if judge and jury took into consideration aggravating and mitigating factors.

Gilmore had murdered a young Provo gas-station attendant in July 1976, shooting him in the head after he surrendered his money and was lying facedown on a rest-room floor. Gilmore had asked to be put to death, but the American Civil Liberties Union had worked frantically to block the execution. Opponents of capital punishment feared that the momentum would now swing toward carrying out death sentences—and they were right.

Gilmore, thirty-six years old, asked for four witnesses to his execution —his uncle, Vern Damico; lawyers Robert Moody and Ron Stanger; and Lawrence Schiller, an agent with rights to his story. Schiller would describe the execution.

We drove to the shed. We saw a black tent to the right which covered the doors. We were informed that Gary already was inside. We then went inside. There was a normal chair, green-covered. Gary was already in it.

There was not tight shackles. I believe they were made of nylon, synthetic, very loose. There was the warden, a priest, a doctor and three or four other additional members around him in red coats. To the left, behind a wooden barricade that had been put up, there were approximately 20 other people. We were asked to stand behind a line.

Gary was talking to the prison officials and the warden. He was calm, I believe direct. We could not overhear his conversation.

We went behind the line and a gentleman from the prison started to pass out cotton. A gentleman came to us and asked us to go over to Gary. He was approximately 25 feet from us.

He could have moved in the chair if he had wished. He did not. I believe the first person was Vern. He spoke to Vern privately. That is a matter between those two. The next was Mr. Moody, who shook his left hand. I was third, and Mr. Stanger, who hugged him around the neck, was fourth, and all of the conversations I believe are private.

We were then asked to return behind the line. The warden then read what I believe was a legal order firmly and to the point. Gary looked at him, holding his own, not quivering.

At this point he looked around the warden into the black line that had neatly sewn horizontal rectangular slits. I did not see anything protruding at that time from the slits.

The warden asked Gary what his last words were, or something to that effect. We could not hear. Gary looked up for an extended period of time, then looked directly, and I believe his words—at my distance, I understood them to be, "Let's do it."

The various parties stepped back behind the line. The warden himself handed out additional cotton to the people who wished it. There was emotional exchanges at that moment.

The priest and the doctor and several other prison people were simultaneously placing the black hood over Gary. He was wearing a black T-shirt, white pants and red, white and blue tennis shoes.

He did not quiver when the hood was placed over him. He did not move or try to deny its coverance. We could not hear anything being said. I believe then additional prison personnel moved away. The priest, Father Meersman, was quite emotional. He gave Gary some rites, I believe, prior to the hood being put on. I believe Gary joked with him. . . .

Rites were then given after the hood was placed. The black target with a white circle was pinned to Gary's black T-shirt.

The priest and other people moved back, and out of the corner of my eye, I believe the warden gave the signal. I did not hear anything, but I saw some type of a movement. . . . Then, bang, bang, bang, three noises. I heard three noises in quick, rapid succession.

There was a slight movement in the hands, not upwardly, not downwardly, but in a very calming manner, and slowly red blood emerged from under the black T-shirt onto the white slacks.

It seemed to me that his body still had a movement in it for approximately 15 to 20 seconds. It is not for me to determine whether that is an after-death or a prior-to-death movement.

I believe the minister and the doctor proceeded towards Gary. I believe the heartbeat was taken first with a stethoscope, then his pulse was taken. . . .

A prison official came towards us and said, "Would you like to leave."

the CAMP DAVID ACCORDS

Egyptian President Anwar Sadat stunned the world in November 1977 with his visit to Jerusalem and his offer of peace with Israel in exchange for its withdrawal from territories occupied since the 1967 war.

The following summer, President Jimmy Carter invited Sadat and Israeli Prime Minister Menachem Begin to Camp David for detailed peacemaking talks.

It would be a tortuous thirteen days in the Maryland hills that September. But when the arguing ended, Carter had prodded the two leaders toward an accord that presaged the signing of a peace treaty at the White House in March 1979. It would be the prime achievement of his administration.

In the detailed diary he kept during the Camp David talks, Carter told how an agreement was salvaged on the final Sunday, when failure seemed imminent.

. . . a serious problem had erupted with the Israelis. Vance had just shown them a copy of our draft letter that would go to Sadat, restating the United States position on Jerusalem, which had been spelled out officially in United Nations debates over the years. There was an absolute furor, and Begin announced that Israel would not sign any document if we wrote any letter to Egypt about Jerusalem.

Hamilton Jordan called to tell me that the Israeli objections to a Jerusalem letter were extremely serious; the Israelis were determined to sign no agreement at all. Vance confirmed Ham's report, and explained that none of the Israelis had understood that we were going to write a letter "criticizing Israel for occupying eastern Jerusalem," even after we had explained the letter exchange last night.

Back at Holly, I had a very unpleasant session there, with Dayan, Weizmann, Barak, Mondale, Vance, and Brzezinski. I asked for a text of our United Nations ambassadors' statements in the debates concerning Jerusalem. Ambassadors Charles Yost, Arthur Goldberg, and William Scranton had spoken on the subject, but I had never read all of what they actually said.

I then asked [Israeli Attorney General Aharon] Barak to walk with me to Aspen to go over the text of our proposed letter, in order to find language which might be acceptable. He was just as adamant as the other Israelis, insisting that the situation was hopeless. However, I proposed that we strike out of our letter all the actual quotations from the United Nations speeches and simply say that the United States position was as it had been expressed by the three ambassadors. Dayan and Barak both agreed to go over this changed text with Begin. It was another tense moment.

Earlier, my secretary, Susan Clough, had brought me some photographs of Begin, Sadat, and me. They had already been signed by President Sadat, and Prime Minister Begin had requested that I autograph them for his grandchildren. Knowing the trouble we were in with the Israelis, Susan suggested that she go and get the actual names of the grandchildren, so that I could personalize each picture. I did this, and walked over to Begin's cabin with them. He was sitting on the front porch, very distraught and nervous because the talks had finally broken down at the last minute.

I handed him the photographs. He took them and thanked me. Then he happened to look down and saw that his granddaughter's name was on the top one. He spoke it aloud, and then looked at each photograph individually, repeating the name of the grandchild I had written on it. His lips trembled, and tears welled up in his eyes. He told me a little about each child, and especially about the one who seemed to be his favorite. We were both emotional as we talked quietly for a few minutes about grandchildren and about war.

Then he asked me to step into his cabin, requesting that everyone else in the room leave. He was quiet, sober, surprisingly friendly. There were no histrionics. He said that the Jerusalem matter was fatal, that he was very sorry but he could not accept our letter to Egypt. I told him I had drafted a new version and submitted it to Dayan and Barak. He had not yet seen it. I suggested he read it over and let me know his decision, but that there was no way I could go back on my commitment to Sadat to exchange letters. The success of any future peace talks might depend on his and Sadat's assessment of my integrity, and I could not violate a promise once it was made.

I walked back to Aspen, very dejected. Sadat was there with [Egyptian Under Secretary of Foreign Affairs Osama] el-Baz, both dressed to go back to Washington. I asked everyone else to leave and told Sadat what was happening. We realized that all of us had done our best, but that prospects were dim indeed.

Then Begin called. He said, "I will accept the letter you have drafted on Jerusalem." I breathed a sigh of relief, because it now seemed that the last obstacle had been removed.

AMERICA HELD HOSTAGE

For 444 days, the United States stood helpless, humiliated as it had not been since Pearl Harbor Sunday.

Iranian students in thrall to the militant Muslim government of the Ayatollah Khomeini invaded the United States Embassy in Teheran on November 4, 1979, and seized sixty-six hostages in response to the United States' admission of the deposed shah for medical treatment.

The Carter administration would become obsessed with obtaining the hostages' release. Diplomatic efforts would be mounted, but they would fail. A rescue attempt would be staged, but it would collapse in a desert helicopter crash leaving eight servicemen dead.

The Iranian hatred of "the great Satan," which would torment Carter and the nation throughout the remainder of his administration, showed its face in a terrifying manner during the first days of the takeover. That's when Sergeant Donald R. Hohman, an army medic at the embassy, was displayed as a trophy.

They took me to the outside of the embassy, removed the blindfold and made me face what looked to me like at least two million screaming Iranians. They were yelling, "Death to the Americans!" over and over and over and over until it was like an earthquake, there was so much vibration from the noise.

It sounded like the walls were going to come down on top of me. The whole building was shaking. I have never been so terrified of anything in my whole life. I must have turned white all over with fear. I muttered to

one of the guards, *"Please, please take me back inside."* And pretty
soon they did.

Soon after the seizure, Elizabeth Montagne, the secretary to
L. Bruce Laingen, the top American diplomat in Iran, was ordered by
a gunman to divulge the combinations of embassy safes. She did not
know what they were, but found it almost impossible to convince the
student holding a pistol to her heart.

*He went click, and the bullet went up one chamber—I could feel it go
up. And then he said, "I'm a very good judge of character, and I know
you're lying to me." And I said, "If you think I'm lying you're a lousy
judge of character, because I'm telling you the truth. I cannot open those
safes." Then he went click and the bullet went up another notch.*

The gunman asked: "Is this worth dying for?"

*I said, "No, it's not," and he went click, and the bullet went up
another notch. And I—this little game must have taken about four, five
minutes, it seemed an eternity—and I can remember my mind being
very, very clear and very, very sharp. I remember my heart trying to
jump out of my chest. He kept pointing the gun at me, and the last—
there was one click to go.*

And he said, "Do you think I'll pull the trigger?"

*And the only thing I could think of was, "I wonder what it would feel
like to have bullets go through my chest." Then I thought, "Well, it can't
hurt for long."*

*We stared at each other, and then he—he put the gun down. He said,
"O.K., so you don't know the combinations."*

I just kind of collapsed.

When the hostages were released en masse—fifty-two in all, fourteen
having been let go earlier—the Iranians flung a final insult at Jimmy
Carter. The captives were set free on January 20, 1981, minutes into
the presidency of Ronald Reagan.

"GERR-EEE, GERR-EEE"

In the spring of 1984, Geraldine Ferraro was an obscure Democratic congresswoman from New York City's borough of Queens. But she would suddenly emerge as a history-maker: the first woman to run for vice president on a major party's ticket.

Her selection as Walter Mondale's running mate was a proud personal moment and a vindication for the women's movement. But Ferraro would look back on the campaign with ruefulness over "the fury, the bigotry, and the sexism my candidacy would unleash."

Questions over the finances of her husband, John Zaccaro, would hound her. She would be asked on "Meet the Press" whether she was "strong enough to push the button." And the Mississippi agriculture commissioner wondered, "Can you bake a blueberry muffin?" Her reply: "I sure can. Can you?"

The Mondale-Ferraro ticket would out-poll President Reagan and Vice President Bush only in the District of Columbia and Mondale's home state of Minnesota. But all that was in the future the night Ferraro stood before the Democratic National Convention in San Francisco to make her acceptance speech.

And then at last it was time for me. As I started toward the podium, the roar began to swell from the Convention floor. "Gerr-eee. Gerr-eee." I'd heard the chant a couple of times before during convention week, but not from ten thousand voices at once. I couldn't believe it. The band broke into the medley of music my staff had suggested. "New York, New York," "The Lady Is a Champ," and Archie Bunker's theme music from "All in the Family," set in my district. What a moment. I shot the thumbs-up sign to John. And I was on.

Speak slowly and don't trip. Don't trip and speak s-l-o-w-l-y. Loftier thoughts should probably have been going through my mind as I walked the last few feet to the podium. After all, this was a moment women had been dreaming of and working toward for generations. Now it was actually happening, and happening not only to me but through me. Yet I wasn't thinking about the extraordinary symbolic significance of this event. I had faced that before deciding to accept the vice-presidential nomination, recognizing the responsibilities of the office and all its implications. What seemed far more important now was to remember not to trip on or off the elevated platform that would raise my five-foot-four-inch frame high enough over the podium to be seen from the convention floor and to s-l-o-w-l-y introduce myself to the entire country. Just in case the TelePrompTers failed, I carried a copy of my speech and my glasses with me.

In the end, you can't worry about these things. You just get out there and do. But perhaps I had talked myself into feeling too comfortable. All I wanted was to deliver my speech well, to communicate with those millions of Americans my ability to help Walter Mondale lead our nation into a more secure and just future—and not to make a mistake. So what happened? I made a whopper, saying in the course of my remarks that I, the daughter of an Italian immigrant, had been chosen to run for President, instead of Vice President, of this great land. Luckily I didn't notice my slipup at the time and kept right on going. Since Fritz didn't get upset about it later, I didn't either. . . .

What a sight. I couldn't make it out too clearly without my glasses but certain homemade signs stood out, like Guam Loves Gerry, El Tiempo Es Ahora ("the time is now"), and one huge cardboard poem: The Republicans May Think They're Hot, But We Have Gerry and They Do Not. An amazing number of children were in the crowd, even little babies, and I worried about them in the crush. Later I was told that many delegates had brought their daughters and even their granddaughters onto the convention floor the night of my nomination to bear witness to this moment in American history. . . .

"I love it," I said to myself, forgetting that the microphone in front of me was sending out my words all over the world. But I meant what I said. I felt so lucky to be standing in for millions and millions of American women. Would I let them down? I certainly hoped not.

ONE MORNING *in* BEIRUT

The taking of American hostages as pawns in Middle Eastern politics had huge political consequences for three presidents, extending from the 1970s to the 1990s. Jimmy Carter was consumed by the seizing of the U.S. Embassy in Iran. Ronald Reagan and George Bush became embroiled in the Iran-contra affair.

The hostage whose plight would be especially remembered was not a government official but a journalist. At 8 A.M. on Saturday, March 16, 1985, Terry Anderson, the chief Middle East correspondent of the Associated Press, was kidnapped on a Beirut street. It was the beginning of a seven-year ordeal.

The green Mercedes, sparkling clean in the weak morning sunlight, drifted to a gentle halt in the narrow road, just a few yards up the hill from the graffiti-covered monument to Gamal Abdul Nasser. Don Mell, the young AP photographer I was dropping off at his apartment after our tennis game, had noticed it earlier at the sports club but hadn't mentioned it—it didn't seem important. Now, though, it struck him as odd, especially the curtains drawn over the rear window.

"A hamster-mobile," he remarked, using the nickname given by journalists to all the armed young men swarming in and around Beirut.

The joke, already worn, seemed even less amusing when three unshaven young men threw open the doors and jumped out, each holding a 9mm pistol in his right hand, hanging loosely by his side.

My mind seemed to stall for a few seconds, and by the time I realized what was happening, one of the men was beside the driver's door of my car, yanking it open and pushing his pistol at my head. "Get out," he said fiercely. "I will shoot. I will shoot."

"Okay," I answered quickly. I pulled the keys from the ignition and dropped them between the seats. "Okay, no problem. No problem."

He reached in and pulled the glasses from my face. As I slid out of the seat, half crouched, he put his hand around my shoulders, forcing me to remain bent over.

"Come, come quickly."

I glanced up at Don, just a vague blur on the other side of the car, willing him to run, but not daring to shout the words. He just stood, frozen.

The young man, dark and very Arab-looking, perhaps twenty or twenty-five, pulled me along beside him toward the Mercedes, just four or five yards away, still forcing me to remain half bent.

"Get in, I will shoot," he hissed at me, pushing me into the back seat. "Get down. Get down."

I tried to crouch in the narrow space between the front and back seats. Another young man jumped in the other door and shoved me to the floor, throwing an old blanket over me, then shoving my head and body down with both his feet. I could feel a gun barrel pushing at my neck. "Get down. Get down."

The car lurched into gear and accelerated madly up the hill a few yards, almost slid around a corner, then another, and up a short hill.

The front-seat passenger leaned over the back of the seat. "Don't worry. It's political," he said in a normal tone as the car lurched back and forth, the driver cutting in and out of traffic.

The strange comment, apparently meant to be reassuring, wasn't. As my mind began to function again, it made me think of the other Americans kidnapped in Beirut for political reasons. William Buckley, missing twelve months. The Reverend Benjamin Weir, missing ten months. Father Lawrence Martin Jenco, missing two months.

There wasn't any real fear yet—it was drowned by adrenaline. Just a loud, repeating mental refrain: Anderson, you stupid shit, you're in deep, deep trouble.

the *CHALLENGER* DISASTER

At the beginning, the stars of the space program were the men with the "right stuff," the cool-nerved test pilots and fighter jocks of the Apollo project.

But with the arrival in 1982 of winged spaceships—the reusable shuttles—the National Aeronautics and Space Administration reached out to foreign astronauts and even gave rides to a few members of Congress.

The seven-member crew of the Challenger shuttle that roared off the pad at Cape Canaveral, Florida, on the frigid morning of January 28,

1986, was a model of diversity—it included one black, an Asian American, and two women.

One of the women was a high-school teacher from Concord, New Hampshire, named Christa McAuliffe, selected by NASA as the first member of the general public to be an astronaut. She had written the most compelling essay in a 1985 nationwide contest inviting teachers to tell why they wanted to go into space.

I remember the excitement in my home when the first satellites were launched. My parents were amazed and I was caught up with their wonder. In school my classes would gather around the TV and try to follow the rocket as it seemed to jump all over the screen. John Kennedy inspired me with his words about placing a man on the moon, and I still remember a cloudy, rainy night driving through Pennsylvania and hearing the news that the astronauts had landed safely.

As a woman I have been envious of those men who could participate in the space program and who were encouraged to excel in the areas of math and science. I felt that women had indeed been left outside of one of the most exciting careers available. When Sally Ride and other women began to train as astronauts, I could look among my students and see ahead of them an ever-increasing list of opportunities.

I cannot join the space program and restart my life as an astronaut, but this opportunity to connect my abilities as an educator with my interests in history and space is a unique opportunity to fulfill my early fantasies. I watched the Space Age being born and I would like to participate.

Much information about the social history of the United States has been found in diaries, travel accounts and personal letters. This social history of the common people, joined with our military, political and economic history, gives my students an awareness of what the whole society was doing at a particular time in history. Just as the pioneer travelers of the Conestoga wagon days kept personal journals, I, as a pioneer space traveler, would do the same.

My journal would be a trilogy. I would like to begin it at the point of selection through the training for the program. The second part would cover the actual flight. Part three would cover my thoughts and reactions after my return.

My perceptions as a nonastronaut would help complete and humanize the technology of the Space Age. Future historians would use my eyewitness accounts to help in their studies of the impact of the Space Age on the general population.

Disaster struck at the seventy-three-second mark of the flight. A flawed seal in one of the two booster rockets leaked hot gases, setting off an explosion. The Challenger disintegrated in front of a national television audience—and Mrs. McAuliffe's students, watching back in Concord.

The shuttle program would resume in 1988, and NASA would fly numerous successful missions after that. But never again would technological wizardry seem so omnipotent.

the AGE *of* AIDS

Among the tens of thousands of AIDS victims, one stands out with particular vividness—a young Florida woman who fit no medical profile for the disease.

Kimberly Bergalis (and four other people) became infected after treatment by a Stuart, Florida, dentist named David Acer who later died of AIDS—the only documented cases of doctor-to-patient transmission.

Bergalis came to personify much of the debate surrounding the AIDS epidemic. Her demand for AIDS testing of health-care workers was welcomed by some, but denounced by others as the impetus for unfounded fears. Her insistence that she never engaged in sexual activity represented for some the distasteful notion that there were "innocent victims" whereas narcotics addicts and homosexuals were deserving of their fate.

In a February 1991 interview, Bergalis unburdened herself of frustration over not being believed by government and health officials investigating her case.

Here I was, 21 years old. Faced with a diagnosis of AIDS. It's a fatal illness. It's hard enough to deal with the stress of having a terminal illness. And I have to deal with people and organizations that don't believe me. They want to believe you were sleeping around.

This is something that didn't have to happen. I'm not asking that we be able to live in a risk-free world. I want people to be able to choose their risks. I didn't have a choice to walk out of the office and seek another dentist.

She recalled the shock back in January 1990 when she learned she had AIDS.

I thought maybe the government was wrong. Maybe you can get it by kissing. That's the only thing that made sense to me, an exchange of saliva or something.

In June 1991, Bergalis's lawyers made public a letter she had addressed, but never sent, to a Florida state health investigator. It was a demand to stop health-care workers, like the dentist who infected her, from spreading the disease. It could not have been more stark in portraying the anguish of the AIDS sufferer.

I have lived to see my hair fall out, my body lose over 40 pounds, blisters on my sides. I lived to see white fungus grow all over the inside of my mouth, the back of my throat, my gums and now my lips. Do you know what it looks like? I'd like to tell you. It looks like white fur and it gives you atrocious breath. Isn't that nice?

Whom do I blame? Do I blame myself? I sure don't. I never used I.V. drugs, never slept with anyone and never had a blood transfusion. I blame Dr. Acer and every single one of you bastards. Anyone who knew Dr. Acer was infected and had full-blown AIDS and stood by not doing a damn thing about it. You are all just as guilty as he was.

Can you imagine what it's like to realize you're losing weight in your fingers and that your body may be using its muscles to try to survive? Or do you know what it's like to look at yourself in a full-length mirror before you shower—and you see only a skeleton? Do you know what I did? I slid to the floor and I cried. Now I shower with a blanket over the mirror.

Like I said—all is forgiven by me—there's no hard feelings anymore. But I will never forget.

You've ruined my life and my family's. If laws are not formed to provide protection, then my suffering and death was in vain. I'm dying, guys. Goodbye.

In September 1991, Bergalis was wheeled into a congressional hearing room to support a bill calling for mandatory AIDS testing of health-care workers who perform invasive procedures. She testified in a weak, slurred voice for fifteen seconds before the House Subcommittee on Health and the Environment.

AIDS is a terrible disease that we must take seriously. I didn't do anything wrong, but I'm being made to suffer like this. My life has been taken away. Please enact legislation so other patients and health care providers don't have to go through the hell that I have. Thank you.

Kimberly Bergalis died on December 8, 1991, at her home in Fort Pierce, Florida. She was twenty-three.

HILL *versus* THOMAS

The imagery was fitting for a Times Square sleaze parlor. But this was no porno shop—it was the stately Senate Caucus Room.

A professor at the University of Oklahoma Law Center was telling the Senate Judiciary Committee—in a most graphic manner—of sexual harassment she had suffered at the hands of her old boss, the former chairman of the Equal Employment Opportunity Commission.

It was October 12, 1991, Anita Hill versus Clarence Thomas, a bizarre day of charges and denials that ranked with the army-McCarthy and Watergate hearings for Capitol Hill drama.

Thomas, the conservative black Federal judge nominated by President Bush for a Supreme Court seat, would deny everything. And

Republican senators would deal harshly with the black woman who leveled the charges, prompting outrage from women's groups and the coining of an enduring phrase to characterize insensitivity—"They just don't get it."

Thomas appeared before the committee during the morning to deny allegations of sexual harassment that Hill had made in earlier statements to the committee and to the FBI.

I have been racking my brains, and eating my insides out trying to think of what I could have said or done to Anita Hill to lead her to allege that I was interested in her in more than a professional way, and that I talked with her about pornographic movies or X-rated films. . . . But I have not said or done the things that Anita Hill has alleged. God has gotten me through the days since September 25, and he is my judge.

In the afternoon, Hill testified at an open committee session for the first time.

He spoke about acts that he had seen in pornographic films involving such matters as women having sex with animals, and films showing group sex or rape scenes. He talked about pornographic materials depicting individuals with large penises, or large breasts, involved in various sex acts. . . .

On several occasions Thomas told me graphically of his own sexual prowess. . . .

One of the oddest episodes I remember was an occasion in which Thomas was drinking a Coke in his office, he got up from the table at which we were working, went over to his desk to get the Coke, looked at the can and asked, "Who has put pubic hair on my Coke?"

On other occasions he referred to the size of his own penis as being larger than normal and he also spoke on some occasions of the pleasures he had given to women with oral sex.

SEN. JOSEPH BIDEN: *Again, it is difficult, but for the record, what substance did he bring up in this instance in the E.E.O.C. in his office? What was the content of what he said?*

HILL: *This was a reference to an individual who had a very large penis and he used the name that he had referred to in the pornographic material—*
BIDEN: *Do you recall what it was?*
HILL: *Yes, I do. The name that was referred to was Long Dong Silver.*

That evening, an outraged Thomas went before the committee once more.

This is a circus. It's a national disgrace. From my standpoint as a black American, it is a high-tech lynching for uppity blacks who in any way deign to think for themselves, to do for themselves.

Thomas was confirmed by the Senate three days later, by fifty-two to forty-eight, at a session enmeshed in issues of race and sex.

The truth of Hill's accusations would never be proved. But the furor surrounding the episode would mark an important moment in the debate over sexual harassment.

the SPECTACLE of the CENTURY

They called it the Trial of the Century, but it was more like mass entertainment. The trial of O. J. Simpson for the murder of his estranged wife, Nicole, and Ronald Goldman became not simply topic No. 1 but topics No. 2, 3, and 4 in America.

Not since the 1935 trial of Richard Bruno Hauptmann for the kidnap-murder of the Lindbergh baby had a criminal case so enthralled the nation.

And now the cast of characters was in everyone's living room. From that Friday night in June 1994 when history's most famous slow-speed chase unfolded—O.J.'s white Bronco pursued by half the Los Angeles Police Department—to the shockingly swift not-guilty verdict, it was all played out on live TV.

One of the victims would leave behind a chilling plea for help— eight months before the murders, on October 25, 1993, Nicole Brown

Simpson made two frantic telephone calls to a Los Angeles police dispatcher.

NICOLE SIMPSON: *Can you send someone to my house?*
POLICE DISPATCHER: *What's the emergency?*
NS: *My ex-husband has just broken into my house and he's ranting and raving outside in the front yard.*
PD: *Has he been drinking or anything?*
NS: *No, but he's crazy.*
PD: *Did he hit you?*
NS: *No.*
PD: *Do you have a restraining order against him?*
NS: *No.*
PD: *What is your name?*
NS: *Nicole Simpson.*

[The call ended, and the dispatcher put out a domestic-violence request for any patrol car to respond to the address at Gretna Green. About fifty seconds later, Nicole Simpson called back.]
NS: *Could you get somebody over here, now, to . . . Gretna Green. He's back. Please.*
PD: *What does he look like?*
NS: *He's O. J. Simpson. I think you know his record. Could you just send somebody over here?*
PD: *What is he doing there?*
NS: *He just drove up again. [She begins to cry.] Could you just send somebody over?*
PD: *What is he driving?*
NS: *He's in a white Bronco, but first of all he broke the back door down to get in.*
PD: *Wait a minute, what's your name?*
NS: *Nicole Simpson.*
PD: *O.K. Is he the sportscaster or whatever?*
NS: *Yeah.*
PD: *Wait a minute, we're sending police. What is he doing? Is he threatening you?*
NS: *He's [expletive deleted] going nuts. [sobs]*

PD: *Has he threatened you or is he just harassing you?*

NS: *You're going to hear him in a minute. He's about to come in again.*

PD: *O.K., just stay on the line.*

NS: *I don't want to stay on the line. He's going to beat the [expletive deleted] out of me.*

PD: *Wait a minute, just stay on the line so we can know what's going on until the police get there. O.K.? O.K., Nicole?*

NS: *Uh-huh.*

PD: *Just a moment. Does he have any weapons?*

NS: *I don't know. He went home. Now he's back. The kids are up there sleeping and I don't want anything to happen.*

PD: *O.K., just a minute. Is he on drugs or anything?*

NS: *No.*

PD: *O.K. What is he saying?*

NS: *Oh, something about some guy I know and hookers and keys and I started this [expletive deleted] before and . . .*

PD: *Um-hum.*

NS: *And it's all my fault and "Now what am I going to do, get the police in on this?" That whole thing. It's all my fault. I started this before. Brother. [crying] I don't want my kids exposed to this.*

PD: *O.K., has he hit you today or . . .*

NS: *No.*

PD: *O.K., you don't need any paramedics or anything.*

NS: *Uh-huh.*

PD: *O.K., you just want him to leave?*

NS: *My door. He broke the whole back door in.*

PD: *And then he left and he came back?*

NS: *He came and he practically knocked my upstairs door down, but he pounded it and he screamed and hollered and I tried to get him out of the bedroom because the kids are sleeping in there.*

PD: *Does he have any weapons with him right now?*

NS: *No, uh-uh.*

PD: *O.K. Where is he standing?*

NS: *In the back doorway, in the house.*

PD: *O.K.*

O. J. SIMPSON: *I don't give a [expletive deleted] anymore. . . .*

NS: *Would you just please, O.J., O.J., O.J., O.J., could you please leave? Please leave.*

O.J.: *I'm leaving with my two [expletive deleted] kids is when I'm leaving.*

PD: *Has this happened before or no?*

NS: *Many times.*

OKLAHOMA CITY

The headlines read "Terror in the Heartland."

Americans had been victimized in a string of terrorist actions overseas—the Iranian hostage episode, the suicide-bomb attack on the Marine barracks in Beirut that killed 241, the destruction of Pan Am flight 103 over Scotland that claimed 270 lives. And there had been terrorist strikes at home, most notably the February 1993 bombing at New York City's World Trade Center by Muslim extremists that killed six persons and the Unabomber devices attributed to a deranged individual.

But nothing had the impact of the car bombing at Oklahoma City's Alfred P. Murrah Federal Building the morning of April 19, 1995.

This was a quiet Southwestern town, seemingly far removed from the murderous grievances that fed other spectacular acts of terrorism. Yet 168 persons would die in Oklahoma City.

Among the victims were children at the America's Kids day-care center on the building's second floor. Twenty-four youngsters were gathered there for breakfast when a thunderous explosion at 9:02 A.M. sent debris crashing down.

Bobby Johnson, a nurse at the South Park Health Care Center, was with a rescue team at the day-care facility.

It was just as bad as anything I'd ever witnessed in Vietnam. The fact it happened here made it seem even worse, the fact that you could see body parts everywhere. All you could see was body parts. Even outside, there were spots of blood. One guy found a child's finger on the sidewalk. I saw part of a little doll house, parts of a tricycle, some Fisher-Price toys. They were all just mingled in with the debris. The only way you could tell they were toys was that the bright colors made them stand out. Every now and then we'd spot a pool of blood.

Lydia Winfrey, a licensed practical nurse, was another would-be rescuer.

Those kids were at ground zero for that blast. They looked like they could have been sitting at a table, and their upper bodies caught the brunt of the blast. One child had no face, just torn skin. With most of them, you couldn't tell whether it was a boy or a girl. They were wearing clothes with little ducks on them, little shoes.

John Avera, an Oklahoma City police sergeant, picked up a child.

We could hear several people back in there crying and hollering. I heard a baby crying and we started moving bricks and rocks back across of them, and we found two babies. The officer I was with took one down one hallway, and I took my baby out the other way.

Fireman Chris Fields grabbed the baby from Avera's arms.

Its little face was covered with insulation and dust. I couldn't tell if the skull was cracked; the head was cut open.

Charles H. Porter IV, a bank clerk who thought at first that demolition crews were tearing down a building, happened to have a camera with him. He snapped a shot of the fireman racing from the building with the bloody child, Baylee Almon—one day past her first birthday. It would be a "signature" photo, encapsulating the horror. Distributed around the world by the Associated Press, the picture would bring Porter a Pulitzer Prize.

Baylee was pronounced dead at the scene. The next day, Baylee's mother, Aren Almon, asked to meet the policeman and fireman who had tried to save her daughter.

Sergeant John Avera:

It worried me that maybe the photo was how she found out her baby was dead. She saw me coming, ran across the yard and hugged my neck. "Thank you, thank you, thank you," that's all she could say. "My waiting is over—not like all the other people who have to wait to find their relatives."

Fireman Chris Fields:

Her aunt gave me a picture of Baylee at her birthday party. That picture will go right up on my locker at the fire station—and stay there until I retire.

Aren Almon:

We heard that they had found a baby with yellow booties, and I knew it was her. She was learning how to walk.
I know my daughter is in heaven. I know she is.

EVERY FOUR YEARS

For those who would menace American democracy by detonating a car bomb or firing a gun, an answer comes on the first Tuesday of each November.
And so, November 5, 1996:

Sioux Falls, South Dakota:

Clinton had finished the final speech of the campaign and worked what seemed to be his last midnight rope line inside the Sioux Falls Arena in South Dakota, and his big blue-and-white plane with The United States of America printed boldly on its side was waiting at the airport to fly him through the early darkness to Little Rock and home. But he could not leave.
He bounded up to the side stage where Jerry Jeff Walker was twanging out "This Land Is Your Land," and clapped along, at one point taking the saxophone from Walker's sax player. He thought about playing it but

decided better, and handed it back and walked down the back stairs, his white hair barely visible back near the curtain.

Then he sauntered up the stairs of the main podium and looked out and waved some more, just standing there, slowly taking it in, this closing moment, 22 years and 10 months after he shook his first hand as a candidate for Congress up in the hills of northwest Arkansas. His eyes reddened and glistened near tears. . . .

The arena was virtually empty now. The cleanup crew was sweeping the floors, the caterers were packing up their carts and trays, and Clinton gestured to some of them—Come on over!—and they ran toward him in their white T-shirts.

He greeted them one by one until he had made contact with the last hand of his last campaign. It belonged to Elsie Fading, a 53-year-old catering assistant who said she thought he was wonderful and that she would vote for him to cancel out her husband's support for Robert J. Dole.

With that, finally, the president disappeared behind the blue curtain, where his staff waited with hugs and high-fives. The last campaign was over. . . .

Russell, Kansas:

Seeming at peace with himself and with the effort he had made to get to the White House, Bob Dole cast his vote for president yesterday at the First Christian Church before flying to Washington to await election returns.

After a marathon 96-hour campaign sprint through 19 states, 29 stops and 10,534 miles, Dole returned to his hometown in the central plains of Kansas. He voted for himself, cracked a few jokes and thanked his friends and neighbors.

While his staff was subdued, Dole seemed happy and relaxed, but not ebullient. Dole and his wife, Elizabeth, entered the first floor of the church, decorated with red, white and blue bunting, at 12:05 P.M.

"How's business? Pretty good? My name's Bob Dole, 1035 Maple Street," he told the five women running the polls. Dole was voter No. 288, his wife was No. 289 of the 763 registered voters in this ward.

Dole used a pencil to mark an X on four ballots—the way voting is done here.

"Never voted for myself for president," he remarked to the women behind the official election table.

Norway, Iowa:

A Union Pacific coal train rumbles by.

They had moved the bright-red fire engine outside the Florence Township station to make room for Election Day 1996, in the form of paper ballots. No machines here.

The firefighters' coats remained inside. "When they have a fire," said Betty Schulte, an election official, "we just get out of the way."

New York City:

Gilda Rodriguez listened intently to the flurry of advice as she made her way to the polls for the first time since coming here from the Dominican Republic 18 years ago.

She looked around at the six women who accompanied her and pumped her fist quickly into the morning air.

"Now we're going to show them the power of women," she said. "We have to go early so nobody will take it away from us."

She turned serious.

"I'm emotional," she said. "I'm voting for the first time in the nation that took me in like a mother does a child," she said as she went into a room crowded with people.

A few minutes later, she emerged.

"I did it!" she said, although she would not say for whom she voted.

Did she feel any different?

"There has to be a difference," she replied. "Because there's one more vote, full of hope."

SOURCES

chapter one—*the* MAKING *of a* NATION

The New World—Verrazano described his explorations along America's East Coast in a letter to King Francis I of France dated July 8, 1524, when he arrived in Dieppe. Account cited in Samuel Eliot Morison, *The European Discovery of America: The Northern Voyages*, A.D. *500–1600* (New York: Oxford University Press, 1971).

Pocahontas to the Rescue—John Smith, *General History of Virginia, New England and the Summer Isles*, 1624.

The Great Harbor—Henry Hudson's account was conveyed by John de Laet, a director of the Dutch West India Company, who had access to his diary.

The First Thanksgiving—*A Relation or Journal of the Beginning and Proceedings of the English Plantation Settled at Plimouth in New England*, known as *Mourt's Relation*, published in 1622 in London and attributed to William Bradford and Edward Winslow.

The Mighty Mississippi—The account is from Father Claude Dablon's *Relation of 1672–1673* and is evidently based on a journal kept by Marquette. The Dablon report was later published in *The Jesuit Relations and Allied Documents: Travels and Explorations of the Jesuit Missionaries in New France, 1610–1791*, 73 vols., ed. Reuben G. Thwaites (Cleveland, 1896–1901).

The Witches of Salem—Cotton Mather, *The Wonders of the Invisible World* (Boston: S. Phillips, 1693).

The Boston Massacre—Richard Palmes, *A Short Narrative of the Horrid Massacre in Boston* (1770). Account by John Tudor cited in *Deacon Tudor's Diary*, ed. William Tudor (Boston, 1896).

The Boston Tea Party—James Hawkes, *A Retrospect of the Boston Tea Party, with a Memoir of George R. T. Hewes a Survivor of the Patriots Who Drowned the Tea in Boston Harbor in 1773* (New York: S. S. Bliss, 1834).

Lexington Green—Deposition of Sylvanus Wood, June 17, 1826, cited in Henry B. Lawson, *Battles of the United States by Sea and Land*, 2 vols. (New York: Johnson, Fry and Company, 1858).

The Declaration of Independence—John Adams to Timothy Pickering, August 6, 1822. Thomas Jefferson to James Madison, August 30, 1823. Jefferson, *Autobiography*, vol. I, 1821. Jefferson to Dr. James Mease, September 26, 1825. Jefferson to Ellen W. Coolidge, November 14, 1825.

Nathan Hale Defiant—Maria Hull Campbell, *Revolutionary Services and Civil Life of General William Hull; Prepared from His Manuscripts* (New York: D. Appleton and Company, 1848).

John Paul Jones Triumphant—Nathaniel Fanning, *Fanning's Narrative; Being the Memoirs of Nathaniel Fanning, an Officer of the Revolutionary Navy*, ed. John S. Barnes (New York: Naval History Society, 1912).

The Battle of Saratoga—Thomas Anburey, *Travels Through the Interior Parts of America: By an Officer* (London: William Lane, 1789). Roger Lamb, *An Original and Authentic Journal of Occurrences During the Late American War* (Dublin: Wilkinson & Courtney, 1809).

Winter at Valley Forge—Joseph Plumb Martin, *A Narrative of Some of the Adventures, Dangers and Sufferings of a Revolutionary Soldier, Interspersed with Anecdotes of Incidents That Occurred Within His Own Observation* (Hallowell, Maine, 1830). George Washington to the President of the Continental Congress, December 23, 1777.

Surrender at Yorktown—James Thacher, *Military Journal of the American Revolution* (Hartford, Conn.: Hurlbut, Williams & Company, 1862).

Washington's Farewell—*Memoir of Colonel Benjamin Tallmadge, Prepared by Himself at the Request of His Children.* (New York: Thomas Holman, 1858).

Shays's Rebellion—General William Shepard to General James Bowdoin, January 26, 1787.

The Founding Fathers—James Madison, *Notes of Debates in the Federal Convention of 1787*. Madison to Thomas Jefferson, June 6, 1787. William Pierce, *Pierce's Relique*. Madison, *Notes*.

Dinner with George and Martha—*The Journal of William Maclay, United States Senator from Pennsylvania, 1789–1791*, ed. Edgar S. Maclay (New York: D. Appleton and Company, 1890).

The Battle of Lake Erie—David C. Bunnell, *Travels and Adventures* (Palmyra, N.Y., 1831).

The British Are Coming! The British Are Coming!—*Memoirs and Letters of Dolley Madison*, ed. Lucia Cutts (New York, 1886).

chapter two—the UNION'S "FIERY TRIAL"

Frontier Politicking—Attributed to David Crockett, *Colonel Crockett's Exploits and Adventures in Texas* (Philadelphia: T. K. and P. G. Collins, 1836).

Jacksonian Democracy—Frances Trollope, *Domestic Manners of the Americans* (London: Billing and Sons, 1832). *The First Forty Years of Washington Society Portrayed by the Family Letters of Mrs. Samuel Harrison Smith*, ed. Gaillard Hunt (New York: C. Scribner's Sons, 1906).

The Iron Horse—William H. Brown, *The First Locomotives in America* (New York: D. Appleton and Company, 1871).

Congressional Manners—Charles Dickens, *American Notes for General Circulation* (London: Chapman & Hall, 1842).

Giants of the Senate—Harriet Martineau, *Retrospect of Western Travel* (London: Saunders & Otley, 1838).

The Virginia Slave Revolt—"Confession" of Nat Turner in jail interview with Thomas R. Gray, November 1–3, 1831.

Remembering the Alamo—Enrique Esparza interview in *San Antonio Express*, May 12, 1907.

Marching into Mexico—Account by George Meade cited in Bernard De Voto, *The Year of Decision: 1846* (Boston: Houghton Mifflin, 1942). Ethan Allen Hitchcock to Elizabeth Nicholls of Georgetown, D.C., March 27, 1847. Peter V. Hagner to Mary M. Hagner, Annapolis, Md., March 30, 1847.

The Bear Flag Revolt—Joseph T. Downey, *The Cruise of the Portsmouth*, cited in Nathan Miller, *The United States Navy: An Illustrated History* (New York: American Heritage Publishing Company, 1977).

Thoreau Behind Bars—Essay known as "Civil Disobedience," originally published as "Resistance to Civil Government: A Lecture Delivered in 1847."

Advocate for the Insane—Dorothea Dix's "Memorial to the Legislature of Massachusetts," 1843.

The Lash of Slavery—Frederick Douglass, *Narrative of the Life of Frederick Douglass, an American Slave, Written by Himself* (Boston: Anti-Slavery Office, 1845).

Sojourner Truth Speaks—*History of Women Suffrage*, vol. I, ed. Elizabeth Cady Stanton, Susan B. Anthony, and Matilda Joslyn Gage (New York: Fowler and Wells, 1881).

The Lincoln-Douglas Debates—Carl Schurz, *The Reminiscences of Carl Schurz* (New York: Charles Scribner's Sons, 1906–8), 3 vols.

The Fall of Fort Sumter—Mary Boykin Chesnut, *A Diary from Dixie*, ed. Isabella D. Martin and Myrta Lockett Avary (New York: D. Appleton and Company, 1905). *The Diary of Edmund Ruffin*, ed. William Kauffman Scarborough (Baton Rouge, La.: Louisiana State University Press, 1972–89). Abner Doubleday, *Reminiscences of Forts Sumter and Moultrie in 1860–61* (New York, 1876). Message by Robert Anderson cited in *War of the Rebellion: A Compilation of the Official Records of the Union and Confederate Armies*, ser. I, vol. 1.

Rout at Bull Run—William H. Russell, *My Diary North and South* (London: Bradbury & Evans, 1863).

"Mine Eyes Have Seen the Glory"—Julia Ward Howe, *Reminiscences, 1819 to 1899* (Boston: Houghton Mifflin, 1899).

Gettysburg—Jesse Bowman Young, *What a Boy Saw in the Army* (New York: Hunt & Eaton, 1894).

Countrymen Again—Ulysses S. Grant, *Personal Memoirs of U.S. Grant* (New York: C. L. Webster, 1885).

"You's Free"—*The American Slave: A Composite Autobiography*, vol. XVI, *Virginia Narratives*, ed. George P. Rawick (Westport, Conn.: Greenwood Press, 1972).

Wartime's Toll—Newspaper dispatch in *The Wound Dresser: A Series of Letters Written from the Hospitals in Washington During the War of the Rebellion by Walt Whitman*, ed. Richard Maurice Bucke (Boston: Smith, Maynard, 1898).

Lincoln's Final Hours—Account by Oliver P. Gatch cited in E. R. Shaw, "The Assassination of Lincoln," *McClure's*, December 1908. Testimony by William Withers cited in W. Emerson Reck, *A. Lincoln—His Last 24 Hours*

(Jefferson, N.C.: McFarland and Company, 1987). Letter from Harry Hawk to his father cited in Allen G. Clark, *Abraham Lincoln in the National Capital* (Washington, D.C.: W. F. Roberts, 1925). James Tanner, "At the Deathbed of Abraham Lincoln," *National Republic*, August 1926. Letter from Elizabeth Dixon to Louisa Wood, May 1, 1865. Account by Dr. Edward Curtis cited in Dorothy Meserve Kunhardt and Philip B. Kunhardt, Jr., *Twenty Days* (New York: Harper & Row, 1965). Account by David R. Locke cited in Carl Sandburg, *Abraham Lincoln: The War Years* (New York: Harcourt, Brace, 1936).

Tracking Down an Assassin—Article by George Alfred Townsend, *New York World*, April 29, 1865.

The South in Ruins—*The American Slave*, vol. VI, *Alabama Narratives*, ed. Rawick.

The Presidency on Trial—Edmund G. Ross, "History of the Impeachment of Andrew Johnson," *Forum*, July 1895.

South Carolina's "Black Parliament"—James Shepherd Pike, *The Prostrate State: South Carolina Under Negro Government* (New York: D. Appleton and Company, 1874).

chapter three—the OLD WEST, *the* NEW AMERICANS

The Donner Party—Diary of Patrick Breen, November 1946–March 1847, ed. Frederick J. Teggart, *Publications of the Academy of Pacific Coast History*, vol. I (1910), cited in George R. Stewart, *Ordeal by Hunger: The Story of the Donner Party* (Boston: Houghton Mifflin, 1936).

Gold!—Charles R. Gillespie, "James Marshall's Account of the Discovery of Gold in California," *Century Magazine*, February 1890.

The Pony Express—William F. Cody, *An Autobiography of Buffalo Bill* (New York: Cosmopolitan Book Corporation, 1920).

Stagecoach to the West—Mark Twain, *Roughing It.* (Hartford, Conn.: American Publishing Company, 1872).

The Golden Spike—Grenville Dodge, *How We Built the Union Pacific Railway* (Washington, D.C.: U.S. Government Printing Office, 1910). *New York Times*, May 10, 1869.

The Great Chicago Fire—Article by John R. Chapin, *Harper's Weekly*, October 28, 1871.

Custer at Little Big Horn—Account by Kate Bighead cited in Thomas B. Marquis, *Custer on the Little Bighorn* (Algonac, Mich.: Reference Publications, 1978). Elizabeth Bacon Custer, *Boots and Saddles, or Life in Dakota with General Custer* (New York: Harper & Brothers, 1885).

Billy the Kid—Federal Writers Project interview with Annie Lesnett, conducted by Edith Crawford, at Carrizozo, N.M., 1938, cited in *First Person America*, ed. Ann Banks (New York: Alfred A. Knopf, 1980). Pat F. Garrett, *The Authentic Life of Billy the Kid* (Santa Fe, N.M.: New Mexican Print and Publishing Company, 1882).

Shootout at the O.K. Corral—R. F. Coleman account cited in *Tombstone Epitaph*, October 27, 1881. Wesley Fuller trial testimony.

Alexander Graham Bell Calling—Recollections of Thomas A. Watson cited in Lincoln Barnett, *The Conquest of Silence* (New York: Harper & Row, 1965).

Edison's Talking Machines—Philip G. Hubert, Jr., "The New Talking-Machines," *Atlantic Monthly*, 1889.

The Brooklyn Bridge—Report of John A. Roebling, C.E., to the President and Directors of the New York Bridge Company, on the Proposed East River Bridge, 1867, cited in David McCullough, *The Great Bridge* (New York: Simon & Schuster, 1972). Account of bridge's opening is from *New York Sun*, May 25, 1883.

The Lady in the Harbor—Juan De Onis, trans., *The America of José Martí* (New York: Noonday, 1953). Edward Corsi, *In the Shadow of Liberty* (New York: Macmillan, 1935). Emma Lazarus, "The New Colossus," 1883.

Ellis Island—H. G. Wells, *The Future in America: A Search After Realities* (London, 1906). Fiorello La Guardia, *The Making of an Insurgent* (Philadelphia: J. B. Lippincott, 1948). Louis Adamic, *Laughing in the Jungle: The Autobiography of an Immigrant in America* (New York: Harper & Brothers, 1932).

The Sweatshops of "Jewtown"—Jacob Riis, *How the Other Half Lives: Case Studies Among the Tenements of New York* (New York: Scribner, 1890.)

The Triangle Fire—Account by William Shepherd, United Press, March 25, 1911, cited in Leon Stein, *The Triangle Fire* (Philadelphia: J. B. Lippincott, 1962). "A Faithful Reader," letter to *Jewish Daily Forward*, cited in *A Bintel Brief*, ed. Isaac Metzker (New York: Doubleday, 1971).

"Honest Graft"—William L. Riordan, *Plunkitt of Tammany Hall* (New York: McClure, Phillips and Company, 1905).

Showdown at Homestead—*Pittsburgh Press*, July 7, 1892.

Revolt of the Miners—Article by James R. Sovereign, *Idaho State Tribune*, Wallace, Idaho, May 3, 1899.

A Cross of Gold—William Jennings Bryan, *The Memoirs of William Jennings Bryan* (Philadelphia, Chicago: John C. Winston Company, 1925). Accounts by Harry Thurston Peck and Charles Warren cited in Mark Sullivan, *Our Times: 1900–1925*, vol. I (New York: Charles Scribner's Sons, 1926).

chapter four—the INTERNATIONAL STAGE

"A Splendid Little War"—Charles Sigsbee, *The Maine: An Account of Her Destruction in Havana Harbor* (New York: Century Company, 1899). Percy H. Epler, *The Life of Clara Barton* (New York: Macmillan, 1915).

The Rough Riders—Theodore Roosevelt to Senator Henry Cabot Lodge, July 19, 1898; to General Leonard Wood, July 4, 1898; to Lodge, December 6, 1898.

Remembering the *Maine*—Account by "Dynamite" Johnny O'Brien cited in J. R. Caldwell, "Most Mournful of Sea Pageants," *Harper's Weekly*, May 11, 1912.

Wings over Kitty Hawk—Orville Wright, "How We Made the First Flight," *Flying*, December 1913.

The Rise of Theodore Roosevelt—Recollection by Samuel Ireland cited in Sullivan, *Our Times*. Lincoln Steffens, *The Autobiography of Lincoln Steffens* (New York: Harcourt, Brace, 1931).

The San Francisco Earthquake—Reports by James Hopper, *San Francisco Call*, cited in Gordon Thomas and Max Morgan Witts, *The San Francisco Earthquake* (New York: Stein and Day, 1971).

"The Birth of a Nation"—Kevin Brownlow, *The Parade's Gone By* (New York: Alfred A. Knopf, 1968).

The Suffragists—Account by Mary I. Nolan cited in Doris Stevens, *Jailed for Freedom: American Women Win the Vote* (New York: Boni and Liveright,

1920). Thomas Marshall, *Recollections of Thomas R. Marshall: A Hoosier Salad* (Indianapolis: Bobbs-Merrill, 1925).

Birth Control Pioneer—Margaret Sanger, *My Fight for Birth Control* (New York: Farrar and Rinehart, 1931).

Soldier for the Lord—Account by Alvin York cited in George Pattullo, "The Second Elder Gives Battle," *Saturday Evening Post*, April 26, 1919.

Captain Harry Gives 'Em Hell—Address by Paul Shaffer to Elks Club of Whittier, California, cited in Lawrence Stallings, *The Doughboys: The Story of the A.E.F., 1917–1918* (New York: Harper & Row, 1963).

Battling the Red Baron—Hamilton Coolidge, *Letters of an American Airman, Being the War Record of Captain Hamilton C. Coolidge, U.S.A., 1917–1918* (Boston: private printing, 1919).

Woodrow Wilson's Failed Crusade—Joseph P. Tumulty, *Woodrow Wilson as I Know Him* (New York: Doubleday, Page and Company, 1921). Speech by Woodrow Wilson at Pueblo, Colorado, September 15, 1919.

chapter five—the ROARING TWENTIES, the DESPERATE THIRTIES

The Black Sox Scandal—Testimony by Joe Jackson before Cook County, Ill., grand jury, September 28, 1920.

The Great Thirst—Stanley Walker, *The Night Club Era* (New York: Frederick A. Stokes, 1935). Izzy Einstein, *Prohibition Agent No. 1* (New York: Frederick A. Stokes, 1932).

Radio Arrives—Account by Leo Rosenberg cited in Edward Bliss, Jr., *Now the News: The Story of Broadcast Journalism* (New York: Columbia University Press, 1961). Robert Saudek, "Program Coming in Fine, Please Play Japanese Sandman," *American Heritage*, August 1965.

The Tube—Account of Elma Farnsworth cited in Michael Winship, *Television* (New York: Random House, 1988).

The Dumbbell Murder—Damon Runyon, "Murder in the Worst Degree," *International News Service*, 1927.

A Mickey Mouse Production—Account by Walt Disney cited in Leonard Mosley, *Disney's World* (New York: Stein and Day, 1985).

The Monkey Trial—H. L. Mencken, "Deep in the Coca-Cola Belt," *Baltimore Evening Sun*, July 13, 1925.

From Horseless Carriage to Model T—Henry Ford in collaboration with Samuel Crowther, *My Life and Work* (New York: Doubleday, Page and Company, 1922).

Lindbergh Alone—Charles Lindbergh, *The Spirit of St. Louis* (New York: Charles Scribner's Sons, 1953).

Panic on Wall Street—Article by Mildred Wohlforth, *New York Times*, December 6, 1987. Richard Whitney, "The Work of the New York Stock Exchange in the Panic of 1929," address to Boston Association of Stock Exchange Firms, June 10, 1930.

The Bonus Army—*Washington Evening Star*, July 28, 1932. Walter W. Waters, as told to William G. White, *The Whole Story of the Bonus Army* (New York: John Day Company, 1933).

The Fireside Chat—Account by Robert Trout cited in Bliss, *Now the News*.

The Dust Bowl—Meridel Le Sueur, "Cows and Horses Are Hungry." *American Mercury*, September 1934.

Pleading for Baby Clothes—Mrs. H. E. C. to Eleanor Roosevelt, January 2, 1935. Eleanor Roosevelt Papers, box 645. Cited in Robert S. McIlvaine, *Down and Out in the Great Depression: Letters from the Forgotten Man* (Chapel Hill: University of North Carolina Press, 1983.)

Public Enemy No. 1—Polly Hamilton, "Dillinger's Last Hours With Me—by His Sweetheart," *Chicago Herald and Examiner*, October 24–27, 1934.

Groucho and the Boys—Groucho Marx and Richard J. Anobile, *The Marx Brothers Scrapbook* (New York: Darien House, 1973).

The *Hindenburg* Aflame—NBC radio broadcast by Herbert Morrison, May 6, 1937.

Martians in Jersey—CBS radio broadcast, *The Mercury Theatre on the Air*, October 30, 1938. Account by Archie Burbank cited in Princeton Radio Project, *The Invasion From Mars* (Princeton, N.J.: Princeton University Press, 1940).

Marian Anderson at the Lincoln Memorial—Walter White, *A Man Called White: The Autobiography of Walter White* (New York: Viking Press, 1948).

"Mr. Hoover, This Is Lepke"—Walter Winchell, "Waiting for Lepke," *New York Daily Mirror*, August 26, 1939.

Royalty on the Hudson—Eleanor Roosevelt, *This I Remember* (New York: Harper & Brothers, 1949).

chapter six—WORLD WAR II YEARS

The Making of GI Joe—Marion Hargrove, *See Here, Private Hargrove* (New York: Henry Holt, 1942).

Pearl Harbor Sunday—Stephen Bower Young, "Out of the Darkness," *United States Naval Institute Proceedings*, December 1965.

Last Word from Corregidor—Message from Irving Strobing, May 5, 1942, as released by United States War Department in June 1942.

Turnabout at Midway—Clarence E. Dickinson and Boyden Sparks, *The Flying Guns* (New York: Charles Scribner's Sons, 1942).

The Japanese Americans—Account by George Akimoto cited in Deborah Gesensway and Mindy Roseman, *Beyond Words: Images from America's Concentration Camps* (Ithaca, N.Y.: Cornell University Press, 1987).

D-Day at Omaha Beach—John Robert Slaughter, "My War Years: 1941–1944," diary typescript.

Afternoon at Warm Springs—*Closest Companion: The Unknown Story of the Intimate Friendship Between Franklin Roosevelt and Margaret Suckley*, ed. by Geoffrey Ward (Boston: Houghton Mifflin, 1995). *1945: Year of Decisions—Memoirs by Harry S. Truman* (New York: Doubleday, 1955). CBS radio broadcast by Arthur Godfrey, April 14, 1945.

The Age of the Atom—New Mexico account by William L. Laurence, *New York Times*, September 26, 1945. Nagasaki account from William L. Laurence, *Men and Atoms* (New York: Simon & Schuster, 1959).

Surrender in Tokyo Bay—Account by Sergeant Dale Kramer cited in Franklin S. Forsberg, *Yank: The G.I. Story of the War* (New York: Duell, Sloan & Pearce, 1947).

chapter seven—COLD WAR CONFLICTS, CIVIL RIGHTS STRUGGLES

Uncle Miltie—Milton Berle with Haskel Frankel, *Milton Berle: An Autobiography* (New York: Delacorte Press, 1974).

The Berlin Airlift—Article by Alfred Wright, *Time*, October, 18,1948.

The Fifth Marines at the Chosin Reservoir—Account by Private First Class Jack Wright cited in Donald Knox, *The Korean War: Pusan to Chosin: An Oral History* (New York: Harcourt Brace Jovanovich, 1985).

The Rosenbergs—Testimony by Harry Gold in United States District Court, Manhattan, March 15, 1951.

The End of Joe McCarthy—Charles E. Potter, *Days of Shame* (New York: Coward-McGann, 1965).

The U-2 Sinks a Summit—Testimony by Francis Gary Powers before the Senate Armed Services Committee, March 6, 1962.

The Great Debates—Douglass Cater, "Notes from Backstage," *Reporter*, November 10, 1960.

The Cuban Missile Crisis—Robert F. Kennedy, *Thirteen Days: A Memoir of the Cuban Missile Crisis* (New York: W. W. Norton, 1969).

Breaking Baseball's Color Barrier—Jackie Robinson and Alfred Duckett, *I Never Had It Made: An Autobiography* (New York: G. P. Putnam's Sons, 1972; reprinted ed., Hopewell, N.J.: Ecco Press, 1995.)

The Montgomery Bus Boycott—Account by Rosa Parks cited in Henry Hampton and Steve Fayer, *Voices of Freedom: An Oral History of the Civil Rights Movement from the 1950's Through the 1980's* (New York: Bantam Books, 1990).

Central High, Little Rock—Melba Pattillo Beals, *Warriors Don't Cry: A Searing Memoir of the Battle to Integrate Little Rock's Central High* (New York: Pocket Books, 1994).

chapter eight—AMERICA in TURMOIL

Dallas, November 22—Testimony by Howard Brennan before the President's Commission on the Assassination of President Kennedy (Warren Commission). Howard Brennan and J. Edward Cherryholmes, *Eyewitness to History: The Kennedy Assassination as Seen by Howard Brennan* (Waco, Tex.: Texian Press, 1987). *Merriman Smith's Book of Presidents*, ed. Timothy G. Smith (New York: W. W. Norton, 1972).

"A Problem That Had No Name"—Betty Friedan, Introduction to the tenth-anniversary edition, *The Feminine Mystique* (New York: W. W. Norton, 1973 [1963]).

Above the Ho Chi Minh Trail—Account by Dick Rutan cited in Harry Maurer, *Strange Ground: Americans in Vietnam, 1945–1975, an Oral History* (New York: Henry Holt, 1989).

Massacre at My Lai—Interview with Paul Meadlo conducted by Mike Wallace for CBS radio, November 24, 1969.

A Balcony in Memphis—Ralph David Abernathy, *And the Walls Came Tumbling Down: An Autobiography* (New York: Harper & Row, 1989).

The Stonewall Raid—Account by Morty Manford cited in Eric Marcus, *Making History: The Struggle for Gay and Lesbian Equal Rights, 1945–1990, an Oral History* (New York: HarperCollins, 1992).

Man on the Moon—National Aeronautics and Space Administration transcript, July 20, 1969.

The Spirit of Woodstock—Account by Miriam Yasgur cited in Joel Makower, *Woodstock: The Oral History* (New York: Doubleday, 1989).

Kent State—Account by Tom Grace cited in Joan Morrison and Robert K. Morrison, *From Camelot to Kent State* (New York: Times Books, 1987).

chapter nine—to the MILLENNIUM

The Watergate Cover-up—Testimony by John Dean before Senate Select Committee on Presidential Campaign Activities (Watergate Committee), June 1973. Transcript of taped Nixon-Dean meeting, March 21, 1973.

Gary Gilmore Faces the Firing Squad—Lawrence Schiller news conference, Point of the Mountain, Utah, January 17, 1977.

The Camp David Accords—Jimmy Carter, *Keeping Faith: Memoirs of a President* (New York: Bantam Books, 1982; reprint ed., Fayetteville: University of Arkansas Press, 1995).

America Held Hostage—Interview with Sergeant Donald R. Hohman, *Sacramento Bee.* Interview with Elizabeth Montagne, NBC News.

"Gerr-eee, Gerr-eee"—Geraldine Ferraro with Linda Bird Francke, *Ferraro: My Story* (New York: Bantam Books, 1985).

One Morning in Beirut—Terry Anderson, *Den of Lions: Memoirs of Seven Years* (New York: Crown Publishers, 1993).

The *Challenger* Disaster—Essay by Christa McAuliffe submitted to National Aeronautics and Space Administration, 1985.

The Age of AIDS—Kimberly Bergalis interview, *New York Times*, February 9, 1991. Bergalis to Florida State Health Department, released June 1991. Bergalis testimony before House Subcommittee on Health and the Environment, September 26, 1991.

Hill versus Thomas—Testimony by Clarence Thomas and Anita Hill before the United States Senate Judiciary Committee, October 12, 1991.

The Spectacle of the Century—Transcript of telephone calls from Nicole Brown Simpson to the Los Angeles Police Department, October 25, 1993.

Oklahoma City—Accounts by Bobby Johnson and Lydia Winfrey cited in *Newsweek*, May 1, 1995. Sergeant John Avera, CNN interview and *People*, May 8, 1995. Fireman Chris Fields quoted by Associated Press and *People*. Aren Almon, *Time*, May 1, 1995.

Every Four Years—Clinton item, *Washington Post;* Dole item, *Boston Globe;* Iowa item, Associated Press; New York City item, *New York Times;* all November 6, 1996.

PERMISSIONS CREDITS

INDEX